D1786009

ALL GLORY TO ŚRĪ GURU AND GAURĀṄGA

ŚRĪMAD BHĀGAVATAM

of

KṚṢṆA-DVAIPĀYANA VYĀSA

एतां स आस्थाय परात्मनिष्ठा-
मध्यासितां पूर्वतमैर्महर्षिभिः ।
अहं तरिष्यामि दुरन्तपारं
तमो मुकुन्दाङ्घ्रिनिषेवयैव ॥५७॥

etāṁ sa āsthāya parātma-niṣṭhām
adhyāsitāṁ pūrvatamair maharṣibhiḥ
ahaṁ tariṣyāmi duranta-pāraṁ
tamo mukundāṅghri-niṣevayaiva

(p. 303)

BOOKS by His Divine Grace A. C. Bhaktivedanta Swami Prabhupāda

Bhagavad-gītā As It Is
Śrīmad-Bhāgavatam, cantos 1–10 (30 vols.)
Śrī Caitanya-caritāmṛta (17 vols.)
Teachings of Lord Caitanya
The Nectar of Devotion
The Nectar of Instruction
Śrī Īśopaniṣad
Easy Journey to Other Planets
Kṛṣṇa Consciousness: The Topmost Yoga System
Kṛṣṇa, the Supreme Personality of Godhead (3 vols.)
Perfect Questions, Perfect Answers
Dialectical Spiritualism—A Vedic View of Western Philosophy
Teachings of Lord Kapila, the Son of Devahūti
Transcendental Teachings of Prahlād Mahārāja
Teachings of Queen Kuntī
Kṛṣṇa, the Reservoir of Pleasure
The Science of Self-Realization
The Path of Perfection
Search for Liberation
Life Comes From Life
The Perfection of Yoga
Beyond Birth and Death
On the Way to Kṛṣṇa
Geetār-gan (Bengali)
Vairāgya-vidyā (Bengali)
Buddhi-yoga (Bengali)
Bhakti-ratna-bolī (Bengali)
Rāja-vidyā: The King of Knowledge
Elevation to Kṛṣṇa Consciousness
Kṛṣṇa Consciousness: The Matchless Gift
Back to Godhead magazine (founder)

A complete catalog is available upon request.

Bhaktivedanta Book Trust
3764 Watseka Avenue
Los Angeles, California 90034

ŚRĪMAD BHĀGAVATAM

Eleventh Canto

"General History"

(Part Four—Chapters 18-24)

With the Original Sanskrit Text,
Its Roman Transliteration, Synonyms,
Translation and Elaborate Purports

The Great Work of

His Divine Grace
A. C. Bhaktivedanta Swami Prabhupāda
Founder-*Ācārya* of the International Society for Krishna Consciousness

Continued by

His Divine Grace
Hridayananda dāsa Goswami Ācāryadeva

Sanskrit Editing by

Gopīparāṇadhana dāsa Adhikārī

THE BHAKTIVEDANTA BOOK TRUST
Los Angeles • London • Paris • Bombay • Sydney • Hong Kong

Readers interested in the subject matter of this book are invited by the International Society for Krishna Consciousness to correspond with its Secretary:

International Society for Krishna Consciousness
3764 Watseka Avenue
Los Angeles, California 90034

First Printing, 1983: 5,000 copies

© 1983 Bhaktivedanta Book Trust
All Rights Reserved
Printed in the United States of America

Library of Congress Cataloging in Publication Data (Revised)

Puranas. Bhāgavatapurāna. English & Sanskrit.
Śrīmad-Bhāgavatam.

Includes bibliographical references and indexes.

Contents: Canto 1. Creation (3 v)— Canto 2. The cosmic manifestation (2 v)— Canto 3. The status quo (4 v)— Canto 4. The creation of the fourth order (4 v)— Canto 5. The creative impetus (2 v)— Canto 6. Prescribed duties for mankind (3 v)— Canto 7. The science of God (3 v)— Canto 8. Withdrawal of the cosmic creations (3 v)— Canto 9. Liberation (3 v)— Canto 10. The summum bonum (3 v)— Canto 11. General history (5 v)

Canto 11- by Hridayananda Goswami Ācāryadeva, completing the great work of His Divine Grace A.C. Bhaktivedanta Swami Prabhupāda; Sanskrit editing by Gopīparāṇadhana Dāsa Adhikārī.

1. Puranas. Bhāgavatapurāṇa—Criticism, interpretation, etc. 2. Chaitanya, 1486–1534. 3. Vaishnavites—India—Biography.

I. Bhaktivedanta Swami, A. C., 1896–1977.
II. Hridayananda Goswami, 1948– .
III. Gopīparāṇadhana Dāsa Adhikārī.
IV. Title.
BL1140.4.B432E5 1972 294.5'925 73-169353
ISBN 0-89213-125-X (Canto 11, v. 4) AACR2

Table of Contents

Preface *ix*

Foreword *xiii*

Introduction *xvii*

CHAPTER EIGHTEEN

Descriptions of *Varṇāśrama-dharma*

Chapter Summary 1

Duties of a *Vānaprastha* 4

Duties of a *Sannyāsī* 14

A *Sannyāsī* Should Travel the Earth Alone 22

The Behavior of a *Paramahaṁsa* 32

Self-Realized Soul Sees Nothing Separate from Kṛṣṇa 41

CHAPTER NINETEEN

The Perfection of Spiritual Knowledge

Chapter Summary 53

Technical Knowledge of Illusion 56

Material Life Compared to Dark Hole Full of Snakes 66

Lord Kṛṣṇa Repeats the Instructions of Bhīṣma 69

Principles for Developing Love for Kṛṣṇa 78

Desirable Qualities for Human Beings 87

CHAPTER TWENTY

Pure Devotional Service Surpasses Knowledge and Detachment

Chapter Summary 95

Good and Bad Qualities of Work 97

The Paths of Knowledge, Work and Devotion 103

Residents of Heaven and Hell Desire Human Birth 111
One Should Bring the Mind Under Control of the Self 119
The Beginning Stage of Pure Devotional Service 128
Piercing the Knot in the Heart 132
Complete Detachment Is the Highest Stage of Freedom 138

CHAPTER TWENTY-ONE
Lord Kṛṣṇa's Explanation of the Vedic Path
Chapter Summary 143
Piety and Impiety 146
Atheistic Philosophy of Modern Science 153
Purity and Impurity 159
Proper Chanting of *Mantras* 166
The Actual Purpose of Vedic Knowledge 178
Worship of Entertainers, Politicians, and Athletes 183
Vedic Sound Is Unlimited, Deep and Unfathomable 188

CHAPTER TWENTY-TWO
Enumeration of the Elements of Material Creation
Chapter Summary 197
Philosophers Disagree on Number of Material Elements 200
Three Modes of Nature 211
Uddhava Inquires About the Difference Between the Body and Soul 223
Is This World Real? 231
Forgetfulness of One's Previous Identity Is Called Death 235
The Body Constantly Undergoes Transformation 241
Experience of Sense Gratification Is Actually False 249

CHAPTER TWENTY-THREE
The Song of the Avantī *Brāhmaṇa*

Chapter Summary 257
A Devotee Tolerates Any Personal Insult 260
Wealth of Misers Causes Self-Torment 268
The Proper Use of Wealth 274
Mind Is the Cause of Happiness and Distress 288
Karma Is Based on Illusory Consciousness 300
The Meaning of *Tridaṇḍa-sannyāsa* 304

CHAPTER TWENTY-FOUR
The Philosophy of Sāṅkhya

Chapter Summary 311
Modern Society's Knowledge Speculative and Changing 314
The Heavenly Planets 322
Material Nature Is the Energy of the Lord 329
Process of Annihilation 332

Appendixes

The Author 339
His Divine Grace A. C. Bhaktivedanta Swami Prabhupāda 341
References 345
Glossary 347
Sanskrit Pronunciation Guide 357
Index of Sanskrit Verses 361
General Index 371

Preface

nama oṁ viṣṇu-pādāya kṛṣṇa-preṣṭhāya bhū-tale
śrīmate bhaktivedānta-svāmin iti nāmine

I offer my most respectful obeisances at the lotus feet of His Divine Grace A. C. Bhaktivedanta Swami Prabhupāda, who is very dear to Lord Kṛṣṇa on this earth, having taken shelter at His lotus feet.

namas te sārasvate deve gaura-vāṇī-pracāriṇe
nirviśeṣa-śūnyavādi-pāścātya-deśa-tāriṇe

I offer my most respectful obeisances unto the lotus feet of His Divine Grace A. C. Bhaktivedanta Swami Prabhupāda, who is the disciple of Śrīla Bhaktisiddhānta Sarasvatī Ṭhākura and who is powerfully distributing the message of Caitanya Mahāprabhu and thus saving the fallen Western countries from impersonalism and voidism.

Śrīmad-Bhāgavatam, with authorized translation and elaborate purports in the English language, is the great work of His Divine Grace Oṁ Viṣṇupāda Paramahaṁsa Parivrājakācārya Aṣṭottara-śata Śrī Śrīmad A. C. Bhaktivedanta Swami Prabhupāda, our beloved spiritual master. Our present publication is a humble attempt by his servants to complete his most cherished work of *Śrīmad-Bhāgavatam.* Just as one may worship the holy Ganges River by offering Ganges water unto the Ganges, similarly, in our attempt to serve our spiritual master, we are offering to him that which he has given to us.

Śrīla Prabhupāda came to America in 1965 at a critical moment in the history of America and the world in general. The story of Śrīla Prabhupāda's arrival and his specific impact on world civilization, and especially Western civilization, has been brilliantly documented by His

Divine Grace Satsvarūpa dāsa Goswami. In Śrīla Satsvarūpa's authorized biography of Śrīla Prabhupāda, called *Śrīla Prabhupāda-līlāmṛta,* the reader can fully understand Śrīla Prabhupāda's purpose, desire and mission in presenting *Śrīmad-Bhāgavatam.* Further, in Śrīla Prabhupāda's own preface to the *Bhāgavatam* (reprinted as the Foreword in this volume), he clearly states that this transcendental literature will provoke a cultural revolution in the world, and that is now underway. I do not wish to be redundant in repeating what Śrīla Prabhupāda has so eloquently stated in his preface, nor that which has been so abundantly documented by Śrīla Satsvarūpa in his authorized biography.

It is necessary to mention, however, that *Śrīmad-Bhāgavatam* is a completely transcendental, liberated sound vibration coming from the spiritual world. And, being absolute, it is not different from the Absolute Truth Himself, Lord Śrī Kṛṣṇa. By understanding *Śrīmad-Bhāgavatam,* consisting of twelve cantos, the reader acquires perfect knowledge by which he or she may live peacefully and progressively on the earth, attending to all material necessities and achieving simultaneously supreme spiritual liberation. In preparing this and other volumes of *Śrīmad-Bhāgavatam,* our intention and methodology has been always to serve faithfully the lotus feet of our spiritual master, carefully trying to translate and comment exactly as he would have, thus preserving the unity and spiritual potency of this edition of *Śrīmad-Bhāgavatam.* In other words, by strictly following the disciplic succession, called in Sanskrit *guru-paramparā,* this edition of the *Bhāgavatam* will continue to be throughout its volumes a liberated work, free from material contamination and capable of elevating the reader to the kingdom of God.

The purport is that we have faithfully followed the commentaries of previous *ācāryas* and exercised a calculated selectivity of material based on the example and mood of Śrīla Prabhupāda. One may write transcendental literature only by the mercy of the Supreme Personality of Godhead, Śrī Kṛṣṇa, and the authorized, liberated spiritual masters coming in disciplic succession. Thus, we humbly fall at the lotus feet of the previous *ācāryas,* offering special gratitude to the great commentators on the *Bhāgavatam,* namely Śrīla Śrīdhara Svāmī, Śrīla Jīva Gosvāmī, Śrīla Viśvanātha Cakravartī Ṭhākura and Śrīla Bhaktisiddhānta Sarasvatī Gosvāmī, the spiritual master of Śrīla Prabhupāda. We also offer our obeisances at the lotus feet of Śrīla Vīrarāghavācārya, Śrīla

Vijayadhvaja Ṭhākura and Śrīla Vaṁśīdhara Ṭhākura, whose commentaries have also helped in this work. Additionally, we offer our humble obeisances at the lotus feet of the great *ācārya* Śrīla Madhva, who has made innumerable learned comments on *Śrīmad-Bhāgavatam*. We further offer our humble obeisances at the lotus feet of the Supreme Personality of Godhead, Śrī Kṛṣṇa Caitanya Mahāprabhu, and to all of His eternally liberated followers, headed by Śrīla Nityānanda Prabhu, Advaita Prabhu, Gadādhara Prabhu and Śrīvāsa Ṭhākura, and to the six Gosvāmīs, Śrīla Rūpa Gosvāmī, Śrīla Sanātana Gosvāmī, Śrīla Raghunātha dāsa Gosvāmī, Śrīla Raghunātha Bhaṭṭa Gosvāmī, Śrīla Jīva Gosvāmī and Śrīla Gopāla Bhaṭṭa Gosvāmī. Finally we offer our most respectful obeisances at the lotus feet of the Absolute Truth, Śrī Śrī Rādhā and Kṛṣṇa, and humbly beg for Their mercy so that this great work of *Śrīmad-Bhāgavatam* can be quickly finished. *Śrīmad-Bhāgavatam* is undoubtedly the most important book within the universe, and the sincere readers of *Śrīmad-Bhāgavatam* will undoubtedly achieve the highest perfection of life, Kṛṣṇa consciousness.

In conclusion, I again remind the reader that *Śrīmad-Bhāgavatam* is the great work of His Divine Grace A. C. Bhaktivedanta Swami Prabhupāda, and that the present volume is the humble attempt of his devoted servants.

Hare Kṛṣṇa

Hridayananda dāsa Goswami

Foreword

We must know the present need of human society. And what is that need? Human society is no longer bounded by geographical limits to particular countries or communities. Human society is broader than in the Middle Ages, and the world tendency is toward one state or one human society. The ideals of spiritual communism, according to *Śrīmad-Bhāgavatam,* are based more or less on the oneness of the entire human society, nay, of the entire energy of living beings. The need is felt by great thinkers to make this a successful ideology. *Śrīmad-Bhāgavatam* will fill this need in human society. It begins, therefore, with the aphorism of Vedānta philosophy *janmādy asya yataḥ* to establish the ideal of a common cause.

Human society, at the present moment, is not in the darkness of oblivion. It has made rapid progress in the field of material comforts, education and economic development throughout the entire world. But there is a pinprick somewhere in the social body at large, and therefore there are large-scale quarrels, even over less important issues. There is need of a clue as to how humanity can become one in peace, friendship and prosperity with a common cause. *Śrīmad-Bhāgavatam* will fill this need, for it is a cultural presentation for the respiritualization of the entire human society.

Śrīmad-Bhāgavatam should be introduced also in the schools and colleges, for it is recommended by the great student-devotee Prahlāda Mahārāja in order to change the demoniac face of society.

kaumāra ācaret prājño
dharmān bhāgavatān iha
durlabhaṁ mānuṣaṁ janma
tad apy adhruvam arthadam
(*Bhāg.* 7.6.1)

Disparity in human society is due to lack of principles in a godless civilization. There is God, or the Almighty One, from whom everything emanates, by whom everything is maintained and in whom everything is merged to rest. Material science has tried to find the ultimate source of creation very insufficiently, but it is a fact that there is one ultimate source of everything that be. This ultimate source is explained rationally and authoritatively in the beautiful *Bhāgavatam*, or *Śrīmad-Bhāgavatam*.

Śrīmad-Bhāgavatam is the transcendental science not only for knowing the ultimate source of everything but also for knowing our relation with Him and our duty toward perfection of the human society on the basis of this perfect knowledge. It is powerful reading matter in the Sanskrit language, and it is now rendered into English elaborately so that simply by a careful reading one will know God perfectly well, so much so that the reader will be sufficiently educated to defend himself from the onslaught of atheists. Over and above this, the reader will be able to convert others to accept God as a concrete principle.

Śrīmad-Bhāgavatam begins with the definition of the ultimate source. It is a bona fide commentary on the *Vedānta-sūtra* by the same author, Śrīla Vyāsadeva, and gradually it develops into nine cantos up to the highest state of God realization. The only qualification one needs to study this great book of transcendental knowledge is to proceed step by step cautiously and not jump forward haphazardly as with an ordinary book. It should be gone through chapter by chapter, one after another. The reading matter is so arranged with its original Sanskrit text, its English transliteration, synonyms, translation and purports so that one is sure to become a God-realized soul at the end of finishing the first nine cantos.

The Tenth Canto is distinct from the first nine cantos because it deals directly with the transcendental activities of the Personality of Godhead, Śrī Kṛṣṇa. One will be unable to capture the effects of the Tenth Canto without going through the first nine cantos. The book is complete in twelve cantos, each independent, but it is good for all to read them in small installments one after another.

I must admit my frailties in presenting *Śrīmad-Bhāgavatam*, but still I am hopeful of its good reception by the thinkers and leaders of society on the strength of the following statement of *Śrīmad-Bhāgavatam* (1.5.11):

tad-vāg-visargo janatāgha-viplavo
yasmin prati-ślokam abaddhavaty api

nāmāny anantasya yaśo 'ṅkitāni yac
chṛṇvanti gāyanti gṛṇanti sādhavaḥ

"On the other hand, that literature which is full with descriptions of the transcendental glories of the name, fame, form and pastimes of the unlimited Supreme Lord is a transcendental creation meant to bring about a revolution in the impious life of a misdirected civilization. Such transcendental literatures, even though irregularly composed, are heard, sung and accepted by purified men who are thoroughly honest."

Oṁ tat sat

A. C. Bhaktivedanta Swami

Introduction

"This *Bhāgavata Purāṇa* is as brilliant as the sun, and it has arisen just after the departure of Lord Kṛṣṇa to His own abode, accompanied by religion, knowledge, etc. Persons who have lost their vision due to the dense darkness of ignorance in the age of Kali shall get light from this *Purāṇa*." (*Śrīmad-Bhāgavatam* 1.3.43)

The timeless wisdom of India is expressed in the *Vedas*, ancient Sanskrit texts that touch upon all fields of human knowledge. Originally preserved through oral tradition, the *Vedas* were first put into writing five thousand years ago by Śrīla Vyāsadeva, the "literary incarnation of God." After compiling the *Vedas*, Vyāsadeva set forth their essence in the aphorisms known as *Vedānta-sūtras*. *Śrīmad-Bhāgavatam* (*Bhāgavata Purāṇa*) is Vyāsadeva's commentary on his own *Vedānta-sūtras*. It was written in the maturity of his spiritual life under the direction of Nārada Muni, his spiritual master. Referred to as "the ripened fruit of the tree of Vedic literature," *Śrīmad-Bhāgavatam* is the most complete and authoritative exposition of Vedic knowledge.

After compiling the *Bhāgavatam*, Vyāsa impressed the synopsis of it upon his son, the sage Śukadeva Gosvāmī. Śukadeva Gosvāmī subsequently recited the entire *Bhāgavatam* to Mahārāja Parīkṣit in an assembly of learned saints on the bank of the Ganges at Hastināpura (now Delhi). Mahārāja Parīkṣit was the emperor of the world and was a great *rājarṣi* (saintly king). Having received a warning that he would die within a week, he renounced his entire kingdom and retired to the bank of the Ganges to fast until death and receive spiritual enlightenment. The *Bhāgavatam* begins with Emperor Parīkṣit's sober inquiry to Śukadeva Gosvāmī: "You are the spiritual master of great saints and devotees. I am therefore begging you to show the way of perfection for all persons, and especially for one who is about to die. Please let me know what a man should hear, chant, remember and worship, and also what he should not do. Please explain all this to me."

Śukadeva Gosvāmī's answer to this question, and numerous other questions posed by Mahārāja Parīkṣit, concerning everything from the nature of the self to the origin of the universe, held the assembled sages in rapt attention continuously for the seven days leading to the king's death. The sage Sūta Gosvāmī, who was present on the bank of the Ganges when Śukadeva Gosvāmī first recited *Śrīmad-Bhāgavatam,* later repeated the *Bhāgavatam* before a gathering of sages in the forest of Naimiṣāraṇya. Those sages, concerned about the spiritual welfare of the people in general, had gathered to perform a long, continuous chain of sacrifices to counteract the degrading influence of the incipient age of Kali. In response to the sages' request that he speak the essence of Vedic wisdom, Sūta Gosvāmī repeated from memory the entire eighteen thousand verses of *Śrīmad-Bhāgavatam,* as spoken by Śukadeva Gosvāmī to Mahārāja Parīkṣit.

The reader of *Śrīmad-Bhāgavatam* hears Sūta Gosvāmī relate the questions of Mahārāja Parīkṣit and the answers of Śukadeva Gosvāmī. Also, Sūta Gosvāmī sometimes responds directly to questions put by Śaunaka Ṛṣi, the spokesman for the sages gathered at Naimiṣāraṇya. One therefore simultaneously hears two dialogues: one between Mahārāja Parīkṣit and Śukadeva Gosvāmī on the bank of the Ganges, and another at Naimiṣāraṇya between Sūta Gosvāmī and the sages at Naimiṣāraṇya Forest, headed by Śaunaka Ṛṣi. Furthermore, while instructing King Parīkṣit, Śukadeva Gosvāmī often relates historical episodes and gives accounts of lengthy philosophical discussions between such great souls as Nārada Muni and Vasudeva. With this understanding of the history of the *Bhāgavatam,* the reader will easily be able to follow its intermingling of dialogues and events from various sources. Since philosophical wisdom, not chronological order, is most important in the text, one need only be attentive to the subject matter of *Śrīmad-Bhāgavatam* to appreciate fully its profound message.

The translator of this edition compares the *Bhāgavatam* to sugar candy—wherever you taste it, you will find it equally sweet and relishable. Therefore, to taste the sweetness of the *Bhāgavatam,* one may begin by reading any of its volumes. After such an introductory taste, however, the serious reader is best advised to go back to Volume One of the First Canto and then proceed through the *Bhāgavatam,* volume after volume, in its natural order.

This edition of the *Bhāgavatam* is the first complete English translation of this important text with an elaborate commentary, and it is the first widely available to the English-speaking public. The first thirty volumes (Canto One through Canto Ten, Volume Three) are the product of the scholarly and devotional effort of His Divine Grace A. C. Bhaktivedanta Swami Prabhupāda, the world's most distinguished teacher of Indian religious and philosophical thought. His consummate Sanskrit scholarship and intimate familiarity with Vedic culture and thought as well as the modern way of life combine to reveal to the West a magnificent exposition of this important classic. Śrīla Prabhupāda departed from this world in 1977, and his monumental work of translating *Śrīmad-Bhāgavatam* is being continued by his disciple His Divine Grace Hridayananda Goswami Ācāryadeva.

Readers will find this work of value for many reasons. For those interested in the classical roots of Indian civilization, it serves as a vast reservoir of detailed information on virtually every one of its aspects. For students of comparative philosophy and religion, the *Bhāgavatam* offers a penetrating view into the meaning of India's profound spiritual heritage. To sociologists and anthropologists, the *Bhāgavatam* reveals the practical workings of a peaceful and scientifically organized Vedic culture, whose institutions were integrated on the basis of a highly developed spiritual world view. Students of literature will discover the *Bhāgavatam* to be a masterpiece of majestic poetry. For students of psychology, the text provides important perspectives on the nature of consciousness, human behavior and the philosophical study of identity. Finally, to those seeking spiritual insight, the *Bhāgavatam* offers simple and practical guidance for attainment of the highest self-knowledge and realization of the Absolute Truth. The entire multivolume text, presented by the Bhaktivedanta Book Trust, promises to occupy a significant place in the intellectual, cultural and spiritual life of modern man for a long time to come.

—The Publishers

CHAPTER EIGHTEEN

Lord Kṛṣṇa's Description of Varṇāśrama-dharma

As related in this chapter, Lord Śrī Kṛṣṇa explained to Uddhava the duties of the *vānaprastha* and *sannyāsa* orders and the religious practices proper to each of these levels of advancement.

One who is taking to the *vānaprastha* stage of life should leave his wife at home in the care of his sons, or else take her along, and with a peaceful mind spend the third quarter of his life in the forest. He should accept as his food whatever bulbs, fruits, roots and so on that grow in the forest, taking sometimes grains cooked by fire and sometimes fruits ripened by time. Furthermore, he should take as his garments tree bark, grass, leaves or the skin of a deer. It is prescribed that he should perform austerities by not cutting his hair, beard, or nails. Nor should he make any special attempt to remove dirt from his limbs. He should bathe three times daily in cold water and sleep upon the ground. During the hot season he should stand beneath the fearsome heat of the sun with fires blazing on four sides. During the rainy season he should stand in the midst of the downpour of rain, and during the cold winter he should submerge himself in water up to his neck. He is absolutely forbidden to clean his teeth, to store food that he has collected at one time to eat at another time, and to worship the Supreme Lord with the flesh of animals. If he can maintain those severe practices for the remainder of his life, the *vānaprastha* will achieve the Tapoloka planet.

The fourth quarter of life is meant for *sannyāsa*. One should develop complete detachment from attaining residence on different planets, up to even Brahmaloka. Such wishes for material elevation are due to desire for the fruits of material activity. When one recognizes that endeavors to achieve residence on the higher planets ultimately award only suffering, then it is enjoined that one should take to *sannyāsa* in a spirit of renunciation. The process of accepting *sannyāsa* involves worshiping the Lord with sacrifice, giving everything one possesses in charity to the priests and establishing within one's own heart the various sacrificial fires. For a *sannyāsī*, association with women or even the sight of women is more undesirable than taking poison. Except in emergencies, the *sannyāsī* should never wear more clothing than a loincloth or some simple covering over his loincloth. He should carry no more than his staff and waterpot. Giving up all violence to living creatures, he should become subdued in the functions of his body, mind and speech. He should remain detached and fixed on the self and travel alone to such pure places as the mountains, rivers and forests. Thus engaged, he should remember the Supreme Personality of Godhead and dwell in a place that is fearless and not heavily populated. He should take his alms each day at seven homes chosen at random from those of the members of the four social classes, avoiding only the homes of those who are cursed or fallen. With a pure heart he should offer to the Supreme Personality of Godhead whatever food he has collected and take the *mahā-prasādam* remnants. In this way he should always be mindful that hankering for sense gratification is bondage and that engaging the objects of the senses in the service of Lord Mādhava is liberation. If one lacks knowledge and renunciation, or continues to be troubled by the unconquered six enemies headed by lust and the all-powerful senses, or if one accepts the *tri-daṇḍa* renounced order simply for the purpose of carrying out a livelihood, then he will achieve as his result only the killing of his own soul.

A *paramahaṁsa* is not under the control of injunctions and prohibitions. He is a devotee of the Supreme Lord, detached from external sense gratification and completely free from desire for even such subtle gratificatory goals as liberation. He is expert in discrimination and, just like a simple child, is free from concepts of pride and insult. Although actually competent, he wanders about like a dull person, and although most learned, he engages himself like an insane fool in incoherent speech. Although actually fixed in the *Vedas*, he behaves in an unordered fashion. He tolerates the evil words of others and never shows contempt for anyone else. He avoids acting as an enemy or vainly indulging in argument. He sees the Supreme Personality of Godhead in all creatures and also all living beings within the Supreme Personality of Godhead. In order to keep his body alive for performing worship of the Lord, he accepts whatever excellent or inferior food, clothing and bedding he can obtain without endeavor. Although he has to make some effort to find food for maintaining his body, he does not become joyful when he finds something, nor does he become depressed when not finding anything. The Supreme Lord Himself, although not at all subject to the Vedic orders and prohibitions, by His own free will executes various prescribed duties; similarly the *paramahaṁsa,* even while on the platform of freedom from subjugation to Vedic rules and prohibitions, carries out various duties. Because his perception of dualities has become completely eradicated by transcendental knowledge, which is focused on the Supreme Lord, he obtains upon the demise of his material body the liberation known as *sārṣṭi,* in which one becomes equal in opulence with the Lord.

The person who desires his own best interest should take shelter of a bona fide spiritual master. Filling his mind with faith, keeping free from enviousness and remaining fixed in devotion, the disciple should serve the spiritual master, whom he should regard as nondifferent from the Supreme Lord. For a *brahmacārī,* the primary duty is service to the spiritual master. The main duties for a householder are protection of living beings and sacrifice, for a *vānaprastha* austerities, and for a *sannyāsī* self-control and nonviolence. Celibacy (practiced by householders at all times except once a month when the wife is fertile), penance, cleanliness, self-satisfaction, friendship with all living beings and above all worship of the Supreme Personality of Godhead are duties meant for every *jīva* soul. One acquires firm devotion for the Supreme Lord by always rendering service to the Supreme Personality of Godhead through one's own particular prescribed duty, by not engaging in the worship of any other personalities, and also by thinking of all creatures as the place of residence of the Supreme Personality of Godhead in His form as the Supersoul. The followers of the *karma-kāṇḍa* section of the *Vedas* can attain the planets of the forefathers and so on by their ritualistic activities, but if they become endowed with devotion for the Supreme Lord, then by these same activities they can achieve the supreme stage of liberation.

TEXT 1

श्रीभगवानुवाच

वनं विविक्षुः पुत्रेषु भार्यां न्यस्य सहैव वा ।
वन एव वसेच्छान्तस्तृतीयं भागमायुषः ॥ १ ॥

śrī-bhagavān uvāca
vanaṁ vivikṣuḥ putreṣu
bhāryāṁ nyasya sahaiva vā
vana eva vasec chāntas
tṛtīyaṁ bhāgam āyuṣaḥ

śrī-bhagavān uvāca—the Supreme Personality of Godhead said; *vanam*—the forest; *vivikṣuḥ*—desiring to enter; *putreṣu*—among the sons; *bhāryām*—wife; *nyasya*—entrusting; *saha*—together with; *eva*—indeed; *vā*—or; *vane*—in the forest; *eva*—certainly; *vaset*—one should dwell; *śāntaḥ*—with a peaceful mind; *tṛtīyam*—the third; *bhāgam*—division; *āyuṣaḥ*—of life.

TRANSLATION

The Supreme Personality of Godhead said: One who desires to adopt the third order of life, *vānaprastha*, should enter the forest with a peaceful mind, leaving his wife with his mature sons, or else taking her along with him.

PURPORT

In Kali-yuga a human being generally cannot live more than one hundred years, and even this is becoming most unusual. A man who has a reasonable expectation of living for one hundred years may adopt the *vānaprastha* order at the age of fifty, and then at the age of seventy-five he may take *sannyāsa* for complete renunciation. Since in Kali-yuga very few people live for one hundred years, one should adjust the schedule accordingly. *Vānaprastha* is intended as a gradual transition from materialistic family life to the stage of complete renunciation.

TEXT 2

कन्दमूलफलैर्वन्यैर्मेध्यैर्वृत्तिं प्रकल्पयेत् ।
वसीत वल्कलं वासस्तृणपर्णाजिनानि च ॥ २ ॥

kanda-mūla-phalair vanyair
medhyair vṛttiṁ prakalpayet
vasīta valkalaṁ vāsas
tṛṇa-parṇājināni vā

kanda—with bulbs; *mūla*—roots; *phalaiḥ*—and fruits; *vanyaiḥ*—growing in the forest; *medhyaiḥ*—pure; *vṛttim*—sustenance; *prakalpayet*—one should arrange; *vasīta*—one should put on; *valkalam*—tree bark; *vāsaḥ*—as clothes; *tṛṇa*—grass; *parṇa*—leaves; *ajināni*—animal skins; *vā*—or.

TRANSLATION

Having adopted the *vānaprastha* order of life, one should arrange one's sustenance by eating uncontaminated bulbs, roots and fruits that grow in the forest. One may dress oneself with tree bark, grass, leaves or animal skins.

PURPORT

A renounced sage in the forest does not kill animals, but rather acquires skins from animals who have suffered natural death. According to a passage from *Manu-saṁhitā*, quoted by Śrīla Bhaktisiddhānta Sarasvatī Ṭhākura, the word *medhyaiḥ*, or "pure," indicates that while residing in the forest a sage may not accept honey-based liquors, animal flesh, fungus, mushrooms, horseradish or any hallucinogenic or intoxicating herbs, even those taken as so-called medicine.

TEXT 3

केशरोमनखश्मश्रुमलानि बिभृयाद् दतः ।
न धावेदप्सु मज्जेत त्रिकालं स्थण्डिलेशयः ॥ ३ ॥

keśa-roma-nakha-śmaśru-
malāni bibhṛyād dataḥ
na dhāved apsu majjeta
tri-kālaṁ sthaṇḍile-śayaḥ

keśa—hair on the head; *roma*—bodily hair; *nakha*—fingernails and toenails; *śmaśru*—facial hair; *malāni*—bodily waste products; *bibhṛyāt*—one should tolerate; *dataḥ*—the teeth; *na dhāvet*—should not clean; *apsu*—in water; *majjeta*—should bathe; *tri-kālam*—three times a day; *sthaṇḍile*—on the earth; *śayaḥ*—lying down.

TRANSLATION

The *vānaprastha* should not groom the hair on his head, body or face, should not manicure his nails, should not pass stool and urine at irregular times and should not make a special endeavor for dental hygiene. He should be content to take bath in water three times daily and should sleep on the ground.

TEXT 4

ग्रीष्मे तप्येत पञ्चाग्नीन् वर्षास्वासारषाड् जले ।
आकण्ठमग्नः शिशिर एवंवृत्तस्तपश्चरेत् ॥ ४ ॥

grīṣme tapyeta pañcāgnīn
varṣāsv āsāra-ṣāḍ jale
ākaṇṭha-magnaḥ śiśira
evaṁ vṛttas tapaś caret

grīṣme—in the summer; *tapyeta*—one should accept as austerity; *pañca-agnīn*—five fires (the overhead sun and fires burning on four sides); *varṣāsu*—during the rainy season; *āsāra*—torrents of rain; *ṣāṭ*—tolerating; *jale*—in water; *ā-kaṇṭha*—up to the neck; *magnaḥ*—submerged; *śiśire*—in the coldest part of winter; *evam*—thus; *vṛttaḥ*—engaged; *tapaḥ*—penance; *caret*—one should execute.

TRANSLATION

Thus engaged as a *vānaprastha*, one should execute penance during the hottest summer days by subjecting oneself to burning fires on four sides and the blazing sun overhead; during the rainy season one should remain outside, subjecting oneself to torrents of rain; and in the freezing winter one should remain submerged in water up to one's neck.

PURPORT

One who engages in sense gratification must perform severe penances at the end of life to counteract his sinful, hedonistic activities. A devotee of the Lord, however, naturally develops Kṛṣṇa consciousness and need not subject himself to such radical penances. As stated in the *Pañcarātra*,

ārādhito yadi haris tapasā tataḥ kiṁ
nārādhito yadi haris tapasā tataḥ kim
antar bahir yadi haris tapasā tataḥ kiṁ
nāntar bahir yadi haris tapasā tataḥ kim

"If one is worshiping the Lord properly, what is the use of severe penances? And if one is not properly worshiping the Lord, what is the use of severe penances? If Śrī Kṛṣṇa is realized within and without everything that exists, what is the use of severe penances? And if Śrī Kṛṣṇa is not seen within and without everything, then what is the use of severe penances?"

TEXT 5

अग्निपक्वं समश्नीयात् कालपक्वमथापि वा ।
उलूखलाश्मकुट्टो वा दन्तोलूखल एव वा ॥ ५ ॥

agni-pakvaṁ samaśnīyāt
kāla-pakvam athāpi vā
ulūkhalāśma-kuṭṭo vā
dantolūkhala eva vā

agni—by fire; *pakvam*—made ready to eat; *samaśnīyāt*—one should eat; *kāla*—by time; *pakvam*—right for eating; *atha*—else; *api*—indeed; *vā*—or; *ulūkhala*—with grinding mortar; *aśma*—and stone; *kuṭṭaḥ*—pulverized, ground up; *vā*—or; *danta*—using the teeth; *ulūkhalaḥ*—as a grinding mortar; *eva*—indeed; *vā*—or, alternatively.

TRANSLATION

One may eat foodstuffs prepared with fire, such as grains, or fruits ripened by time. One may grind one's food with mortar and stone or with one's own teeth.

PURPORT

In Vedic civilization it is recommended that at the end of one's life one should go to a holy place or forest for spiritual perfection. In sacred forests one does not find restaurants, supermarkets, fast-food chains and so on, and thus one must eat simply, reducing sense gratification.

Although in the Western countries people eat processed food, one living simply must himself separate and pulverize grains and other foods before eating. This is referred to here.

TEXT 6

स्वयं संचिनुयात् सर्वमात्मनो वृत्तिकारणम् ।
देशकालबलाभिज्ञो नाददीतान्यदाहृतम् ॥ ६ ॥

svayaṁ sañcinuyāt sarvam
ātmano vṛtti-kāraṇam
deśa-kāla-balābhijño
nādadītānyadāhṛtam

svayam—himself; *sañcinuyāt*—should gather; *sarvam*—everything; *ātmanaḥ*—his own; *vṛtti*—sustenance; *kāraṇam*—facilitating; *deśa*—the particular place; *kāla*—the time; *bala*—and one's strength; *abhijñaḥ*—understanding pragmatically; *na ādadīta*—should not take; *anyadā*—for another time; *āhṛtam*—provisions.

TRANSLATION

The *vānaprastha* should personally collect whatever he requires for his bodily maintenance, carefully considering the time, place and his own capacity. He should never collect provisions for the future.

PURPORT

According to Vedic regulations, one practicing austerity should collect only what he requires for immediate use, and upon receiving gifts of foodstuff he should immediately give up that which he has previously collected, so that there will be no surplus. This regulation is meant to keep one fixed in faithful dependence on the Supreme Lord. One should never stock food or other bodily necessities for future use. The term *deśa-kāla-balābhijña* indicates that in a particularly difficult place, or in time of emergency or personal incapacity, this strict rule need not be followed, as confirmed by Śrīla Viśvanātha Cakravartī Ṭhākura.

Śrīla Bhaktisiddhānta Sarasvatī Ṭhākura points out that unless one is completely incapacitated, one should not depend on others for one's personal maintenance, as this will create a debt that can only be repaid by taking another birth in the material world. This applies only to those endeavoring for personal purification and not to those engaged full time in devotional service to Lord Kṛṣṇa. A pure devotee eats, dresses and speaks only for the service of the Lord, and thus whatever assistance he accepts from others is not for himself. He is fully surrendered to the mission of the Supreme Personality of Godhead. However, one not so surrendered will certainly have to take birth again in the material world to repay all of his debts to others.

TEXT 7

वन्यैश्चरुपुरोडाशैर्निर्वपेत् कालचोदितान् ।
न तु श्रौतेन पशुना मां यजेत वनाश्रमी ॥ ७ ॥

vanyaiś caru-puroḍāśair
nirvapet kāla-coditān
na tu śrautena paśunā
māṁ yajeta vanāśramī

vanyaiḥ—obtained in the forest; *caru*—with oblations of rice, barley and *dāl* beans; *puroḍāśaiḥ*—and sacrificial cakes prepared with wild rice; *nirvapet*—one should offer; *kāla-coditān*—ritualistic sacrifices, such as *āgrayaṇa*, offered according to seasons (*āgrayaṇa* is the offering of the first fruits that appear after the rainy season); *na*—never; *tu*—indeed; *śrautena*—mentioned in the *Vedas; paśunā*—with animal sacrifice; *mām*—Me; *yajeta*—may worship; *vana-āśramī*—one who has gone to the forest, taking the *vānaprastha* order of life.

TRANSLATION

One who has accepted the *vānaprastha* order of life should perform seasonal sacrifices by offering oblations of *caru* and sacrificial cakes prepared from rice and other grains found in the forest. The *vānaprastha,* however, may never offer animal sacrifices to Me, even those sacrifices mentioned in the *Vedas.*

PURPORT

One who has taken the *vānaprastha* order of life should never perform animal sacrifices or eat meat.

TEXT 8

अग्निहोत्रं च दर्शश्च पौर्णमासश्च पूर्ववत् ।
चातुर्मास्यानि च मुनेराम्नातानि च नैगमैः ॥ ८ ॥

agnihotraṁ ca darśaś ca
paurṇamāsaś ca pūrva-vat
cāturmāsyāni ca muner
āmnātāni ca naigamaiḥ

agni-hotram—the fire sacrifice; *ca*—also; *darśaḥ*—the sacrifice performed on the new moon day; *ca*—also; *paurṇa-māsaḥ*—full moon sacrifice; *ca*—also; *pūrva-vat*—as previously, in the *gṛhastha-āśrama; cātuḥ-māsyāni*—the vows and sacrifices of *cāturmāsya; ca*—also; *muneḥ*—of the *vānaprastha; āmnātāni*—enjoined; *ca*—also; *naigamaiḥ*—by expert knowers of the *Vedas.*

TRANSLATION

The *vānaprastha* should perform the *agnihotra, darśa* and *paurṇamāsa* sacrifices, as he did while in the *gṛhastha-āśrama.* He should also perform the vows and sacrifices of *cāturmāsya,* since all of these rituals are enjoined for the *vānaprastha-āśrama* by expert knowers of the *Vedas.*

PURPORT

Śrīla Bhaktisiddhānta Sarasvatī Ṭhākura has given a detailed explanation of the four rituals mentioned here, namely *agnihotra, darśa, paurṇamāsa* and *cāturmāsya.* The conclusion is that everyone should simply chant Hare Kṛṣṇa, Hare Kṛṣṇa, Kṛṣṇa Kṛṣṇa, Hare Hare/ Hare Rāma, Hare Rāma, Rāma Rāma, Hare Hare and avoid the difficult entanglement of Vedic ritualistic ceremonies. If one neither chants Hare Kṛṣṇa nor performs such rituals, one certainly becomes a *pāṣaṇḍī,* an atheistic fool.

TEXT 9

एवं चीर्णेन तपसा मुनिर्धमनिसन्ततः ।
मां तपोमयमाराध्य ऋषिलोकादुपैति माम् ॥ ९ ॥

evaṁ cīrṇena tapasā
munir dhamani-santataḥ
māṁ tapo-mayam ārādhya
ṛṣi-lokād upaiti mām

evam—thus; *cīrṇena*—by the practice; *tapasā*—of austerity; *muniḥ*—the saintly *vānaprastha; dhamani-santataḥ*—emaciated so much that the veins are visible throughout his body; *mām*—Me; *tapaḥ-mayam*—the goal of all penance; *ārādhya*—worshiping; *ṛṣi-lokāt*—beyond Maharloka; *upaiti*—achieves; *mām*—Me.

TRANSLATION

The saintly *vānaprastha*, practicing severe penances and accepting only the bare necessities of life, becomes so emaciated that he appears to be mere skin and bones. Thus worshiping Me through severe penances, he goes to the Maharloka planet and then directly achieves Me.

PURPORT

A *vānaprastha* who develops pure devotional service achieves the Supreme Lord, Kṛṣṇa, while in the *vānaprastha* stage of life. One who does not become completely Kṛṣṇa conscious, however, first goes to the planet Maharloka, or Ṛṣiloka, and from there directly achieves Lord Kṛṣṇa.

One achieves Maharloka, or Ṛṣiloka, through strict observance of positive and negative regulations. However, without developing a taste for chanting and hearing the glories of the Lord (*śravaṇaṁ kīrtanaṁ viṣṇoḥ*), it is not possible to achieve the perfect liberation of going back home, back to Godhead. Therefore, on the Maharloka planet the unsuccessful sage gives more attention to chanting and hearing, and thus he gradually develops pure love of Godhead.

TEXT 10

यस्त्वेतत् कृच्छ्रतश्चीर्णं तपो निःश्रेयसं महत् ।
कामायाल्पीयसे युञ्ज्याद् बालिशः कोऽपरस्ततः ॥१०॥

yas tv etat kṛcchrataś cīrṇaṁ
tapo niḥśreyasaṁ mahat
kāmāyālpīyase yuñjyād
bāliśaḥ ko 'paras tataḥ

yaḥ—one who; *tu*—indeed; *etat*—this; *kṛcchrataḥ*—with great penance; *cīrṇam*—for a long time; *tapaḥ*—austerity; *niḥśreyasam*—awarding ultimate liberation; *mahat*—glorious; *kāmāya*—for sense gratification; *alpīyase*—insignificant; *yuñjyāt*—practices; *bāliśaḥ*—such a fool; *kaḥ*—who; *aparaḥ*—else; *tataḥ*—besides him.

TRANSLATION

One who with long endeavor executes this painful but exalted penance, which awards ultimate liberation, simply to achieve insignificant sense gratification must be considered the greatest fool.

PURPORT

Although the process of *vānaprastha* described by Lord Kṛṣṇa is so glorious that even the consolation prize is promotion to Maharloka, one who consciously performs this process for such promotion to heaven is certainly the greatest fool. The Lord does not want this process to be abused or exploited by materialistic rascals, for the ultimate goal is love of Godhead.

TEXT 11

यदासौ नियमेऽकल्पो जरया जातवेपथुः ।
आत्मन्यग्नीन् समारोप्य मच्चित्तोऽग्निं समाविशेत् ॥११॥

yadāsau niyame 'kalpo
jarayā jāta-vepathuḥ
ātmany agnīn samāropya
mac-citto 'gniṁ samāviśet

yadā—when; *asau*—the saintly *vānaprastha; niyame*—in his prescribed duties; *akalpaḥ*—unable to carry on; *jarayā*—due to old age;

His Divine Grace
A. C. Bhaktivedanta Swami Prabhupāda
Founder-Ācārya of the International Society for Krishna Consciousness

PLATE ONE: The Supersoul

The Supreme Personality of Godhead, Lord Kṛṣṇa, enters within the bodies of all living beings as the four-armed Supersoul. Lord Kṛṣṇa tells His devotee Uddhava, "Just as the moon is reflected in innumerable reservoirs of water, the Supreme Lord, although one, is present within everyone." A saintly person therefore sees all living beings with equal vision. (*p. 36*)

PLATE TWO: The Supreme Personality of Godhead

Kṛṣṇa said, "My dear Uddhava, I am the Supreme Lord of all worlds, and I create and destroy this universe, being its ultimate cause. I am thus the Absolute Truth, and one who worships Me with unfailing devotional service comes to Me." According to the Vedic literatures of India, God is realized in three progressive stages—as the impersonal Brahman effulgence, as the Supersoul within the hearts of all living beings, and finally as the Supreme Personality of Godhead. God's eternal personal form, the object of meditation for the topmost transcendentalists, is described in great detail in the Vedic literature. This painting of Kṛṣṇa is an accurate visual representation of these authoritative descriptions. (*p. 49*)

PLATE THREE: Bhīṣma Instructs King Yudhiṣṭhira

In the aftermath of the Battle of Kurukṣetra, the great upholder of religious principles Bhīṣma lay mortally wounded upon a bed of arrows. King Yudhiṣṭhira, along with His four younger brothers and Lord Kṛṣṇa,

went to his side. Yudhiṣṭhira, overwhelmed by the death of many relatives and friends, listened to the instructions of Bhīṣma, who was an exalted, spiritually advanced devotee of the Supreme Lord. Later Lord Kṛṣṇa would repeat the instructions of Bhīṣma on transcendental knowledge and devotional service to His devotee Uddhava. *(pp. 68–69)*

PLATE FOUR: The Consequences of Material Sense Gratification

Lord Kṛṣṇa instructed Uddhava, "One who accepts material sense objects as desirable certainly becomes attached to them. From such attachment lust arises, and this lust creates quarrel among men. From

quarrel arises intolerable anger, followed by the darkness of ignorance. This ignorance quickly overtakes a man's broad intelligence." Illicit sexual relationships embody the painful progression of emotional states described by the Lord. (*pp. 170–72*)

PLATE FIVE: The Material and Spiritual Energies

The cosmic manifestation is a combination of Lord Kṛṣṇa's material and spiritual energies. The material energy is composed of eight elements, namely earth, water, fire, air, ether, mind, intelligence and false ego. By contact with the Supreme Lord's spiritual energy, these elements interact to form the ever-changing material universe we perceive around us. Similarly, the bodies of all living beings are composed of the same material energy, but without the presence of the soul, they are nothing more than lumps of dead matter. In material consciousness, a person identifies himself with the material body and sees the world as simply a material phenomenon. But an enlightened person understands the actual self to be the soul within the body. Furthermore, he sees the Supreme Soul as the moving force within the material universe. (*pp. 223–33*)

PLATE SIX: Garbhodakaśāyī Viṣṇu

Within each of the myriad material universes, Lord Nārāyaṇa expands Himself as Garbhodakaśāyī Viṣṇu, the Viṣṇu form who lies down upon the ocean within the universal shell. The goddess of fortune, Lakṣmī, massages His lotus feet, and from His navel grows a lotus flower, upon which Lord Brahmā, the chief demigod and first created being within the universe, takes his birth. (*pp. 320–21*)

PLATE SEVEN: The Universal Form

Lord Kṛṣṇa said, "I am the basis of the universal form, which displays endless variety through the repeated creation, maintenance and destruction of the planetary systems." *(p. 330)*

jāta—arisen; *vepathuḥ*—trembling of the body; *ātmani*—within his heart; *agnīn*—the sacrificial fires; *samāropya*—placing; *mat-cittaḥ*—his mind fixed in Me; *agnim*—the fire; *samāviśet*—should enter.

TRANSLATION

If the *vānaprastha* is overtaken by old age and because of his trembling body is no longer able to execute his prescribed duties, he should place the sacrificial fire within his heart by meditation. Then, fixing his mind in Me, he should enter into the fire and give up his body.

PURPORT

Since the process of *vānaprastha* is recommended for those nearing the end of life, there is always the likelihood that one will prematurely succumb to the symptoms of old age and be unable to reach the final stage of *sannyāsa*. If one simply cannot carry on his religious duties due to old age, it is here advised that he fix the mind in Lord Kṛṣṇa and enter into the sacrificial fire. Although this may not be possible in the modern age, we can appreciate the absolute seriousness of going back home, back to Godhead, as evidenced in this verse.

TEXT 12

यदा कर्मविपाकेषु लोकेषु निरयात्मसु ।
विरागो जायते सम्यङ् न्यस्ताग्निः प्रव्रजेत्ततः ॥ १२ ॥

yadā karma-vipākeṣu
lokeṣu nirayātmasu
virāgo jāyate samyaṅ
nyastāgniḥ pravrajet tataḥ

yadā—when; *karma*—by fruitive activities; *vipākeṣu*—in all that which is obtained; *lokeṣu*—including promotion to all the planets of the universe up to Brahmaloka; *niraya-ātmasu*—planets that are actually hellish, being material; *virāgaḥ*—detachment; *jāyate*—is born; *samyak*—completely; *nyasta*—giving up; *agniḥ*—the sacrificial fire of *vānaprastha; pravrajet*—one should take *sannyāsa; tataḥ*—at that point.

TRANSLATION

If the *vānaprastha*, understanding that even promotion to Brahmaloka is a miserable situation, develops complete detachment from all possible results of fruitive activities, then he may take the *sannyāsa* order of life.

TEXT 13

इष्ट्वा यथोपदेशं मां दत्त्वा सर्वस्वमृत्विजे ।
अग्नीन् स्वप्राण आवेश्य निरपेक्षः परिव्रजेत् ॥१३॥

iṣṭvā yathopadeśaṁ māṁ
dattvā sarva-svam ṛtvije
agnīn sva-prāṇa āveśya
nirapekṣaḥ parivrajet

iṣṭvā—having worshiped; *yathā*—according to; *upadeśam*—scriptural injunctions; *mām*—Me; *dattvā*—having given; *sarva-svam*—all one possesses; *ṛtvije*—to the priest; *agnīn*—the sacrificial fire; *sva-prāṇe*—within oneself; *āveśya*—placing; *nirapekṣaḥ*—without attachment; *parivrajet*—one should take *sannyāsa* and set off.

TRANSLATION

Having worshiped Me according to scriptural injunctions and having given all one's property to the sacrificial priest, one should place the fire sacrifice within oneself. Thus, with the mind completely detached, one should enter the *sannyāsa* order of life.

PURPORT

One cannot maintain the *sannyāsa* order of life unless one gives up all materialistic association and engages exclusively in devotional service to the Supreme Lord. Any material desire will gradually prove to be a stumbling block in the prosecution of renounced life. Therefore, a liberated *sannyāsī* must vigilantly keep himself free from the weeds of material desires, which surface principally in the form of attachment to women, money and reputation. One may possess a beautiful garden filled with fruits and flowers, but without vigilant maintenance the garden will be overrun by weeds. Similarly, one who achieves a beautiful state of Kṛṣṇa consciousness takes the *sannyāsa* order of life, but if he does not vigilantly and painstakingly keep his heart clean, there is always the danger of a relapse into illusion.

TEXT 14

विप्रस्य वै संन्यसतो देवा दारादिरूपिणः ।
विघ्नान् कुर्वन्त्ययं ह्यस्मानाक्रम्य समियात् परम् ॥१४॥

viprasya vai sannyasato
devā dārādi-rūpiṇaḥ
vighnān kurvanty ayaṁ hy asmān
ākramya samiyāt param

viprasya—of the saintly person; *vai*—indeed; *sannyasataḥ*—taking *sannyāsa; devāḥ*—the demigods; *dāra-ādi-rūpiṇaḥ*—appearing in the form of his wife or other women and attractive objects; *vighnān*—stumbling blocks; *kurvanti*—create; *ayam*—the *sannyāsī*; *hi*—indeed; *asmān*—them, the demigods; *ākramya*—surpassing; *samiyāt*—should go; *param*—back home, back to Godhead.

TRANSLATION

"This man taking *sannyāsa* is going to surpass us and go back home, back to Godhead." Thus thinking, the demigods create stumbling blocks in the path of the *sannyāsī* by appearing before him in the shape of his former wife or other women and attractive objects. But the *sannyāsī* should pay the demigods and their manifestations no heed.

PURPORT

The demigods are empowered with universal administration and by their potency may appear as the former wife of a *sannyāsī* or as other women, so that the *sannyāsī* gives up his strict vows and becomes entangled in sense gratification. Lord Kṛṣṇa here encourages all *sannyāsīs* by telling them, "Pay no attention to such illusory manifestations. Continue your duties and go back home, back to Godhead."

TEXT 15

बिभृयाच्चेन्मुनिर्वासः कौपीनाच्छादनं परम् ।
त्यक्तं न दण्डपात्राभ्यामन्यत् किञ्चिदनापदि ॥१५॥

bibhṛyāc cen munir vāsaḥ
kaupīnācchādanaṁ param
tyaktaṁ na daṇḍa-pātrābhyām
anyat kiñcid anāpadi

bibhṛyāt—would wear; *cet*—if; *muniḥ*—the *sannyāsī; vāsaḥ*—clothes; *kaupīna*—the thick belt and underwear worn by saintly persons; *ācchādanam*—covering; *param*—other; *tyaktam*—given up; *na*—never; *daṇḍa*—besides his staff; *pātrābhyām*—and waterpot; *anyat*—else; *kiñcit*—anything; *anāpadi*—when there is no emergency.

TRANSLATION

If the *sannyāsī* desires to wear something besides a mere *kaupīna*, he may use another cloth around his waist and hips to cover the *kaupīna*. Otherwise, if there is no emergency, he should not accept anything besides his *daṇḍa* and waterpot.

PURPORT

A *sannyāsī* attracted to material possessions will spoil his worship of Lord Kṛṣṇa.

TEXT 16

दृष्टिपूतं न्यसेत् पादं वस्त्रपूतं पिबेज्जलम् ।
सत्यपूतां वदेद् वाचं मनःपूतं समाचरेत् ॥१६॥

dṛṣṭi-pūtaṁ nyaset pādaṁ
vastra-pūtaṁ pibej jalam
satya-pūtāṁ vaded vācaṁ
manaḥ-pūtaṁ samācaret

dṛṣṭi—by the sight; *pūtam*—ascertained as pure; *nyaset*—he should place; *pādam*—his foot; *vastra*—by his cloth; *pūtam*—filtered; *pibet*—

he should drink; *jalam*—water; *satya*—by truthfulness; *pūtām*—pure; *vadet*—he should speak; *vācam*—words; *manaḥ*—ascertained by the mind; *pūtam*—to be pure; *samācaret*—he should perform.

TRANSLATION

A saintly person should only step or place his foot on the ground after verifying with his eyes that there are no living creatures, such as insects, who might be injured by his foot. He should only drink water after filtering it through a portion of his cloth, and he should only speak words that possess the purity of truth. Similarly, he should only perform an activity that his mind has carefully ascertained to be pure.

PURPORT

While walking, a saintly person is careful not to kill any tiny creatures on the ground. Similarly, he filters his drinking water through cloth to avoid swallowing small creatures living within the water. Speaking untruths simply for sense gratification is detrimental to devotional service and should be avoided. Speaking impersonal philosophy and glorifying the sense gratification of the material world, even that found in heavenly planets, contaminates the heart and must be avoided by those desiring perfection in the loving service of the Lord. By serious consideration one can understand that any activity other than devotional service to Lord Kṛṣṇa has no ultimate value; therefore one should exclusively engage in the purified activities of Kṛṣṇa consciousness.

TEXT 17

मौनानीहानिलायामा दण्डा वाग्देहचेतसाम् ।
न ह्येते यस्य सन्त्यङ्ग वेणुभिर्न भवेद् यतिः ॥१७॥

maunānīhānilāyāmā
daṇḍā vāg-deha-cetasām
na hy ete yasya santy aṅga
veṇubhir na bhaved yatiḥ

mauna—avoiding useless speech; *anīha*—giving up fruitive activities; *anila-āyāmāḥ*—controlling the breathing process; *daṇḍāḥ*—strict disciplines; *vāk*—of the voice; *deha*—of the body; *cetasām*—of the mind; *na*—not; *hi*—indeed; *ete*—these disciplines; *yasya*—of whom; *santi*—exist; *aṅga*—My dear Uddhava; *veṇubhiḥ*—by bamboo rods; *na*—never; *bhavet*—is; *yatiḥ*—a real *sannyāsī.*

TRANSLATION

One who has not accepted the three internal disciplines of avoiding useless speech, avoiding useless activities and controlling the life air can never be considered a *sannyāsī* merely because of his carrying bamboo rods.

PURPORT

The word *daṇḍa* indicates the staff carried by those in the renounced order of life, and *daṇḍa* also indicates severe discipline. The Vaiṣṇava *sannyāsīs* accept a staff made of three bamboo rods, signifying dedication of the body, mind and words to the service of the Supreme Lord. Here Lord Kṛṣṇa says that one must first accept these three *daṇḍas,* or disciplines (namely control of the voice, body and mind), within oneself. The practice of *anilāyāma* (or *prāṇāyāma,* regulating the life air) is meant to control the mind, and one who always thinks of service to Lord Kṛṣṇa has certainly achieved the perfection of *prāṇāyāma.* Merely carrying the three external *daṇḍas* without assimilating the internal *daṇḍas* of bodily, mental and vocal discipline can never make one an actual Vaiṣṇava *sannyāsī,* as explained here by Lord Kṛṣṇa.

In the *Haṁsa-gīta* section of *Mahābhārata* and in Śrīla Rūpa Gosvāmī's *Upadeśāmṛta,* there are instructions regarding the *sannyāsa* order of life. A conditioned soul who adopts only the external ornaments of *tridaṇḍi-sannyāsa* will not actually be able to control the senses. One who takes *sannyāsa* for false prestige, making a show of saintliness without actual advancement in *kṛṣṇa-kīrtana,* will soon be vanquished by the external energy of the Lord.

TEXT 18

भिक्षां चतुर्षु वर्णेषु विगर्ह्यान् वर्जयंश्चरेत् ।
सप्तागारानसंक्लृप्तांस्तुष्येल्लब्धेन तावता ॥१८॥

bhikṣāṁ caturṣu varṇeṣu
vigarhyān varjayaṁś caret
saptāgārān asaṅkḷptāṁs
tuṣyel labdhena tāvatā

bhikṣām—charity obtained by begging; *caturṣu*—among the four; *varṇeṣu*—occupational divisions of society; *vigarhyān*—abominable, impure; *varjayan*—rejecting; *caret*—one should approach; *sapta*—seven; *āgārān*—houses; *asaṅkḷptān*—without calculation or desire; *tuṣyet*—one should be satisfied; *labdhena*—with that obtained; *tāvatā*—with just that amount.

TRANSLATION

Rejecting those houses that are polluted and untouchable, one should approach without previous calculation seven houses and be satisfied with that which is obtained there by begging. According to necessity, one may approach each of the four occupational orders of society.

PURPORT

Saintly persons in the renounced order of life may beg from strict followers of Vedic culture to obtain foodstuffs and other bodily necessities. According to Vedic injunction, a renounced saint should beg from the *brāhmaṇa* community, but if there is danger of his starving, he may beg from *kṣatriyas*, then *vaiśyas*, and even *śūdras* if they are not sinful, as expressed here by the word *vigarhyān*. Śrīla Bhaktisiddhānta Sarasvatī Ṭhākura explains that *asaṅkḷptān* indicates that one should not approach certain houses, calculating, "In that place I can get first-class food. That house has a big reputation among beggars." Without discriminating, one should go to seven houses and be satisfied with whatever may be obtained there. One should beg for one's personal maintenance only from houses where the inhabitants, being sincere followers of the *varṇāśrama* culture, have earned their livelihood by honest means and are free from sinful activities. One may beg alms from such householders. One must not beg alms for one's personal maintenance from those who oppose the Supreme Lord's devotional service, for such service is the whole purpose of *varṇāśrama* culture.

Those who oppose Vedic culture pass laws to make begging by saintly persons a criminal act. They thus insult and persecute saintly beggars, considering them to be ordinary vagrants. A lazy person begging to avoid work is certainly abominable, but a saintly person dedicated to the service of the Lord and practicing the discipline of begging to develop full dependence on the Lord's mercy should be given all facility in human society. Śrīla Bhaktisiddhānta Sarasvatī Ṭhākura explains that there are three forms of collecting alms. *Mādhukara* is the process of imitating the bee, who collects a tiny amount of nectar from each flower. In this way, the saintly person accepts a very small amount from each person, avoiding social conflict. The process mentioned here is *asaṅkḷpta,* by which one indiscriminately approaches seven houses, being satisfied with whatever may be obtained. *Prāk-praṇīta* is that process by which one establishes regular donors and collects one's maintenance from them. In this regard Śrīla Vīrarāghava Ācārya has described the initial stage of *sannyāsa,* called *kuṭīcaka,* as follows. A man accepting the initial stage of *sannyāsa* arranges for his children or other relatives and well-wishers to build him a *kuṭī,* or meditation cottage. He gives up worldly affairs and sits within the cottage, trying to remain free from lust, anger, greed, illusion and so on. According to the prescribed injunctions of regulated life, he accepts a *tri-daṇḍa,* purifies himself with a waterpot, shaves his head (leaving a *śikhā,* or tuft), chants Gāyatrī *mantra* on the sacred thread and wears saffron garments. Bathing regularly, cleansing, performing *ācamana,* chanting *japa,* studying the *Vedas,* remaining celibate and meditating on the Lord, he receives regular supplies of food from his children, friends and relatives. Accepting only the bare necessities of life, he remains fixed in his cottage up to the moment of liberation.

TEXT 19

बहिर्जलाशयं गत्वा तत्रोपस्पृश्य वाग्यतः ।
विभज्य पावितं शेषं भुञ्जीताशेषमाहृतम् ॥१९॥

bahir jalāśayaṁ gatvā
tatropaspṛśya vāg-yataḥ

vibhajya pāvitaṁ śeṣaṁ
bhuñjītāśeṣam āhṛtam

bahiḥ—outside of urban areas, in a secluded place; *jala*—of water; *āśayam*—to a reservoir; *gatvā*—going; *tatra*—there; *upaspṛśya*—being purified by contact with water; *vāk-yataḥ*—without speaking; *vibhajya*—duly distributing; *pāvitam*—purified; *śeṣam*—remnants; *bhuñjīta*—one should eat; *aśeṣam*—completely; *āhṛtam*—gathered by begging.

TRANSLATION

Taking the foodstuffs gathered through begging, one should leave the populated areas and go to a reservoir of water in a secluded place. There, having taken bath and washed one's hands thoroughly, remaining silent, one should distribute portions of the foodstuffs to others who may request it. Then, having thoroughly cleansed the remnants, one should eat everything on one's plate, leaving nothing for future consumption.

PURPORT

Śrīla Bhaktisiddhānta Sarasvatī Ṭhākura explains that a saintly person should not argue or quarrel with materialistic persons who may request or demand part of his foodstuff. The word *vibhajya* indicates that one should give something to such persons to avoid disturbance, and then, offering the remnants to Lord Viṣṇu, one should eat everything on one's plate, without saving food for the future. The word *bahiḥ* indicates that one should not eat in a public place, and *vāg-yata* indicates that one should eat silently, meditating upon the Lord's mercy.

TEXT 20

एकश्चरेन्महीमेतां निःसङ्गः संयतेन्द्रियः ।
आत्मक्रीड आत्मरत आत्मवान् समदर्शनः ॥२०॥

ekaś caren mahīm etāṁ
niḥsaṅgaḥ saṁyatendriyaḥ
ātma-krīḍa ātma-rata
ātma-vān sama-darśanaḥ

ekaḥ—alone; *caret*—one should move about; *mahīm*—the earth; *etām*—this; *niḥsaṅgaḥ*—without any material attachment; *saṁyata-indriyaḥ*—completely controlling the senses; *ātma-krīḍaḥ*—enthusiastic by realization of the Supersoul; *ātma-rataḥ*—completely satisfied in spiritual understanding; *ātma-vān*—steady on the spiritual platform; *sama-darśanaḥ*—with equal vision everywhere.

TRANSLATION

Without any material attachment, with senses fully controlled, remaining enthusiastic, and satisfied in realization of the Supreme Lord and his own self, the saintly person should travel about the earth, alone. Having equal vision everywhere, he should be steady on the spiritual platform.

PURPORT

One who remains attached to material sense gratification cannot be steady in the process of chanting Hare Kṛṣṇa. Being shackled by illusory desires, he is not able to fully control the senses. Actually, one should take shelter of devotional service to Lord Kṛṣṇa twenty-four hours a day, for by such service one remains within the scope of spiritual reality. By chanting and hearing the holy names of the Lord along with the Lord's glories and pastimes, one naturally drifts away from the field of material sense gratification. Good association with Lord Kṛṣṇa and His devotees automatically vanquishes useless material association, and one is able to carry out the Vedic injunctions meant to lift the conditioned soul out of the material field and onto the liberated platform of Kṛṣṇa consciousness. In this regard, Śrīla Rūpa Gosvāmī states in his *Upadeśāmṛta* (4),

dadāti pratigṛhṇāti
guhyam ākhyāti pṛcchati
bhuṅkte bhojayate caiva
ṣaḍ-vidhaṁ prīti-lakṣaṇam

"Offering gifts in charity, accepting charitable gifts, revealing one's mind in confidence, inquiring confidentially, accepting *prasādam* and offering *prasādam* are the six symptoms of love shared by one devotee and another."

One who thus learns to associate with the Lord's devotees actually remains insulated from the contamination of material life. By pure association one gradually understands the name, form, qualities, associates, pastimes and devotional service of Lord Śrī Kṛṣṇa, and thus even in this lifetime one can become a resident of the spiritual world. In the association of pure devotees there is no material contamination and no useless discussion, since all pure devotees are fully engaged twenty-four hours a day in the loving service of the Lord. By the influence of such devotees, one develops equal vision (*sama-darśana*) and sees the realized knowledge of Kṛṣṇa consciousness everywhere. As one begins to understand his eternal relationship with Lord Kṛṣṇa, he becomes *ātma-vān,* situated in his constitutional position. An advanced Vaiṣṇava, constantly enjoying the mellows of loving devotional service and carrying out the mission of the Lord on the earth, is *ātma-krīḍa,* one who enjoys life within the internal potency of the Supreme Lord. The advanced devotee remains constantly attracted to the Supreme Lord and His devotees and is therefore *ātma-rata,* fully satisfied by constant engagement in devotional service. One cannot possibly develop the exalted qualities mentioned here without becoming an unalloyed devotee of Lord Kṛṣṇa. One who is envious of the Lord and His devotees becomes attracted to bad association, gradually loses control of the senses and falls down into the network of impious life. The innumerable varieties of nondevotees are like branches sprouting from the single tree of enviousness of the Supreme Lord, Kṛṣṇa, and their association should be given up by all means.

Without unalloyed devotional service to the Lord, one loses touch with the desire and mission of the Personality of Godhead and becomes attracted to worshiping the wonderful male and female creations of the Lord's illusory energy—demigods, demigoddesses, celebrities, politicians, prostitutes, etc. In this way, one foolishly considers something besides Lord Kṛṣṇa to be supremely wonderful. Actually, Lord Kṛṣṇa is the only true object of worship for those desiring to experience unlimited beauty and pleasure. By seriously taking to Kṛṣṇa consciousness one can realize the transcendental position of Lord Kṛṣṇa and gradually develop all of the qualities mentioned in this verse.

TEXT 21

विविक्तक्षेमशरणो मद्भावविमलाशयः ।
आत्मानं चिन्तयेदेकमभेदेन मया मुनिः ॥२१॥

vivikta-kṣema-śaraṇo
mad-bhāva-vimalāśayaḥ
ātmānaṁ cintayed ekam
abhedena mayā muniḥ

vivikta—solitary; *kṣema*—safe; *śaraṇaḥ*—his dwelling; *mat*—in Me; *bhāva*—by constant thought; *vimala*—purified; *āśayaḥ*—his consciousness; *ātmānam*—on the soul; *cintayet*—he should concentrate; *ekam*—alone; *abhedena*—not different; *mayā*—from Me; *muniḥ*—the sage.

TRANSLATION

Dwelling in a safe and solitary place, his mind purified by constant thought of Me, the sage should concentrate on the soul alone, realizing it to be nondifferent from Me.

PURPORT

One who is engaged exclusively in the devotional service of the Lord in one of the five principal relationships is to be known as a pure Vaiṣṇava. Because of his advanced stage of love of Godhead, a pure devotee is able to constantly chant the glories of the Lord without material hindrance. He is not interested in anything except Lord Kṛṣṇa and never considers himself to be qualitatively different from the Lord. One who is still attracted by the gross material body and subtle material mind, which cover the eternal soul, continues to see himself as different from the Supreme Personality of Godhead. This misconception is due to false identification with matter. With senses purified of material contamination, one must serve the Lord, who is the master of all senses, and thus one's devotional service is considered free from discrepancy.

One who ignores the injunctions of Vedic literature uselessly wastes his sense activity in illusory material activities. He falsely considers himself to be different from Lord Kṛṣṇa and therefore imagines that he possesses an interest independent of the Lord's interest. There is no possibility that such a person can achieve steadiness in life, because the material field of action is constantly being shifted and transformed by the disturbing influence of time. If a devotee begins to cultivate an interest apart from the loving service of the Lord, his meditation on his oneness with the Lord will be disturbed and overturned. When the mind deviates from the lotus feet of the Lord, the duality of material nature again becomes prominent within the mind, and one resumes a work program based on the three modes of material nature. One who is not fixed in one's own relationship with the Supreme Lord cannot be fearless or steady and is deprived of the shelter of Lord Śrī Kṛṣṇa. Therefore one should seriously contemplate, as described in this verse, one's identity as a small particle of consciousness not different from the supreme consciousness, Lord Kṛṣṇa. Thus one should remain steady in Kṛṣṇa consciousness.

TEXT 22

अन्वीक्षेतात्मनो बन्धं मोक्षं च ज्ञाननिष्ठया ।
बन्ध इन्द्रियविक्षेपो मोक्ष एषां च संयमः ॥२२॥

anvīkṣetātmano bandhaṁ
mokṣaṁ ca jñāna-niṣṭhayā
bandha indriya-vikṣepo
mokṣa eṣāṁ ca saṁyamaḥ

anvīkṣeta—one should see by careful study; *ātmanaḥ*—of the soul; *bandham*—the bondage; *mokṣam*—the liberation; *ca*—also; *jñāna*—in knowledge; *niṣṭhayā*—by steadiness; *bandhaḥ*—bondage; *indriya*—of the senses; *vikṣepaḥ*—deviation to sense gratification; *mokṣaḥ*—liberation; *eṣām*—of these senses; *ca*—and; *saṁyamaḥ*—complete control.

TRANSLATION

By steady knowledge a sage should clearly ascertain the nature of the soul's bondage and liberation. Bondage occurs when the senses are deviated to sense gratification, and complete control of the senses constitutes liberation.

PURPORT

By carefully understanding one's eternal nature, one will not again be bound up in the shackles of material energy, and by constant engagement in the service of the Absolute Truth, one is liberated. Then the flickering material senses can no longer drag one into the false consciousness of being a material enjoyer. Such steady sense control gives one relief from the harassment of material sense gratification.

TEXT 23

तस्मान्नियम्य षड्वर्गं मद्भावेन चरेन्मुनिः ।
विरक्तः क्षुद्रकामेभ्यो लब्ध्वात्मनि सुखं महत् ॥२३॥

tasmān niyamya ṣaḍ-vargaṁ
mad-bhāvena caren muniḥ
viraktaḥ kṣudra-kāmebhyo
labdhvātmani sukhaṁ mahat

tasmāt—therefore; *niyamya*—completely controlling; *ṣaṭ-vargam*—the six senses (sight, hearing, smell, touch, taste and the mind); *mat-bhāvena*—by consciousness of Me; *caret*—should live; *muniḥ*—the sage; *viraktaḥ*—detached; *kṣudra*—insignificant; *kāmebhyaḥ*—from sense gratification; *labdhvā*—having experienced; *ātmani*—in the self; *sukham*—happiness; *mahat*—great.

TRANSLATION

Therefore, completely controlling the five senses and the mind by Kṛṣṇa consciousness, a sage, having experienced spiritual bliss within the self, should live detached from insignificant material sense gratification.

TEXT 24

पुरग्रामव्रजान् सार्थान् भिक्षार्थं प्रविशंश्चरेत् ।
पुण्यदेशसरिच्छैलवनाश्रमवतीं महीम् ॥२४॥

pura-grāma-vrajān sārthān
bhikṣārthaṁ praviśaṁś caret

puṇya-deśa-saric-chaila-
vanāśrama-vatīṁ mahīm

pura—cities; *grāma*—towns; *vrajān*—and pasturing grounds; *sa-arthān*—those working for bodily maintenance; *bhikṣā-artham*—for begging alms; *praviśan*—entering; *caret*—he should travel; *puṇya*—pure; *deśa*—places; *sarit*—with rivers; *śaila*—mountains; *vana*—and forests; *āśrama-vatīm*—possessing such residential places; *mahīm*—the earth.

TRANSLATION

The sage should travel in sanctified places, by flowing rivers and within the solitude of mountains and forests. He should enter the cities, towns and pasturing grounds and approach ordinary working men only to beg his bare sustenance.

PURPORT

According to Śrīla Śrīdhara Svāmī, the word *pura* refers to cities and towns with shopping centers, markets and other commercial enterprises, whereas *grāma* refers to smaller towns, lacking such facilities. The *vānaprastha* or *sannyāsī* trying to become free from material attachment should avoid those who are working day and night for sense gratification, approaching them only to engage them in necessary acts of charity. Those who are preaching Kṛṣṇa consciousness all over the world are understood to be liberated souls, and therefore they constantly approach the materialistic living entities to engage them in the devotional service of Lord Kṛṣṇa. However, even such preachers should strictly avoid contact with the materialistic world when not actually necessary for advancing the mission of Kṛṣṇa consciousness. The injunction is that one should not deal unnecessarily with the materialistic world.

TEXT 25

वानप्रस्थाश्रमपदेष्वभीक्ष्णं भैक्ष्यमाचरेत् ।
संसिध्यत्याश्वसंमोहः शुद्धसत्त्वः शिलान्धसा ॥२५॥

vānaprasthāśrama-padeṣv
abhīkṣṇaṁ bhaikṣyam ācaret

saṁsidhyaty āśv asammohaḥ
śuddha-sattvaḥ śilāndhasā

vānaprastha-āśrama—of the *vānaprastha* order of life; *padeṣu*—in the position; *abhīkṣṇam*—always; *bhaikṣyam*—begging; *ācaret*—one should perform; *saṁsidhyati*—one becomes spiritually perfect; *āśu*—quickly; *asammohaḥ*—free from illusion; *śuddha*—purified; *sattvaḥ*—existence; *śila*—obtained by begging or gleaning; *andhasā*—by food.

TRANSLATION

One in the *vānaprastha* order of life should always practice taking charity from others, for one is thereby freed from illusion and quickly becomes perfect in spiritual life. Indeed, one who subsists on food grains obtained in such a humble manner purifies his existence.

PURPORT

In the Western countries people are generally so dull that they cannot distinguish between a saintly beggar and an ordinary hobo or hippie. A saintly beggar is constantly engaged in authorized devotional service to the Supreme Lord and accepts only what he requires for his bare maintenance. The author of this book remembers entering the Kṛṣṇa consciousness society as an arrogant university student and being quickly humbled by the process of begging on the street on behalf of Kṛṣṇa. This process is not theoretical but actually purifies one's existence by forcing one to offer respect to all others. Unless one offers respect to others, one's begging will be fruitless. Also, by begging one will not often eat very sumptuously. This is good because when the tongue is controlled the other senses are quickly pacified. A *vānaprastha* should never give up the purifying process of begging for his food, and ordinary people should not foolishly equate a lazy bum living at the cost of others with a saintly beggar engaged in higher duties for the Supreme Lord.

TEXT 26

नैतद् वस्तुतया पश्येद् दृश्यमानं विनश्यति ।
असक्तचित्तो विरमेदिहामुत्र चिकीर्षितात् ॥२६॥

naitad vastutayā paśyed
dṛśyamānaṁ vinaśyati
asakta-citto viramed
ihāmutra-cikīrṣitāt

na—never; *etat*—this; *vastutayā*—as ultimate reality; *paśyet*—one should see; *dṛśyamānam*—being observed by direct experience; *vinaśyati*—is destroyed; *asakta*—without attachment; *cittaḥ*—whose consciousness; *viramet*—one should be detached; *iha*—in this world; *amutra*—and in one's future life; *cikīrṣitāt*—from activities performed for material advancement.

TRANSLATION

One should never see as ultimate reality those material things which obviously will perish. With consciousness free from material attachment, one should retire from all activities meant for material progress in this life and the next.

PURPORT

One may doubt how a gentleman can retire from family life and live as a beggar, eating meager foodstuffs. The Lord here responds by stating that sumptuous or palatable foods—along with all other material objects, such as the body itself—should never be seen as ultimate reality, since they are obviously perishable items. One should retire from material programs destined to enhance the quality of one's illusion both in this life and the next.

TEXT 27

यदेतदात्मनि जगन्मनोवाक्प्राणसंहतम् ।
सर्वं मायेति तर्केण स्वस्थस्त्यक्त्वा न तत् स्मरेत्॥२७॥

yad etad ātmani jagan
mano-vāk-prāṇa-saṁhatam
sarvaṁ māyeti tarkeṇa
sva-sthas tyaktvā na tat smaret

yat—which; *etat*—this; *ātmani*—in the Supreme Lord; *jagat*—universe; *manaḥ*—of the mind; *vāk*—speech; *prāṇa*—and life air; *saṁhatam*—formed; *sarvam*—all; *māyā*—material illusion; *iti*—thus; *tarkeṇa*—by logic; *sva-sthaḥ*—fixed in the self; *tyaktvā*—giving up; *na*—never; *tat*—that; *smaret*—one should remember.

TRANSLATION

One should logically consider the universe, which is situated within the Lord, and one's own material body, which is composed of mind, speech and life air, to be ultimately products of the Lord's illusory energy. Thus situated in the self, one should give up one's faith in these things and should never again make them the object of one's meditation.

PURPORT

Every conditioned soul considers the material world to be the object of his personal sense gratification and therefore considers the material body to be his actual identity. The word *tyaktvā* indicates that one must give up one's false identification with the material world and the material body, since both are merely products of the illusory potency of the Lord. One should never again meditate on the material world and body as objects of sense gratification but rather should become situated in Kṛṣṇa consciousness. Looking at things from the eternal point of view, this world is simply illusory. The material energy of the Lord is devoid of consciousness and thus cannot be the basis of actual happiness. The Supreme Lord Himself is the only absolutely conscious entity. He is absolutely self-sufficient, standing alone as Viṣṇu, the Personality of Godhead. Only Viṣṇu, and not the insignificant workings of material nature, can give us the actual perfection of life.

TEXT 28

ज्ञाननिष्ठो विरक्तो वा मद्भक्तो वानपेक्षकः ।
सलिङ्गानाश्रमांस्त्यक्त्वा चरेदविधिगोचरः ॥२८॥

jñāna-niṣṭho virakto vā
mad-bhakto vānapekṣakaḥ

sa-liṅgān āśramāṁs tyaktvā
cared avidhi-gocaraḥ

jñāna—to philosophical knowledge; *niṣṭhaḥ*—dedicated; *viraktaḥ*—detached from external manifestations; *vā*—either; *mat-bhaktaḥ*—My devotee; *vā*—or; *anapekṣakaḥ*—not desiring even liberation; *sa-liṅgān*—with their rituals and external regulations; *āśramān*—the duties pertaining to particular statuses of life; *tyaktvā*—giving up; *caret*—one should conduct oneself; *avidhi-gocaraḥ*—beyond the range of rules and regulations.

TRANSLATION

A learned transcendentalist dedicated to the cultivation of knowledge and thus detached from external objects, or My devotee who is detached even from desire for liberation—both neglect those duties based on external rituals or paraphernalia. Thus their conduct is beyond the range of rules and regulations.

PURPORT

This verse describes the *paramahaṁsa* stage of life, in which there is no further need for rituals, external paraphernalia or rules and regulations. A completely realized *jñāna-yogī* pursuing liberation, or beyond that, a perfect devotee of the Lord who does not desire even liberation, has no further desire for material engagement. When one completely purifies the mind, there is no possibility of sinful behavior. Rules and regulations are meant for guiding those who have a tendency to act in ignorance or for personal gratification, but one who is perfect in spiritual consciousness can move freely, as described here by the Lord. One who tends to drive a car recklessly or who is unfamiliar with the local road conditions certainly needs the discipline of elaborate road signs and police enforcement of traffic laws. A perfectly safe driver, however, is thoroughly familiar with the local road conditions. He has no real need for the enforcement officials or the speed limits and caution signs meant for those unfamiliar with the road. A pure devotee of the Lord desires nothing except service to the Lord; he automatically fulfills the purport of all negative and positive injunctions, which is to always remember Kṛṣṇa and never forget Him. One should not, however, artificially imitate the exalted position of a *paramahaṁsa* devotee, for such imitation will quickly ruin one's spiritual career.

In the previous verses the Lord has elaborately described various rituals, paraphernalia and disciplines for the various spiritual orders of life. The *sannyāsī*, for example, carries a *tri-daṇḍa* and a waterpot and eats and lives in a particular way. A *paramahaṁsa* devotee, having completely given up all attachment and interest in the material world, is no longer attracted by such external features of renunciation.

TEXT 29

बुधो बालकवत् क्रीडेत् कुशलो जडवच्चरेत् ।
वदेदुन्मत्तवद् विद्वान् गोचर्यां नैगमश्चरेत् ॥२९॥

budho bālaka-vat krīḍet
kuśalo jaḍa-vac caret
vaded unmatta-vad vidvān
go-caryāṁ naigamaś caret

budhaḥ—although intelligent; *bālaka-vat*—like a child (oblivious to honor and dishonor); *krīḍet*—he should enjoy life; *kuśalaḥ*—although expert; *jaḍa-vat*—like a stunted person; *caret*—he should act; *vadet*—he should speak; *unmatta-vat*—like an insane person; *vidvān*—although most learned; *go-caryām*—unrestricted behavior; *naigamaḥ*—although expert in Vedic injunctions; *caret*—he should perform.

TRANSLATION

Although most wise, the *paramahaṁsa* should enjoy life like a child, oblivious to honor and dishonor; although most expert, he should behave like a stunted, incompetent person; although most learned, he should speak like an insane person; and although a scholar learned in Vedic regulations, he should behave in an unrestricted manner.

PURPORT

A *paramahaṁsa-sannyāsī*, fearing that his mind may be deviated by the tremendous prestige that people sometimes offer to a perfectly self-realized person, conceals his position as described in this verse. A self-realized person does not try to please the mass of people, nor does he desire social prestige, since the mission of his life is to remain detached from the material world and to always please the Supreme Personality of Godhead. Although neglecting ordinary rules and regulations, a *paramahaṁsa* does not ever become sinful or immoral, but rather neglects ritualistic aspects of religious custom, such as dressing in a particular way, performing certain ceremonies or executing specific penances and austerities.

The pure devotees of the Lord who have dedicated their lives to propagating the Lord's holy name must very expertly present Kṛṣṇa consciousness in a way pleasing to the mass of people so that they will accept it. Those who are preaching should try to make Lord Śrī Kṛṣṇa popular without trying to advance their personal prestige in the name of missionary progress. A *paramahaṁsa* not engaged in distributing Kṛṣṇa consciousness, however, should have no attachment whatsoever to public opinion.

TEXT 30

वेदवादरतो न स्यान्न पाषण्डी न हैतुकः ।
शुष्कवादविवादे न कञ्चित् पक्षं समाश्रयेत् ॥३०॥

veda-vāda-rato na syān
na pāṣaṇḍī na haitukaḥ
śuṣka-vāda-vivāde na
kañcit pakṣaṁ samāśrayet

veda-vāda—in the *karma-kāṇḍa* section of the *Vedas; rataḥ*—engaged; *na*—never; *syāt*—should be; *na*—nor; *pāṣaṇḍī*—atheistic, acting against Vedic injunctions; *na*—nor; *haitukaḥ*—a mere logician or skeptic; *śuṣka-vāda*—of useless topics; *vivāde*—in arguments; *na*—never; *kañcit*—any; *pakṣam*—side; *samāśrayet*—should take.

TRANSLATION

A devotee should never engage in the fruitive rituals mentioned in the *karma-kāṇḍa* section of the *Vedas*, nor should he

become atheistic, acting or speaking in opposition to Vedic injunctions. Similarly, he should never speak like a mere logician or skeptic or take any side whatsoever in useless arguments.

PURPORT

Although a *paramahaṁsa* devotee conceals his exalted position, certain activities are forbidden even for one trying to conceal himself. Śrīla Viśvanātha Cakravartī Ṭhākura explains that in the name of concealment one should not become a ghost. The word *pāsaṇḍa* refers to atheistic philosophies opposing the *Vedas,* such as Buddhism, and *haituka* refers to those who accept only that which can be demonstrated by mundane logic or experimentation. Since the whole purpose of the *Vedas* is to understand that which is beyond material experience, a skeptic's so-called logic is irrelevant to spiritual progress. Śrīla Jīva Gosvāmī warns us in this regard that a devotee should not read atheistic literature, even with the purpose of refining arguments against atheism. Such literature should be entirely avoided. The above-mentioned prohibited activities are so detrimental to the advancement of Kṛṣṇa consciousness that they should not be adopted even as a superficial show.

TEXT 31

नोद्विजेत जनाद् धीरो जनं चोद्वेजयेन्न तु ।
अतिवादांस्तितिक्षेत नावमन्येत कञ्चन ।
देहमुद्दिश्य पशुवद् वैरं कुर्यान्न केनचित् ॥३१॥

nodvijeta janād dhīro
janaṁ codvejayen na tu
ati-vādāṁs titikṣeta
nāvamanyeta kañcana
deham uddiśya paśu-vad
vairaṁ kuryān na kenacit

na—never; *udvijeta*—should be disturbed or frightened; *janāt*—because of other people; *dhīraḥ*—a saintly person; *janam*—other people; *ca*—also; *udvejayet*—should frighten or disturb; *na*—never; *tu*—indeed; *ati-vādān*—insulting or harsh words; *titikṣeta*—he should tolerate; *na*—never; *avamanyeta*—should belittle; *kañcana*—anyone; *deham*—the body; *uddiśya*—for the sake of; *paśu-vat*—like an animal; *vairam*—hostility; *kuryāt*—he should create; *na*—never; *kenacit*—with anyone.

TRANSLATION

A saintly person should never let others frighten or disturb him and, similarly, should never frighten or disturb other people. He should tolerate the insults of others and should never himself belittle anyone. He should never create hostility with anyone for the sake of the material body, for he would thus be no better than an animal.

PURPORT

Śrī Caitanya Mahāprabhu has stated,

tṛṇād api su-nīcena
taror iva sahiṣṇunā
amāninā māna-dena
kīrtanīyaḥ sadā hariḥ

"One should chant the holy name of the Lord in a humble state of mind, thinking oneself lower than the straw in the street; one should be more tolerant than a tree, devoid of all sense of false prestige and ready to offer all respect to others. In such a state of mind one can chant the holy name of the Lord constantly."

A Vaiṣṇava should never disturb any other living entity with his body, mind or words. He should always be tolerant and never belittle others. Although a Vaiṣṇava may act powerfully against the demons for Lord Kṛṣṇa's sake—as did Arjuna, Hanumān and many other great devotees—a Vaiṣṇava becomes very meek and humble in regard to his own reputation.

TEXT 32

एक एव परो ह्यात्मा भूतेष्वात्मन्यवस्थितः ।
यथेन्दुरुदपात्रेषु भूतान्येकात्मकानि च ॥३२॥

eka eva paro hy ātmā
bhūteṣv ātmany avasthitaḥ
yathendur uda-pātreṣu
bhūtāny ekātmakāni ca

ekaḥ—one; *eva*—indeed; *paraḥ*—Supreme; *hi*—certainly; *ātmā*—the Personality of Godhead; *bhūteṣu*—within all bodies; *ātmani*—within the living entity; *avasthitaḥ*—situated; *yathā*—just as; *induḥ*—the moon; *uda*—of water; *pātreṣu*—in different reservoirs; *bhūtāni*—all material bodies; *eka*—of the one Supreme Lord; *ātmakāni*—composed of the energy; *ca*—also.

TRANSLATION

The one Supreme Lord is situated within all material bodies and within everyone's soul. Just as the moon is reflected in innumerable reservoirs of water, the Supreme Lord, although one, is present within everyone. Thus every material body is ultimately composed of the energy of the one Supreme Lord.

PURPORT

All material bodies are composed of the same material nature, which is ultimately the potency of the one Supreme Lord. Therefore, one cannot justify feelings of hostility toward any living entity. In carrying out the Lord's mission on earth, the bona fide representatives of God never become envious or hostile toward anyone, even when chastised by those who flagrantly violate the laws of God. Every living being is ultimately the son of God, and God is present within everyone's body. Therefore, saintly persons should be very careful even when dealing with the most insignificant person or creature.

TEXT 33

अलब्ध्वा न विषीदेत काले कालेऽशनं क्वचित् ।
लब्ध्वा न हृष्येद् धृतिमानुभयं दैवतन्त्रितम् ॥३३॥

alabdhvā na viṣīdeta
kāle kāle 'śanaṁ kvacit

labdhvā na hṛṣyed dhṛtimān
ubhayaṁ daiva-tantritam

alabdhvā—not obtaining; *na*—not; *viṣīdeta*—he should be depressed; *kāle kāle*—at different times; *aśanam*—food; *kvacit*—whatever; *labdhvā*—obtaining; *na*—not; *hṛṣyet*—should rejoice; *dhṛti-mān*—fixed in determination; *ubhayam*—both (obtaining and not obtaining good food); *daiva*—of the supreme power of God; *tantritam*—under the control.

TRANSLATION

If at times one does not obtain proper food one should not be depressed, and when one obtains sumptuous food one should not rejoice. Being fixed in determination, one should understand both situations to be under the control of God.

PURPORT

Because we desire to enjoy the material body, the varieties of material experience bring us flickering happiness and inevitable suffering. We foolishly consider ourselves to be controllers and doers, and thus through false egotism we are subjected to the volatile feelings of the material body and mind.

TEXT 34

आहारार्थं समीहेत युक्तं तत् प्राणधारणम् ।
तत्त्वं विमृश्यते तेन तद् विज्ञाय विमुच्यते ॥३४॥

āhārārthaṁ samīheta
yuktaṁ tat-prāṇa-dhāraṇam
tattvaṁ vimṛśyate tena
tad vijñāya vimucyate

āhāra—to eat; *artham*—in order; *samīheta*—one should endeavor; *yuktam*—proper; *tat*—of the person; *prāṇa*—life force; *dhāraṇam*—sustaining; *tattvam*—spiritual truth; *vimṛśyate*—is contemplated; *tena*—by that strength of the mind, senses and life air; *tat*—that truth; *vijñāya*—understanding; *vimucyate*—one is liberated.

TRANSLATION

If required, one should endeavor to get sufficient foodstuffs, because it is always necessary and proper to maintain one's health. When the senses, mind and life air are fit, one can contemplate spiritual truth, and by understanding the truth one is liberated.

PURPORT

If foodstuffs do not come automatically or by token begging, then one should endeavor to keep body and soul together so that one's spiritual program will not be disturbed. Normally, those who are endeavoring in spiritual life cannot maintain steady concentration on the truth if their mind and body are weakened by undereating. On the other hand, extravagant consumption of food is a great impediment for spiritual advancement and should be given up. The word *āhārārtham* in this verse indicates eating only to keep oneself fit for spiritual advancement and does not justify unnecessary collecting or warehousing of so-called alms. If one collects more than necessary for one's spiritual program, the surplus becomes a heavy weight that drags one down to the material platform.

TEXT 35

यदृच्छयोपपन्नान्नमद्याच्छ्रेष्ठमुतापरम् ।
तथा वासस्तथा शय्यां प्राप्तं प्राप्तं भजेन्मुनिः ॥३५॥

yadṛcchayopapannānnam
adyāc chreṣṭham utāparam
tathā vāsas tathā śayyāṁ
prāptaṁ prāptaṁ bhajen muniḥ

yadṛcchayā—of its own accord; *upapanna*—acquired; *annam*—food; *adyāt*—he should eat; *śreṣṭham*—first class; *uta*—or; *aparam*—low class; *tathā*—similarly; *vāsaḥ*—clothing; *tathā*—similarly; *śayyām*—bedding; *prāptam prāptam*—whatever is automatically obtained; *bhajet*—should accept; *muniḥ*—the sage.

TRANSLATION

A sage should accept the food, clothing and bedding—be they of excellent or inferior quality—that come of their own accord.

PURPORT

Sometimes excellent, sumptuous food will come without endeavor, and at other times tasteless food appears. A sage should not become happily excited when a sumptuous plate is brought to him, nor should he angrily refuse ordinary food that comes of its own accord. If no food comes at all, as mentioned in the previous verse, one must endeavor to avoid starvation. From these verses it appears that even a saintly sage must have a good dose of common sense.

TEXT 36

शौचमाचमनं स्नानं न तु चोदनया चरेत् ।
अन्यांश्च नियमाञ्ज्ञानी यथाहं लीलयेश्वरः ॥३६॥

śaucam ācamanaṁ snānaṁ
na tu codanayā caret
anyāṁś ca niyamāñ jñānī
yathāhaṁ līlayeśvaraḥ

śaucam—general cleanliness; *ācamanam*—purifying the hands with water; *snānam*—taking bath; *na*—not; *tu*—indeed; *codanayā*—by force; *caret*—one should perform; *anyān*—other; *ca*—also; *niyamān*—regular duties; *jñānī*—one who has realized knowledge of Me; *yathā*—just as; *aham*—I; *līlayā*—by My own desire; *īśvaraḥ*—the Supreme Lord.

TRANSLATION

Just as I, the Supreme Lord, execute regulative duties by My own free will, similarly, one who has realized knowledge of Me should maintain general cleanliness, purify his hands with water, take bath and execute other regulative duties not by force but by his own free will.

PURPORT

When the Supreme Personality of Godhead descends to the material world, He generally observes the Vedic regulative duties to set a proper example for mankind. The Lord acts by His own free will, since no one can oblige, force or impel the Supreme Personality of Godhead. Similarly, the *jñānī*, or self-realized soul, is fixed on the spiritual platform, beyond the material body, and should therefore execute the regulative duties in relation to the material body by his own free will and not as a servant of the rules and regulations. A self-realized soul is a servant of Lord Kṛṣṇa and not of rules and regulations. Nevertheless, a transcendentalist strictly complies with regular duties for the pleasure of the Supreme Lord. In other words, one who is advanced in loving devotional service to Lord Kṛṣṇa spontaneously moves according to the will of the Supreme. One who is perfectly situated in spiritual realization cannot become a servant of the material body or of rules and regulations concerning the material body. However, this verse and other similar statements in Vedic scriptures should not be ignorantly misinterpreted to justify immoral, whimsical behavior. Lord Kṛṣṇa is discussing the *paramahaṁsa* stage of life, and those who are attached to the material body have nothing to do with this *paramahaṁsa* stage, nor should they exploit its unique privileges and status.

TEXT 37

न हि तस्य विकल्पाख्या या च मद्वीक्षया हता ।
आदेहान्तात् क्वचित् ख्यातिस्ततःसम्पद्यते मया ॥३७॥

na hi tasya vikalpākhyā
yā ca mad-vīkṣayā hatā
ā-dehāntāt kvacit khyātis
tataḥ sampadyate mayā

na—not; *hi*—certainly; *tasya*—for the realized person; *vikalpa*—of something separate from Kṛṣṇa; *ākhyā*—perception; *yā*—which perception; *ca*—also; *mat*—of Me; *vīkṣayā*—by realized knowledge; *hatā*—is destroyed; *ā*—until; *deha*—of the body; *antāt*—the death; *kvacit*—sometimes; *khyātiḥ*—such perception; *tataḥ*—then; *sampadyate*—achieves equal opulences; *mayā*—with Me.

TRANSLATION

A realized soul no longer sees anything as separate from Me, for his realized knowledge of Me has destroyed such illusory perception. Since the material body and mind were previously accustomed to this kind of perception, it may sometimes appear to reoccur; but at the time of death the self-realized soul achieves opulences equal to Mine.

PURPORT

Lord Kṛṣṇa explained in verse 32 of this chapter that all material and spiritual objects are expansions of His potency. By realized knowledge of the Lord one gives up the illusion that anything, anywhere, at any time, can be separate from Lord Kṛṣṇa. Lord Kṛṣṇa has also explained, however, that one must keep the material body and mind fit for executing devotional service; therefore even a self-realized soul may sometimes appear to accept or reject certain conditions or objects within this world. Such brief apparent duality of concentration upon something other than Kṛṣṇa does not change the liberated status of a self-realized soul, who achieves at the time of death the same opulences as Lord Kṛṣṇa in the spiritual world. The function of illusion is to separate one from Lord Kṛṣṇa, but the brief and occasional appearance of duality in the behavior or mentality of a pure devotee never separates him from the Lord. It does not constitute actual illusion, for it lacks the essential function of illusion, namely, the separation of one from Lord Kṛṣṇa.

Śrīla Bhaktisiddhānta Sarasvatī Ṭhākura describes the self-realized devotees as follows. The devotee of the Lord does not see anything as separate from Lord Kṛṣṇa and thus does not consider himself to be a permanent resident of the material world. At every moment the devotee is moved by his desire to serve Lord Kṛṣṇa. Just as those who are inclined to sense gratification pass their time making arrangements for their enjoyment, similarly the devotees are busy throughout the day arranging their devotional service to Lord Kṛṣṇa. Therefore they have no time to act like materialistic sense enjoyers. To ordinary persons it may seem that a pure devotee is seeing something as separate from Kṛṣṇa, but a pure devotee is actually fixed in his status as a liberated soul and is guaranteed to achieve a spiritual body in the kingdom of God. Ordinary, materialistic persons cannot always understand the activities of a pure devotee of the Lord, and thus they may try to minimize his position, considering him to be the same as themselves. At the end of life, however, the results achieved by the devotees of the Lord and ordinary materialists are vastly different.

TEXT 38

दुःखोदर्केषु कामेषु जातनिर्वेद आत्मवान् ।
अजिज्ञासितमद्धर्मो मुनिं गुरुमुपव्रजेत् ॥३८॥

duḥkhodarkeṣu kāmeṣu
jāta-nirveda ātmavān
ajijñāsita-mad-dharmo
muniṁ gurum upavrajet

duḥkha—unhappiness; *udarkeṣu*—in that which brings as its future result; *kāmeṣu*—in sense gratification; *jāta*—arisen; *nirvedaḥ*—detachment; *ātma-vān*—desiring spiritual perfection in life; *ajijñāsita*—one who has not seriously considered; *mat*—Me; *dharmaḥ*—the process of obtaining; *munim*—a wise person; *gurum*—a spiritual master; *upavrajet*—he should approach.

TRANSLATION

One who is detached from sense gratification, knowing its result to be miserable, and who desires spiritual perfection, but has not seriously analyzed the process for obtaining Me, should approach a bona fide and learned spiritual master.

PURPORT

In the previous verses Lord Kṛṣṇa described the duty of one who has developed perfect knowledge. Now Lord Kṛṣṇa discusses the situation of one who, desiring self-realization, has become detached from material life but lacks perfect knowledge of Kṛṣṇa consciousness. Such a detached person desiring self-realization must approach the lotus feet of a bona fide spiritual master in Kṛṣṇa consciousness, and then he will quickly come to the standard of perfect understanding. One who is seriously inclined toward spiritual perfection should not hesitate to adopt the regular discipline necessary for achieving the highest perfection in life.

TEXT 39

तावत् परिचरेद् भक्तः श्रद्धावाननसूयकः ।
यावद् ब्रह्म विजानीयान्मामेव गुरुमादृतः ॥३९॥

tāvat paricared bhaktaḥ
śraddhāvān anasūyakaḥ
yāvad brahma vijānīyān
mām eva gurum ādṛtaḥ

tāvat—that long; *paricaret*—should serve; *bhaktaḥ*—the devotee; *śraddhā-vān*—with great faith; *anasūyakaḥ*—being without envy; *yāvat*—until; *brahma*—spiritual knowledge; *vijānīyāt*—he clearly realizes; *mām*—Me; *eva*—indeed; *gurum*—the spiritual master; *ādṛtaḥ*—with great respect.

TRANSLATION

Until a devotee has clearly realized spiritual knowledge, he should continue with great faith and respect and without envy to render personal service to the *guru*, who is nondifferent from Me.

PURPORT

As stated by Śrīla Viśvanātha Cakravartī Ṭhākura in his *Gurv-aṣṭaka* prayers, *yasya prasādād bhagavat-prasādaḥ:* one receives the mercy of the Supreme Lord through the mercy of the bona fide spiritual master. A devotee who has been blessed by his *guru* with spiritual knowledge becomes qualified to directly engage in the mission of the Supreme Personality of Godhead. Śrīla Prabhupāda always emphasized that service to the spiritual master in separation, pushing on the mission of the *guru*, is the highest form of devotional service. The word *paricaret* in this verse indicates waiting upon one's master by rendering personal service. In other words, one who has not clearly realized the teachings of his spiritual master should remain very close to the *guru* to avoid falling down into illusion, but one who has acquired realized knowledge by the mercy of his spiritual master may expand the spiritual master's mission by traveling around the world to preach Kṛṣṇa consciousness.

TEXTS 40-41

यस्त्वसंयतषड्वर्गः प्रचण्डेन्द्रियसारथिः ।
ज्ञानवैराग्यरहितस्त्रिदण्डमुपजीवति ॥४०॥
सुरानात्मानमात्मस्थं निह्नुते मां च धर्महा ।
अविपक्वकषायोऽस्मादमुष्माच्च विहीयते ॥४१॥

yas tv asaṁyata-ṣaḍ-vargaḥ
pracaṇḍendriya-sārathiḥ
jñāna-vairāgya-rahitas
tri-daṇḍam upajīvati

surān ātmānam ātma-sthaṁ
nihnute māṁ ca dharma-hā
avipakva-kaṣāyo 'smād
amuṣmāc ca vihīyate

yaḥ—one who; *tu*—but; *asaṁyata*—having not controlled; *ṣaṭ*—the six; *vargaḥ*—items of contamination; *pracaṇḍa*—fierce; *indriya*—of the senses; *sārathiḥ*—the driver, intelligence; *jñāna*—of knowledge; *vairāgya*—and detachment; *rahitaḥ*—bereft; *tri-daṇḍam*—the *sannyāsa* order of life; *upajīvati*—utilizing for one's bodily maintenance; *surān*—the worshipable demigods; *ātmānam*—his own self; *ātma-stham*—situated within himself; *nihnute*—denies; *mām*—Me; *ca*—also; *dharma-hā*—ruining religious principles; *avipakva*—not yet dissolved; *kaṣāyaḥ*—contamination; *asmāt*—from this world; *amuṣmāt*—from the next life; *ca*—also; *vihīyate*—he is lost, deviated.

TRANSLATION

One who has not controlled the six forms of illusion [lust, anger, greed, excitement, false pride and intoxication], whose intelligence, the leader of the senses, is extremely attached to material things, who is bereft of knowledge and detachment, who adopts the *sannyāsa* order of life to make a living, who denies the worshipable demigods, his own self and the Supreme Lord

within himself, thus ruining all religious principles, and who is still infected by material contamination, is deviated and lost both in this life and the next.

PURPORT

Lord Kṛṣṇa here condemns bogus personalities who adopt the *sannyāsa* order of life for sense gratification while still maintaining all of the symptoms of gross illusion. A false show of *sannyāsa* is never accepted by intelligent followers of Vedic principles. So-called *sannyāsīs* who ruin all Vedic religious principles sometimes become famous among foolish persons, but they are simply cheating themselves and their followers. These charlatan *sannyāsīs* are never actually engaged in the loving devotional service of Lord Kṛṣṇa.

TEXT 42

भिक्षोर्धर्मः शमोऽहिंसा तप ईक्षा वनौकसः ।
गृहिणो भूतरक्षेज्या द्विजस्याचार्यसेवनम् ॥४२॥

bhikṣor dharmaḥ śamo 'hiṁsā
tapa īkṣā vanaukasaḥ
gṛhiṇo bhūta-rakṣejyā
dvijasyācārya-sevanam

bhikṣoḥ—of a *sannyāsī; dharmaḥ*—the main religious principle; *śamaḥ*—equanimity; *ahiṁsā*—nonviolence; *tapaḥ*—austerity; *īkṣā*—discrimination (between the body and the soul); *vana*—in the forest; *okasaḥ*—of one dwelling, a *vānaprastha; gṛhiṇaḥ*—of a householder; *bhūta-rakṣā*—offering shelter to all living entities; *ijyā*—performance of sacrifice; *dvi-jasya*—of a *brahmacārī; ācārya*—the spiritual master; *sevanam*—serving.

TRANSLATION

The main religious duties of a *sannyāsī* are equanimity and nonviolence, whereas for the *vānaprastha* austerity and philosophical understanding of the difference between the body and

soul are prominent. The main duties of a householder are to give shelter to all living entities and perform sacrifices, and the *brahmacārī* is mainly engaged in serving the spiritual master.

PURPORT

The *brahmacārī* lives in the *āśrama* of the spiritual master and personally assists the *ācārya*. Householders generally are entrusted with the performance of sacrifice and Deity worship and should provide maintenance for all living entities. The *vānaprastha* must clearly understand the difference between body and soul in order to maintain his status of renunciation, and he should also perform austerities. The *sannyāsī* should fully absorb his body, mind and words in self-realization. Having thus achieved equanimity of mind, he is the best well-wisher of all living entities.

TEXT 43

ब्रह्मचर्यं तपः शौचं सन्तोषो भूतसौहृदम् ।
गृहस्थस्याप्यृतौ गन्तुः सर्वेषां मदुपासनम् ॥४३॥

brahmacaryaṁ tapaḥ śaucaṁ
santoṣo bhūta-sauhṛdam
gṛhasthasyāpy ṛtau gantuḥ
sarveṣāṁ mad-upāsanam

brahma-caryam—celibacy; *tapaḥ*—austerity; *śaucam*—purity of mind without attachment or repulsion; *santoṣaḥ*—full satisfaction; *bhūta*—toward all living entities; *sauhṛdam*—friendship; *gṛhasthasya*—of the householder; *api*—also; *ṛtau*—at the proper time; *gantuḥ*—approaching his wife; *sarveṣām*—of all human beings; *mat*—of Me; *upāsanam*—worship.

TRANSLATION

A householder should approach his wife for sex only at the prescribed time and for begetting children. Otherwise, the householder should practice celibacy, austerity, cleanliness of

mind and body, satisfaction in his natural position, and friendship toward all living entities. Worship of Me is to be practiced by all human beings, regardless of social or occupational divisions.

PURPORT

Sarveṣāṁ mad-upāsanam indicates that all followers of the *varṇāśrama* system must worship Lord Kṛṣṇa or risk falling down from their position. As stated in *Śrīmad-Bhāgavatam* (11.5.3), *na bhajanty avajānanti sthānād bhraṣṭāḥ patanty adhaḥ:* even though one may be advanced in the performance of Vedic rituals and customs, without worshiping the Supreme Lord one will certainly fall down.

Those in the householder *āśrama* are not authorized to enjoy life like pigs and dogs, freely exercising their sexual potency. A religious householder should approach his wife at the prescribed time and place and beget a saintly child for the pleasure of the Supreme Lord. Otherwise, it is specifically mentioned here that a householder must practice celibacy along with all of the other members of advanced human civilization. The word *śaucam* indicates cleanliness of mind and body, or else freedom from attachment and repulsion. One who faithfully worships God as the supreme controller experiences *santoṣa,* full satisfaction in whatever situation the Lord arranges. By seeing Lord Kṛṣṇa within everyone, one becomes *bhūta-suhṛt,* the well-wishing friend of all.

TEXT 44

इति मां यः स्वधर्मेण भजेन् नित्यमनन्यभाक् ।
सर्वभूतेषु मद्भावो मद्भक्तिं विन्दते दृढाम् ॥४४॥

iti māṁ yaḥ sva-dharmeṇa
bhajen nityam ananya-bhāk
sarva-bhūteṣu mad-bhāvo
mad-bhaktiṁ vindate dṛḍhām

iti—thus; *mām*—Me; *yaḥ*—one who; *sva-dharmeṇa*—by his prescribed duty; *bhajet*—worships; *nityam*—always; *ananya-bhāk*—with no other object of worship; *sarva-bhūteṣu*—in all living entities; *mat*—of Me; *bhāvaḥ*—being conscious; *mat-bhaktim*—devotional service unto Me; *vindate*—achieves; *dṛḍhām*—unflinching.

TRANSLATION

One who worships Me by his prescribed duty, having no other object of worship, and who remains conscious of Me as present in all living entities, achieves unflinching devotional service unto Me.

PURPORT

It is clearly explained in this verse that loving devotional service unto Lord Kṛṣṇa is the ultimate goal of the entire *varṇāśrama* system, which the Lord has been elaborately explaining. In any social or occupational division of human society one must be a devotee of the Supreme Personality of Godhead and worship Him alone. The bona fide spiritual master is the representative of Lord Kṛṣṇa, and worship of the *ācārya* goes directly to the lotus feet of the Lord. Although ordinary householders are sometimes ordered by Vedic injunctions to worship particular demigods or forefathers, one should remember that Lord Kṛṣṇa is within all living entities. As stated here, *sarva-bhūteṣu mad-bhāvaḥ*. The pure devotees of the Lord worship the Lord alone, and those who cannot come to the standard of pure devotional service should at least meditate upon the Personality of Godhead within the demigods and all other living entities, understanding that all religious processes are ultimately meant for the pleasure of the Lord. In the course of missionary work even pure devotees must deal with government leaders and other prominent members of society, sometimes praising such persons and complying with their orders. Yet because the devotees are always meditating on Lord Kṛṣṇa situated as the Supersoul within everyone, they are therefore acting for the Lord's pleasure and not for the pleasure of any ordinary human being. Those persons dealing with different demigods in the course of their *varṇāśrama* duties should similarly see the Lord as the basis of everything. They should concentrate on pleasing the Supreme Lord by all activities. This stage of life is called love of God, and it brings one to the point of actual liberation.

TEXT 45

भक्त्योद्धवानपायिन्या सर्वलोकमहेश्वरम् ।
सर्वोत्पत्त्यप्ययं ब्रह्म कारणं मोपयाति सः ॥४५॥

bhaktyoddhavānapāyinyā
sarva-loka-maheśvaram
sarvotpatty-apyayaṁ brahma
kāraṇaṁ mopayāti saḥ

bhaktyā—by loving service; *uddhava*—My dear Uddhava; *anapāyinyā*—unfailing; *sarva*—of all; *loka*—worlds; *mahā-īśvaram*—the Supreme Lord; *sarva*—of everything; *utpatti*—the cause of the creation; *apyayam*—and annihilation; *brahma*—the Absolute Truth; *kāraṇam*—the cause of the universe; *mā*—to Me; *upayāti*—comes; *saḥ*—he.

TRANSLATION

My dear Uddhava, I am the Supreme Lord of all worlds, and I create and destroy this universe, being its ultimate cause. I am thus the Absolute Truth, and one who worships Me with unfailing devotional service comes to Me.

PURPORT

As described in the First Canto of *Śrīmad-Bhāgavatam* (1.2.11), Lord Kṛṣṇa is understood in three features—as impersonal Brahman, localized Paramātmā and ultimately the Supreme Personality of Godhead, Śrī Kṛṣṇa, the source of everything. Lord Kṛṣṇa absorbs the impersonal philosophers into the rays of His body, appears before the perfect *yogīs* as the Lord of the heart, and ultimately brings His pure devotees back to His own abode for an eternal life of bliss and knowledge.

TEXT 46

इति स्वधर्मनिर्णिक्तसत्त्वो निर्ज्ञातमद्गतिः ।
ज्ञानविज्ञानसम्पन्नो न चिरात् समुपैति माम् ॥४६॥

iti sva-dharma-nirṇikta-
sattvo nirjñāta-mad-gatiḥ
jñāna-vijñāna-sampanno
na cirāt samupaiti mām

iti—thus; *sva-dharma*—by performing his prescribed duty; *nirṇikta*—having purified; *sattvaḥ*—his existence; *nirjñāta*—completely understanding; *mat-gatiḥ*—My supreme position; *jñāna*—with knowledge of the scriptures; *vijñāna*—and realized knowledge of the soul; *sampannaḥ*—endowed; *na cirāt*—in the near future; *samupaiti*—completely achieves; *mām*—Me.

TRANSLATION

Thus, one who has purified his existence by execution of his prescribed duties, who fully understands My supreme position and who is endowed with scriptural and realized knowledge, very soon achieves Me.

TEXT 47

वर्णाश्रमवतां धर्म एष आचारलक्षणः ।
स एव मद्भक्तियुतो निःश्रेयसकरः परः ॥४७॥

varṇāśramavatāṁ dharma
eṣa ācāra-lakṣaṇaḥ
sa eva mad-bhakti-yuto
niḥśreyasa-karaḥ paraḥ

varṇāśrama-vatām—of the followers of the *varṇāśrama* system; *dharmaḥ*—religious principle; *eṣaḥ*—this; *ācāra*—by proper behavior according to the authorized tradition; *lakṣaṇaḥ*—characterized; *saḥ*—this; *eva*—indeed; *mat-bhakti*—with devotional service to Me; *yutaḥ*—conjoined; *niḥśreyasa*—the highest perfection of life; *karaḥ*—giving; *paraḥ*—supreme.

TRANSLATION

Those who are followers of this *varṇāśrama* system accept religious principles according to authorized traditions of proper conduct. When such *varṇāśrama* duties are dedicated to Me in loving service, they award the supreme perfection of life.

PURPORT

According to the *varṇāśrama* system, the members of different orders and statuses of life have many traditional duties, such as worshiping the forefathers to save them from possible sinful reactions. All such Vedic rituals, sacrifices, austerities and so forth should be offered to the lotus feet of Lord Śrī Kṛṣṇa. They then become the transcendental means for going back home, back to Godhead. In other words, Kṛṣṇa consciousness, or loving service to Lord Śrī Kṛṣṇa, is the sum and substance of progressive human life.

TEXT 48

एतत्तेऽभिहितं साधो भवान् पृच्छति यच्च माम् ।
यथा स्वधर्मसंयुक्तो भक्तो मां समियात् परम् ॥४८॥

etat te 'bhihitaṁ sādho
bhavān pṛcchati yac ca mām
yathā sva-dharma-saṁyukto
bhakto māṁ samiyāt param

etat—this; *te*—unto you; *abhihitam*—described; *sādho*—O saintly Uddhava; *bhavān*—you; *pṛcchati*—have asked; *yat*—which; *ca*—and; *mām*—from Me; *yathā*—the means by which; *sva-dharma*—in one's prescribed duty; *saṁyuktaḥ*—perfectly engaged; *bhaktaḥ*—being a devotee; *mām*—to Me; *samiyāt*—one may come; *param*—the Supreme.

TRANSLATION

My dear saintly Uddhava, I have now described to you, just as you inquired, the means by which My devotee, perfectly engaged in his prescribed duty, can come back to Me, the Supreme Personality of Godhead.

Thus end the purports of the humble servant of His Divine Grace A. C. Bhaktivedanta Swami Prabhupāda to the Eleventh Canto, Eighteenth Chapter, of the Śrīmad-Bhāgavatam, *entitled "Lord Kṛṣṇa's Description of* Varṇāśrama-dharma."

CHAPTER NINETEEN

The Perfection of Spiritual Knowledge

This chapter describes how those who practice speculative knowledge eventually give up their method, whereas the pure devotees remain engaged in devotional service eternally. Also described are the different practices of the *yogīs,* beginning with *yama.*

The Supreme Lord, Śrī Kṛṣṇa, stated to Uddhava, "One who is actually wise, who knows the truth of the self and possesses transcendental insight, rejects this world of dualities and the so-called knowledge meant for facilitating enjoyment of it. He instead engages himself in trying to satisfy the Supreme Personality of Godhead, the master of all. This is pure *bhakti-yoga.* Transcendental knowledge is greater than such ordinary pious activities as chanting of *mantras,* but pure devotional service is greater than even knowledge."

After this, Lord Kṛṣṇa, requested by Śrī Uddhava to describe in full detail pure transcendental knowledge and devotional service, related the same instructions that the greatest of Vaiṣṇavas, Bhīṣmadeva, gave on these topics to Śrī Yudhiṣṭhira on the occasion of the battle at Kurukṣetra. Following this, after being asked about *yama* and the other practices of *yoga,* the Lord enumerated the twelve kinds of *yama,* beginning with nonviolence, and the twelve kinds of *niyama,* beginning with bodily cleanliness.

TEXT 1

श्रीभगवानुवाच
यो विद्याश्रुतसम्पन्न आत्मवान् नानुमानिकः ।
मायामात्रमिदं ज्ञात्वा ज्ञानं च मयि संन्यसेत् ॥ १ ॥

śrī-bhagavān uvāca
yo vidyā-śruta-sampannaḥ
ātmavān nānumānikaḥ

māyā-mātram idaṁ jñātvā
jñānaṁ ca mayi sannyaset

śrī-bhagavān uvāca—the Supreme Personality of Godhead said; *yaḥ*—one who; *vidyā*—with realized knowledge; *śruta*—and preliminary scriptural knowledge; *sampannaḥ*—endowed; *ātma-vān*—self-realized; *na*—not; *ānumānikaḥ*—engaged in impersonal speculation; *māyā*—illusion; *mātram*—only; *idam*—this universe; *jñātvā*—knowing; *jñānam*—such knowledge and the means of achieving it; *ca*—also; *mayi*—to Me; *sannyaset*—one should surrender.

TRANSLATION

The Supreme Personality of Godhead said: A self-realized person who has cultivated scriptural knowledge up to the point of enlightenment and who is free from impersonal speculation, understanding the material universe to be simply illusion, should surrender both that knowledge and the means by which he achieved it unto Me.

PURPORT

Māyā-mātram idaṁ jñātvā indicates knowledge that the eternal spirit soul and the eternal Personality of Godhead are completely separate from the temporary qualities of the material world. The word *vidyā-śruta-sampanna* means that one should cultivate Vedic knowledge for the purpose of enlightenment and not to make a show of mysticism, intellectuality or impersonal speculation. Having neutralized the illusory effects of *māyā,* one should then transfer one's attention to the Supreme Personality of Godhead, surrendering the process of philosophical negation to the Lord Himself. Śrīla Jīva Gosvāmī gives the example that when there is danger the king may issue weapons to private citizens, but after military victory the individual citizens return the weapons to the king.

Śrīla Viśvanātha Cakravartī Ṭhākura explains this point of this verse as follows. Somehow or other the living entity has to free himself from material illusion, which has covered him since time immemorial. Cultivating desirelessness and renunciation by practice of the mystic *yoga* system, the living entity develops knowledge of illusion and may thus lift himself above the reach of material ignorance. However, once one is situated on the transcendental platform, both knowledge of illusion and the process of acquiring such knowledge have no further practical application. Śrīla Viśvanātha Cakravartī Ṭhākura gives the example that a man may be haunted by the ghost of a snake or a tiger. As long as the man is possessed and thinks, "I am a snake" or "I am a tiger," attempts will be made to counteract the ghostly influence by application of jewels, *mantras* and herbs. But when the man is freed from possession by ghosts, he again thinks, "I am Mr. So-and-so, the son of Mr. So-and-so," and returns to his original nature. At that time the jewels, *mantras* and herbs have no further immediate application. The word *vidyā* in this verse thus indicates knowledge acquired through philosophical analysis, mystic *yoga*, austerities and renunciation. Such knowledge of the temporary, illusory nature of this world counteracts ignorance, and there are many Vedic scriptures that train the living entity in such knowledge. Gradually one gives up his false identification with the material body and mind and with those material objects that interact with the body and mind. Having realized such counteractive knowledge, one must engage in the loving service of the Personality of Godhead and become a pure devotee. When one is completely perfect in Kṛṣṇa consciousness, there is naturally little interest in the innumerable details of illusion, and gradually one is transferred to the spiritual world.

TEXT 2

ज्ञानिनस्त्वहमेवेष्टः स्वार्थो हेतुश्च संमतः ।
स्वर्गश्चैवापवर्गश्च नान्योऽर्थो मदृते प्रियः ॥ २ ॥

jñāninas tv aham eveṣṭaḥ
svārtho hetuś ca sammataḥ
svargaś caivāpavargaś ca
nānyo 'rtho mad-ṛte priyaḥ

jñāninaḥ—of a learned self-realized philosopher; *tu*—indeed; *aham*—I; *eva*—alone; *iṣṭaḥ*—the object of worship; *sva-arthaḥ*—the desired goal of life; *hetuḥ*—the means for achieving the goal of life; *ca*—also; *sammataḥ*—the settled conclusion; *svargaḥ*—the cause of all happiness in elevation to heaven; *ca*—also; *eva*—indeed; *apavargaḥ*—freedom from all unhappiness; *ca*—also; *na*—not; *anyaḥ*—any other; *arthaḥ*—purpose; *mat*—Me; *ṛte*—without; *priyaḥ*—dear object.

TRANSLATION

For learned self-realized philosophers I am the only object of worship, the desired goal of life, the means for achieving that goal, and the settled conclusion of all knowledge. Indeed, because I am the cause of their happiness and their freedom from unhappiness, such learned souls have no effective purpose or dear object in life except Me.

PURPORT

In the previous verse Lord Kṛṣṇa stated that one should ultimately surrender unto Him that knowledge by which the material world is seen as illusion. Material attachments are certainly problems for the living entities, since they are diseases of the spirit soul. One who has contracted a skin disease that causes terrible itching gains only flickering relief by scratching the unbearable sores. If he does not scratch he suffers greatly, but by scratching, even though there is an instantaneous sensation of pleasure, unbearable misery follows as the itching increases. Real happiness is not found in scratching one's skin infections but rather in becoming free from such disease. Conditioned souls are harassed by many illusory desires, and in desperation they try to gratify their senses through the hopeless scratching processes of illicit sex, meat-eating, gambling and intoxication. They further try to gain relief through material society, friendship and love, but the result is unbearable suffering. Real happiness is to eliminate completely the itching disease of material desire. Since material desire is a disease of the soul, one must acquire knowledge to treat this disease and eliminate it. Such therapeutic knowledge is essential as long as one is diseased, but when one is fully healthy, such technical medical knowledge is no longer interesting to the healthy person, and he may leave such knowledge to the doctors. Similarly, in the advanced stage of Kṛṣṇa consciousness one need not think continually of one's personal problems but may rather think of the Supreme Personality of Godhead, Lord Kṛṣṇa, with love and devotion. Lord Kṛṣṇa advises in the previous verse that one should eliminate one's personal problems through technical knowledge of illusion. After giving up constant meditation on such problems, one can then become a lover of God. Lord Kṛṣṇa certainly guides each and every sincere devotee internally within the heart and externally through the bona fide spiritual master. In this way, Lord Kṛṣṇa gradually trains His sincere devotees to give up their irrational attachment to dead matter. Once freedom has been achieved, a devotee begins to seriously cultivate his relationship with Lord Kṛṣṇa in the spiritual sky.

One may falsely think that just as at a certain stage of advancement one ceases to concentrate on technical, analytic knowledge of illusion, so, at another stage one may give up loving devotional service to Lord Kṛṣṇa. To nullify such speculation Lord Śrī Kṛṣṇa here states in various ways that He is the supreme eternal goal of all truly learned human beings. Indeed, the most prominent scholars within the universe are the sages, such as the four Kumāras, who accept Lord Kṛṣṇa as their only worshipable object. Because they have discovered that they are eternal fragmental portions of the Supreme Personality of Godhead, Śrī Kṛṣṇa, they are not interested in fruitive activities and mental speculation. Lord Kṛṣṇa awards celestial bliss and freedom from anxiety to His sincere followers, who have no purpose or beloved object in life other than the Lord.

TEXT 3

ज्ञानविज्ञानसंसिद्धाः पदं श्रेष्ठं विदुर्मम ।
ज्ञानी प्रियतमोऽतो मे ज्ञानेनासौ बिभर्ति माम्॥ ३ ॥

jñāna-vijñāna-saṁsiddhāḥ
padaṁ śreṣṭhaṁ vidur mama
jñānī priyatamo 'to me
jñānenāsau bibharti mām

jñāna—in scriptural knowledge; *vijñāna*—and realized spiritual understanding; *saṁsiddhāḥ*—completely perfected; *padam*—the lotus feet; *śreṣṭham*—the supreme object; *viduḥ*—they know; *mama*—My; *jñānī*—a learned transcendentalist; *priya-tamaḥ*—most dear; *ataḥ*—thus; *me*—to Me; *jñānena*—by spiritual knowledge; *asau*—that learned person; *bibharti*—maintains (in happiness); *mām*—Me.

TRANSLATION

Those who have achieved complete perfection through philosophical and realized knowledge recognize My lotus feet to be the supreme transcendental object. Thus the learned transcendentalist is most dear to Me, and by his perfect knowledge he maintains Me in happiness.

PURPORT

The words *padaṁ śreṣṭhaṁ vidur mama* ("they recognize My lotus feet to be supreme") certainly eliminate the impersonalist philosophers from the category of *saṁsiddhāḥ*, or completely perfected philosophers. Lord Kṛṣṇa here refers to such great transcendental scholars as the four Kumāras, Śukadeva Gosvāmī, Śrī Vyāsadeva, Śrīla Bhaktisiddhānta Sarasvatī Ṭhākura and Śrīla A. C. Bhaktivedanta Swami Prabhupāda. The Lord similarly states in *Bhagavad-gītā* (7.17–18),

teṣāṁ jñānī nitya-yukta
eka-bhaktir viśiṣyate
priyo hi jñānino 'ty-artham
ahaṁ sa ca mama priyaḥ

"Of these, the wise one who is in full knowledge in union with Me through pure devotional service is the best. For I am very dear to him, and he is dear to Me."

udārāḥ sarva evaite
jñānī tv ātmaiva me matam
āsthitaḥ sa hi yuktātmā
mām evānuttamāṁ gatim

"All these devotees are undoubtedly magnanimous souls, but he who is situated in knowledge of Me I consider verily to dwell in Me. Being engaged in My transcendental service, he attains Me."

Jñāna refers to an authorized philosophical and analytic perception of reality, and when such knowledge is clearly realized through the sanctification of consciousness the resultant comprehensive experience is called *vijñāna*. Speculative, impersonal knowledge does not actually purify the heart of the living entity but rather merges him ever deeper into forgetfulness of the Supreme Personality of Godhead. Just as a father is always proud of his son's education, similarly, Lord Kṛṣṇa becomes very happy to see the living entities acquiring a sound spiritual education and thus making progress on the way back home, back to Godhead.

TEXT 4

तपस्तीर्थं जपो दानं पवित्राणीतराणि च ।
नालं कुर्वन्ति तां सिद्धिं या ज्ञानकलया कृता ॥ ४ ॥

tapas tīrthaṁ japo dānaṁ
pavitrāṇītarāṇi ca
nālaṁ kurvanti tāṁ siddhiṁ
yā jñāna-kalayā kṛtā

tapaḥ—austerity; *tīrtham*—visiting holy places; *japaḥ*—offering silent prayers; *dānam*—charity; *pavitrāṇi*—pious activities; *itarāṇi*—other; *ca*—also; *na*—not; *alam*—up to the same standard; *kurvanti*—they award; *tām*—this; *siddhim*—perfection; *yā*—which; *jñāna*—of spiritual knowledge; *kalayā*—by a fraction; *kṛtā*—is awarded.

TRANSLATION

That perfection which is produced by a small fraction of spiritual knowledge cannot be duplicated by performing austerities, visiting holy places, chanting silent prayers, giving in charity or engaging in other pious activities.

PURPORT

Jñāna here refers to a clear understanding of the Lord's supreme dominion over all that be, and this realized knowledge is nondifferent from the Supreme Personality of Godhead. That the Lord is supreme is confirmed in the previous verse by the words *padaṁ śreṣṭhaṁ vidur mama.* One may perform penances or visit holy places with a proud mentality or material motivation; similarly, one may chant prayers to God, give charity or perform other externally pious activities with many bizarre, hypocritical or even demoniac motivations. Realized knowledge of the supremacy of Lord Kṛṣṇa, however, is a solid connection with the spiritual world, and if one pursues this holy understanding one is gradually promoted to the highest level of conscious existence, called Vaikuṇṭha, or the kingdom of God.

TEXT 5

तस्माज्ज्ञानेन सहितं ज्ञात्वा स्वात्मानमुद्धव ।
ज्ञानविज्ञानसम्पन्नो भज मां भक्तिभावितः ॥ ५ ॥

tasmāj jñānena sahitaṁ
jñātvā svātmānam uddhava
jñāna-vijñāna-sampanno
bhaja māṁ bhakti-bhāvataḥ

tasmāt—therefore; *jñānena*—knowledge; *sahitam*—with; *jñātvā*—knowing; *sva-ātmānam*—your own self; *uddhava*—My dear Uddhava; *jñāna*—in Vedic knowledge; *vijñāna*—and clear realization; *sampannaḥ*—accomplished; *bhaja*—worship; *mām*—Me; *bhakti*—of loving devotion; *bhāvataḥ*—in the mood.

TRANSLATION

Therefore, My dear Uddhava, through knowledge you should understand your actual self, and then advancing by clear realization of Vedic knowledge you should worship Me in the mood of loving devotion.

PURPORT

The word *vijñāna* indicates realized knowledge of one's original, spiritual form. Every living entity has an eternal spiritual form, which lies dormant until one arouses one's original Kṛṣṇa consciousness. Without knowledge of one's own spiritual personality it is not possible to cultivate love of the Supreme Personality, Lord Kṛṣṇa. Therefore, the words *jñātvā svātmānam* are significant here, indicating that every living entity can realize his full potential as an individual person only in the kingdom of God.

TEXT 6

ज्ञानविज्ञानयज्ञेन मामिष्ट्वात्मानमात्मनि ।
सर्वयज्ञपतिं मां वै संसिद्धिं मुनयोऽगमन् ॥ ६ ॥

jñāna-vijñāna-yajñena
mām iṣṭvātmānam ātmani
sarva-yajña-patiṁ māṁ vai
saṁsiddhiṁ munayo 'gaman

jñāna—of Vedic knowledge; *vijñāna*—and spiritual enlightenment; *yajñena*—by the sacrifice; *mām*—Me; *iṣṭvā*—having worshiped; *ātmānam*—the Supreme Lord within everyone's heart; *ātmani*—within themselves; *sarva*—of all; *yajña*—sacrifices; *patim*—the Lord; *mām*—Me; *vai*—certainly; *saṁsiddhim*—the supreme perfection; *munayaḥ*—the sages; *agaman*—achieved.

TRANSLATION

Formerly, great sages, through the sacrifice of Vedic knowledge and spiritual enlightenment, worshiped Me within themselves, knowing Me to be the Supreme Lord of all sacrifice and the Supersoul in everyone's heart. Thus coming to Me, these sages achieved the supreme perfection.

TEXT 7

त्वय्युद्धवाश्रयति यस्त्रिविधो विकारो
मायान्तरापतति नाद्यपवर्गयोर्यत् ।
जन्मादयोऽस्य यदमी तव तस्य किं स्यु-
राद्यन्तयोर्यदसतोऽस्ति तदेव मध्ये ॥ ७ ॥

tvayy uddhavāśrayati yas tri-vidho vikāro
māyāntarāpatati nādy-apavargayor yat
janmādayo 'sya yad amī tava tasya kiṁ syur
ādy-antayor yad asato 'sti tad eva madhye

tvayi—in you; *uddhava*—O Uddhava; *āśrayati*—enters and remains; *yaḥ*—which; *tri-vidhaḥ*—in three divisions, according to the modes of nature; *vikāraḥ*—(the material body and mind, which are subject to) constant transformation; *māyā*—illusion; *antarā*—during the present; *āpatati*—suddenly appears; *na*—not; *ādi*—in the beginning; *apavargayoḥ*—nor at the end; *yat*—since; *janma*—birth; *ādayaḥ*—and so on (growth, procreation, maintenance, dwindling and death); *asya*—of the body; *yat*—when; *amī*—these; *tava*—in relation to you; *tasya*—in relation to your spiritual nature; *kim*—what relationship; *syuḥ*—could they have; *ādi*—in the beginning; *antayoḥ*—and in the end; *yat*—since; *asataḥ*—of that which does not exist; *asti*—exists; *tat*—that; *eva*—indeed; *madhye*—only in the middle, at present.

TRANSLATION

My dear Uddhava, the material body and mind, composed of the three modes of material nature, attach themselves to you, but they are actually illusion, since they appear only at the present, having no original or ultimate existence. How is it possible, therefore, that the various stages of the body, namely birth, growth, reproduction, maintenance, dwindling and death, can have any relation to your eternal self? These phases relate only to the material body, which previously did not exist and ultimately will not exist. The body exists merely at the present moment.

PURPORT

The example is given that a man walking in the forest may see a rope but consider it to be a snake. Such perception is *māyā,* or illusion, although the rope actually exists and a snake also exists in another place. Illusion thus refers to the false identification of one object with another. The material body exists briefly and then disappears. In the past the body did not exist, and in the future it will not exist; it enjoys a flickering, momentary existence in so-called present time. If we falsely identify ourselves as the material body or mind, we are creating an illusion. One who identifies himself as American, Russian, Chinese, Mexican, black or white, man or woman, communist or capitalist, and so on, accepting such designations as his permanent identity, is certainly in deep illusion. He can be compared to a sleeping man who sees himself acting in a different body while dreaming. In the previous verse Lord Kṛṣṇa told Uddhava that spiritual knowledge is the means of achieving the highest perfection, and now the Lord is explicitly describing such knowledge.

TEXT 8

श्रीउद्धव उवाच
ज्ञानं विशुद्धं विपुलं यथैत-
द्वैराग्यविज्ञानयुतं पुराणम् ।
आख्याहि विश्वेश्वर विश्वमूर्ते
त्वद्भक्तियोगं च महद्विमृग्यम् ॥ ८ ॥

śrī-uddhava uvāca
jñānaṁ viśuddhaṁ vipulaṁ yathaitad
vairāgya-vijñāna-yutaṁ purāṇam
ākhyāhi viśveśvara viśva-mūrte
tvad-bhakti-yogaṁ ca mahad-vimṛgyam

śrī-uddhavaḥ uvāca—Śrī Uddhava said; *jñānam*—knowledge; *viśuddham*—transcendental; *vipulam*—extensive; *yathā*—just as; *etat*—this; *vairāgya*—detachment; *vijñāna*—and direct perception of the truth; *yutam*—including; *purāṇam*—traditional among great philosophers; *ākhyāhi*—please explain; *viśva-īśvara*—O Lord of the universe; *viśva-mūrte*—O form of the universe; *tvat*—unto You; *bhakti-yogam*—loving devotional service; *ca*—also; *mahat*—by great souls; *vimṛgyam*—sought after.

TRANSLATION

Śrī Uddhava said: O Lord of the universe! O form of the universe! Please explain to me that process of knowledge which automatically brings detachment and direct perception of the truth, which is transcendental and is traditional among great spiritual philosophers. This knowledge, sought after by elevated personalities, describes loving devotional service unto Your Lordship.

PURPORT

Those who are able to cross over the darkness of material existence are called *mahat,* or great personalities. Secondary items like cosmic consciousness or universal control do not deviate the attention of such great souls from loving service to the Lord. Śrī Uddhava desires to hear knowledge of the eternal religious principles that are the traditional aim and objective of all superior personalities.

TEXT 9

तापत्रयेणाभिहतस्य घोरे
संतप्यमानस्य भवाध्वनीश ।
पश्यामि नान्यच्छरणं तवाङ्घ्रि-
द्वन्द्वातपत्रादमृताभिवर्षात् ॥ ९ ॥

tāpa-trayeṇābhihatasya ghore
santapyamānasya bhavādhvanīśa
paśyāmi nānyac charaṇaṁ tavāṅghri-
dvandvātapatrād amṛtābhivarṣāt

tāpa—by the miseries; *trayeṇa*—threefold; *abhihatasya*—of one overwhelmed; *ghore*—which is terrible; *santapyamānasya*—being tormented; *bhava*—of material existence; *adhvani*—in the path; *īśa*—O Lord; *paśyāmi*—I see; *na*—none; *anyat*—other; *śaraṇam*—shelter; *tava*—Your; *aṅghri*—lotus feet; *dvandva*—of the two; *ātapatrāt*—than the umbrella; *amṛta*—of nectar; *abhivarṣāt*—the shower.

TRANSLATION

My dear Lord, for one who is being tormented on the terrible path of birth and death and is constantly overwhelmed by the threefold miseries, I do not see any possible shelter other than Your two lotus feet, which are just like a refreshing umbrella that pours down showers of delicious nectar.

PURPORT

Lord Kṛṣṇa, recognizing Uddhava's highly intellectual nature, has repeatedly recommended to him that one should achieve perfection by cultivation of transcendental knowledge. But the Lord has also clearly demonstrated that such knowledge must bring one to the point of loving devotional service to Him, for otherwise it is useless. In this verse Śrī Uddhava corroborates Lord Kṛṣṇa's statements that actual happiness is obtained by surrendering to His lotus feet. When the incarnation of Godhead Pṛthu Mahārāja was crowned, the demigod Vāyu presented him with an umbrella that constantly sprayed fine particles of water. The Lord's two lotus feet are similarly compared here to a wonderful umbrella that produces a constant shower of delicious nectar, the bliss of Kṛṣṇa consciousness. Normally, speculative analytic knowledge terminates in an impersonal conception of the Absolute Truth, but the so-called bliss of merging into impersonal spiritual existence can never be compared to the bliss of Kṛṣṇa consciousness, as stated here by Śrī Uddhava. Kṛṣṇa consciousness thus automatically constitutes perfect knowledge, since Lord Kṛṣṇa is the ultimate shelter of all living entities. The words *abhihatasya* and *abhivarṣāt* are significant in this verse. *Abhihatasya* indicates one who is being defeated on all sides by the onslaught of material nature, whereas *abhivarṣāt* indicates a downpour of nectar that eliminates all of the problems of material existence. By our intelligence we should look beyond the dull material body and nonsensical material mind to observe the unlimited shower of blissful nectar coming from the two lotus feet of Lord Kṛṣṇa. Then our real good fortune will begin.

TEXT 10

दष्टं जनं संपतितं बिलेऽस्मिन्
कालाहिना क्षुद्रसुखोरुतर्षम् ।
समुद्धरैनं कृपयापवर्ग्यै-
र्वचोभिरासिञ्च महानुभाव ॥१०॥

daṣṭaṁ janaṁ sampatitaṁ bile 'smin
kālāhinā kṣudra-sukhoru-tarṣam
samuddharainaṁ kṛpayāpavargyair
vacobhir āsiñca mahānubhāva

daṣṭam—bitten; *janam*—the person; *sampatitam*—hopelessly fallen; *bile*—in the dark hole; *asmin*—this; *kāla*—of time; *ahinā*—by the serpent; *kṣudra*—insignificant; *sukha*—having happiness; *uru*—and tremendous; *tarṣam*—hankering; *samuddhara*—please uplift; *enam*—this person; *kṛpayā*—by Your causeless mercy; *āpavargyaiḥ*—that awaken one to liberation; *vacobhiḥ*—by Your words; *āsiñca*—please pour; *mahā-anubhāva*—O mighty Lord.

TRANSLATION

O almighty Lord, please be merciful and uplift this hopeless living entity who has fallen into the dark hole of material existence, where the snake of time has bitten him. In spite of such abominable conditions, this poor living entity has tremendous desire to relish the most insignificant material happiness. Please save me, my Lord, by pouring down the nectar of Your instructions, which awaken one to spiritual freedom.

PURPORT

Material life, so much cherished by the nondevotees, is here compared to a dark hole filled with poisonous snakes. In material life there is certainly no clear understanding of one's ultimate identity, of God or of the universe. Everything is vague and dark. In material life the poisonous snake of time is always threatening, and at any moment our near and dear ones will be killed by the mortal fangs of the serpent. Ultimately, we ourselves will also be bitten and killed by the poisonous effects of time. The word *sampatitam* indicates that the falldown of the living entity is complete. In other words, he cannot get up again. Śrī Uddhava therefore appeals to the Lord to be kind to these poor fallen souls, humbly represented by his own self. If one receives the Lord's mercy, then even without any further qualification one can go back home, back to Godhead; and without the mercy of Lord Kṛṣṇa, the most learned, austere, powerful, wealthy or beautiful man will be pathetically crushed by the material world's machinery of illusion. The Supreme Personality of Godhead, as described here, is *mahānubhāva,* or the greatest, most powerful and most merciful personality, whose influence extends everywhere. The Lord's mercy is manifest in the form of His nectarean instructions such as *Bhagavad-gītā* and the *Uddhava-gīta,* being spoken here. The word *kṣudra-sukhoru-tarṣam* reveals the irony of material existence. Although material happiness is *kṣudra,* or ridiculous and insignificant, our desire to enjoy it is *uru,* tremendous. Our disproportionate hankering to enjoy dead matter is certainly an illusory state of mind, and it gives us constant distress, keeping us bound up in the dark hole of material existence. Every living entity should put aside his false prestige based on ephemeral bodily qualifications and appeal sincerely to the Supreme Lord, Kṛṣṇa, for His mercy. The Lord hears every sincere appeal, from even the most fallen soul, and the effects of the Lord's mercy are wonderful. Although *jñānīs, yogīs* and fruitive workers are laboriously endeavoring to achieve their respective goals, their position is precarious and uncertain. Simply by achieving the mercy of Lord Kṛṣṇa, however, one can very easily attain the highest perfection of life. If even one who is not a great or pure devotee of Lord Kṛṣṇa sincerely appeals to the Lord for His mercy, the Lord is sure to give it generously.

TEXT 11

श्रीभगवानुवाच
इत्थमेतत् पुरा राजा भीष्मं धर्मभृतां वरम् ।
अजातशत्रुः पप्रच्छ सर्वेषां नोऽनुश‍ृण्वताम् ॥११॥

śrī-bhagavān uvāca
ittham etat purā rājā
bhīṣmaṁ dharma-bhṛtāṁ varam
ajāta-śatruḥ papraccha
sarveṣāṁ no 'nuśṛṇvatām

śrī-bhagavān uvāca—the Supreme Personality of Godhead said; *ittham*—thus; *etat*—this; *purā*—formerly; *rājā*—the King; *bhīṣmam*—unto Bhīṣma; *dharma*—of religious principles; *bhṛtām*—of the upholders; *varam*—unto the best; *ajāta-śatruḥ*—King Yudhiṣṭhira, who considered no one his enemy; *papraccha*—asked; *sarveṣām*—while all; *naḥ*—of us; *anuśṛṇvatām*—were carefully listening.

TRANSLATION

The Supreme Personality of Godhead said: My dear Uddhava, just as you are now inquiring from Me, similarly, in the past King Yudhiṣṭhira, who considered no one his enemy, inquired from

the greatest of the upholders of religious principles, Bhīṣma, while all of us were carefully listening.

TEXT 12

निवृत्ते भारते युद्धे सुहृन्निधनविह्वलः ।
श्रुत्वा धर्मान् बहून् पश्चान्मोक्षधर्मानपृच्छत ॥१२॥

nivṛtte bhārate yuddhe
suhṛn-nidhana-vihvalaḥ
śrutvā dharmān bahūn paścān
mokṣa-dharmān apṛcchata

nivṛtte—when it ended; *bhārate*—of the descendants of Bhārata (the Kurus and Pāṇḍavas); *yuddhe*—the war; *suhṛt*—of his beloved well-wishers; *nidhana*—by the destruction; *vihvalaḥ*—overwhelmed; *śrutvā*—having heard; *dharmān*—religious principles; *bahūn*—many; *paścāt*—at last; *mokṣa*—concerning liberation; *dharmān*—religious principles; *apṛcchata*—asked about.

TRANSLATION

When the great Battle of Kurukṣetra had ended, King Yudhiṣṭhira was overwhelmed by the death of many beloved well-wishers, and thus, after listening to instructions about many religious principles, he finally inquired about the path of liberation.

TEXT 13

तानहं तेऽभिधास्यामि देवव्रतमुखाच्छ्रुतान् ।
ज्ञानवैराग्यविज्ञानश्रद्धाभक्त्युपबृंहितान् ॥१३॥

tān ahaṁ te 'bhidhāsyāmi
deva-vrata-mukhāc chrutān
jñāna-vairāgya-vijñāna-
śraddhā-bhakty-upabṛṁhitān

tān—those; *aham*—I; *te*—unto you; *abhidhāsyāmi*—will describe; *deva-vrata*—of Bhīṣmadeva; *mukhāt*—from the mouth; *śrutān*—heard;

jñāna—Vedic knowledge; *vairāgya*—detachment; *vijñāna*—self-realization; *śraddhā*—faith; *bhakti*—and devotional service; *upa-bṛṁhitān*—consisting of.

TRANSLATION

I will now speak unto you those religous principles of Vedic knowledge, detachment, self-realization, faith and devotional service that were heard directly from the mouth of Bhīṣmadeva.

TEXT 14

नवैकादश पञ्च त्रीन् भावान् भूतेषु येन वै ।
ईक्षेताथैकमप्येषु तज्ज्ञानं मम निश्चितम् ॥१४॥

navaikādaśa pañca trīn
bhāvān bhūteṣu yena vai
īkṣetāthaikam apy eṣu
taj jñānaṁ mama niścitam

nava—nine; *ekādaśa*—eleven; *pañca*—five; *trīn*—and three; *bhāvān*—elements; *bhūteṣu*—in all living beings (from Lord Brahmā down to the immovable living entities); *yena*—by which knowledge; *vai*—certainly; *īkṣeta*—one may see; *atha*—thus; *ekam*—one element; *api*—indeed; *eṣu*—within these twenty-eight elements; *tat*—that; *jñānam*—knowledge; *mama*—by Me; *niścitam*—is authorized.

TRANSLATION

I personally approve of that knowledge by which one sees the combination of nine, eleven, five and three elements in all living entities, and ultimately one element within those twenty-eight.

PURPORT

The nine elements are material nature, the living entity, the *mahat-tattva,* false ego, and the five objects of sense perception, namely sound, touch, form, taste and aroma. The eleven elements are the five working senses (the voice, hands, legs, anus and genital) plus the five knowledge-acquiring senses (the ears, touch, eyes, tongue and nostrils), along with the coordinative sense, the mind. The five elements are the five physical elements, namely earth, water, fire, air and sky, and the three elements are the three modes of material nature—goodness, passion and ignorance. All living entities, from mighty Lord Brahmā down to an insignificant weed, manifest material bodies composed of these twenty-eight elements. The one element within all twenty-eight is the Supreme Personality of Godhead, the Supersoul, who is all-pervading within the material and spiritual worlds.

One can easily understand that the material universe is composed of innumerable causes and effects. Since Lord Kṛṣṇa is the cause of all causes, all secondary causes and their effects are ultimately nondifferent from the Personality of Godhead. This understanding constitutes real knowledge, or *jñāna,* which is essential for perfecting one's life.

TEXT 15

एतदेव हि विज्ञानं न तथैकेन येन यत् ।
स्थित्युत्पत्त्यप्ययान् पश्येद् भावानां त्रिगुणात्मनाम् ॥१५॥

etad eva hi vijñānaṁ
na tathaikena yena yat
sthity-utpatty-apyayān paśyed
bhāvānāṁ tri-guṇātmanām

etat—this; *eva*—indeed; *hi*—actually; *vijñānam*—realized knowledge; *na*—not; *tathā*—in that way; *ekena*—by the one (Personality of Godhead); *yena*—by whom; *yat*—which (universe); *sthiti*—maintenance; *utpatti*—creation; *apyayān*—and annihilation; *paśyet*—one should see; *bhāvānām*—of all material elements; *tri-guṇa*—of the three modes of nature; *ātmanām*—composed.

TRANSLATION

When one no longer sees the twenty-eight separated material elements, which arise from a single cause, but rather sees the cause itself, the Personality of Godhead—at that time one's direct experience is called *vijñāna,* or self-realization.

PURPORT

The difference between *jñāna* (ordinary Vedic knowledge) and *vijñāna* (self-realization) can be understood as follows. A conditioned soul, although cultivating Vedic knowledge, continues to identify himself to some extent with the material body and mind and consequently with the material universe. In trying to understand the world he lives in, the conditioned soul learns through Vedic knowledge that the Supreme Personality of Godhead is the one supreme cause of all material manifestations. He comes to understand the world around him, which he accepts more or less as his world. As he progresses in spiritual realization, breaking through the barrier of bodily identification, and realizes the existence of the eternal soul, he gradually identifies himself as part and parcel of the spiritual world, Vaikuṇṭha. At that time he is no longer interested in the Personality of Godhead merely as the supreme explanation of the material world; rather, he begins to reorient his entire mode of consciousness so that the central object of his attention is the Personality of Godhead. Such a reorientation is required, since the Supreme Lord is the factual center and cause of everything. A self-realized soul in the stage of *vijñāna* thus experiences the Personality of Godhead not merely as the creator of the material world but as the supreme living entity existing blissfully in His own eternal context. As one progresses in one's realization of the Supreme Lord in His own abode in the spiritual sky, one gradually becomes disinterested in the material universe and ceases to define the Supreme Lord in terms of His temporary manifestations. A self-realized soul in the stage of *vijñāna* is not at all attracted by objects that are created, maintained and ultimately destroyed. The stage of *jñāna* is the preliminary stage of knowledge for those still identifying themselves in terms of the material universe, whereas *vijñāna* is the mature stage of knowledge for those who see themselves as part and parcel of the Supreme Lord.

TEXT 16

आदावन्ते च मध्ये च सृज्यात् सृज्यं यदन्वियात् ।
पुनस्तत्प्रतिसंक्रामे यच्छिष्येत तदेव सत् ॥१६॥

ādāv ante ca madhye ca
sṛjyāt sṛjyaṁ yad anviyāt
punas tat-pratisaṅkrāme
yac chiṣyeta tad eva sat

ādau—in the causal stage; *ante*—in the termination of the causal function; *ca*—also; *madhye*—in the phase of maintenance; *ca*—also; *sṛjyāt*—from one production; *sṛjyam*—to another production; *yat*—which; *anviyāt*—accompanies; *punaḥ*—again; *tat*—of all material phases; *pratisaṅkrāme*—in the annihilation; *yat*—which; *śiṣyeta*—remains; *tat*—that; *eva*—indeed; *sat*—the one eternal.

TRANSLATION

Commencement, termination and maintenance are the stages of material causation. That which consistently accompanies all these material phases from one creation to another and remains alone when all material phases are annihilated is the one eternal.

PURPORT

The Lord here reiterates that the one Supreme Personality of Godhead is the basis of unlimited material variety. Material activity is a chain of cause-and-effect relationships by which innumerable objects are produced. A particular material effect is converted into a subsequent cause, and when the causal phase is terminated, the effect disappears. Fire causes firewood to burn to ashes, and when the causal function of fire is finished, fire itself, which was the effect of a previous cause, is also terminated. The simple fact is that all material objects are created, maintained and ultimately annihilated by the supreme potency of the Lord. And when the entire field of material cause and effect is withdrawn, so that all cause-effect relationships vanish, the Personality of Godhead remains in His own abode. Therefore, although innumerable objects may function as causes, they are not the ultimate or supreme cause. Only the Personality of Godhead is the absolute cause. Similarly, although material things may exist, they do not always exist. The Personality of Godhead alone has absolute existence. By the process of *jñāna*, or knowledge, one should understand the supreme position of the Lord.

TEXT 17

श्रुतिः प्रत्यक्षमैतिह्यमनुमानं चतुष्टयम् ।
प्रमाणेष्वनवस्थानाद् विकल्पात् स विरज्यते ॥१७॥

śrutiḥ pratyakṣam aitihyam
anumānaṁ catuṣṭayam
pramāṇeṣv anavasthānād
vikalpāt sa virajyate

śrutiḥ—Vedic knowledge; *pratyakṣam*—direct experience; *aitihyam*—traditional wisdom; *anumānam*—logical induction; *catuṣṭayam*—fourfold; *pramāṇeṣu*—among all types of evidence; *anavasthānāt*—due to the flickering nature; *vikalpāt*—from material diversity; *saḥ*—a person; *virajyate*—becomes detached.

TRANSLATION

From the four types of evidence—Vedic knowledge, direct experience, traditional wisdom and logical induction—one can understand the temporary, insubstantial situation of the material world, by which one becomes detached from the duality of this world.

PURPORT

In the *śruti,* or Vedic literature, it is clearly stated that everything emanates from the Absolute Truth, is maintained by the Absolute Truth and at the end is conserved within the Absolute Truth. Similarly, by direct experience we can observe the creation and destruction of great empires, cities, buildings, bodies and so on. Furthermore, we find all around the world traditional wisdom warning people that things in this world cannot last. Finally, by logical induction we can easily conclude that nothing in this world is permanent. Material sense gratification—up to the highest possible living standard found in the heavenly planets or down to the lowest conditions in the most repugnant precincts of hell—is always unsteady and prone to collapse at any moment. One should therefore develop *vairāgya,* detachment, as stated here.

Another meaning of this verse is that the four types of evidence cited here are often mutually contradictory in their description of the highest truth. One should therefore be detached from the duality of mundane evidence, including the portions of the *Vedas* that deal with the material world. Instead, one should accept the Supreme Personality of Godhead as the actual authority. Both in *Bhagavad-gītā* and here in *Śrīmad-Bhāgavatam* Lord Kṛṣṇa is personally speaking, and thus there is no need to enter into the bewildering network of competing systems of mundane logic. One can directly hear from the Absolute Truth Himself and immediately acquire perfect knowledge. One thereby becomes detached from inferior systems of knowledge, which cause one to hover on the material mental platform.

TEXT 18

कर्मणां परिणामित्वादाविरिञ्च्यादमङ्गलम् ।
विपश्चिन्नश्वरं पश्येददृष्टमपि दृष्टवत् ॥१८॥

karmaṇāṁ pariṇāmitvād
ā-viriñcyād amaṅgalam
vipaścin naśvaraṁ paśyed
adṛṣṭam api dṛṣṭa-vat

karmaṇām—of material activities; *pariṇāmitvāt*—because of being subject to transformation; *ā*—up to; *viriñcyāt*—the planet of Lord Brahmā; *amaṅgalam*—inauspicious unhappiness; *vipaścit*—an intelligent person; *naśvaram*—as temporary; *paśyet*—should see; *adṛṣṭam*—that which he has not yet experienced; *api*—indeed; *dṛṣṭa-vat*—just like that already experienced.

TRANSLATION

An intelligent person should see that any material activity is subject to constant transformation and that even on the planet of Lord Brahmā there is thus simply unhappiness. Indeed, a wise man can understand that just as all that he has seen is temporary, similarly, all things within the universe have a beginning and an end.

PURPORT

The word *adṛṣṭam* indicates the heavenly standard of life available in the higher planets within this universe. Such celestial neighborhoods are not actually experienced on the earth planet, although they are described in the Vedic literatures. One may argue that promotion to material heaven is recommended in the *karma-kāṇḍa* portion of the *Vedas* and that although the happiness available there is not eternal, at least for some time one may enjoy life. Lord Kṛṣṇa here states, however, that even on the planet of Lord Brahmā, which is superior to the heavenly planets, there is no happiness whatsoever. Even in the upper planetary systems there is rivalry, envy, irritation, lamentation and ultimately death itself.

TEXT 19

भक्तियोगः पुरैवोक्तः प्रीयमाणाय तेऽनघ ।
पुनश्च कथयिष्यामि मद्भक्तेः कारणं परम् ॥१९॥

bhakti-yogaḥ puraivoktaḥ
prīyamāṇāya te 'nagha
punaś ca kathayiṣyāmi
mad-bhakteḥ kāraṇaṁ paraṁ

bhakti-yogaḥ—devotional service to the Lord; *purā*—previously; *eva*—indeed; *uktaḥ*—explained; *prīyamāṇāya*—who has developed love; *te*—unto you; *anagha*—O sinless Uddhava; *punaḥ*—again; *ca*—also; *kathayiṣyāmi*—I will explain; *mat*—unto Me; *bhakteḥ*—of devotional service; *kāraṇam*—the actual means; *param*—supreme.

TRANSLATION

O sinless Uddhava, because you love Me, I previously explained to you the process of devotional service. Now I will again explain the supreme process for achieving loving service unto Me.

PURPORT

Although Lord Kṛṣṇa previously described *bhakti-yoga* to Śrī Uddhava, Uddhava is not yet satisfied, because he loves Lord Kṛṣṇa.

Anyone who loves the Lord cannot be fully satiated by discussions of devotional service mixed with decriptions of mere Vedic duties and analytic philosophy. The supreme stage of conscious existence is pure love of Kṛṣṇa, and one who is addicted to Lord Kṛṣṇa desires to constantly drink the nectar of such topics. Lord Kṛṣṇa has given an extensive survey of many aspects of human civilization, including the *varṇāśrama-dharma* system and the processes of distinguishing between matter and spirit, renouncing sense gratification, and so forth. Now Uddhava is hankering to hear specifically about pure devotional service to Lord Kṛṣṇa, and the Lord thus turns to that topic.

TEXTS 20-24

श्रद्धामृतकथायां मे शश्वन्मदनुकीर्तनम् ।
परिनिष्ठा च पूजायां स्तुतिभिः स्तवनं मम ॥२०॥
आदरः परिचर्यायां सर्वाङ्गैरभिवन्दनम् ।
मद्भक्तपूजाभ्यधिका सर्वभूतेषु मन्मतिः ॥२१॥
मदर्थेष्वङ्गचेष्टा च वचसा मद्गुणेरणम् ।
मय्यर्पणं च मनसः सर्वकामविवर्जनम् ॥२२॥
मदर्थेऽर्थपरित्यागो भोगस्य च सुखस्य च ।
इष्टं दत्तं हुतं जप्तं मदर्थं यद् व्रतं तपः ॥२३॥
एवं धर्मैर्मनुष्याणामुद्धवात्मनिवेदिनाम् ।
मयि सञ्जायते भक्तिः कोऽन्योऽर्थोऽस्यावशिष्यते ॥२४॥

śraddhāmṛta-kathāyāṁ me
śaśvan mad-anukīrtanam
pariniṣṭhā ca pūjāyāṁ
stutibhiḥ stavanaṁ mama

ādaraḥ paricaryāyāṁ
sarvāṅgair abhivandanam
mad-bhakta-pūjābhyadhikā
sarva-bhūteṣu man-matiḥ

mad-artheṣv aṅga-ceṣṭā ca
vacasā mad-guṇeraṇam
mayy arpaṇaṁ ca manasaḥ
sarva-kāma-vivarjanam

mad-arthe 'rtha-parityāgo
bhogasya ca sukhasya ca
iṣṭaṁ dattaṁ hutaṁ japtaṁ
mad-arthaṁ yad vrataṁ tapaḥ

evaṁ dharmair manuṣyāṇām
uddhavātma-nivedinām
mayi sañjāyate bhaktiḥ
ko 'nyo 'rtho 'syāvaśiṣyate

śraddhā—faith; *amṛta*—in the nectar; *kathāyām*—of narrations; *me*—about Me; *śaśvat*—always; *mat*—of Me; *anukīrtanam*—chanting the glories; *pariniṣṭhā*—fixed in attachment; *ca*—also; *pūjāyām*—in worshiping Me; *stutibhiḥ*—with beautiful hymns; *stavanam*—formal prayers; *mama*—in relation to Me; *ādaraḥ*—great respect; *paricaryāyām*—for My devotional service; *sarva-aṅgaiḥ*—with all the limbs of the body; *abhivandanam*—offering obeisances; *mat*—My; *bhakta*—of the devotees; *pūjā*—worship; *abhyadhikā*—preeminent; *sarva-bhūteṣu*—in all living entities; *mat*—of Me; *matiḥ*—consciousness; *mat-artheṣu*—for the sake of serving Me; *aṅga-ceṣṭā*—ordinary, bodily activities; *ca*—also; *vacasā*—with words; *mat-guṇa*—My transcendental qualities; *īraṇam*—declaring; *mayi*—in Me; *arpaṇam*—placing; *ca*—also; *manasaḥ*—of the mind; *sarva-kāma*—of all material desires; *vivarjanam*—rejection; *mat-arthe*—for My sake; *artha*—of wealth; *parityāgaḥ*—the giving up; *bhogasya*—of sense gratification; *ca*—also; *sukhasya*—of material happiness; *ca*—also; *iṣṭam*—desirable activities; *dattam*—charity; *hutam*—offering of sacrifice; *japtam*—chanting the holy names of the Lord; *mat-artham*—for the sake of achieving Me; *yat*—which; *vratam*—vows, such as fasting on Ekādaśī; *tapaḥ*—austerities; *evam*—thus; *dharmaiḥ*—by such religious principles; *manuṣyāṇām*—of human beings; *uddhava*—My dear Uddhava; *ātma-nivedinām*—who are surrendered souls; *mayi*—to Me; *sañjāyate*—arises; *bhaktiḥ*—loving devotion; *kaḥ*—what; *anyaḥ*—other; *arthaḥ*—purpose; *asya*—of My devotee; *avaśiṣyate*—remains.

TRANSLATION

Firm faith in the blissful narrations of My pastimes, constant chanting of My glories, unwavering attachment to ceremonial worship of Me, praising Me through beautiful hymns, great respect for My devotional service, offering obeisances with the entire body, performing first-class worship of My devotees, consciousness of Me in all living entities, offering of ordinary, bodily activities in My devotional service, use of words to describe My qualities, offering the mind to Me, rejection of all material desires, giving up wealth for My devotional service, renouncing material sense gratification and happiness, and performing all desirable activities such as charity, sacrifice, chanting, vows and austerities with the purpose of achieving Me—these constitute actual religious principles, by which those human beings who have actually surrendered themselves to Me automatically develop love for Me. What other purpose or goal could remain for My devotee?

PURPORT

The words *mad-bhakta-pūjābhyadhikā* are significant in this verse. *Abhyadhikā* indicates "superior quality." The Lord is extremely satisfied with those who offer worship to His pure devotees, and He rewards them accordingly. Because of the Lord's generous appraisal of His pure devotees, worship of the pure devotees is described as superior to worship of the Lord Himself. The words *mad-artheṣv aṅga-ceṣṭā* state that ordinary, bodily activities such as brushing the teeth, taking bath, eating, etc., should all be offered to the Supreme Lord as devotional service. The words *vacasā mad-guṇeraṇam* indicate that whether one speaks in ordinary, crude language or with learned poetic eloquence, one should describe the glories of the Personality of Godhead. The words *mad-arthe 'rtha-parityāgaḥ* indicate that one should spend one's money for festivals glorifying the Personality of Godhead, such as Ratha-yātrā, Janmāṣṭamī and Gaura-pūrṇimā. Also, one is herein instructed to spend money to assist the mission of one's spiritual master and other Vaiṣṇavas. Wealth that cannot be used properly in the Lord's service and is thus an impediment to one's clear consciousness should be given up entirely. The word *bhogasya* refers to sense gratification, headed by sex enjoyment, and *sukhasya* refers to sentimental material happiness, such as excessive family attachment. The words *dattaṁ hutam* indicate that one should offer to *brāhmaṇas* and Vaiṣṇavas first-class foods cooked in ghee. One should offer the vibration *svāhā* to Lord Viṣṇu in an authorized sacrificial fire along with grains and ghee. The word *japtam* indicates that one should constantly chant the holy names of the Lord.

TEXT 25

यदात्मन्यर्पितं चित्तं शान्तं सत्त्वोपबृंहितम् ।
धर्मं ज्ञानं सवैराग्यमैश्वर्यं चाभिपद्यते ॥२५॥

yadātmany arpitaṁ cittaṁ
śāntaṁ sattvopabṛṁhitam
dharmaṁ jñānaṁ sa vairāgyam
aiśvaryaṁ cābhipadyate

yadā—when; *ātmani*—in the Supreme Lord; *arpitam*—fixed; *cittam*—consciousness; *śāntam*—peaceful; *sattva*—by the mode of goodness; *upabṛṁhitam*—strengthened; *dharmam*—religiosity; *jñānam*—knowledge; *saḥ*—he; *vairāgyam*—detachment; *aiśvaryam*—opulence; *ca*—also; *abhipadyate*—achieves.

TRANSLATION

When one's consciousness, peaceful and strengthened by the mode of goodness, is fixed in the Personality of Godhead, one achieves religiosity, knowledge, detachment and opulence.

PURPORT

A pure devotee becomes peaceful, *śānta*, by desiring everything for the service of the Lord and nothing for himself. He is strengthened by the transcendental, or purified, mode of goodness and thus achieves the supreme religious principle of directly serving the Lord. He also achieves *jñāna*, or knowledge of the Lord's form and his own spiritual body, detachment from material piety and sin, and the opulences of the spiritual world. One who is not a pure devotee of the Lord, however, but whose devotion is mixed with a fascination for mystic knowledge, is strengthened by the material mode of goodness. Through his meditation on the Lord he achieves the lesser results of *dharma* (piety in the mode of goodness), *jñāna* (knowledge of spirit and matter) and *vairāgya* (detachment from the lower modes of nature). Ultimately, one should be a pure devotee of the Lord, since even the best the material world has to offer is most insignificant compared to the kingdom of God.

TEXT 26

यदर्पितं तद् विकल्पे इन्द्रियैः परिधावति ।
रजस्वलं चासन्निष्ठं चित्तं विद्धि विपर्ययम् ॥२६॥

yad arpitaṁ tad vikalpe
indriyaiḥ paridhāvati
rajas-valaṁ cāsan-niṣṭhaṁ
cittaṁ viddhi viparyayam

yat—when; *arpitam*—fixed; *tat*—this (consciousness); *vikalpe*—in material variety (the body, home, family, etc.); *indriyaiḥ*—with the senses; *paridhāvati*—chasing all around; *rajaḥ-valam*—strengthened by the mode of passion; *ca*—also; *asat*—to that which has no permanent reality; *niṣṭham*—dedicated; *cittam*—consciousness; *viddhi*—you should understand; *viparyayam*—the opposite (of what was previously mentioned).

TRANSLATION

When consciousness is fixed in the material body, home and other similar objects of sense gratification, then one spends one's life chasing after material objects with the help of the senses. Consciousness, thus powerfully affected by the mode of passion, becomes dedicated to impermanent things, and in this way irreligion, ignorance, attachment and wretchedness arise.

PURPORT

In the previous verse Lord Kṛṣṇa explained the auspicious results of fixing the mind in Him, and now the opposite is explained. *Rajas-valam* indicates that one's passion grows so strong that one commits sinful activities and reaps all types of misfortune. Although materialistic people are blind to their impending wretchedness, one can confirm by all types of evidence—namely Vedic injunctions, direct observation, traditional wisdom and inductive logic—that the result of violating the laws of God is disastrous.

TEXT 27

धर्मो मद्भक्तिकृत् प्रोक्तो ज्ञानं चैकात्म्यदर्शनम् ।
गुणेष्वसङ्गो वैराग्यमैश्वर्यं चाणिमादयः ॥२७॥

dharmo mad-bhakti-kṛt prokto
jñānaṁ caikātmya-darśanam
guṇesv asaṅgo vairāgyam
aiśvaryaṁ cāṇimādayaḥ

dharmaḥ—religion; *mat*—My; *bhakti*—devotional service; *kṛt*—producing; *proktaḥ*—it is declared; *jñānam*—knowledge; *ca*—also; *aikātmya*—the presence of the Supreme Soul; *darśanam*—seeing; *guṇeṣu*—in the objects of sense gratification; *asaṅgaḥ*—having no interest; *vairāgyam*—detachment; *aiśvaryam*—opulence; *ca*—also; *aṇimā*—the mystic perfection called *aṇimā; ādayaḥ*—and so forth.

TRANSLATION

Actual religious principles are stated to be those that lead one to My devotional service. Real knowledge is the awareness that reveals My all-pervading presence. Detachment is complete disinterest in the objects of material sense gratification, and opulence is the eight mystic perfections, such as *aṇimā-siddhi.*

PURPORT

The Supreme Lord is perfect knowledge; thus one who has been delivered from ignorance automatically engages in the devotional service of the Lord and is called religious. One who becomes detached from the three modes of material nature and the gratificatory objects they produce is considered to be situated in detachment. The eight mystic *yoga* perfections, described previously by the Lord to Uddhava, constitute material power, or opulence, in the highest degree.

TEXTS 28-32

श्री उद्धव उवाच
यमः कतिविधः प्रोक्तो नियमो वारिकर्षन ।
कः शमः को दमः कृष्ण का तितिक्षा धृतिः प्रभो ॥२८॥
किं दानं किं तपः शौर्यं किं सत्यमृतमुच्यते ।
कस्त्यागः किं धनं चेष्टं को यज्ञः का च दक्षिणा ॥२९॥
पुंसः किंस्विद् बलं श्रीमन् भगो लाभश्च केशव ।
का विद्या ह्रीः परा का श्रीः किं सुखं दुःखमेव च ॥३०॥
कः पण्डितः कश्च मूर्खः कः पन्था उत्पथश्च कः ।
कः स्वर्गो नरकः कः स्वित् को बन्धुरुत किं गृहम् ॥३१॥
क आढ्यः को दरिद्रो वा कृपणः कः क ईश्वरः ।
एतान् प्रश्नान् मम ब्रूहि विपरीतांश्च सत्पते ॥३२॥

śrī-uddhava uvāca
yamaḥ kati-vidhaḥ prokto
niyamo vāri-karṣaṇa
kaḥ śamaḥ ko damaḥ kṛṣṇa
kā titikṣā dhṛtiḥ prabho

kiṁ dānaṁ kiṁ tapaḥ śauryaṁ
kim satyam ṛtam ucyate
kas tyāgaḥ kiṁ dhanaṁ ceṣṭaṁ
ko yajñaḥ kā ca dakṣiṇā

puṁsaḥ kiṁ svid balaṁ śrīman
bhago lābhaś ca keśava
kā vidyā hrīḥ parā kā śrīḥ
kiṁ sukhaṁ duḥkham eva ca

kaḥ paṇḍitaḥ kaś ca mūrkhaḥ
kaḥ panthā utpathaś ca kaḥ
kaḥ svargo narakaḥ kaḥ svit
ko bandhur uta kiṁ gṛham

ka āḍhyaḥ ko daridro vā
kṛpaṇaḥ kaḥ ka īśvaraḥ
etān praśnān mama brūhi
viparītāṁś ca sat-pate

śrī-uddhavaḥ uvaca—Śrī Uddhava said; *yamaḥ*—disciplinary regulations; *kati-vidhaḥ*—how many different types; *proktaḥ*—are declared to exist; *niyamaḥ*—regular daily duties; *vā*—or; *ari-karṣaṇa*—O Kṛṣṇa, subduer of the enemy; *kaḥ*—what is; *śamaḥ*—mental equilibrium; *kaḥ*—what is; *damaḥ*—self-control; *kṛṣṇa*—my dear Kṛṣṇa; *kā*—what is; *titikṣā*—tolerance; *dhṛtiḥ*—steadfastness; *prabho*—my Lord; *kim*—what is; *dānam*—charity; *kim*—what is; *tapaḥ*—austerity; *śauryam*—heroism; *kim*—what is; *satyam*—reality; *ṛtam*—truth; *ucyate*—is said; *kaḥ*—what is; *tyāgaḥ*—renunciation; *kim*—what is; *dhanam*—wealth; *ca*—also; *iṣṭam*—desirable; *kaḥ*—what is; *yajñaḥ*—sacrifice; *kā*—what is; *ca*—also; *dakṣiṇā*—religious remuneration; *puṁsaḥ*—of a person; *kim*—what is; *svit*—indeed; *balam*—strength; *śrī-man*—O most fortunate Kṛṣṇa; *bhagaḥ*—opulence; *lābhaḥ*—profit; *ca*—also; *keśava*—my dear Keśava; *kā*—what is; *vidyā*—education; *hrīḥ*—humility; *parā*—supreme; *kā*—what is; *śrīḥ*—beauty; *kim*—what is; *sukham*—happiness; *duḥkham*—unhappiness; *eva*—indeed; *ca*—also; *kaḥ*—who is; *paṇḍitaḥ*—learned; *kaḥ*—who is; *ca*—also; *mūrkhaḥ*—a fool; *kaḥ*—what is; *panthāḥ*—the real path; *utpathaḥ*—the false path; *ca*—also; *kaḥ*—what is; *kaḥ*—what is; *svargaḥ*—heaven; *narakaḥ*—hell; *kaḥ*—what is; *svit*—indeed; *kaḥ*—who is; *bandhuḥ*—a friend; *uta*—and; *kim*—what is; *gṛham*—home; *kaḥ*—who is; *āḍhyaḥ*—wealthy; *kaḥ*—who is; *daridraḥ*—poor; *vā*—or; *kṛpaṇaḥ*—a miser; *kaḥ*—who is; *kaḥ*—who is; *īśvaraḥ*—a controller; *etān*—these; *praśnān*—subject matters of inquiry; *mama*—to me; *brūhi*—please speak; *viparītān*—the opposite qualities; *ca*—also; *sat-pate*—O Lord of the devotees.

TRANSLATION

Śrī Uddhava said: My dear Lord Kṛṣṇa, O chastiser of the enemies, please tell me how many types of disciplinary regulations and regular daily duties there are. Also, my Lord, tell me what is mental equilibrium, what is self-control and what is the actual meaning of tolerance and steadfastness. What are charity,

austerity and heroism, and how are reality and truth to be described? What is renunciation, and what is wealth? What is desirable, what is sacrifice, and what is religious remuneration? My dear Keśava, O most fortunate one, how am I to understand the strength, opulence and profit of a particular person? What is the best education, what is actual humility, and what is real beauty? What are happiness and unhappiness? Who is learned, and who is a fool? What are the true and the false paths in life, and what are heaven and hell? Who is indeed a true friend, and what is one's real home? Who is a rich man, and who is a poor man? Who is wretched, and who is an actual controller? O Lord of the devotees, kindly explain these matters to me, along with their opposites.

PURPORT

All of the items mentioned in these five verses are defined in different ways by different cultures and societies throughout the world. Therefore, Śrī Uddhava is directly approaching the supreme authority, Lord Kṛṣṇa, to obtain the standard definition for these universal aspects of civilized life.

TEXTS 33-35

श्रीभगवानुवाच

अहिंसा सत्यमस्तेयमसङ्गो ह्रीरसञ्चयः ।
आस्तिक्यं ब्रह्मचर्यं च मौनं स्थैर्यं क्षमाभयम् ॥३३॥
शौचं जपस्तपो होमः श्रद्धातिथ्यं मदर्चनम् ।
तीर्थाटनं परार्थेहा तुष्टिराचार्यसेवनम् ॥३४॥
एते यमाः सनियमा उभयोर्द्वादश स्मृताः ।
पुंसामुपासितास्तात यथाकामं दुहन्ति हि ॥३५॥

śrī-bhagavān uvāca
ahiṁsā satyam asteyam
asaṅgo hrīr asañcayaḥ
āstikyaṁ brahmacaryaṁ ca
maunaṁ sthairyaṁ kṣamābhayam

śaucaṁ japas tapo homaḥ
śraddhātithyaṁ mad-arcanam
tīrthāṭanaṁ parārthehā
tuṣṭir ācārya-sevanam

ete yamāḥ sa-niyamā
ubhayor dvādaśa smṛtāḥ
puṁsām upāsitās tāta
yathā-kāmaṁ duhanti hi

śrī-bhagavān uvāca—the Supreme Personality of Godhead said; *ahiṁsā*—nonviolence; *satyam*—truthfulness; *asteyam*—never coveting or stealing the property of others; *asaṅgaḥ*—detachment; *hrīḥ*—humility; *asañcayaḥ*—being nonpossessive; *āstikyam*—trust in the principles of religion; *brahmacaryam*—celibacy; *ca*—also; *maunam*—silence; *sthairyam*—steadiness; *kṣamā*—forgiving; *abhayam*—fearless; *śaucam*—internal and external cleanliness; *japaḥ*—chanting the holy names of the Lord; *tapaḥ*—austerity; *homaḥ*—sacrifice; *śraddhā*—faith; *ātithyam*—hospitality; *mat-arcanam*—worship of Me; *tīrtha-aṭanam*—visiting holy places; *para-artha-īhā*—acting and desiring for the Supreme; *tuṣṭiḥ*—satisfaction; *ācārya-sevanam*—serving the spiritual master; *ete*—these; *yamāḥ*—disciplinary principles; *sa-niyamāḥ*—along with secondary regular duties; *ubhayoḥ*—of each; *dvādaśa*—twelve; *smṛtāḥ*—are understood; *puṁsām*—by human beings; *upāsitāḥ*—being cultivated with devotion; *tāta*—My dear Uddhava; *yathā-kāmam*—according to one's desire; *duhanti*—they supply; *hi*—indeed.

TRANSLATION

The Supreme Personality of Godhead said: Nonviolence, truthfulness, not coveting or stealing the property of others, detachment, humility, freedom from possessiveness, trust in the principles of religion, celibacy, silence, steadiness, forgiveness and fearlessness are the twelve primary disciplinary principles. Internal cleanliness, external cleanliness, chanting the holy names of the Lord, austerity, sacrifice, faith, hospitality, worship of Me, visiting holy places, acting and desiring only for the supreme interest, satisfaction, and service to the spiritual master

are the twelve elements of regular prescribed duties. These twenty-four elements bestow all desired benedictions upon those persons who devotedly cultivate them.

TEXTS 36-39

शमो मन्निष्ठता बुद्धेर्दम इन्द्रियसंयमः ।
तितिक्षा दुःखसंमर्षो जिह्वोपस्थजयो धृतिः ॥३६॥
दण्डन्यासः परं दानं कामत्यागस्तपः स्मृतम् ।
स्वभावविजयः शौर्यं सत्यं च समदर्शनम् ॥३७॥
अन्यच्च सुनृता वाणी कविभिः परिकीर्तिता ।
कर्मस्वसङ्गमः शौचं त्यागः संन्यास उच्यते ॥३८॥
धर्म इष्टं धनं नृणां यज्ञोऽहं भगवत्तमः ।
दक्षिणा ज्ञानसन्देशः प्राणायामः परं बलम् ॥३९॥

śamo man-niṣṭhatā buddher
dama indriya-saṁyamaḥ
titikṣā duḥkha-sammarṣo
jihvopastha-jayo dhṛtiḥ

daṇḍa-nyāsaḥ paraṁ dānaṁ
kāma-tyāgas tapaḥ smṛtam
svabhāva-vijayaḥ śauryaṁ
satyaṁ ca sama-darśanam

anyac ca sunṛtā vāṇī
kavibhiḥ parikīrtitā
karmasv asaṅgamaḥ śaucaṁ
tyāgaḥ sannyāsa ucyate

dharma iṣṭaṁ dhanaṁ nṛṇāṁ
yajño 'haṁ bhagavattamaḥ
dakṣiṇā jñāna-sandeśaḥ
prāṇāyāmaḥ paraṁ balam

śamaḥ—mental equilibrium; *mat*—in Me; *niṣṭhatā*—steady absorption; *buddheḥ*—of the intelligence; *damaḥ*—self-control; *indriya*—of the senses; *saṁyamaḥ*—perfect discipline; *titikṣā*—tolerance; *duḥkha*—unhappiness; *sammarṣaḥ*—tolerating; *jihvā*—the tongue; *upastha*—and genitals; *jayaḥ*—conquering; *dhṛtiḥ*—steadiness; *daṇḍa*—aggression; *nyāsaḥ*—giving up; *param*—the supreme; *dānam*—charity; *kāma*—lust; *tyāgaḥ*—giving up; *tapaḥ*—austerity; *smṛtam*—is considered; *svabhāva*—one's natural tendency to enjoy; *vijayaḥ*—conquering; *śauryam*—heroism; *satyam*—reality; *ca*—also; *sama-darśanam*—seeing the Supreme Lord everywhere; *anyat*—the next element (truthfulness); *ca*—and; *su-nṛtā*—pleasing; *vāṇī*—speech; *kavibhiḥ*—by the sages; *parikīrtitā*—is declared to be; *karmasu*—in fruitive activities; *asaṅgamaḥ*—detachment; *śaucam*—cleanliness; *tyāgaḥ*—renunciation; *sannyāsaḥ*—the *sannyāsa* order of life; *ucyate*—is said to be; *dharmaḥ*—religiousness; *iṣṭam*—desirable; *dhanam*—wealth; *nṝṇām*—for human beings; *yajñaḥ*—sacrifice; *aham*—I am; *bhagavat-tamaḥ*—the Supreme Personality of Godhead; *dakṣiṇā*—religious remuneration; *jñāna-sandeśaḥ*—the instruction of perfect knowledge; *prāṇāyāmaḥ*—the yogic system of controlling the breath; *param*—the supreme; *balam*—strength.

TRANSLATION

Absorbing the intelligence in Me constitutes mental equilibrium, and complete discipline of the senses is self-control. Tolerance means patiently enduring unhappiness, and steadfastness occurs when one conquers the tongue and genitals. The greatest charity is to give up all aggression toward others, and renunciation of lust is understood to be real austerity. Real heroism is to conquer one's natural tendency to enjoy material life, and reality is seeing the Supreme Personality of Godhead everywhere. Truthfulness means to speak the truth in a pleasing way, as declared by great sages. Cleanliness is detachment in fruitive activities, whereas renunciation is the *sannyāsa* order of life. The true desirable wealth for human beings is religiousness, and I, the Supreme Personality of Godhead, am sacrifice. Religious remuneration is devotion to the *ācārya* with the purpose of acquiring spiritual instruction, and the greatest strength is the *prāṇāyāma* system of breath control.

PURPORT

Lord Kṛṣṇa here describes those qualities that are desirable for persons advancing in human life. *Śama,* or "mental equilibrium," means to fix the intelligence in Lord Kṛṣṇa. Mere peacefulness without Kṛṣṇa consciousness is a dull and useless state of mind. *Dama,* or "discipline," means first to control one's own senses. If one wants to discipline one's children, disciples or followers without controlling one's own senses, one becomes a mere laughingstock. Tolerance means to patiently endure unhappiness, such as that provoked by the insults or negligence of others. One must also sometimes accept material inconvenience to carry out the injunctions of scriptures, and that unhappiness must also be patiently endured. If one is not tolerant of the insults and abuse of others, nor tolerant of the inconveniences that may arise from following authorized religious scriptures, it is simply foolishness for him to make a whimsical show of tolerating extreme heat, cold and pain and so on, just to impress others. Concerning steadfastness, if one does not control the tongue and genitals, then any other steadfastness is useless. Real charity means to renounce all aggression toward others. If one gives money to charitable causes but at the same time engages in exploitative business enterprises or abusive political tactics, one's charity is worth nothing at all. Austerity means to give up lust and sense gratification and to observe prescribed vows such as Ekādaśī; it does not mean inventing whimsical methods of torturing the material body. Real heroism is to conquer one's lower nature. Certainly everyone likes to propagate his own fame as a brilliant person, but everyone is also subject to lust, anger, greed and so forth. Therefore, if one can conquer these lower characteristics generated from the modes of passion and ignorance, one is a greater hero than those who merely destroy their political opponents through intrigue and violence.

One can develop equal vision by giving up jealousy and envy and by recognizing the existence of the soul within every material body. This attitude pleases the Supreme Lord, who then reveals Himself, solidifying forever one's equal vision. Merely describing things that exist does not constitute the last word in the perception of reality. One must also see the true spiritual equality of all living entities and all situations. Truthfulness means that one should speak in a pleasing way so that there will be a beneficial effect. If one becomes attached to pointing out the faults of others in the name of truth, then such faultfinding will not be appreciated by saintly persons. The bona fide spiritual master speaks the truth in such a way that people can elevate themselves to the spiritual platform, and one should learn this art of truthfulness. If one is attached to material things, his body and mind are understood to be always polluted. Cleanliness therefore means to give up material attachment, not merely to frequently rinse one's skin with water. Real renunciation is giving up one's false sense of proprietorship over one's relatives and wife, and not just giving away material objects, while real wealth is to be religious. Sacrifice is the Personality of Godhead Himself, because the performer of sacrifice, to be successful, must absorb his consciousness in the Personality of Godhead and not in temporary, material rewards that may accrue from sacrifice. Real religious remuneration means that one should serve saintly persons who can enlighten one with spiritual knowledge. One may offer remuneration to his spiritual master, who has enlightened him, by distributing the same knowledge to others, thereby pleasing the *ācārya*. Preaching work thus constitutes the highest form of remuneration. By performing the *prāṇāyāma* system of respiratory control, the mind is easily subdued, and one who can in this way perfectly control the restless mind is the most powerful person.

TEXTS 40-45

भगो म ऐश्वरो भावो लाभो मद्भक्तिरुत्तमः ।
विद्यात्मनि भिदाबाधो जुगुप्सा ह्रीरकर्मसु ॥४०॥
श्रीर्गुणा नैरपेक्ष्याद्याः सुखं दुःखसुखात्ययः ।
दुःखं कामसुखापेक्षा पण्डितो बन्धमोक्षवित् ॥४१॥
मूर्खो देहाद्यहंबुद्धिः पन्था मन्निगमः स्मृतः ।
उत्पथश्चित्तविक्षेपः स्वर्गः सत्त्वगुणोदयः ॥४२॥
नरकस्तमउन्नाहो बन्धुर्गुरुरहं सखे ।
गृहं शरीरं मानुष्यं गुणाढ्यो ह्याढ्य उच्यते ॥४३॥

दरिद्रो यस्त्वसन्तुष्टः कृपणो योऽजितेन्द्रियः ।
गुणेष्वसक्तधीरीशो गुणसङ्गो विपर्ययः ॥४४॥
एत उद्धव ते प्रश्नाः सर्वे साधु निरूपिताः ।
किं वर्णितेन बहुना लक्षणं गुणदोषयोः ।
गुणदोषदृशिर्दोषो गुणस्तूभयवर्जितः ॥४५॥

bhago ma aiśvaro bhāvo
lābho mad-bhaktir uttamaḥ
vidyātmani bhidā-bādho
jugupsā hrīr akarmasu

śrīr guṇā nairapekṣyādyāḥ
sukhaṁ duḥkha-sukhātyayaḥ
duḥkhaṁ kāma-sukhāpekṣā
paṇḍito bandha-mokṣa-vit

mūrkho dehādy-ahaṁ-buddhiḥ
panthā man-nigamaḥ smṛtaḥ
utpathaś citta-vikṣepaḥ
svargaḥ sattva-guṇodayaḥ

narakas tama-unnāho
bandhur gurur ahaṁ sakhe
gṛhaṁ śarīraṁ mānuṣyaṁ
guṇāḍhyo hy āḍhya ucyate

daridro yas tv asantuṣṭaḥ
kṛpaṇo yo 'jitendriyaḥ
guṇeṣv asakta-dhīr īśo
guṇa-saṅgo viparyayaḥ

eta uddhava te praśnāḥ
sarve sādhu nirūpitāḥ
kiṁ varṇitena bahunā
lakṣaṇaṁ guṇa-doṣayoḥ
guṇa-doṣa-dṛśir doṣo
guṇas tūbhaya-varjitaḥ

bhagaḥ—opulence; *me*—My; *aiśvaraḥ*—divine; *bhāvaḥ*—nature; *lābhaḥ*—gain; *mat-bhaktiḥ*—devotional service unto Me; *uttamaḥ*—supreme; *vidyā*—education; *ātmani*—in the soul; *bhidā*—duality; *bādhaḥ*—nullifying; *jugupsā*—disgust; *hrīḥ*—modesty; *akarmasu*—in sinful activities; *śrīḥ*—beauty; *guṇāḥ*—good qualities; *nairapekṣya*—detachment from material things; *ādyāḥ*—and so on; *sukham*—happiness; *duḥkha*—material unhappiness; *sukha*—and material happiness; *atyayaḥ*—transcending; *duḥkham*—unhappiness; *kāma*—of lust; *sukha*—on the happiness; *apekṣā*—meditating; *paṇḍitaḥ*—a wise man; *bandha*—from bondage; *mokṣa*—liberation; *vit*—one who knows; *mūrkhaḥ*—a fool; *deha*—with the body; *ādi*—and so forth (the mind); *aham-buddhiḥ*—one who identifies himself; *panthāḥ*—the true path; *mat*—to Me; *nigamaḥ*—leading; *smṛtaḥ*—is to be understood; *utpathaḥ*—the wrong path; *citta*—of consciousness; *vikṣepaḥ*—bewilderment; *svargaḥ*—heaven; *sattva-guṇa*—of the mode of goodness; *udayaḥ*—the predominance; *narakaḥ*—hell; *tamaḥ*—of the mode of ignorance; *unnāhaḥ*—the predominance; *bandhuḥ*—the real friend; *guruḥ*—the spiritual master; *aham*—I am; *sakhe*—My dear friend, Uddhava; *gṛham*—one's home; *śarīram*—the body; *mānuṣyam*—human; *guṇa*—with good qualities; *āḍhyaḥ*—enriched; *hi*—indeed; *āḍhyaḥ*—a rich person; *ucyate*—is stated to be; *daridraḥ*—a poor person; *yaḥ*—one who; *tu*—indeed; *asantuṣṭaḥ*—unsatisfied; *kṛpaṇaḥ*—a wretched person; *yaḥ*—one who; *ajita*—has not conquered; *indriyaḥ*—the senses; *guṇeṣu*—in material sense gratification; *asakta*—not attached; *dhīḥ*—whose intelligence; *īśaḥ*—a controller; *guṇa*—to sense gratification; *saṅgaḥ*—attached; *viparyayaḥ*—the opposite, a slave; *ete*—these; *uddhava*—My dear Uddhava; *te*—your; *praśnāḥ*—subjects of inquiry; *sarve*—all; *sādhu*—properly; *nirūpitāḥ*—elucidated; *kim*—what is the value; *varṇitena*—of describing; *bahunā*—elaborately; *lakṣaṇam*—the characteristics; *guṇa*—of good qualities; *doṣayoḥ*—and of bad qualities; *guṇa-doṣa*—good and bad qualities; *dṛśiḥ*—seeing; *doṣaḥ*—a fault; *guṇaḥ*—the real good quality; *tu*—indeed; *ubhaya*—from both of them; *varjitaḥ*—distinct.

TRANSLATION

Actual opulence is My own nature as the Personality of Godhead, through which I exhibit the six unlimited opulences. The supreme gain in life is devotional service to Me, and actual education is nullifying the false perception of duality within the

soul. Real modesty is to be disgusted with improper activities, and beauty is to possess good qualities such as detachment. Real happiness is to transcend material happiness and unhappiness, and real misery is to be implicated in searching for sex pleasure. A wise man is one who knows the process of freedom from bondage, and a fool is one who identifies with his material body and mind. The real path in life is that which leads to Me, and the wrong path is sense gratification, by which consciousness is bewildered. Actual heaven is the predominance of the mode of goodness, whereas hell is the predominance of ignorance. I am everyone's true friend, acting as the spiritual master of the entire universe, and one's home is the human body. My dear friend Uddhava, one who is enriched with good qualities is actually said to be rich, and one who is unsatisfied in life is actually poor. A wretched person is one who cannot control his senses, whereas one who is not attached to sense gratification is a real controller. One who attaches himself to sense gratification is the opposite, a slave. Thus, Uddhava, I have elucidated all of the matters about which you inquired. There is no need for a more elaborate description of these good and bad qualities, since to constantly see good and bad is itself a bad quality. The best quality is to transcend material good and evil.

PURPORT

The Supreme Personality of Godhead is naturally full of six opulences, namely unlimited beauty, wealth, fame, knowledge, strength and renunciation. Therefore the greatest profit in life is to achieve personal loving service to the Lord, who is naturally the reservoir of all pleasure. Real education means to give up the false idea that anything is separate from the Lord, the source of all potencies. Similarly, one should not falsely consider the individual soul to be different or separate from the Supreme Soul. Mere bashfulness does not constitute modesty. One should spontaneously withdraw in disgust from sinful activities; then one is actually modest or humble. One who is satisfied in Kṛṣṇa consciousness and thus does not seek material pleasure or suffer material unhappiness is considered to be actually situated in happiness. The most wretched person is one addicted to sex pleasure, and a wise man is one who knows the process of freedom from such material bondage. A fool is one who gives up his eternal friendship with Lord Kṛṣṇa and instead identifies himself with his own temporary material body, mind, society, community and family. The real path in life is not simply a modern interstate highway or, in more simple cultures, a footpath free of thorns and mud. It is that path that leads to Lord Kṛṣṇa. The wrong path in life is not simply a road having many thieves or tollbooths; it is that path that leads one to utter confusion in material sense gratification. A heavenly situation is that in which the mode of goodness predominates, rather than that found on the planet of Indra, where passion and ignorance sometimes disturb the celestial atmosphere. Hell is anywhere the mode of ignorance is predominant, and not merely the hellish planets, where, according to Lord Śiva, a pure devotee can think of Kṛṣṇa and remain happy. Our actual friend in life is the bona fide spiritual master, who saves us from all dangers. Among all *gurus*, Lord Kṛṣṇa is Himself the *jagat-guru*, or spiritual master of the entire universe. In material life our own material body is our immediate home, rather than some structure of bricks, cement, stone and wood. A rich man is one who possesses innumerable good qualities; he is not a neurotic fool with a large bank account. A poor man is one who is unsatisfied, which is self-explanatory. One who cannot control his senses is certainly wretched and miserable in life, whereas one who detaches himself from material life is actually a lord or controller. In modern times there are remnants of aristocracy in Europe and other countries, but such so-called lords often display the habits of lower forms of life. A real lord is one who conquers material existence by rising to the spiritual platform. A person who is attached to material life will undoubtedly manifest the opposites of all the good qualities mentioned here, and he is thus the symbol of going backward in life. The Lord concludes His analysis by stating that there is no need for further elaboration of these good and bad qualities. Indeed, the purpose of life is to transcend materially good and bad qualities and come to the liberated platform of pure Kṛṣṇa consciousness. This point will be further explained in the following chapter.

Thus end the purports of the humble servant of His Divine Grace A. C. Bhaktivedanta Swami Prabhupāda to the Eleventh Canto, Nineteenth Chapter, of the Śrīmad-Bhāgavatam, *entitled "The Perfection of Spiritual Knowledge."*

CHAPTER TWENTY

Pure Devotional Service Surpasses Knowledge and Detachment

The processes of *karma-yoga, jñāna-yoga* and *bhakti-yoga* are explained in this chapter, in terms of the presence of different good and bad qualities in particular candidates.

The Vedic *śāstras* are the words expressing the order of the Supreme Personality of Godhead. In these Vedic literatures is found an outlook of duality, based on such concepts as the *varṇāśrama* system, and at the same time the *Vedas* reject this dualistic vision. Uddhava, desiring to understand the reason why the scriptures contain such conflicting ideas, and how these might be reconciled, inquired from Lord Śrī Kṛṣṇa about this matter. In response the Supreme Lord replied that the *Vedas* describe the processes of *karma-yoga, jñāna-yoga* and *bhakti-yoga* for facilitating the attainment of liberation. *Karma-yoga* is designated for those persons who are not detached and who are full of gross desires; *jñāna-yoga* is for those who are detached from the fruits of activity and have given up material endeavors; and *bhakti-yoga* is for those persons who have taken to the principle of *yukta-vairāgya,* appropriate renunciation. As long as one has not become uninterested in enjoying the fruits of one's work, or as long as one's faith in the topics of discussion of the Supreme Personality of Godhead on the path of devotional service has not awakened, then one must continue to fulfill all the prescribed duties of his *karma.* But neither the renunciant nor the devotee of the Supreme Lord need carry out ritualistic duties.

Persons who follow their own duty, who abandon that which is forbidden and who are free from greed and other unhealthy characteristics attain either monistic knowledge or else, if they are fortunate, devotion to the Supreme Personality of Godhead. Such knowledge and devotion can be achieved in the human form of life, which is therefore a desirable object both for those living in hell and for the demigods. The human body, even though it awards the whole purpose of existence in the form of knowledge and devotion, is ephemeral; therefore one who is discriminating should soberly strive for liberation before death comes. The human body is like a boat, Śrī Gurudeva is the helmsman, and the mercy of the Supreme Lord is the favorable breeze. If the person who has attained such a rare boat in the form of the human body does not desire to cross over the ocean of material existence, he is in fact the killer of the soul. The mind is fickle, but one should not indifferently allow it to act as it will. Rather, one should conquer the senses and the vital air and by intelligence endowed with the qualities of goodness should bring the mind under control.

Until the mind finally becomes stable, one should continue to meditate about the process of the creation of all material things in sequence from subtle to gross and of their destruction in reverse sequence of gross to subtle. One who has a sense of detachment and renunciation can give up false identification with the body and other sense objects by constantly studying the instructions of his spiritual master. By the *yoga* practice of *yama, niyama* and so forth, by cultivation of transcendental knowledge and by worship of and meditation upon the Supreme Personality of Godhead, one can remember the Supersoul.

Virtue, or *guṇa,* means to remain steadfast in the object of one's particular platform of qualification. By developing the desire to reject one's accumulated material association by pursuing the injunctions of what is good and what is bad, all of one's inauspicious material activities become diminished. By devotional service to the Supreme Personality of Godhead all perfections are achieved. Anyone who renders service to the Supreme Lord by constant devotional service will be able to steadily fix his mind upon the Supreme Lord, and thus all desires for sense gratification sitting within the heart will be destroyed to the root. When one directly perceives the presence of the Supreme Lord, his false ego becomes completely eradicated; all of his doubts are shattered, and heaps of material activities become diminished to nil. For this reason the devotees of the Supreme Personality of Godhead do not consider knowledge and renunciation to be the means for achieving the highest benefit. Only in the heart of a person who is devoid of material desire and disinterested in material things can devotional service to the Lord arise. The piety and impiety that result from ritualistic injunctions and prohibitions cannot be applied to the unalloyed pure devotees of the Supreme Lord.

TEXT 1

श्री उद्धव उवाच
विधिश्च प्रतिषेधश्च निगमो हीश्वरस्य ते ।
अवेक्षतेऽरविन्दाक्ष गुणं दोषं च कर्मणाम् ॥ १ ॥

śrī-uddhava uvāca
vidhiś ca pratiṣedhaś ca
nigamo hīśvarasya te
avekṣate 'ravindākṣa
guṇaṁ doṣaṁ ca karmaṇām

śrī-uddhavaḥ uvāca—Śrī Uddhava said; *vidhiḥ*—positive injunction; *ca*—also; *pratiṣedhaḥ*—prohibitive injunction; *ca*—and; *nigamaḥ*—the Vedic literature; *hi*—indeed; *īśvarasya*—of the Lord; *te*—of You; *avekṣate*—focuses upon; *aravinda-akṣa*—O lotus-eyed one; *guṇam*—good or pious qualities; *doṣam*—bad or sinful qualities; *ca*—also; *karmaṇām*—of activities.

TRANSLATION

Śrī Uddhava said: My dear lotus-eyed Kṛṣṇa, You are the Supreme Lord, and thus the Vedic literatures, consisting of positive and negative injunctions, constitute Your order. Such literatures focus upon the good and bad qualities of work.

PURPORT

At the end of the previous chapter, Lord Kṛṣṇa stated, *guṇa-doṣa-dṛśir doṣo guṇas tūbhaya-varjitaḥ:* "Focusing upon material piety and sin is itself a discrepancy, since actual piety means to transcend both of them." Śrī Uddhava now pursues this point so that Lord Kṛṣṇa will give a more elaborate explanation of this difficult subject matter. Śrī Uddhava here states that the Vedic literatures, which constitute the laws of God, deal with piety and sin; therefore, it must be clarified how one transcends activities recommended in the Vedas. According to Śrīla Viśvanātha Cakravartī Ṭhākura, Uddhava suddenly understood Lord Kṛṣṇa's purpose in the words He had just spoken, and to induce the Lord to elaborate upon this interesting point Uddhava outwardly challenged the Lord's statement.

TEXT 2

वर्णाश्रमविकल्पं च प्रतिलोमानुलोमजम् ।
द्रव्यदेशवयःकालान् स्वर्गं नरकमेव च ॥ २ ॥

varṇāśrama-vikalpaṁ ca
pratilomānulomajam
dravya-deśa-vayaḥ-kālān
svargaṁ narakam eva ca

varṇa-āśrama—of the *varṇāśrama* system; *vikalpam*—the variety of superior and inferior positions created by piety and sin; *ca*—and; *pratiloma*—birth in a mixed family wherein the father is inferior in social status to the mother; *anuloma-jam*—birth in a mixed family in which the father is superior in social status to the mother; *dravya*—material objects or possessions; *deśa*—the place; *vayaḥ*—one's age; *kālān*—the time; *svargam*—heaven; *narakam*—hell; *eva*—indeed; *ca*—also.

TRANSLATION

According to Vedic literature, the superior and inferior varieties found in the human social system, *varṇāśrama,* are due to pious and sinful modes of family planning. Thus piety and sin are constant points of reference in the Vedic analysis of the components of a given situation—namely the material ingredients, place, age and time. Indeed, the *Vedas* reveal the existence of material heaven and hell, which are certainly based on piety and sin.

PURPORT

Pratiloma indicates the combination of a superior woman with an inferior man. For example, the *vaidehaka* community consists of those born of a *śūdra* father and *brāhmaṇa* mother, whereas the *sūtas* are those born from a *kṣatriya* father and a *brāhmaṇa* mother or from a *śūdra* father and *kṣatriya* mother. *Anuloma* indicates those born from a superior father and inferior mother. The *mūrdhāvasikta* are those born of a *brāhmaṇa* father and *kṣatriya* mother. *Ambaṣṭhas* are those born from a *brāhmaṇa* father and *vaiśya* mother, and they often become medical men. *Karaṇa* indicates those born of a *vaiśya* father and *śūdra* mother or of a *kṣatriya* father and *vaiśya* mother. That such mixing of castes is not very much appreciated in the Vedic culture is demonstrated in the first chapter of *Bhagavad-gītā.* Arjuna was very worried that the death of so many *kṣatriyas* on the battlefield would lead to the mixing of superior women with inferior men, and on those grounds he objected to fighting. In any case, the entire Vedic social system is based on distinguishing between piety and sin, and Śrī Uddhava is encouraging the Lord to explain more elaborately His statement that one should transcend both piety and sin.

TEXT 3

गुणदोषभिदादृष्टिमन्तरेण वचस्तव ।
निःश्रेयसं कथं नृणां निषेधविधिलक्षणम् ॥ ३ ॥

guṇa-doṣa-bhidā-dṛṣṭim
antareṇa vacas tava
niḥśreyasaṁ kathaṁ nṝṇāṁ
niṣedha-vidhi-lakṣaṇam

guṇa—piety; *doṣa*—sin; *bhidā*—the difference between; *dṛṣṭim*—seeing; *antareṇa*—without; *vacaḥ*—words; *tava*—Your; *niḥśreyasam*—perfection of life, liberation; *katham*—how is it possible; *nṝṇām*—for human beings; *niṣedha*—prohibitions; *vidhi*—positive injunctions; *lakṣaṇam*—characterized by.

TRANSLATION

Without seeing the difference between piety and sin, how can one understand Your own instructions in the form of Vedic literatures, which order one to act piously and forbid one to act sinfully? Furthermore, without such authorized Vedic literatures, which ultimately award liberation, how can human beings achieve the perfection of life?

PURPORT

If one does not accept the necessity of performing pious activities and avoiding sinful activities, it becomes very difficult to understand authorized religious scriptures; and without such scriptures, how can human beings attain salvation? This is the essence of Śrī Uddhava's question.

TEXT 4

पितृदेवमनुष्याणां वेदश्चक्षुस्तवेश्वर ।
श्रेयस्त्वनुपलब्धेऽर्थे साध्यसाधनयोरपि ॥ ४ ॥

pitṛ-deva-manuṣyāṇāṁ
vedaś cakṣus taveśvara
śreyas tv anupalabdhe 'rthe
sādhya-sādhanayor api

pitṛ—of the forefathers; *deva*—of the demigods; *manuṣyāṇām*—of the human beings; *vedaḥ*—the Vedic knowledge; *cakṣuḥ*—is the eye; *tava*—emanating from You; *īśvara*—O Supreme Lord; *śreyaḥ*—superior; *tu*—indeed; *anupalabdhe*—in that which cannot be directly perceived; *arthe*—in the goals of human life, such as sense gratification, liberation, and attainment of heaven; *sādhya-sādhanayoḥ*—both in the means and the end; *api*—indeed.

TRANSLATION

My dear Lord, in order to understand those things beyond direct experience—such as spiritual liberation or attainment of heaven and other material enjoyments beyond our present capacity—and in general to understand the means and end of all things, the forefathers, demigods and human beings must consult the Vedic literatures, which are Your own laws, for these constitute the highest evidence and revelation.

PURPORT

One might argue that while human beings are certainly prone to ignorance, the elevated forefathers and demigods are considered to be all-knowing within universal affairs. If such superior beings would communicate with the earth, then everyone could bypass Vedic knowledge in achieving his personal desire. This concept is denied here by the words *vedaś cakṣuḥ*. Even the demigods and forefathers have at best an ambiguous conception of supreme liberation, and even in material affairs they are subject to personal frustration. Although the demigods are all-powerful in awarding material benedictions to inferior species such as human beings, they are sometimes thwarted in their personal programs of sense gratification. A rich businessman, for example, may have no difficulty paying the insignificant salary of one of his innumerable workers, but the same wealthy man may be completely frustrated in his dealings with his own family and friends and may also be defeated in his attempts to expand his fortune by further investments. Although a rich man appears to be all-powerful to his subordinate workers, he must personally struggle to fulfill his personal desires. Similarly, the demigods and forefathers encounter many difficulties in maintaining and expanding their celestial standard of living. They must therefore constantly take shelter of superior Vedic knowledge. Even in the administration of cosmic affairs, they strictly follow the guidelines of the *Vedas,* which are the laws of God. If such fabulous entities as demigods must take shelter of the *Vedas,* we can just imagine the position of human beings, who are frustrated at virtually every step of their lives. Every human being should accept Vedic knowledge as the highest evidence in material and spiritual affairs. Uddhava points out to the Lord that if one accepts the authority of Vedic knowledge, it is seemingly impossible to reject the concept of material piety and sin. Thus Uddhava persists in examining the Lord's controversial statement at the end of the last chapter.

TEXT 5

गुणदोषभिदादृष्टिर्निगमात्ते न हि स्वतः ।
निगमेनापवादश्च भिदाया इति ह भ्रमः ॥ ५ ॥

guṇa-doṣa-bhidā-dṛṣṭir
nigamāt te na hi svataḥ
nigamenāpavādaś ca
bhidāyā iti ha bhramaḥ

guṇa—piety; *doṣa*—sin; *bhidā*—the difference between; *dṛṣṭiḥ*—seeing; *nigamāt*—from Vedic knowledge; *te*—Your; *na*—not; *hi*—

indeed; *svataḥ*—automatically; *nigamena*—by the *Vedas; apavādaḥ*—nullification; *ca*—also; *bhidāyāḥ*—of such distinction; *iti*—thus; *ha*—clearly; *bhramaḥ*—confusion.

TRANSLATION

My dear Lord, the distinction observed between piety and sin comes from Your own Vedic knowledge and does not arise by itself. If the same Vedic literature subsequently nullifies such distinction between piety and sin, there will certainly be confusion.

PURPORT

In the *Bhagavad-gītā* (15.15) Lord Kṛṣṇa states, *vedaś ca sarvair aham eva vedyaḥ:* "By all the *Vedas* I am to be known. Indeed, I am the compiler of *Vedānta,* and I know the *Veda* as it is." Vedic knowledge emanates from the breathing of the Personality of Godhead; therefore, whatever Lord Kṛṣṇa speaks is *Veda,* or perfect knowledge. The Vedic literatures are full of descriptions of piety and sin, but Lord Kṛṣṇa's statement that one should transcend piety and sin is also to be understood as Vedic knowledge. Śrī Uddhava has understood this point and therefore requests Lord Kṛṣṇa to clear up an apparent contradiction. Ultimately, the material world gives the living entities a chance to satisfy their perverted desires and at the same time gradually achieve the liberation of going back home, back to Godhead. Thus material piety must be considered a means and never an absolute end, since the material world itself is not absolute, being temporary and limited. The Personality of Godhead is Himself the reservoir of all virtue and goodness. Those persons and activities that please the Lord are to be considered virtuous, and those that displease Him are to be considered sinful. There cannot be any other permanent definition of these terms. If one becomes a mundane moralist, forgetting the Supreme Lord, one's position is certainly imperfect, and one will not achieve the ultimate goal of piety, going back home, back to Godhead. On the other hand, there is great fear among moralists that if the distinction between piety and sin is minimized, people will commit many atrocities in the name of God. In the modern world there is no clear understanding of spiritual authority, and moral men consider any appeal to transcend morality to be an invitation to fanaticism, anarchy, violence and corruption. Thus they regard material moral principles as more important than directly trying to please God. Because this point is controversial, Uddhava is anxiously requesting the Lord to give a clear explanation.

TEXT 6

श्रीभगवानुवाच
योगास्त्रयो मया प्रोक्ता नृणां श्रेयोविधित्सया ।
ज्ञानं कर्म च भक्तिश्च नोपायोऽन्योऽस्ति कुत्रचित् ॥६॥

śrī-bhagavān uvāca
yogās trayo mayā proktā
nṝṇāṁ śreyo-vidhitsayā
jñānaṁ karma ca bhaktiś ca
nopāyo 'nyo 'sti kutracit

śrī-bhagavān uvāca—the Supreme Personality of Godhead said; *yogāḥ*—processes; *trayaḥ*—three; *mayā*—by Me; *proktāḥ*—described; *nṝṇam*—of human beings; *śreyaḥ*—perfection; *vidhitsayā*—desiring to bestow; *jñānam*—the path of philosophy; *karma*—the path of work; *ca*—also; *bhaktiḥ*—the path of devotion; *ca*—also; *na*—no; *upāyaḥ*—means; *anyaḥ*—other; *asti*—exists; *kutracit*—whatsoever.

TRANSLATION

The Supreme Personality of Godhead said: My dear Uddhava, because I desire that human beings may achieve perfection, I have presented three paths of advancement—the path of knowledge, the path of work and the path of devotion. Besides these three there is absolutely no other means of elevation.

PURPORT

Ultimately, the goal of philosophical speculation, pious regulated work and devotional service is the same—Kṛṣṇa consciousness. As stated by the Lord in *Bhagavad-gītā* (4.11),

ye yathā māṁ prapadyante
tāṁs tathaiva bhajāmy aham

mama vartmānuvartante
manuṣyāḥ pārtha sarvaśaḥ

"All of them—as they surrender unto Me—I reward accordingly. Everyone follows My path in all respects, O son of Pṛthā." Although all authorized processes of human perfection ultimately lead to Kṛṣṇa consciousness, or love of God, various performers have specific propensities and qualifications and thus gravitate to different methods of self-realization. Lord Kṛṣṇa here describes the three authorized processes together in order to emphasize that their ultimate goal is one. At the same time, philosophical speculation and regulated pious work can never be considered equal to pure love of Godhead, as the Lord has elaborately clarified in the previous chapters. The word *trayaḥ*, or "three," indicates that despite their ultimate oneness of purpose, the three paths display diversity in progress and achievement. One cannot achieve the same result by mere speculation or piety that one achieves by directly surrendering to the Personality of Godhead, depending completely on His mercy and friendship. The word *karma* here indicates work dedicated to the Personality of Godhead. As described in *Bhagavad-gītā* (3.9),

yajñārthāt karmaṇo 'nyatra
loko 'yaṁ karma-bandhanaḥ
tad-arthaṁ karma kaunteya
mukta-saṅgaḥ samācara

"Work done as a sacrifice for Viṣṇu has to be performed, otherwise work binds one to this material world. Therefore, O son of Kuntī, perform your prescribed duties for His satisfaction, and in that way you will always remain unattached and free from bondage." In the process of *jñāna*, one seeks impersonal liberation by merging into the glaring effulgence of the Personality of Godhead. Such liberation is considered hellish by the devotees, because by merging one loses all awareness of the supreme blissful feature of the Lord as Bhagavān, the supreme person. The performers of *karma*, or regulated work, seek the three aspects of human progress other than liberation—namely religiosity, economic development and sense gratification. The fruitive workers think that by exhausting each of their innumerable material desires they will gradually come out of the dark tunnel of material existence into the clear light of spiritual liberation. This process is very dangerous and uncertain, because not only is there virtually no limit to material desires, but even a slight flaw in the process of regulated work constitutes sin and throws one off the path of progressive life. The devotees directly aim for love of Godhead and are therefore most pleasing to the Supreme Lord. In any case, all three divisions of Vedic elevation depend completely on the mercy of Lord Kṛṣṇa. One cannot progress along any one of these paths without the blessings of the Lord. Other Vedic processes, such as austerity, charity and so forth, are included within the three primary divisions described here.

TEXT 7

निर्विण्णानां ज्ञानयोगो न्यासिनामिह कर्मसु ।
तेष्वनिर्विण्णचित्तानां कर्मयोगस्तु कामिनाम् ॥ ७ ॥

nirviṇṇānāṁ jñāna-yogo
nyāsinām iha karmasu
teṣv anirviṇṇa-cittānāṁ
karma-yogas tu kāminām

nirviṇṇānām—for those who are disgusted; *jñāna-yogaḥ*—the path of philosophical speculation; *nyāsinām*—for those who are renounced; *iha*—among these three paths; *karmasu*—in ordinary material activities; *teṣu*—in those activities; *anirviṇṇa*—not disgusted; *cittānām*—for those who have consciousness; *karma-yogaḥ*—the path of *karma-yoga;* *tu*—indeed; *kāminām*—for those who still desire material happiness.

TRANSLATION

Among these three paths, *jñāna-yoga*, the path of philosophical speculation, is recommended for those who are disgusted with material life and are thus detached from ordinary, fruitive activities. Those who are not disgusted with material life, having many desires yet to fulfill, should seek perfection through the path of *karma-yoga*.

PURPORT

In this verse the Lord reveals the different propensities that lead human beings to adopt different processes of perfection. Those who are frustrated in the ordinary material life of society, friendship and love, and who understand that promotion to heaven simply brings further domestic miseries, take directly to the path of knowledge. Through authorized philosophical discrimination they transcend the bonds of material existence. Those who are still desirous of enjoying material society, friendship and love, and who are excited by the prospect of going with their relatives to material heavenly planets, cannot take directly to the path of rigorous philosophical advancement, which requires great austerity. Such persons are advised to remain in family life and offer the fruits of their work to the Supreme. In this way, they also can become perfect and gradually learn detachment from material life.

TEXT 8

यदृच्छया मत्कथादौ जातश्रद्धस्तु यः पुमान् ।
न निर्विण्णो नातिसक्तो भक्तियोगोऽस्य सिद्धिदः ॥८॥

yadṛcchayā mat-kathādau
jāta-śraddhas tu yaḥ pumān
na nirviṇṇo nāti-sakto
bhakti-yogo 'sya siddhi-daḥ

yadṛcchayā—somehow or other by good fortune; *mat-kathā-ādau*—in the narrations, songs, philosophy, dramatical performances, etc., that describe My glories; *jāta*—awakened; *śraddhaḥ*—faith; *tu*—indeed; *yaḥ*—one who; *pumān*—a person; *na*—not; *nirviṇṇaḥ*—disgusted; *na*—not; *ati-saktaḥ*—very attached; *bhakti-yogaḥ*—the path of loving devotion; *asya*—his; *siddhi-daḥ*—will award perfection.

TRANSLATION

If somehow or other by good fortune one develops faith in hearing and chanting My glories, such a person, being neither very disgusted with nor attached to material life, should achieve perfection through the path of loving devotion to Me.

PURPORT

If somehow or other one gets the association of pure devotees of the Lord and hears from them the transcendental message of Lord Kṛṣṇa, then one has the chance to become a devotee of the Lord. As mentioned in the previous verse, those who become disgusted with material life take to impersonal philosophical speculation and rigorously try to stamp out any trace of personal existence. Those who are still attached to material sense gratification try to purify themselves by offering the fruits of their ordinary activities to the Supreme. A first-class candidate for pure devotional service, on the other hand, is neither completely disgusted with nor attached to material life. He does not desire to pursue ordinary material existence any further, because it cannot award real happiness. Nevertheless, a candidate for devotional service does not give up all hope for perfecting personal existence. A person who avoids the two extremes of material attachment and impersonal reaction to material attachment and who somehow or other gets the association of pure devotees, faithfully hearing their message, is a good candidate for going back home, back to Godhead, as described here by the Lord.

TEXT 9

तावत् कर्माणि कुर्वीत न निर्विद्येत यावता ।
मत्कथाश्रवणादौ वा श्रद्धा यावन्न जायते ॥ ९ ॥

tāvat karmāṇi kurvīta
na nirvidyeta yāvatā
mat-kathā-śravaṇādau vā
śraddhā yāvan na jāyate

tāvat—up to that time; *karmāṇi*—fruitive activities; *kurvīta*—one should execute; *na nirvidyeta*—is not satiated; *yāvatā*—as long as; *mat-kathā*—of discourses about Me; *śravaṇa-ādau*—in the matter of *śravaṇam, kīrtanam* and so on; *vā*—or; *śraddhā*—faith; *yāvat*—as long as; *na*—not; *jāyate*—is awakened.

TRANSLATION

As long as one is not satiated by fruitive activity and has not awakened his taste for devotional service by *śravaṇaṁ kīrtanaṁ*

***viṣṇoḥ*, one has to act according to the regulative principles of the Vedic injunctions.**

PURPORT

Unless one has developed firm faith in Lord Kṛṣṇa by association with pure devotees and is thus engaged full time in the devotional service of the Lord, one should not neglect ordinary Vedic principles and duties. As stated by the Lord Himself,

śruti-smṛtī mamaivājñe
yas te ullaṅghya vartate
ājñā-cchedī mama dveṣī
mad-bhakto 'pi na vaiṣṇavaḥ

"The *śruti* and *smṛti* literatures are to be understood as My injunctions, and one who violates such codes is to be understood as violating My will and thus opposing Me. Although such a person may claim to be My devotee, he is not actually a Vaiṣṇava." The Lord here states that if one has not developed firm faith in the process of chanting and hearing, one must comply with the ordinary injunctions of Vedic literatures. There are many symptoms by which one can recognize an advanced devotee of the Lord. In the First Canto of *Śrīmad-Bhāgavatam* (1.2.7) it is stated,

vāsudeve bhagavati
bhakti-yogaḥ prayojitaḥ
janayaty āśu vairāgyaṁ
jñānaṁ ca yad ahaitukam

One who is actually engaged in advanced devotional service immediately develops both clear knowledge of Kṛṣṇa consciousness and detachment from nondevotional activities. One who is not situated on this platform must comply with the ordinary injunctions of Vedic literature or risk becoming inimical to the Supreme Personality of Godhead. On the other hand, one who has developed great faith in the devotional service of Lord Kṛṣṇa does not hesitate to do anything that will further the mission of the Lord. As stated in the Eleventh Canto of *Śrīmad-Bhāgavatam* (11.5.41),

devarṣi-bhūtāpta-nṛṇāṁ pitṝṇāṁ
na kiṅkaro nāyam ṛṇī ca rājan
sarvātmanā yaḥ śaraṇaṁ śaraṇyaṁ
gato mukundaṁ parihṛtya kartam

"Anyone who has taken shelter of the lotus feet of Mukunda, the giver of liberation, giving up all kinds of obligation, and has taken to the path in all seriousness, owes neither duties nor obligations to the demigods, sages, general living entities, family members, humankind or forefathers."

Śrīla Jīva Gosvāmī points out in this regard that when a person fully surrenders to Lord Kṛṣṇa, he takes shelter of the Lord's promise to liquidate all other responsibilities and debts of the surrendered soul. The devotee thus becomes fearless by meditating on the Lord's promise of protection. Those, however, who are materially attached are frightened by the prospect of full surrender to the Supreme Personality of Godhead, thereby revealing their inimical mentality toward the Lord.

TEXT 10

स्वधर्मस्थो यजन् यज्ञैरनाशीःकाम उद्धव ।
न याति स्वर्गनरकौ यद्यन्यन्न समाचरेत् ॥१०॥

sva-dharma-stho yajan yajñair
anāśīḥ-kāma uddhava
na yāti svarga-narakau
yady anyan na samācaret

sva-dharma—in one's prescribed duties; *sthaḥ*—situated; *yajan*—worshiping; *yajñaiḥ*—by prescribed sacrifices; *anāśīḥ-kāmaḥ*—not desiring fruitive results; *uddhava*—My dear Uddhava; *na*—does not; *yāti*—go; *svarga*—to heaven; *narakau*—or to hell; *yadi*—if; *anyat*—something other than his prescribed duty; *na*—does not; *samācaret*—perform.

TRANSLATION

My dear Uddhava, a person who is situated in his prescribed duty, properly worshiping by Vedic sacrifices but not desiring

the fruitive result of such worship, will not go to the heavenly planets; similarly, by not performing forbidden activities he will not go to hell.

PURPORT

The perfection of *karma-yoga* is described here. One who does not desire fruitive rewards for his religious activities does not waste time going to the heavenly planets for celestial sense gratification. Similarly, one who does not neglect his prescribed duty or perform forbidden activities will not be bothered by going to hell for punishment. Thus avoiding material rewards and punishments, such a desireless person can be promoted to the platform of pure devotional service to Lord Kṛṣṇa.

TEXT 11

अस्मिँल्लोके वर्तमानः स्वधर्मस्थोऽनघः शुचिः ।
ज्ञानं विशुद्धमाप्नोति मद्भक्तिं वा यदृच्छया ॥११॥

asmil̐ loke vartamānaḥ
sva-dharma-stho 'naghaḥ śuciḥ
jñānaṁ viśuddham āpnoti
mad-bhaktiṁ vā yadṛcchayā

asmin—in this; *loke*—world; *vartamānaḥ*—existing; *sva-dharma*—in one's prescribed duty; *sthaḥ*—situated; *anaghaḥ*—free from sinful activities; *śuciḥ*—cleansed of material contamination; *jñānam*—knowledge; *viśuddham*—transcendental; *āpnoti*—obtains; *mat*—to Me; *bhaktim*—devotional service; *vā*—or; *yadṛcchayā*—according to one's fortune.

TRANSLATION

One who is situated in his prescribed duty, free from sinful activities and cleansed of material contamination, in this very life obtains transcendental knowledge or, by fortune, devotional service unto Me.

PURPORT

Asmin loke indicates one's present duration of life. Before the death of one's present body one can obtain transcendental knowledge or, by great fortune, pure devotional service to the Supreme Lord. The word *yadṛc-chayā* indicates that if one somehow or other gets the association of pure devotees and hears from them faithfully, one can achieve Kṛṣṇa consciousness, the highest perfection of life. According to Śrīla Viśvanātha Cakravartī Ṭhākura, through transcendental knowledge one obtains liberation, whereas through pure devotional service one can achieve love of Godhead, in which liberation is automatically included. Both results are certainly superior to ordinary, fruitive activities, by which one tries to enjoy much the same things that animals do. If one's devotional service is mixed with a tendency toward fruitive activities or mental speculation, then one may achieve the neutral stage of love of Godhead, whereas those who are inclined to serve only Lord Kṛṣṇa advance to the higher stages of love of Godhead in servitude, friendship, parental love and the conjugal relationship.

TEXT 12

स्वर्गिणोऽप्येतमिच्छन्ति लोकं निरयिणस्तथा ।
साधकं ज्ञानभक्तिभ्यामुभयं तदसाधकम् ॥१२॥

svargiṇo 'py etam icchanti
lokaṁ nirayiṇas tathā
sādhakaṁ jñāna-bhaktibhyām
ubhayaṁ tad-asādhakam

svargiṇaḥ—the residents of the heavenly planets; *api*—even; *etam*—this; *icchanti*—desire; *lokam*—earth planet; *nirayiṇaḥ*—the residents of hell; *tathā*—in the same way; *sādhakam*—leading to achievement; *jñāna-bhaktibhyām*—of transcendental knowledge and love of Godhead; *ubhayam*—both (heaven and hell); *tat*—for that perfection; *asādhakam*—not useful.

TRANSLATION

The residents of both heaven and hell desire human birth on the earth planet because human life facilitates the achievement of transcendental knowledge and love of Godhead, whereas neither heavenly nor hellish bodies efficiently provide such opportunities.

PURPORT

Śrīla Jīva Gosvāmī points out that in material heaven one becomes absorbed in extraordinary sense gratification and in hell one is absorbed in suffering. In both cases there is little impetus to acquire transcendental knowledge or pure love of Godhead. Excessive suffering or excessive enjoyment are thus impediments to spiritual advancement.

TEXT 13

न नरः स्वर्गतिं काङ्क्षेन्नारकीं वा विचक्षणः ।
नेमं लोकं च काङ्क्षेत देहावेशात् प्रमाद्यति ॥१३॥

na naraḥ svar-gatiṁ kāṅkṣen
nārakīṁ vā vicakṣaṇaḥ
nemaṁ lokaṁ ca kāṅkṣeta
dehāveśāt pramādyati

na—never; *naraḥ*—a human being; *svaḥ-gatim*—promotion to heaven; *kāṅkṣet*—should desire; *nārakīm*—to hell; *vā*—or; *vicakṣaṇaḥ*—a learned person; *na*—nor; *imam*—this; *lokam*—earth planet; *ca*—also; *kāṅkṣeta*—one should desire; *deha*—in the material body; *āveśāt*—from absorption; *pramādyati*—one becomes a fool.

TRANSLATION

A human being who is wise should never desire promotion to heavenly planets or residence in hell. Indeed, a human being should also never desire permanent residence on the earth, for by such absorption in the material body one becomes foolishly negligent of one's actual self-interest.

PURPORT

One who has achieved human life on the earth has an excellent opportunity to attain spiritual liberation through Kṛṣṇa consciousness, or devotional service to the Lord. Thus one should not desire promotion to heaven or risk residence in hell, where excessive enjoyment or punishment deviate one's mind from self-realization. On the other hand, one should not think, "The earth is so nice, I can stay here forever." One should develop thorough detachment from all aspects and categories of material existence and go back home, back to Godhead, where life is eternal and full of bliss and knowledge.

Lord Kṛṣṇa now begins to develop His conclusive proof that actual human progress lies beyond material piety and sin. The Lord first clarified that there are basically three methods of human elevation, namely *jñāna, karma* and *bhakti,* and that the goal is transcendental knowledge and ultimately love of Godhead. Now the Lord explains that promotion to heavenly planets (the final goal of piety) as well as residence in hell (the result of sinful activities) are both useless in fulfilling the actual purpose of life. Neither material piety nor sin establish the eternal living entity in his constitutional position; therefore something more is required to achieve the actual perfection of life.

TEXT 14

एतद् विद्वान् पुरा मृत्योरभवाय घटेत सः ।
अप्रमत्त इदं ज्ञात्वा मर्त्यमप्यर्थसिद्धिदम् ॥१४॥

etad vidvān purā mṛtyor
abhavāya ghaṭeta saḥ
apramatta idaṁ jñātvā
martyam apy artha-siddhi-dam

etat—this; *vidvān*—knowing; *purā*—before; *mṛtyoḥ*—death; *abhavāya*—to transcend material existence; *ghaṭeta*—should act; *saḥ*—he; *apramattaḥ*—without laziness or foolishness; *idam*—this; *jñātvā*—knowing; *martyam*—subject to death; *api*—even though; *artha*—of the goal of life; *siddhi-dam*—giving the perfection.

TRANSLATION

A wise person, knowing that although the material body is subject to death it can still award the perfection of one's life, should not foolishly neglect to take advantage of this opportunity before death arrives.

TEXT 15

छिद्यमानं यमैरेतैः कृतनीडं वनस्पतिम् ।
खगः स्वकेतमुत्सृज्य क्षेमं याति ह्यलम्पटः ॥१५॥

chidyamānaṁ yamair etaiḥ
kṛta-nīḍaṁ vanaspatim
khagaḥ sva-ketam utsṛjya
kṣemaṁ yāti hy alampaṭaḥ

chidyamānam—being cut down; *yamaiḥ*—by cruel men, who are like death personified; *etaiḥ*—by these; *kṛta-nīḍam*—in which he has constructed his nest; *vanaspatim*—a tree; *khagaḥ*—a bird; *sva-ketam*—his home; *utsṛjya*—giving up; *kṣemam*—happiness; *yāti*—achieves; *hi*—indeed; *alampaṭaḥ*—without attachment.

TRANSLATION

Without attachment, a bird gives up the tree in which his nest was constructed when that tree is cut down by cruel men who are like death personified, and thus the bird achieves happiness in another place.

PURPORT

Here the example is given of detachment from the bodily concept of life. The living entity resides within the body just as a bird dwells within a tree. When thoughtless men cut down the tree, the bird, without lamenting the loss of its previous nest, does not hesitate to establish its residence in another place.

TEXT 16

अहोरात्रैश्छिद्यमानं बुद्ध्वायुर्भयवेपथुः ।
मुक्तसङ्गः परं बुद्ध्वा निरीह उपशाम्यति ॥१६॥

aho-rātraiś chidyamānaṁ
buddhvāyur bhaya-vepathuḥ
mukta-saṅgaḥ paraṁ buddhvā
nirīha upaśāmyati

ahaḥ—by days; *rātraiḥ*—by nights; *chidyamānam*—being cut down; *buddhvā*—knowing; *āyuḥ*—the duration of life; *bhaya*—with fear; *vepathuḥ*—trembling; *mukta-saṅgaḥ*—free from attachment; *param*—the Supreme Lord; *buddhvā*—understanding; *nirīhaḥ*—without material desire; *upaśāmyati*—achieves perfect peace.

TRANSLATION

Knowing that one's duration of life is being similarly cut down by the passing of days and nights, one should be shaken by fear. In this way, giving up all material attachment and desire, one understands the Supreme Lord and achieves perfect peace.

PURPORT

An intelligent devotee knows that the passing days and nights are exhausting one's duration of life, and he therefore gives up his futile attachment to material sense objects. Instead, he strives to achieve permanent benefit in life. Just as the detached bird immediately gives up its nest and goes to another tree, similarly, a devotee knows that there is no permanent opportunity for residence within the material world. Instead he dedicates his working energy to achieving eternal residence in the kingdom of God. Transcending the modes of material nature by attaining Kṛṣṇa's own spiritual nature, the devotee at last obtains perfect peace.

TEXT 17

नृदेहमाद्यं सुलभं सुदुर्लभं
प्लवं सुकल्पं गुरुकर्णधारम् ।
मयानुकूलेन नभस्वतेरितं
पुमान् भवाब्धिं न तरेत् स आत्महा ॥१७॥

nṛ-deham ādyaṁ su-labhaṁ su-durlabhaṁ
plavaṁ su-kalpaṁ guru-karṇadhāram
mayānukūlena nabhasvateritaṁ
pumān bhavābdhiṁ na taret sa ātma-hā

nṛ—human; *deham*—body; *ādyam*—the source of all favorable results; *su-labham*—effortlessly obtained; *su-durlabham*—although impossible to obtain even with great endeavor; *plavam*—a boat; *su-kalpam*—extremely well suited for its purpose; *guru*—having the spiritual master; *karṇa-dhāram*—as the captain of the boat; *mayā*—by Me; *anukūlena*—with favorable; *nabhasvatā*—winds; *īritam*—impelled; *pumān*—a person; *bhava*—of material existence; *abdhim*—the ocean; *na*—does not; *taret*—cross over; *saḥ*—he; *ātma-hā*—the killer of his own soul.

TRANSLATION

The human body, which can award all benefit in life, is automatically obtained by the laws of nature, although it is a very rare achievement. This human body can be compared to a perfectly constructed boat having the spiritual master as the captain and the instructions of the Personality of Godhead as favorable winds impelling it on its course. Considering all these advantages, a human being who does not utilize his human life to cross the ocean of material existence must be considered the killer of his own soul.

PURPORT

The human body, which is obtained after passing through many inferior forms, is created in such a way that it can award the highest perfection of life. A human being is supposed to serve the Supreme Personality of Godhead, and the bona fide spiritual master is the appropriate guide for such service. The causeless mercy of Lord Kṛṣṇa is compared to favorable winds that help the boat of the body to ply smoothly on the course back home, back to Godhead. Lord Kṛṣṇa gives His personal instructions in Vedic literature, speaks through the bona fide spiritual master, and encourages, warns and protects His sincere devotee from within the devotee's heart. Such merciful guidance of the Lord moves a sincere soul quickly on the path back to Godhead. But one who cannot understand that the human body is a suitable boat for crossing the ocean of material existence will see no need to accept a captain in the form of the spiritual master and will not at all appreciate the favorable winds of the Lord's mercy. He has no chance of achieving the goal of human life. Acting against his own self-interest, he gradually becomes the killer of his own soul.

TEXT 18

यदारम्भेषु निर्विण्णो विरक्तः संयतेन्द्रियः ।
अभ्यासेनात्मनो योगी धारयेदचलं मनः ॥१८॥

yadārambheṣu nirviṇṇo
viraktaḥ saṁyatendriyaḥ
abhyāsenātmano yogī
dhārayed acalaṁ manaḥ

yadā—when; *ārambheṣu*—in material endeavors; *nirviṇṇaḥ*—hopeless; *viraktaḥ*—detached; *saṁyata*—completely controlling; *indriyaḥ*—the senses; *abhyāsena*—by practice; *ātmanaḥ*—of the soul; *yogī*—the transcendentalist; *dhārayet*—should concentrate; *acalam*—steady; *manaḥ*—the mind.

TRANSLATION

A transcendentalist, having become disgusted and hopeless in all endeavors for material happiness, completely controls the senses and develops detachment. By spiritual practice he should then fix the mind on the spiritual platform without deviation.

PURPORT

The inevitable result of material sense gratification is disappointment and pain that sears the heart. One becomes gradually hopeless and despondent in material life; then, receiving good instructions from the Lord or His devotee, one transforms one's material disappointment into spiritual success. Actually, Lord Kṛṣṇa is our only true friend, and this simple understanding can bring one to a new life of spiritual happiness in the company of the Lord.

TEXT 19

धार्यमाणं मनो यर्हि भ्राम्यदाश्वनवस्थितम् ।
अतन्द्रितोऽनुरोधेन मार्गेणात्मवशं नयेत् ॥१९॥

dhāryamāṇaṁ mano yarhi
bhrāmyad āśv anavasthitam
atandrito 'nurodhena
mārgeṇātma-vaśaṁ nayet

dhāryamāṇam—being concentrated on the spiritual platform; *manaḥ*—the mind; *yarhi*—when; *bhrāmyat*—is deviated; *āśu*—suddenly;

anavasthitam—not situated on the spiritual platform; *atandritaḥ*—carefully; *anurodhena*—according to the prescribed regulations; *mārgeṇa*—by the process; *ātma*—of the soul; *vaśam*—under the control; *nayet*—one should bring.

TRANSLATION

Whenever the mind, being concentrated on the spiritual platform, is suddenly deviated from its spiritual position, one should carefully bring it under the control of the self by following the prescribed means.

PURPORT

Although one is seriously engaging the mind in Kṛṣṇa consciousness, the mind is so flickering that it may suddenly be deviated from its spiritual position. One should then carefully bring the mind back under the control of the self. It is stated in *Bhagavad-gītā* that if one is too austere or too sensuous one cannot control the mind. Sometimes one may bring the mind under control by allowing the material senses limited satisfaction. For example, although one may eat austerely, from time to time one may accept a reasonable amount of *mahā-prasādam*, opulent foods offered to the temple Deities, so that the mind will not become disturbed. Similarly, one may occasionally relax with other transcendentalists through joking, swimming and so forth. But if such activities are performed excessively, they will lead to a setback in spiritual life. When the mind desires sinful gratification such as illicit sex or intoxication, one must simply tolerate the mind's foolishness and by strenuous effort push on with Kṛṣṇa consciousness. Then the waves of illusion will soon subside, and the path of advancement will again open wide.

TEXT 20

मनोगतिं न विसृजेज्जितप्राणो जितेन्द्रियः ।
सत्त्वसम्पन्नया बुद्ध्या मन आत्मवशं नयेत् ॥२०॥

mano-gatiṁ na visṛjej
jita-prāṇo jitendriyaḥ

sattva-sampannayā buddhyā
mana ātma-vaśaṁ nayet

manaḥ—of the mind; *gatim*—goal; *na*—not; *visṛjet*—should lose sight of; *jita-prāṇaḥ*—one who has conquered the breath; *jita-indriyaḥ*—who has conquered his senses; *sattva*—of the mode of goodness; *sampannayā*—characterized by flourishing; *buddhyā*—by the intelligence; *manaḥ*—the mind; *ātma-vaśam*—under the control of the self; *nayet*—one should bring.

TRANSLATION

One should never lose sight of the actual goal of mental activities, but rather, conquering the life air and senses and utilizing intelligence strengthened by the mode of goodness, one should bring the mind under the control of the self.

PURPORT

Although the mind may suddenly wander outside the jurisdiction of self-realization, one must bring the mind back under control by clear intelligence in the mode of goodness. The best solution is to keep the mind always busy in the service of Lord Kṛṣṇa so that the mind cannot wander onto the dangerous path of sense gratification, headed by sex attraction. The material mind is naturally inclined to accept material objects at every moment. Therefore unless the mind is seriously brought under control there is no possibility of becoming steady on the path of spiritual advancement.

TEXT 21

एष वै परमो योगो मनसः संग्रहः स्मृतः ।
हृदयज्ञत्वमन्विच्छन् दम्यस्येवार्वतो मुहुः ॥२१॥

eṣa vai paramo yogo
manasaḥ saṅgrahaḥ smṛtaḥ
hṛdaya-jñatvam anvicchan
damyasyevārvato muhuḥ

eṣaḥ—this; *vai*—indeed; *paramaḥ*—supreme; *yogaḥ*—*yoga* process; *manasaḥ*—of the mind; *saṅgrahaḥ*—complete control; *smṛtaḥ*—thus declared; *hṛdaya-jñatvam*—the characteristic of knowing intimately; *anvicchan*—carefully watching; *damyasya*—which is to be subdued; *iva*—like; *arvataḥ*—of a horse; *muhuḥ*—always.

TRANSLATION

An expert horseman, desiring to tame a headstrong horse, first lets the horse have his way for a moment and then, pulling the reins, gradually places the horse on the desired path. Similarly, the supreme *yoga* process is that by which one carefully observes the movements and desires of the mind and gradually brings them under full control.

PURPORT

Just as an expert rider intimately knows the propensities of an untamed horse and gradually brings the horse under control, an expert *yogī* allows the mind to reveal its materialistic propensities and then controls them through superior intelligence. A learned transcendentalist withholds and supplies sense objects so that the mind and senses remain fully controlled, just as the horseman sometimes pulls sharply on the reins and sometimes allows the horse to run freely. The rider never forgets his actual goal or destination, and eventually places the horse on the right path. Similarly, a learned transcendentalist, even though sometimes allowing the senses to act, never forgets the goal of self-realization, nor does he allow the senses to engage in sinful activity. Excessive austerity or restriction may result in great mental disturbance, just as pulling excessively on the reins of a horse may cause the horse to rear up against the rider. The path of self-realization depends upon clear intelligence, and the easiest way to acquire such expertise is surrender to Lord Kṛṣṇa. The Lord says in *Bhagavad-gītā* (10.10),

teṣāṁ satata-yuktānāṁ
bhajatāṁ prīti-pūrvakam
dadāmi buddhi-yogaṁ taṁ
yena mām upayānti te

One may not be a great scholar or spiritual intellect, but if one is sincerely engaged in loving service to the Lord without personal envy or personal motivation the Lord will reveal from within the heart the methodology required to control the mind. Expertly riding the waves of mental desire, a Kṛṣṇa conscious person does not fall from the saddle, and he eventually rides all the way back home, back to Godhead.

TEXT 22

सांख्येन सर्वभावानां प्रतिलोमानुलोमतः ।
भवाप्ययावनुध्यायेन्मनो यावत् प्रसीदति ॥२२॥

sāṅkhyena sarva-bhāvānāṁ
pratilomānulomataḥ
bhavāpyayāv anudhyāyen
mano yāvat prasīdati

sāṅkhyena—by analytic study; *sarva*—of all; *bhāvānām*—material elements (cosmic, earthly and atomic); *pratiloma*—by regressive function; *anulomataḥ*—by progressive function; *bhava*—creation; *apyayau*—annihilation; *anudhyāyet*—should constantly observe; *manaḥ*—the mind; *yāvat*—until; *prasīdati*—is spiritually satisfied.

TRANSLATION

Until one's mind is fixed in spiritual satisfaction, one should analytically study the temporary nature of all material objects, whether cosmic, earthly or atomic. One should constantly observe the process of creation through the natural progressive function and the process of annihilation through the regressive function.

PURPORT

There is a saying that whatever goes up must come down. Similarly, Lord Kṛṣṇa states in the *Bhagavad-gītā* (2.27),

jātasya hi dhruvo mṛtyur
dhruvaṁ janma mṛtasya ca

tasmād aparihārye 'rthe
na tvaṁ śocitum arhasi

"For one who has taken his birth, death is certain; and for one who is dead, birth is certain. Therefore, in the unavoidable discharge of your duty, you should not lament." *Mano yāvat prasīdati:* Until one has established one's consciousness on the liberated platform of perfect knowledge, one must constantly ward off the attacks of illusion through rigid analytic observation of material nature. The material mind may be attracted to sex; therefore by spiritual intelligence one should scrutinize the temporary nature of one's own body and the body that has artificially become the object of one's material lust. One may apply this rigid analysis to all material bodies, from the fantastic cosmic body of Lord Brahmā down to that of the most insignificant germ. As previously stated by Lord Kṛṣṇa, one who is advanced in Kṛṣṇa consciousness spontaneously avoids sense gratification and is constantly drawn by spiritual love into his relationship with Lord Kṛṣṇa. One who has not achieved the platform of spontaneous Kṛṣṇa consciousness must remain constantly vigilant so as not to be grossly cheated by the material energy of the Lord. One who tries to exploit the material energy ruins his spiritual life and experiences varieties of misery.

TEXT 23

निर्विण्णस्य विरक्तस्य पुरुषस्योक्तवेदिनः ।
मनस्त्यजति दौरात्म्यं चिन्तितस्यानुचिन्तया ॥२३॥

nirviṇṇasya viraktasya
puruṣasyokta-vedinaḥ
manas tyajati daurātmyaṁ
cintitasyānucintayā

nirviṇṇasya—of one who is disgusted with the illusory nature of the material world; *viraktasya*—and who is therefore detached; *puruṣasya*—of such a person; *ukta-vedinaḥ*—who is guided by the instructions of his spiritual master; *manaḥ*—the mind; *tyajati*—gives up; *daurātmyam*—

the false identification with the material body and mind; *cintitasya*—of that which is contemplated; *anucintayā*—by constant analysis.

TRANSLATION

When a person is disgusted with the temporary, illusory nature of this world and is thus detached from it, his mind, guided by the instructions of his spiritual master, considers again and again the nature of this world and eventually gives up the false identification with matter.

PURPORT

Although it is difficult to control the mind, by constant practice the mind can be spiritualized in Kṛṣṇa consciousness. A sincere disciple constantly remembers the instructions of his spiritual master and thereby faces again and again the stark truth that the material world is not the ultimate reality. By detachment and perseverence the mind gradually gives up its propensity toward sense gratification; thus illusion loses its grip on a sincere Kṛṣṇa conscious devotee. Gradually the purified mind completely gives up the false identification with this world and transfers its attention to the spiritual platform. Then one is considered to be perfect in the *yoga* system.

TEXT 24

यमादिभिर्योगपथैरान्वीक्षिक्या च विद्यया ।
ममार्चोपासनाभिर्वा नान्यैर्योग्यं स्मरेन्मनः ॥२४॥

yamādibhir yoga-pathair
ānvīkṣikyā ca vidyayā
mamārcopāsanābhir vā
nānyair yogyaṁ smaren manaḥ

yama-ādibhiḥ—by disciplinary regulations, etc.; *yoga-pathaiḥ*—by the procedures of the *yoga* system; *ānvīkṣikyā*—by logical analysis; *ca*—also; *vidyayā*—by spiritual knowledge; *mama*—My; *arcā*—worship; *upāsanābhiḥ*—by adoration, etc.; *vā*—or; *na*—never; *anyaiḥ*—by other (means); *yogyam*—the Supreme Personality of Godhead, the object of meditation; *smaret*—one should focus on; *manaḥ*—the mind.

TRANSLATION

Through the various disciplinary regulations and the purificatory procedures of the *yoga* system, through logic and spiritual education or through worship and adoration of Me, one should constantly engage his mind in remembering the Personality of Godhead, the goal of *yoga*. No other means should be employed for this purpose.

PURPORT

The word *vā* is significant in this verse, for it indicates that one engaged in the worship and adoration of the Personality of Godhead need not trouble himself with the disciplinary, regulatory and purificatory procedures of *yoga*, nor with the grueling intricacies of Vedic studies and logic. *Yogyam*, or the most appropriate object of meditation, is the Supreme Personality of Godhead, as confirmed throughout Vedic literature. One who directly takes to the worship of the Lord should not employ other methods, for full dependence on the Lord is in itself the supreme process of perfection.

TEXT 25

यदि कुर्यात् प्रमादेन योगी कर्म विगर्हितम् ।
योगेनैव दहेदंहो नान्यत्तत्र कदाचन ॥२५॥

yadi kuryāt pramādena
yogī karma vigarhitam
yogenaiva dahed aṁho
nānyat tatra kadācana

yadi—if; *kuryāt*—should perform; *pramādena*—due to negligence; *yogī*—the *yogī; karma*—an activity; *vigarhitam*—abominable; *yogena*—by the *yoga* process; *eva*—only; *dahet*—he should burn up; *aṁhaḥ*—that sin; *na*—no; *anyat*—other means; *tatra*—in this matter; *kadācana*—at any time (should be employed).

TRANSLATION

If a *yogī* because of momentary inattention accidentally commits an abominable activity, then by the very practice of *yoga* he should burn to ashes the sinful reaction, without at any time employing any other procedure.

PURPORT

The word *yogena* here indicates *jñānena yogena* and *bhaktyā yogena,* since these two transcendental systems have the power to burn sinful reactions to ashes. It should be clearly understood that the word *aṁhas,* or "sin," here refers to an accidental falldown against one's desire. Premeditated exploitation of the mercy of the Lord can never be excused.

Significantly, the Lord forbids any extraneous purificatory rites, since the transcendental *yoga* systems are themselves the most purifying processes, especially *bhakti-yoga.* If one gives up one's regular prescribed duties to perform a special ritual or penance, trying to purify a sinful reaction, then one will be guilty of the additional fault of giving up one's prescribed duties. One should pick oneself up from an accidental falldown and go on vigorously with one's prescribed duties in life without being unnecessarily discouraged. One should certainly lament and feel ashamed, or there will be no purification. However, if one becomes overly depressed at an accidental falldown one will not have the enthusiasm to go on to perfection. Lord Kṛṣṇa also states in the *Bhagavad-gītā* (9.30),

api cet su-durācāro
bhajate mām ananya-bhāk
sādhur eva sa mantavyaḥ
samyag vyavasito hi saḥ

"Even if one commits the most abominable actions, if he is engaged in devotional sevice, he is to be considered saintly because he is properly situated." The most important point is that one should be properly engaged in the devotional service of the Lord, for then the Lord will excuse and purify an accidental falldown. One should, however, be most cautious to avoid such an unhappy event.

TEXT 26

स्वे स्वेऽधिकारे या निष्ठा स गुणः परिकीर्तितः ।
कर्मणां जात्यशुद्धानामनेन नियमः कृतः ।
गुणदोषविधानेन सङ्गानां त्याजनेच्छया ॥२६॥

sve sve 'dhikāre yā niṣṭhā
sa guṇaḥ parikīrtitaḥ
karmaṇāṁ jāty-aśuddhānām
anena niyamaḥ kṛtaḥ
guṇa-doṣa-vidhānena
saṅgānāṁ tyājanecchayā

sve sve—each in his own; *adhikāre*—position; *yā*—which; *niṣṭhā*—steady practice; *saḥ*—this; *guṇaḥ*—piety; *parikīrtitaḥ*—is thoroughly declared; *karmaṇām*—of fruitive activities; *jāti*—by nature; *aśuddhānām*—impure; *anena*—by this; *niyamaḥ*—disciplinary control; *kṛtaḥ*—is established; *guṇa*—of piety; *doṣa*—of sin; *vidhānena*—by the rule; *saṅgānām*—of association with different types of sense gratification; *tyājana*—of renunciation; *icchayā*—by the desire.

TRANSLATION

It is firmly declared that the steady adherence of transcendentalists to their respective spiritual positions constitutes real piety and that sin occurs when a transcendentalist neglects his prescribed duty. One who adopts this standard of piety and sin, sincerely desiring to give up all past association with sense gratification, is able to subdue materialistic activities, which are by nature impure.

PURPORT

Lord Kṛṣṇa here explains more clearly that those persons directly engaged in self-realization either through *jñāna-yoga* or *bhakti-yoga* need not give up their regular duties and perform special penances to atone for an accidental falldown. The actual purpose of Vedic literature is to direct one back home, back to Godhead, and not to encourage material sense gratification. Although the *Vedas* recommend innumerable rituals for promotion to heavenly planets and enjoyment of all varieties of material opulence, such materialistic rewards are meant only to engage materialistic people, who otherwise would become demoniac. To purify an accidental falldown, one who is engaged in transcendental realization need not adopt any procedure beyond his own spiritual practice. The words *saṅgānāṁ tyājanecchayā* indicate that one should not practice Kṛṣṇa consciousness or self-realization superficially or casually; rather, one should sincerely and earnestly desire freedom from one's past sinful life. Similarly, the words *yā niṣṭhā* indicate that one must constantly practice Kṛṣṇa consciousness. Thus, essential piety is to give up material sense gratification and engage in the loving service of the Lord. One who engages his senses, mind and intelligence twenty-four hours a day in the Lord's service is the most pious person, and the Lord personally protects such a surrendered soul.

TEXTS 27-28

जातश्रद्धो मत्कथासु निर्विण्णः सर्वकर्मसु ।
वेद दुःखात्मकान् कामान् परित्यागेऽप्यनीश्वरः ॥२७॥
ततो भजेत मां प्रीतः श्रद्धालुर्दृढनिश्चयः ।
जुषमाणश्च तान् कामान् दुःखोदर्कांश्च गर्हयन् ॥२८॥

jāta-śraddho mat-kathāsu
nirviṇṇaḥ sarva-karmasu
veda duḥkhātmakān kāmān
parityāge 'py anīśvaraḥ

tato bhajeta māṁ prītaḥ
śraddhālur dṛḍha-niścayaḥ
juṣamāṇaś ca tān kāmān
duḥkhodarkāṁś ca garhayan

jāta—one who has awakened; *śraddhaḥ*—faith; *mat-kathāsu*—in the descriptions of My glories; *nirviṇṇaḥ*—disgusted; *sarva*—with all; *karmasu*—activities; *veda*—he knows; *duḥkha*—misery; *ātmakān*—constituted of; *kāmān*—all types of sense gratification; *parityāge*—in the process of renouncing; *api*—although; *anīśvaraḥ*—unable; *tataḥ*—due to such faith; *bhajeta*—he should worship; *mām*—Me; *prītaḥ*—remaining happy; *śraddhāluḥ*—being faithful; *dṛḍha*—resolute; *niś-cayaḥ*—conviction; *juṣamāṇaḥ*—engaging in; *ca*—also; *tān*—that; *kāmān*—sense gratification; *duḥkha*—misery; *udarkān*—leading to; *ca*—also; *garhayan*—repenting of.

TRANSLATION

Having awakened faith in the narrations of My glories, being disgusted with all material activities, knowing that all sense gratification leads to misery, but still being unable to renounce all sense enjoyment, My devotee should remain happy and worship Me with great faith and conviction. Even though he is sometimes engaged in sense enjoyment, My devotee knows that all sense gratification leads to a miserable result, and he sincerely repents such activities.

PURPORT

The beginning stage of pure devotional service is described here by the Lord. A sincere devotee has practically seen that all material activities lead only to sense gratification and all sense gratification leads only to misery. Thus a devotee's sincere desire is to engage twenty-four hours a day in the loving service of Lord Kṛṣṇa without any personal motivation. The devotee sincerely desires to be established in his constitutional position as the Lord's eternal servitor, and he prays to the Lord to elevate him to this exalted position. The word *anīśvara* indicates that because of one's past sinful activities and bad habits one may not immediately be able to completely extinguish the enjoying spirit. The Lord here encourages such a devotee not to be overly depressed or morose but to remain enthusiastic and to go on with his loving service. The word *nirviṇṇa* indicates that a sincere devotee, although somewhat entangled in the remnants of sense gratification, is completely disgusted with material life and under no circumstances willingly commits sinful activities. In fact, he avoids every kind of materialistic activity. The word *kāmān* basically refers to sex attraction and its by-products in the form of children, home and so forth. Within the material world, the sex impulse is so strong that even a sincere candidate in the loving service of the Lord may sometimes be disturbed by sex attraction or by lingering sentiments for wife and children. A pure devotee certainly feels spiritual affection for all living entities, including the so-called wife and children, but he knows that material bodily attraction leads to no good, for it simply entangles one and one's so-called relatives in a miserable chain reaction of fruitive activities. The word *dṛḍha-niścaya* ("steadfast conviction") indicates that in any circumstance a devotee is completely determined to go on with his prescribed duties for Kṛṣṇa. Thus he thinks, "By my previous shameful life my heart is polluted with many illusory attachments. Personally I have no power to stop them. Only Lord Kṛṣṇa within my heart can remove such inauspicious contamination. But whether the Lord removes such attachments immediately or lets me go on being afflicted by them, I will never give up my devotional service to Him. Even if the Lord places millions of obstacles in my path, and even if because of my offenses I go to hell, I will never for a moment stop serving Lord Kṛṣṇa. I am not interested in mental speculation and fruitive activities; even if Lord Brahmā personally comes before me offering such engagements, I will not be even slightly interested. Although I am attached to material things I can see very clearly that they lead to no good because they simply give me trouble and disturb my devotional service to the Lord. Therefore, I sincerely repent my foolish attachments to so many material things, and I am patiently awaiting Lord Kṛṣṇa's mercy."

The word *prīta* indicates that a devotee feels exactly like the son or subject of the Supreme Personality of Godhead and is very attached to his relationship with the Lord. Therefore, although sincerely lamenting occasional lapses into sense enjoyment, he never gives up his enthusiasm to serve Lord Kṛṣṇa. If a devotee becomes too morose or discouraged in devotional service, he may drift into an impersonal consciousness or give up his devotional service to the Lord. Therefore, the Lord here advises that although one should sincerely repent, he should not become chronically depressed. One should understand that because of his past sins he must occasionally suffer disturbances from the material mind and senses, but one should not therefore become a devotee of detachment, as do the speculative philosophers. Although one may desire detachment to purify one's devotional service to the Lord, if one becomes more concerned with renunciation than with acting for the pleasure of Lord Kṛṣṇa, he is misunderstanding the position of loving devotional sevice. Faith in Lord Kṛṣṇa is so powerful that in due course of time it will automatically award detachment and perfect knowledge. If one gives up Lord Kṛṣṇa as the central object of one's worship and concentrates more on knowledge and detachment, one will become deviated from one's progress in going back home, back to Godhead. A sincere devotee of the Lord must be sincerely convinced that simply by the strength of devotional service and the mercy of Lord Kṛṣṇa he will achieve everything auspicious in life. One must believe that Lord Kṛṣṇa is all-merciful and that He is the only real goal of one's life. Such determined faith combined with a sincere desire to give up sense enjoyment will carry one past the obstacles of this world.

The words *jāta-śraddhaḥ mat-kathāsu* are most significant here. By faithful hearing of the mercy and glories of the Lord one will gradually be freed from all material desire and clearly see at every moment the utter frustration of sense gratification. Chanting the glories of the Lord with firm faith and conviction is a tremendously powerful spiritual process that enables one to give up all material association.

There is actually nothing inauspicious in the devotional service of the Lord. Occasional difficulties experienced by a devotee are due to his previous material activities. On the other hand, the endeavor for sense gratification is completely inauspicious. Thus sense gratification and devotional service are directly opposed to each other. In all circumstances one should therefore remain the Lord's sincere servant, always believing in His mercy. Then one will certainly go back home, back to Godhead.

TEXT 29

प्रोक्तेन भक्तियोगेन भजतो मासकृन्मुनेः ।
कामा हृदय्या नश्यन्ति सर्वे मयि हृदि स्थिते ॥२९॥

proktena bhakti-yogena
bhajato māsakṛn muneḥ
kāmā hṛdayyā naśyanti
sarve mayi hṛdi sthite

proktena—which has been described; *bhakti-yogena*—by devotional service; *bhajataḥ*—who is worshiping; *mā*—Me; *asakṛt*—constantly; *muneḥ*—of the sage; *kāmāḥ*—material desires; *hṛdayyāḥ*—in the heart;

naśyanti—are destroyed; *sarve*—all of them; *mayi*—in Me; *hṛdi*—when the heart; *sthite*—is firmly situated.

TRANSLATION

When an intelligent person engages constantly in worshiping Me through loving devotional service as described by Me, his heart becomes firmly situated in Me. Thus all material desires within the heart are destroyed.

PURPORT

The material senses are engaged in gratifying the concoctions of the mind, causing many types of material desires to become prominent, one after another. One who constantly engages in the devotional service of the Lord by hearing and chanting the Lord's transcendental glories with firm faith gets relief from the harassment of material desires. By serving the Lord one becomes strengthened in the conviction that Śrī Kṛṣṇa is the only actual enjoyer and all others are meant to share the Lord's pleasure through devotional service. A devotee of the Lord situates Śrī Kṛṣṇa on a beautiful throne within his heart and there offers the Lord constant service. Just as the rising sun gradually eliminates all trace of darkness, the Lord's presence within the heart causes all material desires there to weaken and eventually disappear. The words *mayi hṛdi sthite* ("when the heart is situated in Me") indicate that an advanced devotee sees Lord Kṛṣṇa not only within his own heart but within the hearts of all living creatures. Thus a sincere devotee who chants and hears the glories of Śrī Kṛṣṇa should not be discouraged by the remnants of material desires within the heart. He should faithfully wait for the devotional process to naturally purify the heart of all contamination.

TEXT 30

भिद्यते हृदयग्रन्थिश्छिद्यन्ते सर्वसंशयाः ।
क्षीयन्ते चास्य कर्माणि मयि दृष्टेऽखिलात्मनि ॥३०॥

bhidyate hṛdaya-granthiś
chidyante sarva-saṁśayāḥ
kṣīyante cāsya karmāṇi
mayi dṛṣṭe 'khilātmani

bhidyate—pierced; *hṛdaya*—heart; *granthiḥ*—knots; *chidyante*—cut to pieces; *sarva*—all; *saṁśayāḥ*—misgivings; *kṣīyante*—terminated; *ca*—and; *asya*—his; *karmāṇi*—chain of fruitive actions; *mayi*—when I; *dṛṣṭe*—am seen; *akhila-ātmani*—as the Supreme Personality of Godhead.

TRANSLATION

The knot in the heart is pierced, all misgivings are cut to pieces and the chain of fruitive actions is terminated when I am seen as the Supreme Personality of Godhead.

PURPORT

Hṛdaya-granthi indicates that one's heart is bound to illusion by false identification with the material body. One thus becomes absorbed in material sex pleasure, dreaming of innumerable combinations of male and female bodies. A person intoxicated by sex attraction cannot understand that the Supreme Personality of Godhead is the reservoir of all pleasure and the supreme enjoyer. When a devotee achieves steadiness in devotional service, feeling transcendental pleasure at every moment in the execution of his loving service to the Lord, the knot of false identification is pierced and all his misgivings are cut to pieces. In illusion we imagine that the living entity cannot be fully satisfied without material sense gratification and speculative doubting of the Absolute Truth. Materialistic persons consider sense enjoyment and speculative doubting to be essential for civilized life. A pure devotee, however, realizes that Lord Kṛṣṇa is an unlimited ocean of happiness and the personification of all knowledge. This realization of Lord Kṛṣṇa completely eradicates the twin tendencies of sense gratification and mental speculation. Thus the chain of fruitive activities, or *karma,* automatically collapses, just as a fire collapses and goes out when its fuel is removed.

Advanced devotional service automatically awards one liberation from material bondage, as confirmed by Lord Kapila: *jarayaty āśu yā kośaṁ nigīrṇam analo yathā.* "*Bhakti,* devotional service, dissolves the subtle body of the living entity without separate effort, just as fire in the stomach digests all that we eat." (*Bhāg.* 3.25.33) Śrīla Prabhupāda states in his purport to this verse, "A devotee does not have to try separately to attain liberation. That very service to the Supreme Personality of Godhead is the process of liberation, because to engage oneself in the service of the Lord is to liberate oneself from material entanglement. Śrī Bilvamaṅgala Ṭhākura explained this position very nicely. He said, 'If I have unflinching devotion unto the lotus feet of the Supreme Lord, then *mukti*, or liberation, serves me as my maidservant. *Mukti* the maidservant is always ready to do whatever I ask.' For a devotee, liberation is no problem at all. Liberation takes place without separate endeavor."

TEXT 31

तस्मान्मद्भक्तियुक्तस्य योगिनो वै मदात्मनः ।
न ज्ञानं न च वैराग्यं प्रायः श्रेयो भवेदिह ॥३१॥

tasmān mad-bhakti-yuktasya
yogino vai mad-ātmanaḥ
na jñānaṁ na ca vairāgyaṁ
prāyaḥ śreyo bhaved iha

tasmāt—therefore; *mat-bhakti-yuktasya*—of one who is engaged in My loving service; *yoginaḥ*—of a devotee; *vai*—certainly; *mat-ātmanaḥ*—whose mind is fixed in Me; *na*—not; *jñānam*—the cultivation of knowledge; *na*—nor; *ca*—also; *vairāgyam*—the cultivation of renunciation; *prāyaḥ*—generally; *śreyaḥ*—the means of achieving perfection; *bhavet*—may be; *iha*—in this world.

TRANSLATION

Therefore, for a devotee engaged in My loving service, with mind fixed in Me, the cultivation of knowledge and renunciation is generally not the means of achieving the highest perfection within this world.

PURPORT

A surrendered devotee of Lord Kṛṣṇa does not seek perfection through the cultivation of knowledge and renunciation outside the loving service of the Lord. Devotional service to Lord Kṛṣṇa, being itself the supreme transcendental process, never depends upon the secondary methods involving the cultivation of knowledge and renunciation. By chanting and hearing the glories of the Personality of Godhead a devotee automatically realizes all knowledge, and as the devotee's attachment to the Lord increases, he automatically gives up attachment for the inferior material nature. The Lord has explicitly declared in the previous verses that a devotee should not try to solve his lingering problems by means other than devotional service. Although a sincere devotee has surrendered heart and soul in loving service to the Lord, there may be lingering material attachments that prevent the devotee from perfectly realizing transcendental knowledge. Devotional service, however, will automatically eradicate such lingering attachments in due course of time. If the devotee tries to purify himself through cultivation of knowledge and renunciation, which fall outside the scope of devotional service, there is danger of his being deviated from the Lord's lotus feet and falling down completely from the transcendental path. One who endeavors for purification outside the loving service of the Lord has not actually understood the transcendental potency of *bhakti-yoga* and does not appreciate the extent of Lord Kṛṣṇa's mercy.

Within this world one's heart is bound by sex attraction, which disturbs one's meditation on the lotus feet of Lord Kṛṣṇa. Intoxicated by contact with women, the conditioned soul becomes artificially proud and forgets his loving servitude to the Lord. Through determined cultivation of knowledge and detachment, a conditioned soul may try to purify himself without the mercy of Lord Kṛṣṇa, but such false pride is to be given up, just as one must give up the false pride of material attraction. When pure devotional service to the Lord is available to a conditioned soul, attraction to other processes is certainly a deviation in his devotional career. Material desire stubbornly residing within the heart can be vanquished by taking full shelter of the Supreme Personality of Godhead. Without false confidence in one's own cultivation of knowledge and renunciation, one should depend fully on the mercy of Lord Kṛṣṇa and at the same time strictly follow the rules and regulations of *bhakti-yoga*, as instructed by the Lord Himself.

TEXTS 32-33

यत् कर्मभिर्यत्तपसा ज्ञानवैराग्यतश्च यत् ।
योगेन दानधर्मेण श्रेयोभिरितरैरपि ॥३२॥

सर्वं मद्भक्तियोगेन मद्भक्तो लभतेऽञ्जसा ।
स्वर्गापवर्गं मद्धाम कथञ्चिद् यदि वाञ्छति ॥३३॥

yat karmabhir yat tapasā
jñāna-vairāgyataś ca yat
yogena dāna-dharmeṇa
śreyobhir itarair api

sarvaṁ mad-bhakti-yogena
mad-bhakto labhate 'ñjasā
svargāpavargaṁ mad-dhāma
kathañcid yadi vāñchati

yat—that which is obtained; *karmabhiḥ*—by fruitive activities; *yat*—that which; *tapasā*—by penance; *jñāna*—by cultivation of knowledge; *vairāgyataḥ*—by detachment; *ca*—also; *yat*—that which is achieved; *yogena*—by the mystic *yoga* system; *dāna*—by charity; *dharmeṇa*—by religious duties; *śreyobhiḥ*—by processes for making life auspicious; *itaraiḥ*—by others; *api*—indeed; *sarvam*—all; *mat-bhakti-yogena*—by loving service unto Me; *mat-bhaktaḥ*—My devotee; *labhate*—achieves; *añjasā*—easily; *svarga*—promotion to heaven; *apavargam*—liberation from all misery; *mat-dhāma*—residence in My abode; *kathañcit*—somehow or other; *yadi*—if; *vāñchati*—he desires.

TRANSLATION

Everything that can be achieved by fruitive activities, penance, knowledge, detachment, mystic *yoga*, charity, religious duties and all other means of perfecting life is easily achieved by My devotee through loving service unto Me. If somehow or other My devotee desires promotion to heaven, liberation, or residence in My abode, he easily achieves such benedictions.

PURPORT

Lord Kṛṣṇa here reveals the transcendental glories of devotional service to the Lord. Although pure devotees are desireless, desiring only the Lord's service, sometimes a great devotee may desire the Lord's benediction to facilitate his loving service. In the Sixth Canto of the

Bhāgavatam we find that Śrī Citraketu, a great devotee of the Lord, desired promotion to heaven so that accompanied by the most attractive ladies of the Vidyādhara planet he could beautifully chant the glories of the Lord. Similarly, Śrī Śukadeva Gosvāmī, the great narrator of *Śrīmad-Bhāgavatam*, desiring to avoid entanglement in the illusory potency of the Lord, would not come out of his mother's womb. In other words, Śukadeva Gosvāmī desired *apavargam,* or liberation from *māyā,* so that his devotional service would not be disturbed. Lord Kṛṣṇa personally sent the illusory energy far away so that Śukadeva Gosvāmī would come out of his mother's womb. Because of intense loving desire to serve the lotus feet of the Lord, a devotee may also desire promotion to the spiritual world.

According to Śrīla Viśvanātha Cakravartī Ṭhākura, a devotee, having given up the independent cultivation of knowledge and detachment, may have firm faith in the devotional service of the Lord and yet remain slightly attached to the fruits of such activities. By expert fruitive activities one gains residence in material heaven, and by cultivation of detachment one is relieved of all bodily distress. If Lord Kṛṣṇa detects within a devotee's heart the desire for such benedictions, the Lord can easily award them to His devotee.

The word *itaraiḥ* in this verse indicates visiting holy places, accepting religious vows and so forth. Several auspicious processes of elevation are mentioned in the verse preceding this, but all the auspicious results of these processes are easily achieved by loving service to the Lord. Thus all devotees of the Lord, in whatever stage of advancement, should dedicate their energy exclusively to the Lord's service, as affirmed in the Second Canto of *Śrīmad-Bhāgavatam* by Śrī Śukadeva Gosvāmī:

akāmaḥ sarva-kāmo vā
mokṣa-kāma udāra-dhīḥ
tīvreṇa bhakti-yogena
yajeta puruṣaṁ param

"A person who has broader intelligence, whether he be full of all material desire, without any material desire or desiring liberation, must by all means worship the supreme whole, the Personality of Godhead." (*Bhāg*. 2.3.10)

TEXT 34

न किञ्चित् साधवो धीरा भक्ता ह्येकान्तिनो मम ।
वाञ्छन्त्यपि मया दत्तं कैवल्यमपुनर्भवम् ॥३४॥

na kiñcit sādhavo dhīrā
bhaktā hy ekāntino mama
vāñchanty api mayā dattaṁ
kaivalyam apunar-bhavam

na—never; *kiñcit*—anything; *sādhavaḥ*—saintly persons; *dhīrāḥ*—with deep intelligence; *bhaktāḥ*—devotees; *hi*—certainly; *ekāntinaḥ*—completely dedicated; *mama*—unto Me; *vāñchanti*—desire; *api*—indeed; *mayā*—by Me; *dattam*—given; *kaivalyam*—liberation; *apunaḥ-bhavam*—freedom from birth and death.

TRANSLATION

Because My devotees possess saintly behavior and deep intelligence they completely dedicate themselves to Me and do not desire anything besides Me. Indeed, even if I offer them liberation from birth and death, they do not accept it.

PURPORT

The words *ekāntino mama* indicate that the pure devotees of the Lord, being saintly and most intelligent, dedicate themselves exclusively to the devotional service of the Personality of Godhead. Even when the Lord offers them personal liberation from birth and death, the devotees will not accept it. A pure devotee automatically gains an eternal life of bliss and knowledge in the Lord's personal abode and thus considers mere liberation without the loving service of the Lord to be most abominable. One who chants Lord Kṛṣṇa's holy name or superficially serves the Lord with the motive of achieving impersonal liberation or material sense gratification cannot be considered a transcendental devotee of the Lord. As long as one desires mundane religiosity, economic development, sense gratification or liberation, one cannot achieve the platform of *samādhi*, or perfect self-realization. Every living entity is actually the eternal servant of Lord Kṛṣṇa and is constitutionally meant to engage in the loving service of the Lord without personal desire. This pure and supreme status of life is described in this verse by the Lord Himself.

TEXT 35

नैरपेक्ष्यं परं प्राहुर्निःश्रेयसमनल्पकम् ।
तस्मान्निराशिषो भक्तिर्निरपेक्षस्य मे भवेत् ॥३५॥

nairapekṣyaṁ paraṁ prāhur
niḥśreyasam analpakam
tasmān nirāśiṣo bhaktir
nirapekṣasya me bhavet

nairapekṣyam—not desiring anything except devotional sevice; *param*—the best; *prāhuḥ*—it is said; *niḥśreyasam*—highest stage of liberation; *analpakam*—great; *tasmāt*—therefore; *nirāśiṣaḥ*—of one who does not seek personal rewards; *bhaktiḥ*—loving devotional service; *nirapekṣasya*—of one who only sees Me; *me*—unto Me; *bhavet*—may arise.

TRANSLATION

It is said that complete detachment is the highest stage of freedom. Therefore, one who has no personal desire and does not pursue personal rewards can achieve loving devotional service unto Me.

PURPORT

As stated in *Śrīmad-Bhāgavatam* (2.3.10),

akāmaḥ sarva-kāmo vā
mokṣa-kāma udāra-dhīḥ
tīvreṇa bhakti-yogena
yajeta puruṣaṁ param

"A person who has broader intelligence, whether he be full of all material desire, without any material desire or desiring liberation, must by all means worship the supreme whole, the Personality of Godhead." In this statement by Śukadeva Gosvāmī, the words *tīvreṇa bhakti-yogena* are very significant. Śrīla Prabhupāda remarks in this regard, "As the unmixed sun ray is very forceful and is therefore called *tīvra*, similarly, unmixed *bhakti-yoga* of hearing, chanting, etc., may be performed by one and all regardless of inner motive." Undoubtedly, in this age of Kali people are generally very fallen and polluted by material lust, greed, anger, lamentation and so forth. In this age most people are *sarva-kāma*, or full of material desires. Still we must understand that simply by taking shelter of Lord Kṛṣṇa we will achieve everything in life. The living entity should not engage in any process except the loving service of the Lord. One must accept that Lord Kṛṣṇa is the reservoir of all pleasure and that only Lord Kṛṣṇa within our heart can fulfill our real desire. This simple faith that one will achieve everything by approaching Lord Kṛṣṇa is the essence of all knowledge and carries even a fallen person over the painful hurdles of this difficult age.

TEXT 36

न मय्येकान्तभक्तानां गुणदोषोद्भवा गुणाः ।
साधूनां समचित्तानां बुद्धेः परमुपेयुषाम् ॥३६॥

na mayy ekānta-bhaktānāṁ
guṇa-doṣodbhavā guṇāḥ
sādhūnāṁ sama-cittānāṁ
buddheḥ param upeyuṣām

na—not; *mayi*—in Me; *eka-anta*—unalloyed; *bhaktānām*—of the devotees; *guṇa*—recommended as good; *doṣa*—forbidden as unfavorable; *udbhavāḥ*—arising from such things; *guṇāḥ*—piety and sin; *sādhūnām*—of those who are free from material hankering; *sama-cittānām*—who maintain steady spiritual consciousness in all circumstances; *buddheḥ*—that which can be conceived by material intelligence; *param*—beyond; *upeyuṣām*—of those who have achieved.

TRANSLATION

Material piety and sin, which arise from the good and evil of this world, cannot exist within My unalloyed devotees, who, being free from material hankering, maintain steady spiritual consciousness in all circumstances. Indeed, such devotees have

achieved Me, the Supreme Lord, who am beyond anything that can be conceived by material intelligence.

PURPORT

The words *buddheḥ param* indicate that the material modes of nature cannot be found within a pure devotee absorbed in the transcendental qualities of the Lord. In the Second Chapter of *Bhagavad-gītā,* Lord Kṛṣṇa clearly explains that a pure devotee is recognized by complete detachment from personal desire; therefore, a pure devotee constantly engaged in selfless service to Lord Kṛṣṇa may not always observe the innumerable details of Vedic rituals and regulations. Such occasional negligence is not to be considered a transgression. Similarly, observance of ordinary material piety does not constitute the ultimate qualification of a soul surrendered to God. Love of Kṛṣṇa and absolute surrender to the Lord's will raise one immediately to the transcendental platform, where activities performed on the Lord's behalf are absolute, being an expression of God's will. Ordinary materialistic persons sometimes falsely claim this exalted status for their whimsical, immoral activities and cause a great disturbance in society. However, just as an ordinary person should not falsely claim the executive privileges of the personal assistants of a national leader, similarly, an ordinary conditioned soul may not foolishly claim that his immoral, whimsical or speculative activities are sheltered by divine right, being the will of God. One must actually be a pure devotee of the Lord, empowered by the Lord Himself and completely surrendered to the will of the Lord, before one may be accepted as transcendental to ordinary piety and sin.

There are cases of highly elevated devotees who momentarily fell down from the saintly platform of devotional service. The Lord instructs in *Bhagavad-gītā* (9.30),

api cet su-durācāro
bhajate mām ananya-bhāk
sādhur eva sa mantavyaḥ
samyag vyavasito hi saḥ

A momentary falldown by a sincere devotee of the Lord cannot change the Lord's feelings toward such a person. Even an ordinary father or mother quickly excuses a momentary transgression by their child. Just as children and parents enjoy mutual love, the Lord's surrendered servants enjoy a loving relationship with the Lord. An unpremeditated, accidental falldown is quickly excused by the Lord, and all members of society must share in the Lord's own feelings, excusing such a sincere devotee. An advanced devotee should not be branded as materialistic or sinful because of accidental falldown. A devotee immediately returns to the platform of saintly service and begs the Lord's forgiveness. However, one who permanently remains in a fallen condition can no longer be accepted as a highly elevated devotee of the Lord.

TEXT 37

एवमेतान् मया दिष्टाननुतिष्ठन्ति मे पथः ।
क्षेमं विन्दन्ति मत्स्थानं यद् ब्रह्म परमं विदुः ॥३७॥

evam etān mayā diṣṭān
anutiṣṭhanti me pathaḥ
kṣemaṁ vindanti mat-sthānaṁ
yad brahma paramaṁ viduḥ

evam—thus; *etān*—these; *mayā*—by Me; *diṣṭān*—instructed; *anutiṣṭhanti*—those who follow; *me*—Me; *pathaḥ*—the means of achieving; *kṣemam*—freedom from illusion; *vindanti*—they achieve; *mat-sthānam*—My personal abode; *yat*—that which; *brahma paramam*—the Absolute Truth; *viduḥ*—they directly know.

TRANSLATION

Those who seriously follow the methods of achieving Me that I have personally taught attain freedom from illusion, and upon reaching My personal abode at last perfectly understand the Absolute Truth.

Thus end the purports of the humble servant of His Divine Grace A. C. Bhaktivedanta Swami Prabhupāda to the Eleventh Canto, Twentieth Chapter, of the Śrīmad-Bhāgavatam, *entitled "Pure Devotional Service Surpasses Knowledge and Detachment."*

CHAPTER TWENTY-ONE

Lord Kṛṣṇa's Explanation of the Vedic Path

There are persons who are unfit for all three of the forms of *yoga*—*karma, jñāna* and *bhakti*. They are inimical to Lord Kṛṣṇa, attached to sense gratification, and are dominated by fruitive activities aimed at fulfillment of material desires. This chapter describes their faults in terms of place, time, substance and beneficiary of actions.

For those who are perfect in knowledge and devotion to the Lord, there are no materially good qualities or faults. But for a candidate endeavoring on the platform of *karma* to achieve cessation of material life, execution of regular and special fruitive duties is good and the failure to execute such is evil. That which counteracts sinful reaction is also good for him.

For one on the platform of knowledge in the pure mode of goodness and for one on the platform of devotion, the proper actions are, respectively, cultivation of knowledge and practice of devotional service consisting of hearing, chanting and so forth. For both, everything detrimental to their proper actions is bad. But for persons who are not candidates for transcendental advancement or who are not perfected souls, namely those who are completely inimical to spiritual life and are devoted exclusively to fruitive work for fulfillment of lusty desires, there are numerous considerations of purity and impurity and auspiciousness and inauspiciousness. These are to be made in terms of one's body, the place of activity, the time, the objects utilized, the performer, the *mantras* chanted and the particular activity.

In actuality, virtue and fault are not absolute but are relative to one's particular platform of advancement. Remaining fixed in the type of discrimination suitable to one's level of advancement is good, and anything else is bad. This is the basic understanding of virtue and fault. Even among objects belonging to the same category, there are different considerations of their purity or impurity in relation to performance of religious duties, worldly transactions, and the maintenance of one's life. These distinctions are described in various scriptures.

The doctrine of *varṇāśrama* codifies precepts of bodily purity and impurity. With respect to place, purity and impurity are distinguished by such facts as the presence of black deer. In connection with time, there are distinctions of purity and impurity either in terms of the time itself or in terms of its specific relation with various objects. In connection with physical substances, distinctions of purity and impurity are made in terms of sanctification of objects and words and by such activities as bathing, giving charity, performing austere penances and remembering the Supreme Lord. There are also distinctions of the purity and impurity of the performers of actions. When one's knowledge of *mantras* is received from the lips of the bona fide spiritual master, one's *mantra* is considered pure, and one's work is purified by offering it unto the Supreme Personality of Godhead. If the six factors of place, time and so forth are purified, then there is *dharma,* or virtue, but otherwise there is *adharma,* or fault.

Ultimately, there is no substantial basis in distinctions of virtue and fault, because they transform according to place, time, beneficiary and so on. In regard to the execution of prescribed duties for sense gratification, the actual intent of all the scriptures is the subduing of materialistic propensities; such is the actual principle of religion that destroys sorrow, confusion and fear and bestows all good fortune. Work performed for sense gratification is not actually beneficial. The descriptions of such fruitive benefits offered in various *phala-śrutis* are actually meant to help one gradually cultivate a taste for the highest benefit. But persons of inferior intelligence take the flowery benedictory verses of the scriptures to be the actual purport of the *Vedas;* this opinion, however, is never held by those in factual knowledge of the truth of the *Vedas.* Persons whose minds are agitated by the flowery words of the *Vedas* have no attraction for hearing topics about Lord Hari. It should be understood that there is no inner purport to the *Vedas* apart from the original Personality of Godhead. The *Vedas* focus exclusively upon the Supreme Absolute Truth, the Personality of Godhead. Because this material world is simply the illusory energy of the Supreme Lord, it is by refuting material existence that one gains disassociation from matter.

TEXT 1

श्रीभगवानुवाच
य एतान् मत्पथो हित्वा भक्तिज्ञानक्रियात्मकान् ।
क्षुद्रान् कामांश्चलैः प्राणैर्जुषन्तः संसरन्ति ते ॥ १ ॥

śrī-bhagavān uvāca
ya etān mat-patho hitvā
bhakti-jñāna-kriyātmakān
kṣudrān kāmāṁś calaiḥ prāṇair
juṣantaḥ saṁsaranti te

śrī-bhagavān uvāca—the Supreme Personality of Godhead said; *ye*—those who; *etān*—these; *mat-pathaḥ*—means for achieving Me; *hitvā*—giving up; *bhakti*—devotional service; *jñāna*—analytic philosophy; *kriyā*—regulated work; *ātmakān*—consisting of; *kṣudrān*—insignificant; *kāmān*—sense gratification; *calaiḥ*—by the flickering; *prāṇaiḥ*—senses; *juṣantaḥ*—cultivating; *saṁsaranti*—undergo material existence; *te*—they.

TRANSLATION

The Supreme Personality of Godhead said: Those who give up the methods for achieving Me, which consist of devotional service, analytic philosophy and regulated execution of prescribed duties, and instead, being moved by the material senses, cultivate insignificant sense gratification, certainly undergo the continual cycle of material existence.

PURPORT

As clearly explained by Lord Kṛṣṇa in the previous chapters, philosophical analysis and also the performance of prescribed duties are ultimately meant for achieving Kṛṣṇa consciousness, or pure love of God. Devotional service, based on hearing and chanting the glories of the Lord, directly engages the conditioned soul in the Lord's loving service and thus is the most efficient means of achieving the Lord. All three processes, however, share a common goal, Kṛṣṇa consciousness. Now the Lord describes those who, being completely absorbed in material sense gratification, do not adopt any authorized means to achieve the Lord's mercy. Currently, hundreds of millions of unfortunate human beings fit squarely into this category and, as described here, perpetually suffer the bondage of material existence.

TEXT 2

स्वे स्वेऽधिकारे या निष्ठा स गुणः परिकीर्तितः ।
विपर्ययस्तु दोषः स्यादुभयोरेष निश्चयः ॥ २ ॥

sve sve 'dhikāre yā niṣṭhā
sa guṇaḥ parikīrtitaḥ
viparyayas tu doṣaḥ syād
ubhayor eṣa niścayaḥ

sve sve—each in his own; *adhikāre*—position; *yā*—such; *niṣṭhā*—steadiness; *saḥ*—this; *guṇaḥ*—piety; *parikīrtitaḥ*—is declared to be; *viparyayaḥ*—the opposite; *tu*—indeed; *doṣaḥ*—impiety; *syāt*—is; *ubhayoḥ*—of the two; *eṣaḥ*—this; *niścayaḥ*—the definite conclusion.

TRANSLATION

Steadiness in one's own position is declared to be actual piety, whereas deviation from one's position is considered impiety. In this way the two are definitely ascertained.

PURPORT

In the previous verse Lord Kṛṣṇa explained that the path of spiritual progress begins with working without fruitive desires, advances to the stage of realized spiritual knowledge, and culminates in direct engagement in the devotional service of the Lord. Here the Lord emphasizes that a conditioned soul should not artificially disrupt the natural evolution of his Kṛṣṇa consciousness by deviating from those duties prescribed by the Lord Himself. In the lower stages of human life one is entangled in false identification with the gross material body and desires to execute material fruitive activities based on society, friendship and love. When such materialistic activities are offered in sacrifice to the Supreme Lord, one becomes situated in *karma-yoga*. By regulated sacrifice one gradually gives up the gross bodily concept of life and advances to the stage of realization of spiritual knowledge, whereby one understands oneself to be an eternal spirit soul completely different from the material body and mind. Feeling relief from the pangs of materialism one becomes very attached to one's spiritual knowledge, and thus one is situated in the stage of *jñāna-yoga*. As the candidate further advances on the spiritual path, he understands himself to be part and parcel of the Supreme Soul, the Personality of Godhead, Lord Kṛṣṇa. He then sees that his conditional life as well as his spiritual knowledge was obtained from the Personality of Godhead, who awards the results of all types of activities, both pious and sinful. By directly engaging in the loving service of the Supreme Lord and understanding oneself to be the Lord's eternal servant, one's attachment evolves into pure love of Godhead. Thus one first gives up the lower stage of attachment to the material body and then subsequently gives up attachment to cultivation of spiritual knowledge. This relieves one of material life. Finally one recognizes the Lord Himself as the resting place of one's eternal love and fully surrenders to God in full Kṛṣṇa consciousness.

Lord Kṛṣṇa explains in this verse that one who is still attached to the material body and mind cannot artificially give up the prescribed duties of *karma-yoga*. In the same way, one who is a spiritual neophyte, just beginning to realize the illusion of material life, should not artificially try to think of the Lord's intimate pastimes twenty-four hours a day, imitating the stage of *prema-bhakti*. Rather, he should cultivate analytic knowledge of the material world, by which one gives up attachment to the material body and mind. In *Śrīmad-Bhāgavatam* we find many analytic descriptions of the material world, and they can free the conditioned soul from false identification with matter. One who has achieved the perfect stage of love of Godhead, however, being freed from all gross and subtle attachments to the material world, may give up the lower stages of *karma-yoga* and *jñāna-yoga* and engage directly in the Lord's loving service.

In Chapter Nineteen, verse 45, Lord Kṛṣṇa states, *guṇa-doṣa-dṛśir doṣo guṇas tūbhaya-varjitaḥ*. One should not see material good and evil within a devotee of the Lord. Indeed, one becomes pious by giving up such mundane conceptions. Śrīla Viśvanātha Cakravartī Ṭhākura points out that occasionally a neophyte devotee may be polluted by association with those enthusiastically executing fruitive activities and mental speculation. Such a devotee's religious activities may be affected by mundane tendencies. Similarly, an ordinary person who observes the exalted status of a pure devotee sometimes externally imitates the devotee's activities, considering himself to be on the same exalted platform of pure devotional service. These imperfect practitioners of *bhakti-yoga* are not exempt from criticism, since their fruitive activities, mental speculation and false prestige are material intrusions in the pure loving service of the Lord. A pure devotee engaged exclusively in the Lord's service should not be criticized, but a devotee whose devotional service is mixed with material qualities may be corrected so that he can rise to the platform of pure devotional service. Innocent persons should not be misled by the mixed devotional service of those not engaged exclusively in the *bhakti-yoga* system, but those unable to fully engage in Kṛṣṇa consciousness should nevertheless not give up their regular prescribed duties, declaring them to be illusion. For example, one unable to fully engage in pure Kṛṣṇa consciousness should not give up his family, considering it an illusion, for by doing so he will fall into illicit sex life. Material piety and analytic knowledge of the material world must therefore be cultivated until one comes to the stage of directly practicing Kṛṣṇa consciousness.

TEXT 3

शुद्ध्यशुद्धी विधीयेते समानेष्वपि वस्तुषु ।
द्रव्यस्य विचिकित्सार्थं गुणदोषौ शुभाशुभौ ।
धर्मार्थं व्यवहारार्थं यात्रार्थमिति चानघ ॥ ३ ॥

śuddhy-aśuddhī vidhīyete
samāneṣv api vastuṣu
dravyasya vicikitsārthaṁ
guṇa-doṣau śubhāśubhau
dharmārthaṁ vyavahārārthaṁ
yātrārtham iti cānagha

śuddhi—purity; *aśuddhī*—and impurity; *vidhīyete*—are established; *samāneṣu*—of the same category; *api*—indeed; *vastuṣu*—among objects; *dravyasya*—of a particular object; *vicikitsā*—evaluation; *artham*—for the purpose of; *guṇa-doṣau*—good and bad qualities; *śubha-aśubhau*—auspicious and inauspicious; *dharma-artham*—for the purpose of religious activities; *vyavahāra-artham*—for the purpose of ordinary dealings; *yātrā-artham*—for one's physical survival; *iti*—thus; *ca*—also; *anagha*—O sinless one.

TRANSLATION

O sinless Uddhava, in order to understand what is proper in life one must evaluate a given object within its particular category. Thus, in analyzing religious principles one must consider purity and impurity. Similarly, in one's ordinary dealings one must distinguish between good and bad, and to insure one's physical survival one must recognize that which is auspicious and inauspicious.

PURPORT

In religious activities, ordinary dealings and personal survival one cannot avoid value judgments. Morality and religion are perennial necessities in civilized society; therefore distinctions between purity and impurity, piety and impiety, morality and immorality must somehow be ascertained. Similarly, in our ordinary, worldly activities we distinguish between palatable and tasteless food, good and bad business, high-class and low-class residences, good and bad friends, and so forth. And to insure our physical health and survival, we must constantly distinguish between what is safe and unsafe, healthy and unhealthy, profitable and unprofitable. Even a learned person must constantly distinguish between good and bad within the material world, but at the same time he must understand the transcendental position of Kṛṣṇa consciousness. Despite one's careful calculation of that which is materially healthy and unhealthy, the physical body will collapse and die. Despite careful scrutiny of the socially favorable and unfavorable, one's entire social milieu will vanish with the passing of time. In the same way, great religions arise and disappear in the course of history. Thus mere religiosity, social and financial expertise or physical fitness cannot award the actual perfection of life. There is a transcendental good beyond the relative good of the material world. Any sane person accepts the practical and immediate necessity of material discrimination; yet one must come ultimately to the transcendental stage of Kṛṣṇa consciousness, where life is eternal, full of bliss and knowledge. Lord Kṛṣṇa, in His elaborate teachings to Śrī Uddhava, is gradually clarifying the transcendental position of Kṛṣṇa consciousness beyond the endless variety of material good and evil.

TEXT 4

दर्शितोऽयं मयाचारो धर्ममुद्वहतां धुरम् ॥ ४ ॥

darśito 'yaṁ mayācāro
dharmam udvahatāṁ dhuram

darśitaḥ—revealed; *ayam*—this; *mayā*—by Me; *ācāraḥ*—way of life; *dharmam*—religious principles; *udvahatām*—for those who are bearing; *dhuram*—the burden.

TRANSLATION

I have revealed this way of life for those bearing the burden of mundane religious principles.

PURPORT

Ordinary religious principles, prescribing innumerable rules, regulations and prohibitions, are undoubtedly a great burden for those bereft of Kṛṣṇa consciousness. In the First Canto of *Śrīmad-Bhāgavatam* (1.1.11) it is stated, *bhūrīṇi bhūri-karmāṇi śrotavyāni vibhāgaśaḥ:* there are countless religious scriptures in the world prescribing countless religious duties. The authorized scriptures are those spoken by the Lord Himself or His representatives, as stated in this verse. In the last chapter of *Bhagavad-gītā* (18.66) Lord Kṛṣṇa states, *sarva-dharmān parityajya mām ekaṁ śaraṇaṁ vraja:* one should give up the troublesome burden of mundane piety and directly take to the loving service of the Lord, in which everything is simplified. Lord Kṛṣṇa also states in *Bhagavad-gītā* (9.2), *su-sukhaṁ kartum avyayam:* the *bhakti-yoga* process, which depends completely upon the mercy of the Lord, is very joyful and easily performed. Similarly, Locana dāsa Ṭhākura sings,

parama karuṇa, pahuṅ dui jana,
nitāi-gauracandra
saba avatāra-, sāra-śiromaṇi,
kevala ānanda-kāṇḍa

Śrī Caitanya Mahāprabhu, who is Lord Kṛṣṇa Himself, appeared five hundred years ago to distribute the sublime method of chanting the holy names of the Lord. In this way, rather than bearing the burden of artificial austerity, one can directly take to the Lord's service, cleansing one's heart and immediately experiencing transcendental bliss. Those who have taken to Caitanya Mahāprabhu's movement follow four basic principles: no illicit sex, no eating of meat, fish or eggs, no intoxication and no gambling. They rise early in the morning, chant Hare Kṛṣṇa and spend the day happily engaged in the Lord's service. Those who follow the ritualistic *karma-kāṇḍa* section of the *Vedas*, however, are burdened with innumerable regulations, rituals and ceremonies, which must be personally performed by the worshipers or performed on their behalf by qualified *brāhmaṇas*. At any moment there is danger of discrepancy resulting in the total loss of their accumulated piety. Similarly, those on the philosophical path must painstakingly define, refine and adjust philosophical categories, a process that generally ends in confusion and hopelessness. The practitioners of mystic *yoga* undergo grueling penances, subjecting themselves to severe heat and cold, near starvation and so on. All such materialistic persons have personal desires to fulfill, whereas the devotees of the Lord, who desire the Lord's pleasure, simply depend upon the Lord's mercy and go back home, back to Godhead. In the previous verse the Lord mentioned that in the material world there are endless distinctions and value judgments to be made in the course of one's life. A devotee, however, sees Kṛṣṇa within everything and everything within Kṛṣṇa, remaining humble, simple and blissful in the Lord's service. He does not perform elaborate religious ceremonies, nor does he become antisocial or immoral. The devotee simply chants the holy name of Kṛṣṇa and easily achieves the highest perfection of life. Ordinary persons endeavor for bodily maintenance, but a devotee is automatically maintained by the Lord's mercy. A devotee's ordinary dealings and religious activities are also all dedicated to the Personality of Godhead; thus there is nothing but Kṛṣṇa in a devotee's life. Kṛṣṇa gives all protection and maintenance, and the devotee gives everything to Kṛṣṇa. This natural liberated situation is called Kṛṣṇa consciousness. It is the ultimate absolute good, as explained by the Lord throughout this canto.

TEXT 5

भूम्यम्ब्वग्न्यनिलाकाशा भूतानां पञ्च धातवः ।
आब्रह्मस्थावरादीनां शारीरा आत्मसंयुताः ॥ ५ ॥

bhūmy-ambv-agny-anilākāśā
bhūtānāṁ pañca-dhātavaḥ
ā-brahma-sthāvarādīnāṁ
śārīrā ātma-saṁyutāḥ

bhūmi—earth; *ambu*—water; *agni*—fire; *anila*—air; *ākāśāḥ*—sky or ether; *bhūtānām*—of all conditioned souls; *pañca*—the five; *dhātavaḥ*—basic elements; *ā-brahma*—from Lord Brahmā; *sthāvara-ādīnām*—down to the nonmoving creatures; *śārīrāḥ*—used for the construction of the material bodies; *ātma*—to the Supreme Soul; *saṁyutāḥ*—equally related.

TRANSLATION

Earth, water, fire, air and ether are the five basic elements that constitute the bodies of all conditioned souls, from Lord Brahmā himself down to the nonmoving creatures. These elements all emanate from the one Personality of Godhead.

PURPORT

All material bodies are composed of different proportions of the same five gross elements, which emanate from the one Personality of Godhead and cover the living entities, who are all in the *jīva* category.

The concepts of good and bad depend on the choice of the Supreme Lord and not on inherent qualitative differences in material objects. A Kṛṣṇa conscious person ultimately sees all material phenomena as one. The devotee's good behavior, intelligent discrimination and artistic sense within the material world are all based on the will of God. The material elements, being emanations from the Supreme Lord, are ultimately all nondifferent. However, advocates of mundane piety fear that if the material duality of good and bad is minimized, people will become immoral or anarchistic. Certainly the impersonal and atheistic philosophy preached by modern scientists, in which material variety is reduced to mere mathematical descriptions of molecular and atomic particles, leads to immoral society. Although both material science and Vedic knowledge uncover the illusion of material variety and reveal the ultimate oneness of all material energy, only the devotees of Lord Kṛṣṇa are surrendered to the supreme absolute piety of God's will. Thus they always act for the benefit of all living entities, accepting material variety in the Lord's service, according to the Lord's desire. Without Kṛṣṇa consciousness, or God consciousness, people cannot understand the absolute position of spiritual goodness; instead they artificially try to construct a civilization based on interdependent self-interest on the material platform. Such a foolish arrangement easily collapses, as evidenced by widespread social conflict and chaos in the modern age. All members of a civilized society must accept the absolute authority of the Supreme Personality of Godhead, and then social peace and harmony will not rest on the flimsy relative platform of mundane piety and sin.

TEXT 6

वेदेन नामरूपाणि विषमाणि समेष्वपि ।
धातुषूद्धव कल्प्यन्त एतेषां स्वार्थसिद्धये ॥ ६ ॥

vedena nāma-rūpāṇi
viṣamāṇi sameṣv api
dhātuṣūddhava kalpyanta
eteṣāṁ svārtha-siddhaye

vedena—by Vedic literature; *nāma*—names; *rūpāṇi*—and forms; *viṣamāṇi*—different; *sameṣu*—which are equal; *api*—indeed; *dhātuṣu*—in (material bodies composed of) the five elements; *uddhava*—My dear Uddhava; *kalpyante*—are conceived of; *eteṣām*—of them, the living entities; *sva-artha*—of self-interest; *siddhaye*—for the achievement.

TRANSLATION

My dear Uddhava, although all material bodies are composed of the same five elements and are thus equal, the Vedic literatures conceive of different names and forms in relation to such bodies so that the living entities may achieve their goal of life.

PURPORT

The words *nāma-rūpāṇi viṣamāṇi* refer to the system of *varṇāśrama-dharma,* in which members of human society are designated according to four social and four occupational divisions. Those dedicated to intellectual or religious perfection are called *brāhmaṇas,* those dedicated to political perfection are called *kṣatriyas,* those dedicated to financial perfection are called *vaiśyas,* and those dedicated to eating, sleeping, sex and honest work are called *śūdras.* Such propensities arise from the three modes of material nature (goodness, passion and ignorance), because the pure soul is not materially intellectual, ambitious for power, enterprising or servile. Rather, the pure soul is always absorbed in loving devotion to the Supreme Lord. If the various propensities of a conditioned soul are not engaged in the *varṇāśrama* system, they will certainly be misused, and thus that person will fall down from the standard of human life. The Vedic system is designed by the Lord so that conditioned souls may pursue their individual achievements and at the same time advance toward the ultimate goal of life, Kṛṣṇa consciousness. Just as a doctor deals with a crazy man by speaking to him sympathetically in terms of his false conception of life, one who understands the Vedic literature engages the living entities according to their illusory identification with the elements of matter. Although all material bodies are composed of the same material elements and are thus qualitatively identical, as described here by the word *sameṣu,* the Vedic social system, *varṇāśrama,* is created to engage all human beings in Kṛṣṇa consciousness according to their various degrees of material identification. The absolute good is the Supreme Lord Himself, and that which approaches the Supreme Lord becomes similarly good. Because the sun is the source of heat within this world, an object that approaches the sun becomes hotter and hotter until it merges into fire. In the same manner, as we approach the transcendental nature of the Personality of Godhead, we automatically become surcharged with absolute goodness.

Although this knowledge is the real basis of the Vedic literature, mundane piety is enjoined and sin is prohibited so that one can gradually come to the platform of material goodness, whereupon spiritual knowledge becomes visible.

TEXT 7

देशकालादिभावानां वस्तूनां मम सत्तम ।
गुणदोषौ विधीयेते नियमार्थं हि कर्मणाम् ॥ ७ ॥

deśa-kālādi-bhāvānāṁ
vastūnāṁ mama sattama
guṇa-doṣau vidhīyete
niyamārthaṁ hi karmaṇām

deśa—of space; *kāla*—time; *ādi*—and so on; *bhāvānām*—of such states of existence; *vastūnām*—of things; *mama*—by Me; *sat-tama*—O most saintly Uddhava; *guṇa-doṣau*—piety and sin; *vidhīyete*—are established; *niyama-artham*—for the restriction; *hi*—certainly; *karmaṇām*—of fruitive activities.

TRANSLATION

O saintly Uddhava, in order to restrict materialistic activities, I have established that which is proper and improper among all material things, including time, space and all physical objects.

PURPORT

The word *niyamārtham* ("in order to restrict") is significant in this verse. A conditioned soul falsely identifies with his material senses and thus considers anything giving immediate satisfaction to the body to be good and anything inconvenient or disturbing to be bad. By higher intelligence, however, one recognizes long-term self-interest and danger. For example, medicine may be immediately bitter, but by calculating one's long-term interest one accepts the bitter medicine to cure a disease that is not immediately troublesome but ultimately fatal. Similarly, Vedic literature restricts the sinful propensities of human beings by establishing what is proper and what is improper among all the objects and activities of the material world. Because everyone must eat, the *Vedas* prescribe foods in the mode of goodness and not those which are sinful, such as meat, fish and eggs. Similarly, one is advised to live in a peaceful and pious community and not in association with sinful persons, nor in an unclean or turbulent environment. By designating and restricting the exploitation of the material world, Vedic knowledge gradually brings a conditioned soul to the platform of material goodness. At that stage one becomes eligible to serve the Supreme Personality of Godhead and enter the transcendental stage of life. It should be remembered that such mere eligibility does not constitute actual qualification; without Kṛṣṇa consciousness mere mundane piety can never qualify a conditioned soul to go back home, back to Godhead. Within this world we are all infected by false pride, which must be diminished through submission to the Vedic injunctions. One who is completely engaged in the loving service of the Lord need not adopt these preliminary methods, for he directly contacts the Personality of Godhead through the spontaneous process of surrender. In the previous verse the Lord explained why Vedic literatures assign different values to the bodies of different living entities, and here the Lord explains the Vedic value system in regard to the material objects that interact with these bodies.

TEXT 8

अकृष्णसारो देशानामब्रह्मण्योऽशुचिर्भवेत् ।
कृष्णसारोऽप्यसौवीरकीकटासंस्कृतेरिणम् ॥ ८ ॥

akṛṣṇa-sāro deśānām
abrahmaṇyo 'sucir bhavet
kṛṣṇa-sāro 'py asauvīra-
kīkaṭāsaṁskṛteriṇam

akṛṣṇa-sāraḥ—without spotted antelopes; *deśānām*—among places; *abrahmaṇyaḥ*—where there is no devotion to the *brāhmaṇas; aśuciḥ*—contaminated; *bhavet*—is; *kṛṣṇa-sāraḥ*—possessing spotted antelopes; *api*—even; *asauvīra*—without saintly cultured men; *kīkaṭa*—(a place of low-class men, such as) the state of Gayā; *asaṁskṛta*—where people do not practice cleanliness or purificatory ceremonies; *īraṇam*—where the land is barren.

TRANSLATION

Among places, those bereft of the spotted antelope, those devoid of devotion to the *brāhmaṇas*, those possessing spotted antelopes but bereft of respectable men, provinces like Kīkaṭa and places where cleanliness and purificatory rites are neglected, where meat-eaters are prominent or where the earth is barren, are all considered to be contaminated lands.

PURPORT

The word *kṛṣṇa-sāra* refers to the spotted antelope, whose hide is used by *brahmacārīs* while residing in the *āśrama* of the spiritual master. *Brahmacārīs* never hunt in the forest, but rather accept skins from those animals already deceased. The skin of the black or spotted antelope is also used as a garment by those receiving instruction in the execution of Vedic sacrifice. Therefore, since sacrifice cannot be properly performed in areas bereft of such creatures, these places are impure. Furthermore, although the inhabitants of a particular place may be expert in performing fruitive activities and ritualistic sacrifices, if they are inimical to the devotional service of the Lord, such a place is also polluted. Śrīla Bhaktisiddhānta Sarasvatī Ṭhākura explains that previously the provinces of Bihar and Bengal were bereft of devotional service to the Lord and were considered impure. Then great Vaiṣṇavas such as Jayadeva appeared in these territories, converting them into holy places.

The word *asauvīra* indicates those places without *suvīras*, respectable saintly persons. Ordinarily, a person who obeys the state laws is considered a respectable citizen. In the same way, one who strictly obeys the law of God is considered to be a cultured or decent man, *suvīra*. The place where such intelligent persons reside is called *sauvīram*. Kīkaṭa refers to the modern state of Bihar, which traditionally has been known as a territory of uncivilized men. Even in such provinces, however, any place where saintly persons gather is considered to be holy. On the other hand, a province of generally respectable persons is immediately polluted by the presence of sinful men. *Asaṁskṛta* indicates lack of external cleanliness, as well as the absence of purificatory ceremonies for internal cleanliness. Śrīla Madhvācārya quotes from the *Skanda Purāṇa* as follows: "Religious persons should reside within an eight-mile radius of rivers, oceans, mountains, hermitages, forests, spiritual cities or places where the *śālagrāma-śilā* is found. All other places should be considered *kīkaṭa*, or contaminated. But if even in such contaminated places black and spotted antelopes are found, one may reside there as long as sinful persons are not also present. Even if sinful persons are present, if the civil power rests with respectable authorities, one may remain. Similarly, one may dwell wherever the Deity of Viṣṇu is duly installed and worshiped."

The Lord here elaborates upon the theme of piety and sin, which are based on purity and impurity. Thus pure and contaminated places of residence are described here.

TEXT 9

कर्मण्यो गुणवान् कालो द्रव्यतः स्वत एव वा ।
यतो निवर्तते कर्म स दोषोऽकर्मकः स्मृतः ॥ ९ ॥

karmaṇyo guṇavān kālo
dravyataḥ svata eva vā
yato nivartate karma
sa doṣo 'karmakaḥ smṛtaḥ

karmaṇyaḥ—suitable for executing one's prescribed duty; *guṇavān*—pure; *kālaḥ*—time; *dravyataḥ*—by achievement of auspicious objects; *svataḥ*—by its own nature; *eva*—indeed; *vā*—or; *yataḥ*—due to which (time); *nivartate*—is impeded; *karma*—one's duty; *saḥ*—this (time); *doṣaḥ*—impure; *akarmakaḥ*—inappropriate for working properly; *smṛtaḥ*—is considered.

TRANSLATION

A specific time is considered pure when it is appropriate, either by its own nature or through achievement of suitable paraphernalia, for the performance of one's prescribed duty. That time which impedes the performance of one's duty is considered impure.

PURPORT

Having discussed pure and impure places, the Lord now discusses different qualities of time. Certain times, such as the *brāhma-muhūrta*, the last few hours before sunrise, are always auspicious for spiritual advancement. Other times, not auspicious in themselves, become so by achievement of material prosperity that facilitates one's mission in life.

Political, social or economic disturbances that obstruct the execution of one's religious duties are considered inauspicious times. Similarly, a woman is considered contaminated just after childbirth or during her menstrual period. She cannot perform ordinary religious activities at such times, which are therefore inauspicious and impure. Śrīla Bhaktisiddhānta Sarasvatī Ṭhākura explains that the most auspicious of all times is the moment one achieves the mercy of the Supreme Personality of Godhead. If one neglects the loving service of the Lord, being carried away by sense gratification, he is certainly living in most inauspicious times. Therefore that moment in which one achieves the association of the Supreme Lord or the Lord's pure devotee is the most auspicious time, whereas the moment of losing such association is most inauspicious. In other words, the perfection of life is simply Kṛṣṇa consciousness, by which one transcends the dualities of time and space caused by the three modes of material nature.

TEXT 10

द्रव्यस्य शुद्ध्यशुद्धी च द्रव्येण वचनेन च ।
संस्कारेणाथ कालेन महत्त्वाल्पतयाथवा ॥१०॥

dravyasya śuddhy-aśuddhī ca
dravyeṇa vacanena ca
saṁskāreṇātha kālena
mahatvālpatayātha vā

dravyasya—of an object; *śuddhi*—purity; *aśuddhī*—or impurity; *ca*—and; *dravyeṇa*—by another object; *vacanena*—by speech; *ca*—and; *saṁskāreṇa*—by ritual performance; *atha*—or else; *kālena*—by time; *mahatva-alpatayā*—by greatness or smallness; *atha vā*—or else.

TRANSLATION

An object's purity or impurity is established by application of another object, by words, by rituals, by the effects of time or according to relative magnitude.

PURPORT

Cloth is purified by application of clean water and contaminated by application of urine. The words of a saintly *brāhmaṇa* are pure, but the sound vibration of a materialistic person is contaminated by lust and envy. A saintly devotee explains actual purity to others, whereas a nondevotee makes false propaganda that leads innocent people to commit polluted, sinful activities. Pure rituals are those meant for the satisfaction of the Supreme Lord, while materialistic ceremonies are those that lead their followers into materialistic and demoniac activities. The word *saṁskāreṇa* also indicates that the purity or impurity of a particular object is ascertained according to the regulations of ritualistic performances. For example, a flower to be offered to the Deity must be purified with water. Flowers or food cannot be offered to the Deity, however, if they have been contaminated by being smelled or tasted before the offering. The word *kālena* indicates that certain substances are purified by time and others contaminated by time. Rainwater, for example, is considered pure after ten days' time, and after three days in cases of emergency. On the other hand, certain foods decay in time and thus become impure. *Mahatva* indicates that great bodies of water do not become contaminated, and *alpatayā* means that a small amount of water can easily become polluted or stagnant. In the same way, a great soul is not polluted by occasional contact with materialistic persons, whereas one whose devotion to God is very small is easily carried away and put into doubt by bad association. In terms of combination with other substances, and in terms of speech, ritual, time and magnitude, the purity and impurity of all objects can be ascertained.

Śrīla Viśvanātha Cakravartī Ṭhākura remarks that impure or decayed food is certainly forbidden for normal persons but is permissible for those who have no other means of subsistence.

TEXT 11

शक्त्याशक्त्याथ वा बुद्ध्या समृद्ध्या च यदात्मने ।
अघं कुर्वन्ति हि यथा देशावस्थानुसारतः ॥११॥

śaktyāśaktyātha vā buddhyā
samṛddhyā ca yad ātmane
aghaṁ kurvanti hi yathā
deśāvasthānusārataḥ

śaktyā—by relative potency; *aśaktyā*—impotence; *atha vā*—or; *buddhyā*—in terms of understanding; *samṛddhyā*—opulence; *ca*—and; *yat*—which; *ātmane*—to oneself; *agham*—sinful reaction; *kurvanti*—cause; *hi*—indeed; *yathā*—in actuality; *deśa*—place; *avasthā*—or one's condition; *anusārataḥ*—in accordance with.

TRANSLATION

Impure things may or may not impose sinful reactions upon a person, depending on that person's strength or weakness, intelligence, wealth, location and physical condition.

PURPORT

The Lord has described the purity and impurity of different places, times and material objects. According to the laws of nature, that which is impure contaminates a particular person in accordance with that person's situation, as described here. For example, on certain occasions, such as a solar eclipse or just after childbirth, one must restrict the intake of food according to ritualistic injunctions. One who is physically weak, however, may eat without being considered impious. Ordinary persons consider the ten days following childbirth to be most auspicious, whereas one who is learned knows that this period is actually impure. Ignorance of the law does not save one from being punished, but one who consciously commits sinful activities is considered most fallen. Concerning opulence (*samṛddhi*), worn-out, dirty clothing or a messy residence are considered impure for a rich man but acceptable for one who is poor. The word *deśa* indicates that in a safe and peaceful place one is obligated to strictly perform religious rituals, whereas in a dangerous or chaotic situation one may be excused for occasional negligence of secondary principles. One who is physically healthy must offer obeisances to the Deities, attend religious functions and execute his prescribed duties, but a young child or sickly person may be excused from such activities, as indicated by the word *avasthā*. Ultimately, as Śrīla Rūpa Gosvāmī states,

anyābhilāṣitā-śūnyaṁ
jñāna-karmādy-anāvṛtam
ānukūlyena kṛṣṇānu-
śīlanaṁ bhaktir uttamā

"One should render transcendental loving service to the Supreme Lord Kṛṣṇa favorably and without desire for material profit or gain through fruitive activities or philosophical speculation. That is called pure devotional service." (*Bhakti-rasāmṛta-sindhu* 1.1.11) One should accept everything which is favorable for the devotional service of Lord Kṛṣṇa and reject whatever is unfavorable. One must learn the process of serving God from the bona fide spiritual master and thus always maintain one's existence pure and free from anxiety. In general, however, when considering the relative purity and impurity of material things, all of the above-mentioned factors must be calculated.

TEXT 12

धान्यदार्वस्थितन्तूनां रसतैजसचर्मणाम् ।
कालवाय्वग्निमृत्तोयैः पार्थिवानां युतायुतैः ॥१२॥

dhānya-dārv-asthi-tantūnāṁ
rasa-taijasa-carmaṇām
kāla-vāyv-agni-mṛt-toyaiḥ
pārthivānāṁ yutāyutaiḥ

dhānya—of grains; *dāru*—of wood (in the form of both ordinary objects and sacred utensils); *asthi*—bone (such as elephant tusks); *tantūnām*—and thread; *rasa*—of liquids (oil, ghee, etc.); *taijasa*—fiery objects (gold, etc.); *carmaṇām*—and skins; *kāla*—by time; *vāyu*—by air; *agni*—by fire; *mṛt*—by earth; *toyaiḥ*—and by water; *pārthivānām*—(also) of earthen objects (such as chariot wheels, mud, pots, bricks, etc.); *yuta*—in combination; *ayutaiḥ*—or separately.

TRANSLATION

Various objects such as grains, wooden utensils, things made of bone, thread, liquids, objects derived from fire, skins and earthy objects are all purified by time, by the wind, by fire, by earth and by water, either separately or in combination.

PURPORT

The word *kāla*, or "time," is mentioned here, since all purificatory processes take place within time.

TEXT 13

अमेध्यलिप्तं यद् येन गन्धलेपं व्यपोहति ।
भजते प्रकृतिं तस्य तच्छौचं तावदिष्यते ॥१३॥

amedhya-liptaṁ yad yena
gandha-lepaṁ vyapohati
bhajate prakṛtiṁ tasya
tac chaucaṁ tāvad iṣyate

amedhya—by something impure; *liptam*—touched; *yat*—that thing which; *yena*—by which; *gandha*—the bad smell; *lepam*—and the impure covering; *vyapohati*—gives up; *bhajate*—the contaminated object again assumes; *prakṛtim*—its original nature; *tasya*—of that object; *tat*—that application; *śaucam*—purification; *tāvat*—to that extent; *iṣyate*—is considered.

TRANSLATION

A particular purifying agent is considered appropriate when its application removes the bad odor or dirty covering of some contaminated object and makes it resume its original nature.

PURPORT

Furniture, kitchen utensils, clothing and other objects are purified by application of abrasion, alkali, acid, water and so on. One thereby removes the bad fragrance or impure coating of such objects, restoring them to their original clean appearance.

TEXT 14

स्नानदानतपोऽवस्थावीर्यसंस्कारकर्मभिः ।
मत्स्मृत्या चात्मनः शौचं शुद्धः कर्माचरेद् द्विजः ॥१४॥

snāna-dāna-tapo-'vasthā-
vīrya-saṁskāra-karmabhiḥ
mat-smṛtyā cātmanaḥ śaucaṁ
śuddhaḥ karmācared dvijaḥ

snāna—by bathing; *dāna*—charity; *tapaḥ*—austerity; *avasthā*—by virtue of one's age; *vīrya*—potency; *saṁskāra*—execution of ritual purification; *karmabhiḥ*—and prescribed duties; *mat-smṛtyā*—by remembrance of Me; *ca*—also; *ātmanaḥ*—of the self; *śaucam*—cleanliness; *śuddhaḥ*—pure; *karma*—activity; *ācaret*—he should perform; *dvijaḥ*—a twice-born man.

TRANSLATION

The self can be cleansed by bathing, charity, austerity, age, personal strength, purificatory rituals, prescribed duties and, above all, by remembrance of Me. The *brāhmaṇa* and other twice-born men should be duly purified before performing their specific activities.

PURPORT

The word *avasthā* indicates that when boys and girls are young they are kept pure by youthful innocence and that as they grow up they are kept pure through proper education and engagement. By one's individual potency one should avoid sinful activities and the association of those inclined toward sense gratification. The word *karma* here refers to prescribed duties, such as worshiping the spiritual master and the Deity, chanting the Gāyatrī *mantra* three times daily and accepting spiritual initiation. The prescribed duties of the *varṇāśrama* system automatically purify one from the covering of false ego by dovetailing one's bodily designation in appropriate religious activities. There are specific duties for *brāhmaṇas, kṣatriyas, vaiśyas, śūdras, brahmacārīs, gṛhasthas, vānaprasthas* and *sannyāsīs*, as described previously in this canto by the Lord Himself. The most significant word here is *mat-smṛtyā* ("by remembrance of Me"). Ultimately, one cannot avoid the infection of illusion through any process except Kṛṣṇa consciousness. The three modes of nature perpetually interact, and one must sometimes fall into the mode of ignorance and sometimes rise to the mode of goodness, uselessly rotating within the kingdom of illusion. But by Kṛṣṇa consciousness, remembrance of the Personality of Godhead, one can actually uproot one's tendency to act against the will of the Absolute Truth. Then one becomes freed from the clutches of *māyā* and goes back home, back to Godhead. As stated in the *Garuḍa Purāṇa,*

apavitraḥ pavitro vā
sarvāvasthāṁ gato 'pi vā
yaḥ smaret puṇḍarīkākṣaṁ
sa bāhyābhyantare śuciḥ

"Whether one is pure or contaminated, and regardless of one's external situation, simply by remembering the lotus-eyed Personality of Godhead one can internally and externally cleanse one's existence."

Lord Caitanya recommended that we constantly remember the Supreme Lord by chanting His holy names, Hare Kṛṣṇa, Hare Kṛṣṇa, Kṛṣṇa Kṛṣṇa, Hare Hare/ Hare Rāma, Hare Rāma, Rāma Rāma, Hare Hare. This sublime process is essential for every human actually desirous of purifying his existence.

TEXT 15

मन्त्रस्य च परिज्ञानं कर्मशुद्धिर्मदर्पणम् ।
धर्मः सम्पद्यते षड्भिरधर्मस्तु विपर्ययः ॥१५॥

mantrasya ca parijñānaṁ
karma-śuddhir mad-arpaṇam
dharmaḥ sampadyate ṣaḍbhir
adharmas tu viparyayaḥ

mantrasya—(the purification) of a *mantra; ca*—and; *parijñānam*—correct knowledge; *karma*—of work; *śuddhiḥ*—the purification; *mat-arpaṇam*—offering unto Me; *dharmaḥ*—religiousness; *sampadyate*—is achieved; *ṣaḍbhiḥ*—by the six (purification of place, time, substance, the doer, the *mantras* and the work); *adharmaḥ*—irreligiosity; *tu*—but; *viparyayaḥ*—otherwise.

TRANSLATION

A *mantra* is purified when chanted with proper knowledge, and one's work is purified when offered unto Me. Thus by purification of the place, time, substance, the doer, *mantras* and work, one becomes religious, and by negligence of these six methods one is considered irreligious.

PURPORT

One receives a *mantra* from the mouth of a bona fide spiritual master, who instructs the disciple in the method, meaning and ultimate purpose of the *mantra.* The bona fide spiritual master in this age gives his disciple the *mahā-mantra,* or holy names of God, Hare Kṛṣṇa, Hare Kṛṣṇa, Kṛṣṇa Kṛṣṇa, Hare Hare/ Hare Rāma, Hare Rāma, Rāma Rāma, Hare Hare. One who chants this *mantra,* considering himself to be the eternal servant of the Lord, gradually learns to chant offenselessly and by such purified chanting quickly achieves the highest perfection of life. The Lord here summarizes His discussion of purity and impurity, which manifest ultimately in religious and irreligious life.

TEXT 16

क्वचिद् गुणोऽपि दोषः स्याद् दोषोऽपि विधिना गुणः।
गुणदोषार्थनियमस्तद्भिदामेव बाधते ॥१६॥

kvacid guṇo 'pi doṣaḥ syād
doṣo 'pi vidhinā guṇaḥ
guṇa-doṣārtha-niyamas
tad-bhidām eva bādhate

kvacit—sometimes; *guṇaḥ*—piety; *api*—even; *doṣaḥ*—sin; *syāt*—becomes; *doṣaḥ*—sin; *api*—also; *vidhinā*—on the strength of Vedic injunction; *guṇaḥ*—piety; *guṇa-doṣa*—to piety and sin; *artha*—regarding; *niyamaḥ*—restrictive regulation; *tat*—of them; *bhidām*—the distinction; *eva*—actually; *bādhate*—undoes.

TRANSLATION

Sometimes piety becomes sin, and sometimes what is ordinarily sin becomes piety on the strength of Vedic injunctions. Such special rules in effect eradicate the clear distinction between piety and sin.

PURPORT

The Lord clearly explains here that material piety and sin are always relative considerations. For example, if a neighbor's house is on fire and one chops a hole in the roof so that the trapped family may escape, one is considered to be a pious hero because of the dangerous condition. In normal conditions, however, if one chops a hole in his neighbor's roof or breaks the neighbor's windows, he is considered a criminal. Similarly, one who abandons one's wife and children is certainly irresponsible and thoughtless. If one takes *sannyāsa,* however, and remains fixed on a higher spiritual platform, he is considered to be a most saintly person. Piety and sin therefore depend upon particular circumstances and are at times difficult to distinguish.

According to Śrīla Madhvācārya, persons above the age of fourteen are considered capable of distinguishing between good and bad and are thus responsible for their pious and sinful activities. Animals, on the other hand, being merged in ignorance, cannot be blamed for their offenses or praised for their so-called good qualities, which all arise ultimately from ignorance. Human beings who act like animals, with the idea that one should not feel any guilt but should do whatever one likes, will certainly take birth as animals absorbed in ignorance. And there are other foolish people who, observing the relativity of material piety and sin, conclude that there is no absolute good. It should be understood, however, that Kṛṣṇa consciousness is absolutely good because it involves complete obedience to the Absolute Truth, the Supreme Personality of Godhead, whose goodness is eternal and absolute. Those who are inclined to study material piety and sin ultimately experience frustration due to the relativity and variability of the subject matter. One should therefore come to the transcendental platform of Kṛṣṇa consciousness, which is valid and perfect in all circumstances.

TEXT 17

समानकर्माचरणं पतितानां न पातकम् ।
औत्पत्तिको गुणः सङ्गो न शयानः पतत्यधः ॥१७॥

samāna-karmācaraṇaṁ
patitānāṁ na pātakam
autpattiko guṇaḥ saṅgo
na śayānaḥ pataty adhaḥ

samāna—equal; *karma*—of work; *ācaraṇam*—the performance; *patitānām*—for those who are fallen; *na*—is not; *pātakam*—a cause of falldown; *autpattikaḥ*—dictated by one's nature; *guṇaḥ*—becomes a good quality; *saṅgaḥ*—material association; *na*—does not; *śayānaḥ*—one who is lying down; *patati*—fall; *adhaḥ*—further down.

TRANSLATION

The same activities that would degrade an elevated person do not cause falldown for those who are already fallen. Indeed, one who is lying on the ground cannot possibly fall further. The material association that is dictated by one's own nature is considered a good quality.

PURPORT

The Lord here further describes the ambiguity in ascertaining material piety and sin. Although intimate association with women is most abominable for a renounced *sannyāsī*, the same association is pious for a householder, who is ordered by Vedic injunction to approach his wife at the suitable time for procreation. Similarly, a *brāhmaṇa* who drinks liquor is considered to be committing a most abominable act, whereas a *śūdra*, a low-class man, who can moderate his drinking is considered to be self-controlled. Piety and sin on the material level are thus relative considerations. Any member of society, however, who receives *dīkṣā*, initiation into the chanting of the Lord's holy names, must strictly obey the four regulative principles: no eating of meat, fish or eggs, no illicit sex, no intoxication and no gambling. A spiritually initiated person neglecting these principles will certainly fall from his elevated position of liberation.

TEXT 18

यतो यतो निवर्तेत विमुच्येत ततस्ततः ।
एष धर्मो नृणां क्षेमः शोकमोहभयापहः ॥१८॥

yato yato nivarteta
vimucyeta tatas tataḥ
eṣa dharmo nṛṇāṁ kṣemaḥ
śoka-moha-bhayāpahaḥ

yataḥ yataḥ—from whatever; *nivarteta*—one desists; *vimucyeta*—he becomes liberated; *tataḥ tataḥ*—from that; *eṣaḥ*—this; *dharmaḥ*—the system of religion; *nṛṇām*—for humans; *kṣemaḥ*—the path of auspiciousness; *śoka*—suffering; *moha*—delusion; *bhaya*—and fear; *apahaḥ*—which takes away.

TRANSLATION

By refraining from a particular sinful or materialistic activity, one becomes freed from its bondage. Such renunciation is the basis of religious and auspicious life for human beings and drives away all suffering, illusion and fear.

PURPORT

In *Caitanya-caritāmṛta* (*Antya-līlā* 6.220) it is stated,

mahāprabhura bhakta-gaṇera vairāgya pradhāna
yāhā dekhi' prīta hana gaura-bhagavān

"Renunciation is the basic principle sustaining the lives of Śrī Caitanya Mahāprabhu's devotees. Seeing this renunciation, Śrī Caitanya Mahāprabhu, the Supreme Personality of Godhead, is extremely satisfied."

Because of false ego one considers oneself to be the proprietor and enjoyer of one's activities. Actually, Lord Kṛṣṇa, the Personality of Godhead, is the proprietor and enjoyer of our activities; recognition of this fact in Kṛṣṇa consciousness leads one to real renunciation. Every human being should perform his prescribed duty as an offering to the Supreme Lord. Then there will be no possibility of material entanglement. Lord Kṛṣṇa clearly explains in *Bhagavad-gītā* that prescribed duties performed as an offering to the Lord award liberation from material bondage. Sinful activities cannot be offered to the Lord but must be given up altogether. In effect, the distinction between piety and sin is made so that the living entities will become pious and eligible to surrender to the Supreme Lord. As explained in *Bhagavad-gītā* (7.28),

yeṣāṁ tv anta-gataṁ pāpaṁ
janānāṁ puṇya-karmaṇām
te dvandva-moha-nirmuktā
bhajante māṁ dṛḍha-vratāḥ

"Persons who have acted piously in previous lives and in this life, whose sinful actions are completely eradicated and who are freed from the duality of delusion, engage themselves in My service with determination."

By thorough piety one's life becomes auspicious and freed from lamentation, illusion and fear, and one can then take to the path of Kṛṣṇa consciousness.

TEXT 19

विषयेषु गुणाध्यासात् पुंसः सङ्गस्ततो भवेत् ।
सङ्गात्तत्र भवेत् कामः कामादेव कलिर्नृणाम्॥१९॥

viṣayeṣu guṇādhyāsāt
puṁsaḥ saṅgas tato bhavet
saṅgāt tatra bhavet kāmaḥ
kāmād eva kalir nṛṇām

viṣayeṣu—in material objects of sense gratification; *guṇa-adhyāsāt*—because of presuming them to be good; *puṁsaḥ*—of a person; *saṅgaḥ*—attachment; *tataḥ*—from that presumption; *bhavet*—comes into being;

saṅgāt—from that material association; *tatra*—thus; *bhavet*—arises; *kāmaḥ*—lust; *kāmāt*—from lust; *eva*—also; *kaliḥ*—quarrel; *nṛṇām*—among men.

TRANSLATION

One who accepts material sense objects as desirable certainly becomes attached to them. From such attachment lust arises, and this lust creates quarrel among men.

PURPORT

The actual goal of human life should not be material sense gratification, for it is the basis of conflict in human society. Although the Vedic literature sometimes sanctions sense gratification, the ultimate purpose of the *Vedas* is renunciation, since Vedic culture cannot possibly recommend anything that disturbs human life. A lusty person is easily angered and becomes inimical to anyone frustrating his lusty desires. Since his sex desire can never be satisfied, a lusty person ultimately becomes frustrated with his own sex partner, and thus a "love-hate" relationship develops. A lusty person considers himself to be the enjoyer of God's creation and is therefore full of pride and false prestige. The lusty, proud person will not be attracted to the process of humble submission at the lotus feet of the bona fide spiritual master. Attraction to illicit sex is thus the direct enemy of Kṛṣṇa consciousness, which depends upon humble submission to the representative of the Supreme Lord. Lord Kṛṣṇa also states in *Bhagavad-gītā* that desire for illicit sex is the all-devouring, sinful enemy of this world.

Because modern society sanctions unrestricted mixing of men and women, its citizens cannot possibly achieve peace; rather, the regulation of conflict becomes the basis of social survival. This is the symptom of an ignorant society falsely accepting the material body as the highest good, as described here by the words *viṣayeṣu guṇādhyāsāt*. One who is too affectionate to his own body will inevitably be seized by sex desire.

TEXT 20

कलेर्दुर्विषहः क्रोधस्तमस्तमनुवर्तते ।
तमसा ग्रस्यते पुंसश्चेतना व्यापिनी द्रुतम् ॥२०॥

kaler durviṣahaḥ krodhas
tamas tam anuvartate
tamasā grasyate puṁsaś
cetanā vyāpinī drutam

kaleḥ—from quarrel; *durviṣahaḥ*—intolerable; *krodhaḥ*—anger; *tamaḥ*—ignorance; *tam*—that anger; *anuvartate*—follows; *tamasā*—by ignorance; *grasyate*—is seized; *puṁsaḥ*—of a man; *cetanā*—the consciousness; *vyāpinī*—broad; *drutam*—swiftly.

TRANSLATION

From quarrel arises intolerable anger, followed by the darkness of ignorance. This ignorance quickly overtakes a man's broad intelligence.

PURPORT

The desire for material association arises from one's propensity to deny that everything is God's energy. Falsely imagining material sense objects to be separate from the Supreme Lord, one desires to enjoy them; such desire gives rise to conflict and quarrel in human society. This conflict inevitably gives rise to great anger, which makes human beings become foolish and destructive. Thus the actual goal of human life is quickly forgotten.

TEXT 21

तया विरहितः साधो जन्तुः शून्याय कल्पते ।
ततोऽस्य स्वार्थविभ्रंशो मूर्च्छितस्य मृतस्य च ॥२१॥

tayā virahitaḥ sādho
jantuḥ śūnyāya kalpate
tato 'sya svārtha-vibhraṁśo
mūrcchitasya mṛtasya ca

tayā—of that intelligence; *virahitaḥ*—deprived; *sādho*—O saintly Uddhava; *jantuḥ*—a living creature; *śūnyāya*—practically void; *kalpate*—

becomes; *tataḥ*—consequently; *asya*—his; *sva-artha*—from the goals of life; *vibhraṁśaḥ*—downfall; *mūrcchitasya*—of him who has become like dull matter; *mṛtasya*—virtually dead; *ca*—and.

TRANSLATION

O saintly Uddhava, a person bereft of real intelligence is considered to have lost everything. Deviated from the actual purpose of his life, he becomes dull, just like a dead person.

PURPORT

Kṛṣṇa consciousness is so vital and essential that one who has deviated from this progressive path of self-realization is considered to be virtually unconscious, or like a dead person. Since every living entity is part and parcel of Kṛṣṇa, anyone who falsely identifies with the external body is actually unconscious of his real position. Thus it is stated, *śūnyāya kalpate:* pursuing that which has no factual existence, he is devoid of any tangible progress or benefit in life. One whose consciousness is absorbed in the nonexistent becomes himself practically nonexistent. In this way, the eternal living entities become fallen, lost in the ocean of material existence, and it is only by the special mercy of the pure devotees of the Lord that they can be rescued. The Lord's devotees therefore instruct the fallen people to chant Hare Kṛṣṇa, Hare Kṛṣṇa, Kṛṣṇa Kṛṣṇa, Hare Hare/ Hare Rāma, Hare Rāma, Rāma Rāma, Hare Hare. By this process our real consciousness and life can be quickly revived.

TEXT 22

विषयाभिनिवेशेन नात्मानं वेद नापरम् ।
वृक्षजीविकया जीवन् व्यर्थं भस्त्रेव यः श्वसन् ॥२२॥

viṣayābhiniveśena
nātmānaṁ veda nāparam
vṛkṣa-jīvikayā jīvan
vyarthaṁ bhastreva yaḥ śvasan

viṣaya—in sense gratification; *abhiniveśena*—by overabsorption; *na*—not; *ātmānam*—himself; *veda*—knows; *na*—nor; *aparam*—another; *vṛkṣa*—of a tree; *jīvakayā*—by the life-style; *jīvan*—living; *vyartham*—in vain; *bhastrā iva*—just like a bellows; *yaḥ*—who; *śvasan*—is breathing.

TRANSLATION

Because of absorption in sense gratification, one cannot recognize himself or others. Living uselessly in ignorance like a tree, one is merely breathing just like a bellows.

PURPORT

Just as trees, having no means of defending themselves, are always being cut down, similarly, the conditioned souls are constantly being cut down by the cruel laws of nature, which impose innumerable miseries culminating in sudden death. Although foolish people think they are helping themselves and others, they actually do not know their own identity, nor the identities of their so-called friends and relatives. Absorbed in gratifying the senses of the external body, they spend their lives uselessly, without spiritual profit. This useless life-style can be transformed into a perfect life simply by chanting the holy names of God in Kṛṣṇa consciousness, as recommended by Śrī Caitanya Mahāprabhu.

TEXT 23

फलश्रुतिरियं नृणां न श्रेयो रोचनं परम् ।
श्रेयोविवक्षया प्रोक्तं यथा भैषज्यरोचनम् ॥२३॥

phala-śrutir iyaṁ nṛṇāṁ
na śreyo rocanaṁ param
śreyo-vivakṣayā proktaṁ
yathā bhaiṣajya-rocanam

phala-śrutiḥ—the statements of scripture promising rewards; *iyam*—these; *nṛṇām*—for men; *na*—are not; *śreyaḥ*—the highest good; *rocanam*—enticement; *param*—merely; *śreyaḥ*—the ultimate good; *vivakṣayā*—with the idea of saying; *proktam*—spoken; *yathā*—just as; *bhaiṣajya*—for taking medicine; *rocanam*—inducement.

TRANSLATION

Those statements of scripture promising fruitive rewards do not prescribe the ultimate good for men but are merely enticements for executing beneficial religious duties, like promises of candy spoken to induce a child to take beneficial medicine.

PURPORT

In the previous verse Lord Kṛṣṇa stated that persons absorbed in sense gratification certainly deviate from the real purpose of human life. But since the *Vedas* themselves promise heavenly sense gratification as the result of sacrifice and austerity, how can such promotion to heaven be considered a deviation from the goal of life? The Lord here explains that the fruitive rewards offered in religious scriptures are merely inducements, like candy that is used to induce a child to take medicine. It is actually the medicine that is beneficial, and not the candy. Similarly, in fruitive sacrifices it is the worship of Lord Viṣṇu that is beneficial, not the fruitive reward itself. According to *Bhagavad-gītā*, those professing fruitive rewards to be the ultimate goal of religious scripture are certainly less intelligent fools inimical to the purpose of the Supreme Personality of Godhead. The Lord desires that all conditioned souls be purified and come back home, back to Godhead, for an eternal life of bliss and knowledge. One who opposes the Lord's purpose in the name of religiosity is certainly bewildered about the purpose of life.

TEXT 24

उत्पत्त्यैव हि कामेषु प्राणेषु स्वजनेषु च ।
आसक्तमनसो मर्त्या आत्मनोऽनर्थहेतुषु ॥२४॥

utpattyaiva hi kāmeṣu
prāṇeṣu sva-janeṣu ca
āsakta-manaso martyā
ātmano 'nartha-hetuṣu

utpattyā eva—simply by birth; *hi*—indeed; *kāmeṣu*—in objects of selfish desires; *prāṇeṣu*—in vital functions (such as one's duration of life, sense activities, physical strength and sexual potency); *sva-janeṣu*—in his family members; *ca*—and; *āsakta-manasaḥ*—having become attached within the mind; *martyāḥ*—mortal human beings; *ātmanaḥ*—of their real self; *anartha*—of defeating the purpose; *hetuṣu*—which are the causes.

TRANSLATION

Simply by material birth, human beings become attached within their minds to personal sense gratification, long duration of life, sense activities, bodily strength, sexual potency and friends and family. Their minds are thus absorbed in that which defeats their actual self-interest.

PURPORT

Our attachment to the material body and the bodies of family and friends inevitably leads to unbearable anxiety and suffering. The mind absorbed in the bodily concept of life cannot possibly advance in self-realization, and thus one's hope for an eternal life of bliss and knowledge is defeated by the objects of one's so-called affection. Activities performed in ignorance are beneficial neither for oneself nor others, just as the charitable activities one may perform in a dream bestow no tangible benefit on real people. The conditioned soul is dreaming of a world separate from God, but any advancement experienced in this dream world is merely hallucination. The Lord states in *Bhagavad-gītā*, *sarva-loka-maheśvaram:* He is the supreme enjoyer and Lord of all planets and worlds. Only by Kṛṣṇa consciousness, recognition of the supremacy of God, can one make actual progress in life.

TEXT 25

नतानविदुषः स्वार्थं भ्राम्यतो वृजिनाध्वनि ।
कथं युञ्ज्यात्पुनस्तेषु तांस्तमो विशतो बुधः ॥२५॥

natān aviduṣaḥ svārthaṁ
bhrāmyato vṛjinādhvani
kathaṁ yuñjyāt punas teṣu
tāṁs tamo viśato budhaḥ

natān—submissive; *aviduṣaḥ*—ignorant; *sva-artham*—of their own interest; *bhrāmyataḥ*—wandering; *vṛjina*—of danger; *adhvani*—upon the path; *katham*—for what purpose; *yuñjyāt*—would cause to engage; *punaḥ*—further; *teṣu*—in those (modes of sense gratification); *tān*—them; *tamaḥ*—darkness; *viśataḥ*—who are entering; *budhaḥ*—the intelligent (Vedic authority).

TRANSLATION

Those ignorant of their real self-interest are wandering on the path of material existence, gradually heading toward darkness. Why would the *Vedas* further encourage them in sense gratification if they, although foolish, submissively pay heed to Vedic injunctions?

PURPORT

Materialistic persons are not prepared to renounce society, friendship and love, which are all based on sex indulgence, to instead take to a life of renunciation and self-realization. In order to bring such foolish persons under the canopy of Vedic injunctions, the *Vedas* promise innumerable material rewards, even promotion to heavenly planets, to those who faithfully execute the Vedic injunctions. As explained by the Lord, such rewards are like the candy offered to a child, who then faithfully takes his medicine. Material enjoyment is certainly the cause of suffering, since all enjoyable objects are subject to destruction along with the so-called enjoyer. Material life is simply painful and full of anxiety, frustration and lamentation. We become agitated by seeing a so-called enjoyable object, such as the naked body of a woman, a beautiful residence, a sumptuous tray of food or the expansion of our own prestige, but actually such imagined happiness is simply the intense expectation of a satisfaction that never comes. One remains perpetually frustrated in material existence, and the more one tries to enjoy, the more one's frustration increases. Therefore, the Vedic knowledge, which aims at ultimate peace and happiness on the spiritual platform, cannot possibly authorize the materialistic way of life. Material rewards are employed by the *Vedas* merely as inducements for the conditioned soul to take the medicine, submission to the Supreme Lord, Viṣṇu, through various types of sacrifice. Those who are *veda-vāda-rata* claim that religious scriptures are meant to facilitate sense gratification in the ignorance of conditioned life. The true goal of religion, however, is spiritual liberation, in which material sense gratification ceases to exist.

The darkness of bodily attachment cannot exist in the effulgent light of spiritual knowledge. In the ocean of spiritual bliss, the anxiety-ridden apparent pleasure of this world vanishes completely. The true meaning of *veda*, or perfect knowledge, is to surrender to the Supreme Lord in full Kṛṣṇa consciousness for an eternal life of bliss and knowledge as the Lord's faithful servant.

TEXT 26

एवं व्यवसितं केचिदविज्ञाय कुबुद्धयः ।
फलश्रुतिं कुसुमितां न वेदज्ञा वदन्ति हि ॥२६॥

evaṁ vyavasitaṁ kecid
avijñāya kubuddhayaḥ
phala-śrutiṁ kusumitāṁ
na veda-jñā vadanti hi

evam—in this way; *vyavasitam*—the actual conclusion; *kecit*—some people; *avijñāya*—not understanding; *ku-buddhayaḥ*—having perverted intelligence; *phala-śrutim*—the scriptural statements promising material rewards; *kusumitām*—flowery; *na*—do not; *veda-jñāḥ*—those in full knowledge of the *Vedas; vadanti*—speak; *hi*—indeed.

TRANSLATION

Persons with perverted intelligence do not understand this actual purpose of Vedic knowledge and instead propagate as the highest Vedic truth the flowery statements of the *Vedas* that promise material rewards. Those in actual knowledge of the *Vedas* never speak in that way.

PURPORT

The followers of the *karma-mīmāṁsā* philosophy declare that there is no eternal kingdom of God beyond this universe and that one should therefore become a professional performer of Vedic rituals in order to keep oneself in a material heavenly planet. As explained by the Lord to Śrī Uddhava in a previous chapter, there is no actual happiness in the material world, since one will inevitably rotate throughout the various planetary environments stretching from heaven to hell and thus always be disturbed within the material atmosphere. Although the doctor may give a child candy-covered medicine, one who urges the child to eat the candy and throw away the medicine is certainly a great fool. In the same way, the flowery statements of the *Vedas* describing heavenly enjoyment do not award the real fruit of Vedic knowledge but merely supply decorative blossoms of sense gratification. As stated in the *Vedas* (*Ṛg Veda* 1.22.20), *tad viṣṇoḥ paramaṁ padaṁ sadā paśyanti sūrayaḥ*. Even the demigods, who are permanent residents of heaven, are always looking to the eternal abode of the Supreme Lord. Foolish people who admire the standard of living in material heaven should therefore note that the demigods themselves are devotees of the Supreme Lord. One should not become a bogus propagator of so-called Vedic knowledge but should take to Kṛṣṇa consciousness and make a genuine solution to the problem of progressing in life.

TEXT 27

कामिनः कृपणा लुब्धाः पुष्पेषु फलबुद्धयः ।
अग्निमुग्धा धूमतान्ताः स्वं लोकं न विदन्ति ते ॥२७॥

kāminaḥ kṛpaṇā lubdhāḥ
puṣpeṣu phala-buddhayaḥ
agni-mugdhā dhūma-tāntāḥ
svaṁ lokaṁ na vidanti te

kāminaḥ—lusty persons; *kṛpaṇāḥ*—miserly; *lubdhāḥ*—greedy; *puṣpeṣu*—flowers; *phala-buddhayaḥ*—thinking to be the ultimate fruits; *agni*—by fire; *mugdhāḥ*—bewildered; *dhūma-tāntāḥ*—suffocating from smoke; *svam*—their own; *lokam*—identity; *na vidanti*—do not recognize; *te*—they.

TRANSLATION

Those who are full of lust, avarice and greed mistake mere flowers to be the actual fruit of life. Bewildered by the glare of fire and suffocated by its smoke, they cannot recognize their own true identity.

PURPORT

Those attached to female association become proud separatists; desiring everything for their personal gratification and that of their lady friends, they become greedy misers, full of anxiety and envy. Such unfortunate persons mistake the flowery statements of the *Vedas* to be the highest perfection of life. The word *agni-mugdhāḥ,* "bewildered by fire," indicates that such persons consider Vedic fire sacrifices awarding material benefit to be the highest religious truth, and thus they merge into ignorance. Fire produces smoke, which obscures one's vision. Similarly, the path of fruitive fire sacrifices is cloudy and obscure, without clear understanding of the spirit soul. The Lord here clearly states that fruitive religionists cannot understand their actual spiritual identity, nor do they realize the genuine shelter of the spirit soul in the kingdom of God.

Lord Kṛṣṇa states in *Bhagavad-gītā* (15.15), *vedaiś ca sarvair aham eva vedyaḥ:* all Vedic knowledge is actually meant to lead one to pure love of Godhead. Lord Kṛṣṇa is certainly the Absolute Truth, and to love Him is the ultimate purpose of our existence. The Vedic knowledge patiently tries to bring the conditioned soul to this perfection of pure Kṛṣṇa consciousness.

TEXT 28

न ते मामङ्ग जानन्ति हृदिस्थं य इदं यतः ।
उक्थशस्त्रा ह्यसुतृपो यथा नीहारचक्षुषः ॥२८॥

na te mām aṅga jānanti
hṛdi-sthaṁ ya idaṁ yataḥ
uktha-śastrā hy asu-tṛpo
yathā nīhāra-cakṣuṣaḥ

na—do not; *te*—they; *mām*—Me; *aṅga*—My dear Uddhava; *jānanti*—know; *hṛdi-stham*—seated within the heart; *yaḥ*—who is; *idam*—this created universe; *yataḥ*—from whom it comes; *uktha-śastrāḥ*—who consider Vedic ritual activities to be praiseworthy, or else, for whom their own ritualistic performances are like the weapon that kills the sacrificial animal; *hi*—indeed; *asu-tṛpaḥ*—interested only in sense gratification; *yathā*—just as; *nīhāra*—in fog; *cakṣuṣaḥ*—those whose eyes.

TRANSLATION

My dear Uddhava, persons dedicated to sense gratification obtained through honoring the Vedic rituals cannot understand that I am situated in everyone's heart and that the entire universe is nondifferent from Me and emanates from Me. Indeed, they are just like persons whose eyes are covered by fog.

PURPORT

The word *uktha-śastrāḥ* refers to the chanting of certain Vedic hymns, by which one obtains fruitive results in this world and the next. The word *śastra* also indicates a weapon, and thus *uktha-śastra* also means the weapon used in Vedic sacrifice to kill the sacrificial animal. Persons exploiting Vedic knowledge for bodily gratification are slaughtering themselves with the weapon of materialistic religious principles. They are also compared to those trying to see within a dense fog. The false bodily concept of life, in which one ignores the eternal soul within the body, is a dense fog of ignorance that blocks our vision of God. Lord Kṛṣṇa therefore begins His instruction in *Bhagavad-gītā* by clearing away the dense ignorance of the bodily concept of life. Religion means the law of God. The Lord's final order, or law, is that every conditioned soul surrender unto Him, learn to serve and love Him, and thus go back home, back to Godhead. This is the process of Kṛṣṇa consciousness.

TEXTS 29-30

ते मे मतमविज्ञाय परोक्षं विषयात्मकाः ।
हिंसायां यदि रागः स्याद् यज्ञ एव न चोदना ॥२९॥
हिंसाविहारा ह्यालब्धैः पशुभिः स्वसुखेच्छया ।
यजन्ते देवता यज्ञैः पितृभूतपतीन् खलाः ॥३०॥

te me matam avijñāya
parokṣaṁ viṣayātmakāḥ
hiṁsāyāṁ yadi rāgaḥ syād
yajña eva na codanā

hiṁsā-vihārā hy ālabdhaiḥ
paśubhiḥ sva-sukhecchayā

yajante devatā yajñaiḥ
pitṛ-bhūta-patīn khalāḥ

te—they; *me*—My; *matam*—conclusion; *avijñāya*—without understanding; *parokṣam*—confidential; *viṣaya-ātmakāḥ*—absorbed in sense gratification; *hiṁsāyām*—to violence; *yadi*—if; *rāgaḥ*—attachment; *syāt*—may be; *yajñe*—in the sacrificial prescriptions; *eva*—certainly; *na*—there is not; *codanā*—encouragement; *hiṁsā-vihārāḥ*—those who take pleasure in violence; *hi*—indeed; *ālabdhaiḥ*—which have been slaughtered; *paśubhiḥ*—by means of the animals; *sva-sukha*—for their own happiness; *icchayā*—with the desire; *yajante*—they worship; *devatāḥ*—the demigods; *yajñaiḥ*—by sacrificial rituals; *pitṛ*—the forefathers; *bhūta-patīn*—and the leaders among the ghostly spirits; *khalāḥ*—cruel persons.

TRANSLATION

Those who are sworn to sense gratification cannot understand the confidential conclusion of Vedic knowledge as explained by Me. Taking pleasure in violence, they cruelly slaughter innocent animals in sacrifice for their own sense gratification and thus worship demigods, forefathers and leaders among ghostly creatures. Such passion for violence, however, is never encouraged within the process of Vedic sacrifice.

PURPORT

The Vedic scriptures sanction occasional animal sacrifice to satisfy cruel, low-class men who cannot live without the taste of flesh and blood. Such concessions, however, are restricted by rigorous obligatory rituals and are meant to gradually discourage animal-killing, just as the exorbitant cost of a liquor license restricts the number of retail outlets selling alcoholic beverages. But unscrupulous persons misconstrue such restrictive sanctions and declare that Vedic sacrifice is meant for killing animals in order to enjoy sense gratification. Being materialistic, they desire to attain the planets of the forefathers or demigods and thus worship such beings. Sometimes materialistic persons are attracted to the subtle life-style of ghosts and worship ghostly creatures. These methods constitute gross ignorance of the Supreme Personality of

Godhead, who is the actual enjoyer of all sacrifice and austerity. The demons perform Vedic sacrifice but are inimical to Lord Nārāyaṇa, for they consider the demigods, the forefathers or Lord Śiva to be equal to God. Although understanding the authority of Vedic rituals, they do not accept the ultimate Vedic conclusion and therefore never surrender to God. Thus false religious principles flourish in the demoniac societies of the animal-killers. Although in countries like America people outwardly profess to be followers of God alone, actual worship and glorification is offered to innumerable popular heroes such as entertainers, politicians, athletes and other equally insignificant persons. Animal-killers, being grossly materialistic, are inevitably attracted to the extraordinary features of material illusion; they cannot understand the real platform of Kṛṣṇa consciousness, or spiritual life.

TEXT 31

स्वप्नोपममसुं लोकमसन्तं श्रवणप्रियम् ।
आशिषो हृदि सङ्कल्प्य त्यजन्त्यर्थान् यथा वणिक् ॥३१॥

svapnopamam amuṁ lokam
asantaṁ śravaṇa-priyam
āśiṣo hṛdi saṅkalpya
tyajanty arthān yathā vaṇik

svapna—a dream; *upamam*—equal to; *amum*—that; *lokam*—world (after death); *asantam*—unreal; *śravaṇa-priyam*—only enchanting to hear about; *āśiṣaḥ*—mundane achievements in this life; *hṛdi*—in their hearts; *saṅkalpya*—imagining; *tyajanti*—they give up; *arthān*—their wealth; *yathā*—like; *vaṇik*—a businessman.

TRANSLATION

Just as a foolish businessman gives up his real wealth in useless business speculation, foolish persons give up all that is actually valuable in life and instead pursue promotion to material heaven, which although pleasing to hear about is actually unreal, like a dream. Such bewildered persons imagine within their hearts that they will achieve all material blessings.

PURPORT

All over the world people are working hard to achieve perfect sense gratification in this life or the next. As eternal living beings, part and parcel of Lord Kṛṣṇa, we are naturally endowed with all bliss and knowledge in the association of the Lord. But giving up this exalted position of spiritual bliss and knowledge, we foolishly waste our time pursuing the phantasmagoria of bodily happiness, just like a foolish businessman who squanders his real assets in imaginary business ventures that deliver no real profit.

TEXT 32

रजःसत्त्वतमोनिष्ठा रजःसत्त्वतमोजुषः ।
उपासत इन्द्रमुख्यान् देवादीन् न यथैव माम् ॥३२॥

rajaḥ-sattva-tamo-niṣṭhā
rajaḥ-sattva-tamo-juṣaḥ
upāsata indra-mukhyān
devādīn na yathaiva mām

rajaḥ—in the mode of passion; *sattva*—goodness; *tamaḥ*—or ignorance; *niṣṭhāḥ*—established; *rajaḥ*—passion; *sattva*—goodness; *tamaḥ*—or ignorance; *juṣaḥ*—who manifest; *upāsate*—they worship; *indra-mukhyān*—headed by Lord Indra; *deva-ādīn*—the demigods and other deities; *na*—but not; *yathā eva*—in the proper way; *mām*—Me.

TRANSLATION

Those established in material passion, goodness and ignorance worship the particular demigods and other deities, headed by Indra, who manifest the same modes of passion, goodness or ignorance. They fail, however, to properly worship Me.

PURPORT

Although the demigods are part and parcel of the Supreme Personality of Godhead, demigod worship fosters the false idea that the demigods exist apart from the Supreme Lord. Such worship is *avidhi-pūrvakam*, or an improper approach to the Absolute Truth. Śrīla Madhvācārya quotes from the *Hari-vaṁśa* that among those primarily in the mode of ignorance there are sometimes manifestations of passion and goodness. Ignorant persons possessing a tendency toward goodness may go to hell but are also allowed a little heavenly pleasure. Thus it can be seen that a man suffering in miserable financial or political conditions sometimes enjoys the company of a beautiful wife, though his general condition is hellish. Those in ignorance mixed slightly with passion simply go to hell, and those purely in the mode of ignorance glide down to the darkest region of hell. Those devoid of devotion to the Supreme Lord are in ignorance in these three categories. Sometimes persons situated in the mode of goodness accept the supremacy of the Supreme Lord but are more attracted to the demigods, believing that through Vedic rituals they can achieve the same standard of living as the demigods. This proud tendency is certainly an obstacle in the loving service of the Supreme Lord and ultimately causes falldown.

TEXTS 33-34

इष्ट्वेह देवता यज्ञैर्गत्वा रंस्यामहे दिवि ।
तस्यान्त इह भूयास्म महाशाला महाकुलाः ॥३३॥
एवं पुष्पितया वाचा व्याक्षिप्तमनसां नृणाम् ।
मानिनां चातिलुब्धानां मद्वार्तापि न रोचते ॥३४॥

iṣṭveha devatā yajñair
gatvā raṁsyāmahe divi
tasyānta iha bhūyāsma
mahā-śālā mahā-kulāḥ

evaṁ puṣpitayā vācā
vyākṣipta-manasāṁ nṛṇām
māninām cāti-lubdhānāṁ
mad-vārtāpi na rocate

iṣṭvā—offering sacrifice; *iha*—in this world; *devatāḥ*—to the demigods; *yajñaiḥ*—by our sacrifices; *gatvā*—going; *raṁsyāmahe*—we shall enjoy; *divi*—in heaven; *tasya*—of that enjoyment; *ante*—at the end; *iha*—on this earth; *bhūyāsmaḥ*—we shall become; *mahā-śālāḥ*—great householders; *mahā-kulāḥ*—members of aristocratic families; *evam*—thus; *puṣpitayā*—by the flowery; *vācā*—words; *vyākṣipta-manasām*—for those whose minds are bewildered; *nṛṇām*—men; *māninām*—very proud; *ca*—and; *ati-lubdhānām*—extremely greedy; *mad-vārtā*—topics about Me; *api*—even; *na rocate*—have no attraction.

TRANSLATION

The worshipers of demigods think: "We shall worship the demigods in this life, and by our sacrifices we shall go to heaven and enjoy there. When that enjoyment is finished we shall return to this world and take birth as great householders in aristocratic families." Being excessively proud and greedy, the minds of such persons are bewildered by the flowery words of the *Vedas*. They are not attracted to topics about Me, the Supreme Lord.

PURPORT

Real pleasure is found in the transcendental form of the Lord, who is the supreme Cupid, engaging in pastimes of love in the spiritual world. Neglecting the eternal bliss of the Lord's pastimes, the foolish worshipers of the demigods dream of becoming like the Lord, but they achieve exactly the opposite result. In other words, they continue perpetually in the cycle of birth and death.

TEXT 35

वेदा ब्रह्मात्मविषयास्त्रिकाण्डविषया इमे ।
परोक्षवादा ऋषयः परोक्षं मम च प्रियम् ॥३५॥

vedā brahmātma-viṣayās
tri-kāṇḍa-viṣayā ime
parokṣa-vādā ṛṣayaḥ
parokṣaṁ mama ca priyam

vedāḥ—the *Vedas*; *brahma-ātma*—the understanding that the soul is pure spirit; *viṣayāḥ*—having as their subject matter; *tri-kāṇḍa-viṣayāḥ*—divided into three sections (which represent fruitive work, worship of demigods and realization of the Absolute Truth); *ime*—these; *parokṣa-vādāḥ*—speaking esoterically; *ṛṣayaḥ*—the Vedic authorities; *parokṣam*—indirect explanation; *mama*—to Me; *ca*—also; *priyam*—dear.

TRANSLATION

The *Vedas*, divided into three divisions, ultimately reveal the living entity as pure spirit soul. The Vedic seers and *mantras*, however, deal in esoteric terms, and I also am pleased by such confidential descriptions.

PURPORT

In the previous verses Lord Kṛṣṇa clearly refuted the concept that Vedic knowledge is meant for material enjoyment, and here the Lord summarizes the actual purpose of Vedic literature: self-realization. Although the conditioned souls are struggling in the network of material energy, their actual existence is transcendental freedom in the kingdom of God. The *Vedas* gradually lift the conditioned soul out of the darkness of illusion and establish him in the eternal loving service of the Lord. As stated in the *Vedānta-sūtra* (4.4.23), *anāvṛttiḥ śabdāt:* "One who properly hears Vedic knowledge does not have to return to the cycle of birth and death."

One may ask why the Lord Himself as well as the Lord's representatives, the Vedic seers and *mantras,* speak in esoteric or indirect terms. As the Lord states in *Bhagavad-gītā, nāhaṁ prakāśaḥ sarvasya:* the Supreme Lord does not allow Himself to be taken cheaply, and thus He is not manifest to superficial or inimical people. Those who are polluted by the material atmosphere are induced to purify themselves through Vedic rituals that offer fruitive results, just as a child is induced to take medicine by the offer of a candy reward. Because of the confidential nature of Vedic exposition, less intelligent persons cannot appreciate the ultimate transcendental purpose of the *Vedas,* and consequently they fall down to the platform of sense gratification.

The term *brahmātma* ("spirit soul") ultimately indicates the Supreme Personality of Godhead, who states in *Bhagavad-gītā* that knowledge of Him is *rāja-guhyam,* the most confidential of all secrets. One who depends upon material sense perception remains in gross ignorance of the Absolute Truth. One who depends upon mental and intellectual speculation may get a clue that the eternal soul and Supersoul are both within the material body. But one who depends upon the Lord Himself, faithfully hearing the Lord's own message in *Bhagavad-gītā*, perfectly understands the entire situation and goes back home, back to Godhead, having fulfilled the true purpose of Vedic knowledge.

TEXT 36

शब्दब्रह्म सुदुर्बोधं प्राणेन्द्रियमनोमयम् ।
अनन्तपारं गम्भीरं दुर्विगाह्यं समुद्रवत् ॥३६॥

śabda-brahma su-durbodhaṁ
prāṇendriya-mano-mayam
ananta-pāraṁ gambhīraṁ
durvigāhyaṁ samudra-vat

śabda-brahma—the transcendental sound of the *Vedas; su-durbodham*—extremely difficult to comprehend; *prāṇa*—of the vital air; *indriya*—senses; *manaḥ*—and mind; *mayam*—manifesting on the different levels; *ananta-pāram*—without limit; *gambhīram*—deep; *durvigāhyam*—unfathomable; *samudra-vat*—like the ocean.

TRANSLATION

The transcendental sound of the *Vedas* is very difficult to comprehend and manifests on different levels within the *prāṇa*, senses and mind. This Vedic sound is unlimited, very deep and unfathomable, just like the ocean.

PURPORT

According to Vedic knowledge, the Vedic sound is divided into four phases, which can be understood only by the most intelligent *brāhmaṇas*. This is because three of the divisions are internally situated within the living entity and only the fourth division is externally manifested, as speech. Even this fourth phase of Vedic sound, called *vaikharī*, is very difficult to understand for ordinary human beings. Śrīla Viśvanātha Cakravartī Ṭhākura explains these divisions as follows. The *prāṇa* phase of Vedic sound, known as *parā*, is situated in the *ādhāra-cakra;* the mental phase, known as *paśyantī,* is situated in the area of the navel, on the *maṇipūraka-cakra;* the intellectual phase, known as *madhyamā,* is situated in the heart area, in the *anāhata-cakra.* Finally, the manifest sensory phase of Vedic sound is called *vaikharī.*

Such Vedic sound is *ananta-pāra* because it comprehends all vital energies within the universe and beyond and is thus undivided by time or space. Actually, Vedic sound vibration is so subtle, unfathomable and deep that only the Lord Himself and His empowered followers such as Vyāsa and Nārada can understand its actual form and meaning. Ordinary human beings cannot comprehend all of the intricacies and subtleties of Vedic sound, but if one takes to Kṛṣṇa consciousness one can immediately understand the conclusion of all Vedic knowledge, namely Lord Kṛṣṇa Himself, the original source of Vedic knowledge. Foolish persons devote their vital air, senses and mind to sense gratification and thus do not understand the transcendental value of the holy name of God. Ultimately, the essence of all Vedic sound is the holy name of the Supreme Lord, which is not different from the Lord Himself. Since the Lord is unlimited, His holy name is equally unlimited. No one can understand the transcendental glories of the Lord without the Lord's direct mercy. By offenselessly chanting the holy names Hare Kṛṣṇa, Hare Kṛṣṇa, Kṛṣṇa Kṛṣṇa, Hare Hare/ Hare Rāma, Hare Rāma, Rāma Rāma, Hare Hare, one can enter into the transcendental mysteries of Vedic sound. Otherwise the knowledge of the *Vedas* will remain *durvigāhyam,* or impossible to penetrate.

TEXT 37

मयोपबृंहितं भूम्ना ब्रह्मणानन्तशक्तिना ।
भूतेषु घोषरूपेण बिसेषूर्णेव लक्ष्यते ॥३७॥

mayopabṛṁhitaṁ bhūmnā
brahmaṇānanta-śaktinā
bhūteṣu ghoṣa-rūpeṇa
viseṣūrṇeva lakṣyate

mayā—by Me; *upabṛṁhitam*—established; *bhūmnā*—by the unlimited; *brahmaṇā*—the changeless Absolute; *ananta-śaktinā*—whose potencies have no end; *bhūteṣu*—within the living beings; *ghoṣa-rūpeṇa*—

in the form of subtle sound, the *oṁkāra; viseṣu*—in the subtle fibrous covering of a lotus stalk; *ūrṇā*—one thread; *iva*—as; *lakṣyate*—appears.

TRANSLATION

As the unlimited, unchanging and omnipotent Personality of Godhead dwelling within all living beings, I personally establish the Vedic sound vibration in the form of *oṁkāra* within all living entities. It is thus perceived subtly, just like a single strand of fiber on a lotus stalk.

PURPORT

The Supreme Personality of Godhead personally resides within the heart of every living entity, and from this verse we can understand that the seed of all Vedic knowledge is also situated within all living beings. In this way, the process of awakening Vedic knowledge, and thereby awakening one's eternal relationship with God, is natural and necessary for everyone. All perfection is found within the heart of the living being; as soon as the heart is purified by chanting the holy names of God, that perfection, Kṛṣṇa consciousness, immediately awakens.

TEXTS 38-40

यथोर्णनाभिर्हृदयादूर्णामुद्वमते मुखात् ।
आकाशाद् घोषवान् प्राणो मनसा स्पर्शरूपिणा ॥३८॥
छन्दोमयोऽमृतमयः सहस्रपदवीं प्रभुः ।
ओङ्काराद् व्यञ्जितस्पर्शस्वरोष्मान्तस्थभूषिताम् ॥३९॥
विचित्रभाषाविततां छन्दोभिश्चतुरुत्तरैः ।
अनन्तपारां बृहतीं सृजत्याक्षिपते स्वयम् ॥४०॥

yathorṇanābhir hṛdayād
ūrṇām udvamate mukhāt
ākāśād ghoṣavān prāṇo
manasā sparśa-rūpiṇā

chando-mayo 'mṛta-mayaḥ
sahasra-padavīṁ prabhuḥ

oṁkārād vyañjita-sparśa-
svaroṣmāntastha-bhūṣitām

vicitra-bhāṣā-vitatāṁ
chandobhiś catur-uttaraiḥ
ananta-pārāṁ bṛhatīṁ
sṛjaty ākṣipate svayam

yathā—just as; *ūrṇa-nābhiḥ*—a spider; *hṛdayāt*—from its heart; *ūrṇām*—its web; *udvamate*—emits; *mukhāt*—through its mouth; *ākāśāt*—from the ether; *ghoṣa-vān*—manifesting sound vibration; *prāṇaḥ*—the Lord in the form of the original life air; *manasā*—by means of the primeval mind; *sparśa-rūpiṇā*—which exhibits the forms of the different phonemes of the alphabet, beginning with the *sparśa* letters; *chandaḥ-mayaḥ*—comprising all the sacred Vedic meters; *amṛta-mayaḥ*—full of transcendental pleasure; *sahasra-padavīm*—which branches out in thousands of directions; *prabhuḥ*—the Supreme Personality of Godhead; *oṁkārāt*—from the subtle vibration *oṁkāra; vyañjita*—expanded; *sparśa*—with the consonant stops; *svara*—vowels; *uṣma*—sibilants; *anta-stha*—and semivowels; *bhūṣitām*—decorated; *vicitra*—variegated; *bhāṣā*—by verbal expressions; *vitatām*—elaborated; *chandobhiḥ*—along with the metrical arrangements; *catuḥ-uttaraiḥ*—each having four syllables more than the previous; *ananta-pārām*—limitless; *bṛhatīm*—the great expanse of Vedic literature; *sṛjati*—He creates; *ākṣipate*—and withdraws; *svayam*—Himself.

TRANSLATION

Just as a spider brings forth from its heart its web and emits it through its mouth, the Supreme Personality of Godhead manifests Himself as the reverberating primeval vital air, comprising all sacred Vedic meters and full of transcendental pleasure. Thus the Lord, from the ethereal sky of His heart, creates the great and limitless Vedic sound by the agency of His mind, which conceives of variegated sounds such as the *sparśas*. The Vedic sound branches out in thousands of directions, adorned with the different letters expanded from the syllable *oṁ:* the consonants, vowels, sibilants and semivowels. The *Veda* is then elaborated by many verbal varieties, expressed in different meters, each having

four more syllables than the previous one. Ultimately the Lord again withdraws His manifestation of Vedic sound within Himself.

PURPORT

Śrīla Śrīdhara Svāmī has given an elaborate technical explanation of these three verses, the understanding of which requires extensive linguistic knowledge of the Sanskrit language. The essential point is that transcendental knowledge is expressed through Vedic sound vibration, which is itself a manifestation of the Absolute Truth, the Personality of Godhead. Vedic sound emanates from the Supreme Lord and is vibrated to glorify and understand Him. The conclusion of all Vedic sound vibration is found in *Bhagavad-gītā,* wherein the Lord states, *vedaiś ca sarvair aham eva vedyaḥ:* all Vedic knowledge is simply meant to teach us to know and love God. One who always thinks of Lord Kṛṣṇa, who becomes the Lord's devotee and who bows down to and worships the Lord with faith and devotion, chanting His holy name, has certainly achieved a perfect understanding of all that is indicated by the word *veda* ("knowledge").

TEXT 41

गायत्र्युष्णिगनुष्टुप् च बृहती पङ्क्तिरेव च ।
त्रिष्टुब्जगत्यतिच्छन्दो ह्यत्यष्ट्यतिजगद्विराट् ॥४१॥

gāyatry uṣṇig anuṣṭup ca
bṛhatī paṅktir eva ca
triṣṭub jagaty aticchando
hy atyaṣṭy-atijagad-virāṭ

gāyatrī uṣṇik anuṣṭup ca—known as Gāyatrī, Uṣṇik and Anuṣṭup; *bṛhatī paṅktiḥ*—Bṛhatī and Paṅkti; *eva ca*—also; *triṣṭup jagatī aticchandaḥ*—Triṣṭup, Jagatī and Aticchanda; *hi*—indeed; *atyaṣṭi-atijagat-virāṭ*—Atyaṣṭi, Atijagatī and Ativirāṭ.

TRANSLATION

The Vedic meters are Gāyatrī, Uṣṇik, Anuṣṭup, Bṛhatī, Paṅkti, Triṣṭup, Jagatī, Aticchanda, Atyaṣṭi, Atijagatī and Ativirāṭ.

PURPORT

The Gāyatrī meter has twenty-four syllables, the Uṣṇik twenty-eight, the Anuṣṭup thirty-two, and so on, each meter having four more syllables than the previous one. Vedic sound is called *bṛhatī,* or most expansive, and thus it is not possible for ordinary living entities to understand all the technical details in this matter.

TEXT 42

किं विधत्ते किमाचष्टे किमनूद्य विकल्पयेत् ।
इत्यस्या हृदयं लोके नान्यो मद् वेद कश्चन ॥४२॥

kiṁ vidhatte kim ācaṣṭe
kim anūdya vikalpayet
ity asyā hṛdayaṁ loke
nānyo mad veda kaścana

kim—what; *vidhatte*—enjoins (in the ritualistic *karma-kāṇḍa*); *kim*—what; *ācaṣṭe*—indicates (as the object of worship in the *devatā-kāṇḍa*); *kim*—what; *anūdya*—describing in different aspects; *vikalpayet*—raises the possibility of alternatives (in the *jñāna-kāṇḍa*); *iti*—thus; *asyāḥ*—of Vedic literature; *hṛdayam*—the heart, or confidential purpose; *loke*—in this world; *na*—does not; *anyaḥ*—other; *mat*—than Me; *veda*—know; *kaścana*—anyone.

TRANSLATION

In the entire world no one but Me actually understands the confidential purpose of Vedic knowledge. Thus people do not know what the *Veda* is actually prescribing in the ritualistic injunctions of *karma-kāṇḍa,* nor what object is actually being indicated in the formulas of worship found in the *upāsanā-kāṇḍa,* nor that which is elaborately discussed through various hypotheses in the *jñāna-kāṇḍa* section of the *Veda.*

PURPORT

The Supreme Personality of Godhead is the Absolute Truth, Lord Śrī Kṛṣṇa. Since the Lord is the source, maintainer and ultimate goal of

Vedic knowledge, He is *veda-vit,* or the only true knower of Vedic knowledge. So-called philosophers, either Vedic scholars or ordinary men, may give their sectarian opinion, but it is the Lord Himself who knows the confidential purpose of the *Vedas.* The Lord is the only actual shelter and lovable object for all living entities. As He states in the Tenth Chapter of *Bhagavad-gītā* (10.41):

yad yad vibhūtimat sattvaṁ
śrīmad ūrjitam eva vā
tad tad evāvagaccha tvaṁ
mama tejo-'ṁśa-sambhavam

"Know that all beautiful, glorious and mighty creations spring from but a spark of My splendor." All beautiful, extraordinary and powerful manifestations are insignificant displays of the Lord's own opulences. Although ordinary people may quarrel over the purpose of religion, the actual purpose is one, Kṛṣṇa consciousness, or pure love of Godhead. All Vedic formulas are understood to be preliminary stages leading to the perfect stage of Kṛṣṇa consciousness, in which one fully surrenders to the devotional service of the Lord. The pure devotees of the Lord represent Him within this world and never speak anything which is not authorized by the Lord. Because they are repeating the Lord's own words, they are also to be understood as true knowers of the *Veda.*

TEXT 43

मां विधत्तेऽभिधत्ते मां विकल्प्यापोह्यते त्वहम् ।
एतावान् सर्ववेदार्थः शब्द आस्थाय मां भिदाम् ।
मायामात्रमनूद्यान्ते प्रतिषिध्य प्रसीदति ॥४३॥

māṁ vidhatte 'bhidhatte māṁ
vikalpyāpohyate tv aham
etāvān sarva-vedārthaḥ
śabda āsthāya māṁ bhidām
māyā-mātram anūdyānte
pratiṣidhya prasīdati

mām—Me; *vidhatte*—enjoins in sacrifice; *abhidhatte*—designates as the object of worship; *mām*—Me; *vikalpya*—presented as alternate hypothesis; *apohyate*—am refuted; *tu*—also; *aham*—I; *etāvān*—thus; *sarva-veda*—of all the *Vedas; arthaḥ*—the meaning; *śabdaḥ*—the transcendental sound vibration; *āsthāya*—establishing; *mām*—Me; *bhidām*—material duality; *māyā-mātram*—as simply illusion; *anūdya*—describing elaborately in different aspects; *ante*—ultimately; *pratiṣidhya*—negating; *prasīdati*—becomes satisfied.

TRANSLATION

I am the ritualistic sacrifice enjoined by the *Vedas*, and I am the worshipable Deity. It is I who am presented as various philosohical hypotheses, and it is I alone who am then refuted by philosophical analysis. The transcendental sound vibration thus establishes Me as the essential meaning of all Vedic knowledge. The *Vedas*, elaborately analyzing all material duality as nothing but My illusory potency, ultimately completely negate this duality and achieve their own satisfaction.

PURPORT

The Lord declared in the previous verse that He alone knows the ultimate purpose of the *Vedas*, and now the Lord reveals that He alone is the ultimate basis and purpose of all Vedic knowledge. The *karma-kāṇḍa* section of the *Vedas* prescribes ritualistic sacrifices for promotion to heaven. Such sacrifices are the Lord Himself. Similarly, the *upāsanā-kāṇḍa* section of the *Vedas* designates different demigods as objects of ritualistic worship, and these deities are not different from the Lord Himself, being expansions of the Lord's body. In the *jñāna-kāṇḍa* section of the *Vedas* different philosophical methods of analysis are presented and refuted. Such knowledge, which analyzes the potency of the Supreme Lord, is not different from Him. Ultimately Lord Kṛṣṇa is everything, because everything is part and parcel of the Lord's multipotencies. Although Vedic literature entices those absorbed in material duality to begin the Vedic way of life by offering them materially desirable rewards, the *Vedas* eventually refute all material duality by bringing one to the stage of God consciousness, wherein there is nothing different from the Supreme Lord.

Within the Vedic literature there are various injunctions stating that at a particular stage of life one should give up fruitive rituals and take to the path of knowledge. Similarly, other injunctions declare that a self-realized soul should give up the path of speculative knowledge and take directly to the shelter of the Absolute Truth, the Personality of Godhead. But nowhere is there an injunction recommending that one give up the loving service of the Lord, because that is the eternal constitutional position of every living entity. Different philosophical theses are presented and rejected in the *Vedas*, since one who is progressing must give up each previous stage in the advancement of knowledge. For example, one who is addicted to sex enjoyment is taught to accept religious marriage and enjoy sex pleasure with his wife. Such ritualistic knowledge is to be given up when one attains the stage of detachment, whereupon one is recommended to take the renounced order of life. In that stage of life one is forbidden to see or speak with women. When, however, one reaches the perfection of Kṛṣṇa consciousness, wherein the Lord is manifest everywhere, one may engage all living entities, including women, in the loving service of the Lord without danger of spiritual falldown. Thus different injunctions based on progressive stages of spiritual vision are presented and refuted in Vedic literature. Since all such injunctions and processes are ultimately meant for the achievement of Kṛṣṇa consciousness, the loving service of the Lord, they are not different from Lord Kṛṣṇa Himself. The conditioned soul, therefore, should not prematurely stop his progressive march back home, back to Godhead, by foolishly mistaking an intermediate or preliminary stage of advancement as the actual goal of life. One must understand that the Supreme Personality of Godhead, Śrī Kṛṣṇa, is the source, maintenance and resting place of everything, and that every living entity is the Lord's eternal servant. In this way one should continue on the Vedic path all the way back home, back to Godhead, for eternal life of bliss and knowledge.

Thus end the purports of the humble servant of His Divine Grace A. C. Bhaktivedanta Swami Prabhupāda to the Eleventh Canto, Twenty-first Chapter, of the Śrīmad-Bhāgavatam, *entitled "Lord Kṛṣṇa's Explanation of the Vedic Path."*

CHAPTER TWENTY-TWO

Enumeration of the Elements of Material Creation

This chapter enumerates and categorizes the natural elements, explains the difference between the male and female natures and describes birth and death.

There are many opinions concerning the number of material elements. But this difference of opinions, brought about by the influence of the illusory energy, is not illogical. All the elements of nature exist everywhere; so authorities who have accepted the illusory potency of the Supreme Personality may propose a variety of theories. The insurmountable illusory energy of God is the root cause of their mutually contradictory arguments.

There is no difference between the ultimate enjoyer and the supreme controller. To presuppose any distinction between them is senseless. Ordinary knowledge is simply a quality of material nature, not of the soul proper. The raw substance of material nature is designated according to its different phases. In the mode of goodness, it is known as knowledge, in the mode of passion as activity, and in the mode of darkness as ignorance. Time is another name of the Supreme Personality of Godhead, and another name for material propensity is *sūtra* or *mahat-tattva.* The twenty-five elements of nature are the Lord, nature, the *mahat,* false ego, ether, air, fire, water, earth, the eyes, the ears, the nose, the tongue, the skin, speech, the hands, the feet, the genitals, the anus, the mind, sound, touch, form, taste and smell.

The unmanifest Supreme Personality merely glances at nature. Material nature, which is under the control of the Supreme Lord, then assumes the forms of causes and effects and carries out the creation, maintenance and destruction of the material world. Even though the *puruṣa* and *prakṛti* appear nondifferent to superficial vision, there is an ultimate difference between the two. Material creation is produced from the modes of *prakṛti,* and its quality is transformation. The living entities who are inimical to the Supreme Personality of Godhead take on and give up various kinds of material bodies through the agency of their own material work. But those who are ignorant of the self, because of being bewildered by illusion, do not understand this. The mind, which is filled with ideas of fruitive work, simply takes the senses with it from one body to another, while the soul follows along. Nevertheless, on account of being totally absorbed in sense gratification, one cannot remember his past existence.

The body undergoes nine stages of manifestation, which are brought about by association with the qualities of material nature. These are impregnation, gestation, birth, childhood, youth, maturity, middle age, old age and death. From the death of one's father and the birth of one's son, a person can easily comprehend the rise and fall of his own body. The soul, who is the perceiver, is different from this body. But when there is no knowledge of the true facts, the living entity, confused by the objects of sense gratification, achieves his destinations within the cycle of material existence. Thus the living entity continuously wanders under the spell of material work, taking birth as a sage or a demigod when he is predominated by the mode of goodness, among the demons or human beings when he is predominantly influenced by the mode of passion, and in the species of ghosts, spirits or animals when he is predominated by the mode of ignorance. The spirit soul does not engage in the enjoyment of sense objects; rather, it is the senses that perform this activity. Therefore the living being has no actual need for sense gratificatory pleasures. With the exception of those peaceful personalities who have taken shelter of the lotus feet of the Supreme Personality of Godhead and are dedicated to the divine duty of His service, everyone, including so-called learned scholars, is inevitably overcome by the all-powerful material nature.

TEXTS 1-3

श्री उद्धव उवाच

कति तत्त्वानि विश्वेश संख्यातान्यृषिभिः प्रभो ।
नवैकादश पञ्च त्रीण्यात्थ त्वमिह शुश्रुम ॥ १ ॥
केचित् षड्विंशतिं प्राहुरपरे पञ्चविंशतिम् ।
सप्तैके नव षट् केचिच्चत्वार्येकादशापरे ।

केचित् सप्तदश प्राहुः षोडशैके त्रयोदश ॥ २ ॥
एतावत्त्वं हि संख्यानामृषयो यद्विवक्षया ।
गायन्ति पृथगायुष्मन्निदं नो वक्तुमर्हसि ॥ ३ ॥

śrī-uddhava uvāca
kati tattvāni viśveśa
saṅkhyātāny ṛṣibhiḥ prabho
navaikādaśa pañca trīṇy
āttha tvam iha śuśruma

kecit ṣaḍ-viṁśatiṁ prāhur
apare pañca-viṁśatiṁ
saptaike nava ṣaṭ kecic
catvāry ekādaśāpare
kecit saptadaśa prāhuḥ
ṣoḍaśaike trayodaśa

etāvattvaṁ hi saṅkhyānām
ṛṣayo yad-vivakṣayā
gāyanti pṛthag āyuṣmann
idaṁ no vaktum arhasi

śrī-uddhavaḥ uvāca—Śrī Uddhava said; *kati*—how many; *tattvāni*—basic elements of creation; *viśva-īśa*—O Lord of the universe; *saṅkhyātāni*—have been enumerated; *ṛṣibhiḥ*—by great authorities; *prabho*—O my master; *nava*—nine (God, the individual soul, the *mahat-tattva,* false ego and the five gross elements); *ekākaśa*—plus eleven (the ten knowledge-acquiring and working senses together with the mind); *pañca*—plus five (the subtle forms of the sense objects); *trīṇi*—plus three (the modes of goodness, passion and ignorance, making altogether a total of twenty-eight); *āttha*—have stated; *tvam*—You; *iha*—during Your appearance in this world; *śuśruma*—so I have heard; *kecit*—some; *ṣaṭ-viṁśatim*—twenty-six; *prāhuḥ*—they say; *apare*—others; *pañca-viṁśatim*—twenty-five; *sapta*—seven; *eke*—some; *nava*—nine; *ṣaṭ*—six; *kecit*—some; *catvāri*—four; *ekādaśa*—eleven; *apare*—still others; *kecit*—some; *saptadaśa*—seventeen; *prāhuḥ*—say; *ṣoḍaśa*—sixteen; *eke*—some; *trayodaśa*—thirteen; *etāvattvam*—such calculations; *hi*—indeed; *saṅkhyānām*—of the different ways of counting the elements; *ṛṣayaḥ*—

the sages; *yat-vivakṣayā*—with the intention of expressing what ideas; *gāyanti*—they have declared; *pṛthak*—in various manners; *āyuḥ-man*—O supreme eternal; *idam*—this; *naḥ*—to us; *vaktum*—to explain; *arhasi*—You should please.

TRANSLATION

Uddhava inquired: My dear Lord, O master of the universe, how many different elements of creation have been enumerated by the great sages? I have heard You personally describe a total of twenty-eight—God, the *jīva* soul, the *mahat-tattva*, false ego, the five gross elements, the ten senses, the mind, the five subtle objects of perception and the three modes of nature. But some authorities say that there are twenty-six elements, while others cite twenty-five or else seven, nine, six, four or eleven, and even others say that there are seventeen, sixteen or thirteen. What did each of these sages have in mind when he calculated the creative elements in such different ways? O supreme eternal, kindly explain this to me.

PURPORT

Lord Kṛṣṇa thoroughly explained in the previous chapter that Vedic knowledge is not meant for sense gratification but for liberation from material bondage. Now Uddhava presents some intermediate questions that must be answered so the path of liberation will be clear. Different philosophers have historically disagreed over the exact number of material elements, about the existence and nonexistence of particular external objects and about the existence of the soul itself. The *jñāna-kāṇḍa* section of the *Vedas* aims at liberation through analytic understanding of the material world and of the spirit soul as a transcendental element beyond matter. Ultimately the Supreme Lord Himself stands above all elements and maintains them by His personal potency. Uddhava mentions in numerical terms different methodologies of various sages, citing first the Lord's own opinion. The word *āyuṣman,* or "possessing eternal form," is significant in this regard. Since Lord Kṛṣṇa is eternal, He possesses all knowledge of past, present and future and is thus the original and supreme philosopher.

According to Śrīla Viśvanātha Carkavartī Ṭhākura, the different analytic approaches mentioned by Śrī Uddhava are actually not contradictory, since they are different methods of categorizing the same reality. Atheistic speculation on reality does not recognize the existence of God; consequently it is a worthless attempt to explain the truth. The Lord Himself empowers different living entities to speculate and speak on reality in different ways. The actual reality, however, is the Lord Himself, who will now speak to Śrī Uddhava.

TEXT 4

श्रीभगवानुवाच
युक्तं च सन्ति सर्वत्र भाषन्ते ब्राह्मणा यथा ।
मायां मदीयामुद्गृह्य वदतां किं नु दुर्घटम् ॥ ४ ॥

śrī-bhagavān uvāca
yuktaṁ ca santi sarvatra
bhāṣante brāhmaṇā yathā
māyāṁ madīyām udgṛhya
vadatāṁ kiṁ nu durghaṭam

śrī-bhagavān uvāca—the Supreme Personality of Godhead said; *yuktam*—reasonably; *ca*—even; *santi*—they are present; *sarvatra*—everywhere; *bhāṣante*—they speak; *brāhmaṇāḥ*—*brāhmaṇas; yathā*—how; *māyām*—the mystic energy; *madīyām*—My; *udgṛhya*—resorting to; *vadatām*—of those who speak; *kim*—what; *nu*—after all; *durghaṭam*—will be impossible.

TRANSLATION

Lord Kṛṣṇa replied: Because all material elements are present everywhere, it is reasonable that different learned *brāhmaṇas* have analyzed them in different ways. All such philosophers spoke under the shelter of My mystic potency, and thus they could say anything without contradicting the truth.

PURPORT

The words *santi sarvatra* in this verse indicate that all material elements are found within each other in gross and subtle forms. In this way there are innumerable ways to categorically describe them. The material world is ultimately illusory, undergoing constant transformation. It may be measured in different ways, just as the mirage of an oasis may be described in different ways, but the Lord's own analysis of twenty-eight elements is perfect and should be accepted. Śrīla Jīva Gosvāmī states that the word *māyā* in this verse does not refer to *mahā-māyā,* or the potency of ignorance, but to the Lord's inconceivable mystic power, which shelters the learned followers of Vedic knowledge. Each of the philosophers mentioned here reveals a particular aspect of truth, and their theories are not contradictory, since they are simply describing the same phenomena with different categorical systems. Such philosophical disagreement is endless within the material world; thus everyone should unite on the platform of the Lord's own opinion, as stated in this verse. Similarly, in *Bhagavad-gītā* Lord Kṛṣṇa requests all conditioned souls to give up their various forms of worship and surrender unto Him in full Kṛṣṇa consciousness, becoming His devotees. Thus the whole universe can be united in love of Godhead by chanting Hare Kṛṣṇa, Hare Kṛṣṇa, Kṛṣṇa Kṛṣṇa, Hare Hare/ Hare Rāma, Hare Rāma, Rāma Rāma, Hare Hare. By the Lord's revealing Himself to a sincere devotee, the controversy of analytic philosophy is ended.

TEXT 5

नैतदेवं यथात्थ त्वं यदहं वच्मि तत्तथा ।
एवं विवदतां हेतुं शक्तयो मे दुरत्यया: ॥ ५ ॥

naitad evaṁ yathāttha tvaṁ
yad ahaṁ vacmi tat tathā
evaṁ vivadatāṁ hetuṁ
śaktayo me duratyayāḥ

na—it is not; *etat*—this; *evam*—so; *yathā*—as; *āttha*—say; *tvam*—you; *yat*—which; *aham*—I; *vacmi*—am saying; *tat*—that; *tathā*—thus; *evam*—in this way; *vivadatām*—for those who argue; *hetum*—over logical reasons; *śaktayaḥ*—the energies (are impelling); *me*—My; *duratyayāḥ*—unsurpassable.

TRANSLATION

When philosophers argue, "I don't choose to analyze this particular case in the same way as you have," it is simply My own insurmountable energies that are motivating their analytic disagreements.

PURPORT

Because of the material potencies of the Supreme Lord, mundane philosophers are perpetually arguing about which came first, the chicken or the egg. By the influence of the modes of goodness, passion and ignorance, different philosophers are attracted to different views; and by the influence of the material atmosphere created by the Lord, these philosophers perpetually disagree with one another. The Supreme Lord Himself, however, has given the clear explanation. As stated in *Śrīmad-Bhāgavatam* (6.4.31),

yac-chaktayo vadatāṁ vādināṁ vai
vivāda-saṁvāda-bhuvo bhavanti
kurvanti caiṣāṁ muhur ātma-mohaṁ
tasmai namo 'nanta-guṇāya bhūmne

"Let me offer my respectful obeisances unto the all-pervading Supreme Personality of Godhead, who possesses unlimited transcendental qualities. Acting from within the cores of the hearts of all philosophers, who propagate various views, He caused them to forget their own souls while sometimes agreeing and sometimes disagreeing among themselves. Thus He creates within this material world a situation in which they are unable to come to a conclusion. I offer my respectful obeisances unto Him."

TEXT 6

यासां व्यतिकरादासीद् विकल्पो वदतां पदम् ।
प्राप्ते शमदमेऽप्येति वादस्तमनुशाम्यति ॥ ६ ॥

yāsāṁ vyatikarād āsīd
vikalpo vadatāṁ padam
prāpte śama-dame 'pyeti
vādas tam anu śāmyati

yāsām—of which (energies of Mine); *vyatikarāt*—by the interaction; *āsīt*—has arisen; *vikalpaḥ*—difference of opinion; *vadatām*—of those arguing; *padam*—the subject of discussion; *prāpte*—when one has achieved; *śama*—the ability to fix his intelligence on Me; *dame*—and control of his external senses; *apyeti*—disappears (that difference of opinion); *vādaḥ*—the argument itself; *tam anu*—consequently; *śāmyati*—subsides.

TRANSLATION

By interaction of My energies different opinions arise. But for those who have fixed their intelligence in Me, controlling the senses, differences of perception disappear, and consequently the very cause for argument is removed.

PURPORT

Conflicting varieties of perception are created by the interaction of the Lord's material energies in the minds of different philosophers, who staunchly defend their opinions, stating, "This may be the case or perhaps that or the other; or this may not be the case, or perhaps that is not the case." Such logical or rational proposing, doubting, counter-proposing, counteracting, etc., take thousands of different forms and become the basis of argument. Actually, the Supreme Personality of Godhead, Lord Kṛṣṇa, is the basis of all existence, since everything emanates from the Lord, is maintained by the Lord and at the end is merged to rest within the Lord. Lord Kṛṣṇa is *para-tattva,* the highest truth underlying all other dependent truths. In a society of learned persons who have understood the Personality of Godhead to be everything, there is no further cause of philosophical quarrel. Such unity of opinion is not based on the absence of philosophical inquiry, nor on the stifling of rational discussion, but is the natural result of spiritual enlightenment. So-called philosophers proudly boast that they are searching and researching for the Absolute Truth, yet they somehow consider one who has found the Absolute Truth to be less intelligent than one who has not found it but is searching. Because Lord Kṛṣṇa is the Absolute Truth, one who fully surrenders to the Lord becomes the most learned person.

TEXT 7

परस्परानुप्रवेशात् तत्त्वानां पुरुषर्षभ ।
पौर्वापर्यप्रसंख्यानं यथा वक्तुर्विवक्षितम् ॥ ७ ॥

parasparānupraveśāt
tattvānāṁ puruṣarṣabha
paurvāparya-prasaṅkhyānaṁ
yathā vaktur vivakṣitam

paraspara—mutual; *anupraveśāt*—because of the entrance (as subtle causes within gross manifestations, and vice versa); *tattvānām*—of the various elements; *puruṣa-ṛṣabha*—O best among men (Uddhava); *paurva*—in terms of prior causes; *aparya*—or of resultant products; *prasaṅkhyānam*—enumeration; *yathā*—however; *vaktuḥ*—the speaker; *vivakṣitam*—wants to describe.

TRANSLATION

O best among men, because subtle and gross elements mutually enter into one another, philosophers may calculate the number of basic material elements in different ways, according to their personal desire.

PURPORT

Material creation takes place as a chain reaction in which subtle elements expand and transform into progressively denser elements. Since a cause is in a sense present within its effect, and the effect is subtly present within the cause, all subtle and gross elements have entered within one another. Thus one may categorize basic material elements in many different ways, assigning various numbers and names according to one's methodology. Although material philosophers proudly assume their individual theories to be supreme, they are all speculating according to their personal proclivities, as described in this and the following verse.

TEXT 8

एकस्मिन्नपि दृश्यन्ते प्रविष्टानीतराणि च ।
पूर्वस्मिन् वा परस्मिन् वा तत्त्वे तत्त्वानि सर्वशः ॥ ८ ॥

ekasminn api dṛśyante
praviṣṭānītarāṇi ca

pūrvasmin vā parasmin vā
tattve tattvāni sarvaśaḥ

ekasmin—in one (element); *api*—even; *dṛśyante*—there are seen; *praviṣṭāni*—entered within; *itarāṇi*—others; *ca*—also; *pūrvasmin*—in a prior (subtle causal element, such as the dormant presence of ether within its cause, sound); *vā*—either; *parasmin*—or in a later (produced element, such as the subtle presence of sound within its further product, air); *vā*—or; *tattve*—in some element; *tattvāni*—other elements; *sarvaśaḥ*—in the cases of each of the different enumerations.

TRANSLATION

All subtle material elements are actually present within their gross effects; similarly, all gross elements are present within their subtle causes, since material creation takes place by progressive manifestation of elements from subtle to gross. Thus we can find all material elements within any single element.

PURPORT

Since material elements are present within each other, there are innumerable ways to construe and categorize the material creation of God. Ultimately, however, the significant element is God Himself, who is the basis of all the transformations and permutations of the material cosmos. The creation of the material world takes place by a progression from subtle to gross elements, as explained in the *sāṅkhya-yoga* system of Lord Kapila. The example may be given that we find the dormant existence of an earthen pot within mud and also the existence of mud within the earthen pot. Similarly, one element is present within another, and ultimately all elements rest within the Supreme Personality of Godhead, who is simultaneously within everything. By such explanations, Kṛṣṇa consciousness constitutes the ultimate scientific methodology for factually understanding this universe.

TEXT 9

पौर्वापर्यमतोऽमीषां प्रसंख्यानमभीप्सताम् ।
यथा विविक्तं यद्वक्त्रं गृह्णीमो युक्तिसम्भवात् ॥ ९ ॥

paurvāparyam ato 'mīṣāṁ
prasaṅkhyānam abhīpsatām
yathā viviktaṁ yad-vaktraṁ
gṛhṇīmo yukti-sambhavāt

paurva—considering causal elements to include their manifest products; *aparyam*—or assuming elements to include their subtle causes; *ataḥ*—therefore; *amīṣām*—of these thinkers; *prasaṅkhyānam*—the counting; *abhīpsatām*—who are intending; *yathā*—how; *viviktam*—ascertained; *yat-vaktram*—from whose mouth; *gṛhṇīmaḥ*—We accept it; *yukti*—of reason; *sambhavāt*—because of the possibility.

TRANSLATION

Therefore, no matter which of these thinkers is speaking, and regardless of whether in their calculations they include material elements within their previous subtle causes or else within their subsequent manifest products, I accept their conclusions as authoritative, because a logical explanation can always be given for each of the different theories.

PURPORT

Although innumerable philosophers may rationally describe the material creation from different points of view, one cannot perfect one's knowledge without Kṛṣṇa consciousness. An intellectual person should therefore not be falsely proud simply because he has ascertained a particular truth within the material world. The Lord here states that one who follows the Vedic way of analysis will undoubtedly have many insights concerning the material creation. Ultimately, however, one must become a devotee of the Supreme Lord and perfect one's knowledge in Kṛṣṇa consciousness.

TEXT 10

अनाद्यविद्यायुक्तस्य पुरुषस्यात्मवेदनम् ।
स्वतो न सम्भवादन्यस्तत्त्वज्ञो ज्ञानदो भवेत् ॥ १० ॥

anādy-avidyā-yuktasya
puruṣasyātma-vedanam

svato na sambhavād anyas
tattva-jño jñāna-do bhavet

anādi—without beginning; *avidyā*—with ignorance; *yuktasya*—who is joined; *puruṣasya*—of a person; *ātma-vedanam*—the process of self-realization; *svataḥ*—by his own ability; *na sambhavāt*—because it cannot occur; *anyaḥ*—another person; *tattva-jñaḥ*—the knower of transcendental reality; *jñāna-daḥ*—the bestower of real knowledge; *bhavet*—must be.

TRANSLATION

Because a person who has been covered by ignorance since time immemorial is not capable of effecting his own self-realization, there must be some other personality who is in factual knowledge of the Absolute Truth and can impart this knowledge to him.

PURPORT

Although the Lord tolerates different methods of calculating material causes within their effects and material effects within their causes, there cannot be any speculation regarding the two spiritual elements found in this universe, namely the individual soul and the Supersoul. Lord Kṛṣṇa clearly states in this verse that the living entity is incapable of effecting his own enlightenment. The Supreme Lord is *tattva-jña,* omniscient, and *jñāna-da,* the spiritual master of the entire universe. Śrī Uddhava mentioned that some philosophers describe twenty-five elements and others twenty-six. The difference is that the twenty-six elements include a separate category for the individual soul and the Supreme Soul, Lord Kṛṣṇa, whereas the proponents of twenty-five elements artificially merge the two transcendental categories of *jīva-tattva* and *viṣṇu-tattva,* hiding the eternal supremacy of the Personality of Godhead.

Knowledge based on the three modes of material nature cannot rise to the transcendental platform, where the Personality of Godhead exists as the supreme enjoyer of eternal spiritual varieties of form, color, flavor, musical sounds and loving affairs. Mundane philosophers simply bounce back and forth between material enjoyment and material renunciation. Being victims of Māyāvāda (impersonal) perception of the Absolute Truth, they cannot achieve the shelter of the Personality of Godhead and thus cannot understand Him. Because foolish, impersonal philosophers consider themselves supreme, they are unable to appreciate that loving service exists on the spiritual platform. Stubbornly rejecting subservience to the Personality of Godhead, the impersonalists are eventually overwhelmed by the illusory potency of the Lord and undergo the miseries of material existence. The Vaiṣṇavas, on the other hand, are not envious of the Personality of Godhead. They gladly accept His shelter and supremacy, and thus the Lord personally takes charge of His devotees and enlightens them, filling them with His own transcendental bliss. Spiritual service to the Supreme Lord is in this way free from the disappointment and repression of material service.

TEXT 11

पुरुषेश्वरयोरत्र न वैलक्षण्यमण्वपि ।
तदन्यकल्पनापार्था ज्ञानं च प्रकृतेर्गुणः ॥११॥

puruṣeśvarayor atra
na vailakṣaṇyam aṇv api
tad-anya-kalpanāpārthā
jñānaṁ ca prakṛter guṇaḥ

puruṣa—between the enjoyer; *īśvarayoḥ*—and the supreme controller; *atra*—herein; *na*—there is no; *vailakṣaṇyam*—dissimilarity; *aṇu*—minute; *api*—even; *tat*—of them; *anya*—as being completely different; *kalpanā*—the imagined idea; *apārthā*—useless; *jñānam*—knowledge; *ca*—and; *prakṛteḥ*—of material nature; *guṇaḥ*—a quality.

TRANSLATION

According to knowledge in the material mode of goodness, there is no qualitative difference between the living entity and the supreme controller. The imagination of qualitative difference between them is useless speculation.

PURPORT

According to certain philosophers there are twenty-five elements, among which a single category is stipulated for both the individual living entity and the Supreme Lord. Such impersonal knowledge is declared by the Lord to be material: *jñānaṁ ca prakṛter guṇaḥ*. Such knowledge can, however, be accepted to establish the qualitative identity of the Supreme Lord and the living entities who expand from Him. Materialistic persons sometimes believe that there is a supreme spirit in heaven but also think that human beings are identical with their material bodies and thus qualitatively and perpetually separated from the Supreme Lord. Knowledge of the Lord's qualitative oneness with the living entity, as described in this verse, refutes the materialistic concept of life and partially establishes the Absolute Truth. Śrī Caitanya Mahāprabhu described the actual situation as *acintya-bhedābheda-tattva:* the supreme controller and the controlled living entities are simultaneously one and different. In the material mode of goodness the oneness is perceived. As one proceeds further, to the stage of *viśuddha-sattva,* or purified spiritual goodness, one finds spiritual variety within the qualitative oneness, completing one's knowledge of the Absolute Truth. The words *na vailakṣaṇyam aṇv api* boldly affirm that the individual living entity is indisputably part and parcel of the Supreme Lord and qualitatively one with Him. Any philosophical attempt to separate the living entity from the Supreme Lord and deny his eternal servitude to the Lord is thus refuted. Speculation arriving at the conclusion that the living entity has independent existence separate from the Lord is described here as *apārthā,* useless. Nevertheless, the theory of twenty-five elements is acceptable to the Lord as a preliminary phase in the evolution of spiritual knowledge.

TEXT 12

प्रकृतिर्गुणसाम्यं वै प्रकृतेर्नात्मनो गुणाः ।
सत्त्वं रजस्तम इति स्थित्युत्पत्त्यन्तहेतवः ॥१२॥

prakṛtir guṇa-sāmyaṁ vai
prakṛter nātmano guṇāḥ
sattvaṁ rajas tama iti
sthity-utpatty-anta-hetavaḥ

prakṛtiḥ—material nature; *guṇa*—of the three modes; *sāmyam*—the original equilibrium; *vai*—indeed; *prakṛteḥ*—of nature; *na ātmanaḥ*—not of the spirit soul; *guṇāḥ*—these modes; *sattvam*—goodness; *rajaḥ*—passion; *tamaḥ*—ignorance; *iti*—thus called; *sthiti*—of the maintenance of universal creation; *utpatti*—its production; *anta*—and its annihilation; *hetavaḥ*—the causes.

TRANSLATION

Nature exists originally as the equilibrium of the three material modes, which pertain only to nature, not to the transcendental spirit soul. These modes—goodness, passion and ignorance—are the effective causes of the creation, maintenance and destruction of this universe.

PURPORT

In *Bhagavad-gītā* (3.27) it is stated,

prakṛteḥ kriyamāṇāni
guṇaiḥ karmāṇi sarvaśaḥ
ahaṅkāra-vimūḍhātmā
kartāham iti manyate

"The bewildered spirit soul, under the influence of the three modes of material nature, thinks himself to be the doer of activities, which are in actuality carried out by nature."

The three modes of nature, in their original state of equilibrium, as well as the subsequent creation generated from the modes, are vastly more powerful than the tiny living entity who is controlled by them. The living entity thus cannot be accepted as the actual doer or creator within the material world. The mode of goodness is symptomized by the experience of knowledge, the mode of passion by the experience of work, and the mode of ignorance by the experience of darkness. These modes of material knowledge, work and darkness have no real relation with the transcendental spirit soul, who exhibits his own qualities of eternality, bliss and knowledge (the *sandhinī, saṁvit* and *hlādinī* potencies of the Supreme Lord). The material modes have no access within the kingdom of God, in the unbounded atmosphere of which the eternal living entity is meant to live.

TEXT 13

सत्त्वं ज्ञानं रजः कर्म तमोऽज्ञानमिहोच्यते ।
गुणव्यतिकरः कालः स्वभावः सूत्रमेव च ॥१३॥

sattvaṁ jñānaṁ rajaḥ karma
tamo 'jñānam ihocyate
guṇa-vyatikaraḥ kālaḥ
svabhāvaḥ sūtram eva ca

sattvam—the mode of goodness; *jñānam*—knowledge; *rajaḥ*—the mode of passion; *karma*—fruitive work; *tamaḥ*—the mode of ignorance; *ajñānam*—foolishness; *iha*—in this world; *ucyate*—is called; *guṇa*—of the modes; *vyatikaraḥ*—the agitated transformation; *kālaḥ*—time; *svabhāvaḥ*—innate tendency, nature; *sūtram*—the *mahat-tattva; eva*—indeed; *ca*—also.

TRANSLATION

In this world the mode of goodness is recognized as knowledge, the mode of passion as fruitive work, and the mode of darkness as ignorance. Time is perceived as the agitated interaction of the material modes, and the totality of functional propensity is embodied by the primeval *sūtra*, or *mahat-tattva.*

PURPORT

The impetus for the interaction of the material elements is the forward movement of time. Because time is passing, the embryo grows within the womb, gradually comes out, grows up, produces by-products, dwindles and dies. All of this is due to the pushing of time. In the absence of the time factor, the material elements do not interact but remain inert in the form of *pradhāna*. Lord Kṛṣṇa is establishing the basic categories of the material world so that human beings can conceive of the Lord's creation. Were the categories not condensed, analysis and conceptualization would be impossible, since the Lord's potencies are infinite. Although there are numerous divisions of material elements within the basic divisions, the spirit soul is always to be understood as a distinct transcendental element, meant for residence in the kindgom of God.

TEXT 14

पुरुषः प्रकृतिर्व्यक्तमहङ्कारो नभोऽनिलः ।
ज्योतिरापः क्षितिरिति तत्त्वान्युक्तानि मे नव ॥१४॥

puruṣaḥ prakṛtir vyaktam
ahaṅkāro nabho 'nilaḥ
jyotir āpaḥ kṣitir iti
tattvāny uktāni me nava

puruṣaḥ—the enjoyer; *prakṛtiḥ*—nature; *vyaktam*—the primeval manifestation of matter; *ahaṅkāraḥ*—false ego; *nabhaḥ*—ether; *anilaḥ*—air; *jyotiḥ*—fire; *āpaḥ*—water; *kṣitiḥ*—earth; *iti*—thus; *tattvāni*—the elements of creation; *uktāni*—have been described; *me*—by Me; *nava*—nine.

TRANSLATION

I have described the nine basic elements as the enjoying soul, nature, its primeval manifestation of the *mahat-tattva,* false ego, ether, air, fire, water and earth.

PURPORT

Prakṛti, or nature, is originally unmanifest and later becomes manifest as the *mahat-tattva.* Although the living entity is *puruṣa,* an enjoyer, the real process by which he can enjoy is by satisfying the transcendental senses of the Lord, just as the hand eats by supplying food to the stomach. Within material nature the living entity becomes a false enjoyer, forgetting his subservience to the Lord. The material elements as well as the living entity and the Supersoul are thus systematically analyzed to demonstrate to the conditioned soul his actual constitutional position beyond material nature.

TEXT 15

श्रोत्रं त्वग्दर्शनं घ्राणो जिह्वेति ज्ञानशक्तयः ।
वाक्पाण्युपस्थपाय्वङ्घ्रिः कर्माण्यङ्गोभयं मनः ॥१५॥

śrotraṁ tvag darśanaṁ ghrāṇo
jihveti jñāna-śaktayaḥ
vāk-pāṇy-upastha-pāyv-aṅghriḥ
karmāṇy aṅgobhayaṁ manaḥ

śrotram—the sense of hearing; *tvak*—the sense of touch, experienced upon the skin; *darśanam*—sight; *ghrāṇaḥ*—smell; *jihvā*—the sense of taste, experienced upon the tongue; *iti*—thus; *jñāna-śaktayaḥ*—the knowledge-acquiring senses; *vāk*—speech; *pāṇi*—the hands; *upastha*—the genitals; *pāyu*—the anus; *aṅghriḥ*—and the legs; *karmāṇi*—the working senses; *aṅga*—My dear Uddhava; *ubhayam*—belonging to both these categories; *manaḥ*—the mind.

TRANSLATION

Hearing, touch, sight, smell and taste are the five knowledge-acquiring senses, My dear Uddhava, and speech, the hands, the genitals, the anus and the legs constitute the five working senses. The mind belongs to both these categories.

PURPORT

Eleven elements are mentioned in this verse.

TEXT 16

शब्दः स्पर्शो रसो गन्धो रूपं चेत्यर्थजातयः ।
गत्युक्त्युत्सर्गशिल्पानि कर्मायतनसिद्धयः ॥१६॥

śabdaḥ sparśo raso gandho
rūpaṁ cety artha-jātayaḥ
gaty-ukty-utsarga-śilpāni
karmāyatana-siddhayaḥ

śabdaḥ—sound; *sparśaḥ*—touch; *rasaḥ*—taste; *gandhaḥ*—fragrance; *rūpam*—form; *ca*—and; *iti*—thus; *artha*—of sense objects; *jātayaḥ*—the categories; *gati*—movement; *ukti*—speech; *utsarga*—excretion (by both the genitals and anus); *śilpāni*—and manufacture; *karma-āyatana*—by the above-mentioned working senses; *siddhayaḥ*—accomplished.

TRANSLATION

Sound, touch, taste, smell and form are the objects of the knowledge-acquiring senses, and movement, speech, excretion and manufacture are functions of the working senses.

PURPORT

Here the word *utsarga* refers to evacuation by the genitals and anus, and thus constitutes two elements. In this way ten elements are listed here in two sets of five.

TEXT 17

सर्गादौ प्रकृतिर्ह्यस्य कार्यकारणरूपिणी ।
सत्त्वादिभिर्गुणैर्धत्ते पुरुषोऽव्यक्त ईक्षते ॥१७॥

sargādau prakṛtir hy asya
kārya-kāraṇa-rūpiṇī
sattvādibhir guṇair dhatte
puruṣo 'vyakta īkṣate

sarga—of creation; *ādau*—in the beginning; *prakṛtiḥ*—the material nature; *hi*—indeed; *asya*—of this universe; *kārya*—the manifest products; *kāraṇa*—and subtle causes; *rūpiṇī*—embodying; *sattva-ādibhiḥ*—by means of goodness, passion and ignorance; *guṇaiḥ*—the modes; *dhatte*—assumes its position; *puruṣaḥ*—the Supreme Lord; *avyaktaḥ*—not involved in material manifestation; *īkṣate*—witnesses.

TRANSLATION

In the beginning of creation nature assumes, by the modes of goodness, passion and ignorance, its form as the embodiment of all subtle causes and gross manifestations within the universe. The Supreme Personality of Godhead does not enter the interaction of material manifestation but merely glances upon nature.

PURPORT

The Personality of Godhead is not subject to transformation like the subtle and gross material elements. Thus the Lord is *avyakta,* or not materially manifest at any stage of cosmic evolution. Regardless of the specific method of cataloging the material elements, the Lord remains the ultimate creator, maintainer and annihilator of the total cosmic situation.

TEXT 18

व्यक्तादयो विकुर्वाणा धातवः पुरुषेक्षया ।
लब्धवीर्याः सृजन्त्यण्डं संहताः प्रकृतेर्बलात् ॥१८॥

vyaktādayo vikurvāṇā
dhātavaḥ puruṣekṣayā
labdha-vīryāḥ sṛjanty aṇḍaṁ
saṁhatāḥ prakṛter balāt

vyakta-ādayaḥ—the *mahat-tattva* and so on; *vikurvāṇāḥ*—undergoing transformation; *dhātavaḥ*—the elements; *puruṣa*—of the Lord; *īkṣayā*—by the glance; *labdha*—having attained; *vīryāḥ*—their potencies; *sṛjanti*—they create; *aṇḍam*—the egg of the universe; *saṁhatāḥ*—amalgamated; *prakṛteḥ*—of nature; *balāt*—by the power.

TRANSLATION

The material elements headed by the *mahat-tattva*, undergoing transformation, receive their specific potencies from the glance of the Supreme Lord and being amalgamated by the power of nature create the universal egg.

TEXT 19

सप्तैव धातव इति तत्रार्थाः पञ्च खादयः ।
ज्ञानमात्मोभयाधारस्ततो देहेन्द्रियासवः ॥१९॥

saptaiva dhātava iti
tatrārthāḥ pañca khādayaḥ
jñānam ātmobhayādhāras
tato dehendriyāsavaḥ

sapta—seven; *eva*—indeed; *dhātavaḥ*—elements; *iti*—thus saying; *tatra*—therein; *arthāḥ*—the physical elements; *pañca*—five; *kha-ādayaḥ*—

beginning with ether; *jñānam*—the spirit soul, who is the possessor of knowledge; *ātmā*—the Supreme Soul; *ubhaya*—of both (the seen nature and the *jīva* who is its seer); *ādhāraḥ*—the fundamental basis; *tataḥ*—from these; *deha*—the body; *indriya*—senses; *asavaḥ*—and vital airs.

TRANSLATION

According to some philosophers there are seven elements, namely earth, water, fire, air and ether, along with the conscious spirit soul and the Supreme Soul, who is the basis of both the material elements and the ordinary spirit soul. According to this theory, the body, senses, life air and all material phenomena are produced from these seven elements.

PURPORT

Having explained His own viewpoint, the Lord now summarizes various other analytic methodologies.

TEXT 20

षडित्यत्रापि भूतानि पञ्च षष्ठः परः पुमान् ।
तैर्युक्त आत्मसम्भूतैः सृष्ट्वेदं समुपाविशत् ॥२०॥

ṣaḍ ity atrāpi bhūtāni
pañca ṣaṣṭhaḥ paraḥ pumān
tair yukta ātma-sambhūtaiḥ
sṛṣṭvedaṁ samupāviśat

ṣaṭ—six; *iti*—thus; *atra*—in this theory; *api*—also; *bhūtāni*—the elements; *pañca*—five; *ṣaṣṭhaḥ*—the sixth; *paraḥ*—the transcendental; *pumān*—Supreme Personality; *taiḥ*—with those (five gross elements); *yuktaḥ*—conjoined; *ātma*—from Himself; *sambhūtaiḥ*—created; *sṛṣṭvā*—sending forth; *idam*—this creation; *samupāviśat*—He entered within it.

TRANSLATION

Other philosophers state that there are six elements—the five physical elements (earth, water, fire, air and ether) and the sixth

element, the Supreme Personality of Godhead. That Supreme Lord, endowed with the elements that He has brought forth from Himself, creates this universe and then personally enters within it.

PURPORT

Śrīla Śrīdhara Svāmī states that according to this philosophy, the ordinary living entity is included within the category of the Supersoul. This theory thus accepts only the Supreme Personality of Godhead and the five physical elements.

TEXT 21

चत्वार्येवेति तत्रापि तेज आपोऽन्नमात्मनः ।
जातानि तैरिदं जातं जन्मावयविनः खलु ॥२१॥

catvāry eveti tatrāpi
teja āpo 'nnam ātmanaḥ
jātāni tair idaṁ jātaṁ
janmāvayavinaḥ khalu

catvāri—four; *eva*—also; *iti*—thus; *tatra*—in that case; *api*—even; *tejaḥ*—fire; *āpaḥ*—water; *annam*—earth; *ātmanaḥ*—from the Self; *jātāni*—all arising; *taiḥ*—by them; *idam*—this cosmos; *jātam*—has come about; *janma*—the birth; *avayavinaḥ*—of the manifest product; *khalu*—indeed.

TRANSLATION

Some philosophers propose the existence of four basic elements, of which three—fire, water and earth—emanate from the fourth, the Self. Once existing, these elements producc the cosmic manifestation, in which all material creation takes place.

TEXT 22

संख्याने सप्तदशके भूतमात्रेन्द्रियाणि च ।
पञ्च पञ्चैकमनसा आत्मा सप्तदशः स्मृतः ॥२२॥

saṅkhyāne saptadaśake
bhūta-mātrendriyāṇi ca
pañca pañcaika-manasā
ātmā saptadaśaḥ smṛtaḥ

saṅkhyāne—in the enumeration; *saptadaśake*—in terms of seventeen elements; *bhūta*—the five gross elements; *mātra*—the five subtle perceptions pertaining to each; *indriyāṇi*—and the five corresponding senses; *ca*—also; *pañca pañca*—in groups of five; *eka-manasā*—along with the one mind; *ātmā*—the soul; *saptadaśaḥ*—as the seventeenth; *smṛtaḥ*—is so considered.

TRANSLATION

Some calculate the existence of seventeen basic elements, namely the five gross elements, the five objects of perception, the five sensory organs, the mind, and the soul as the seventeenth element.

TEXT 23

तद्वत् षोडशसंख्याने आत्मैव मन उच्यते ।
भूतेन्द्रियाणि पञ्चैव मन आत्मा त्रयोदश ॥२३॥

tadvat ṣoḍaśa-saṅkhyāne
ātmaiva mana ucyate
bhūtendriyāṇi pañcaiva
mana ātmā trayodaśa

tadvat—similarly; *ṣoḍaśa-saṅkhyāne*—in counting sixteen; *ātmā*—the soul; *eva*—indeed; *manaḥ*—as the mind; *ucyate*—is identified; *bhūta*—the five gross elements; *indriyāṇi*—the senses; *pañca*—five; *eva*—certainly; *manaḥ*—the mind; *ātmā*—the soul (both the individual soul and the Supersoul); *trayodaśa*—thirteen.

TRANSLATION

According to the calculation of sixteen elements, the only difference from the previous theory is that the soul is identified

with the mind. If we think in terms of five physical elements, five senses, the mind, the individual soul and the Supreme Lord, there are thirteen elements.

PURPORT

According to the theory of thirteen elements, the sense objects—aroma, taste, form, touch and sound—are considered by-products of the interaction of the senses and physical matter.

TEXT 24

एकादशत्व आत्मासौ महाभूतेन्द्रियाणि च ।
अष्टौ प्रकृतयश्चैव पुरुषश्च नवेत्यथ ॥२४॥

ekādaśatva ātmāsau
mahā-bhūtendriyāṇi ca
aṣṭau prakṛtayaś caiva
puruṣaś ca navety atha

ekādaśatve—in the consideration of eleven; *ātmā*—the soul; *asau*—this; *mahā-bhūta*—the gross elements; *indriyāṇi*—the senses; *ca*—and; *aṣṭau*—eight; *prakṛtayaḥ*—natural elements (earth, water, fire, air, ether, mind, intelligence and false ego); *ca*—also; *eva*—certainly; *puruṣaḥ*—the Supreme Lord; *ca*—and; *nava*—nine; *iti*—thus; *atha*—furthermore.

TRANSLATION

Counting eleven, there are the soul, the gross elements and the senses. Eight gross and subtle elements plus the Supreme Lord would make nine.

TEXT 25

इति नानाप्रसंख्यानं तत्त्वानामृषिभिः कृतम् ।
सर्वं न्याय्यं युक्तिमत्त्वाद् विदुषां किमशोभनम् ॥२५॥

iti nānā-prasaṅkhyānaṁ
tattvānām ṛṣibhiḥ kṛtam
sarvaṁ nyāyyaṁ yuktimattvād
viduṣāṁ kim aśobhanam

iti—in these ways; *nānā*—various; *prasaṅkhyānam*—enumeration; *tattvānām*—of the elements; *ṛṣibhiḥ*—by the sages; *kṛtam*—has been done; *sarvam*—all this; *nyāyyam*—logical; *yukti-mattvāt*—because of the presentation of rational arguments; *viduṣām*—of those who are learned; *kim*—what; *aśobhanam*—lack of brilliance.

TRANSLATION

Thus great philosophers have analyzed the material elements in many different ways. All of their proposals are reasonable, since they are all presented with ample logic. Indeed, such philosophical brilliance is expected of the truly learned.

PURPORT

The material world has been analyzed in innumerable ways by innumerable brilliant philosophers, but the conclusion is always one—the Supreme Personality of Godhead, Vāsudeva. Aspiring philosophers need not waste their precious time showing off their intellectual brilliance, because there is little left to analyze on the material platform. One should simply surrender to the Absolute Truth, the supreme element, Lord Śrī Kṛṣṇa, and uncover one's eternal consciousness of God.

TEXT 26

श्री उद्धव उवाच
प्रकृतिः पुरुषश्चोभौ यद्यप्यात्मविलक्षणौ ।
अन्योन्यापाश्रयात् कृष्ण दृश्यते न भिदा तयोः ।
प्रकृतौ लक्ष्यते ह्यात्मा प्रकृतिश्च तथात्मनि ॥२६॥

śrī-uddhava uvāca
prakṛtiḥ puruṣaś cobhau
yady apy ātma-vilakṣaṇau

anyonyāpāśrayāt kṛṣṇa
dṛśyate na bhidā tayoḥ
prakṛtau lakṣyate hy ātmā
prakṛtiś ca tathātmani

śrī-uddhavaḥ uvāca—Śrī Uddhava said; *prakṛtiḥ*—nature; *puruṣaḥ*—the enjoyer, or living entity; *ca*—and; *ubhau*—both; *yadi api*—although; *ātma*—constitutionally; *vilakṣaṇau*—distinct; *anyonya*—mutual; *apāśrayāt*—because of shelter; *kṛṣṇa*—O Lord Kṛṣṇa; *dṛśyate na*—it does not appear; *bhidā*—any difference; *tayoḥ*—between them; *prakṛtau*—within nature; *lakṣyate*—is apparently seen; *hi*—indeed; *ātmā*—the soul; *prakrtiḥ*—nature; *ca*—and; *tathā*—also; *ātmani*—in the soul.

TRANSLATION

Śrī Uddhava inquired: Although nature and the living entity are constitutionally distinct, O Lord Kṛṣṇa, there appears to be no difference between them, because they are found residing within one another. Thus the soul appears to be within nature and nature within the soul.

PURPORT

Śrī Uddhava here expresses the doubt that arises in the heart of an ordinary conditioned soul. Although the Vedic scriptures declare that the material body is a temporary fabrication of the material modes of nature, the conscious living entity within the body is actually an eternal spirit soul. In *Bhagavad-gītā* Lord Kṛṣṇa has declared the material elements constituting the body to be His separated, inferior energy, whereas the living entity is the superior, conscious energy of the Lord. Still, in conditioned life the material body and conditioned soul appear inseparable and thus nondifferent. Because the living entity enters the womb of a mother and gradually comes out in a developed body, the soul appears to have entered deeply within material nature. Similarly, by the soul's identification with the material body, the body appears to enter deeply within the consciousness of the soul. What is more, the body cannot exist without the presence of the soul. By this apparent mutual dependence, the difference between the body and soul is obscured. Śrī Uddhava therefore questions the Lord in order to clarify this issue.

TEXT 27

एवं मे पुण्डरीकाक्ष महान्तं संशयं हृदि ।
छेत्तुमर्हसि सर्वज्ञ वचोभिर्नयनैपुणैः ॥२७॥

evaṁ me puṇḍarīkākṣa
mahāntaṁ saṁśayaṁ hṛdi
chettum arhasi sarva-jña
vacobhir naya-naipuṇaiḥ

evam—thus; *me*—my; *puṇḍarīka-akṣa*—O lotus-eyed Lord; *mahāntam*—great; *saṁśayam*—doubt; *hṛdi*—within my heart; *chettum*—cut; *arhasi*—You should please; *sarva-jña*—O omniscient one; *vacobhiḥ*—with Your words; *naya*—in reasoning; *naipuṇaiḥ*—very expert.

TRANSLATION

O lotus-eyed Kṛṣṇa, O omniscient Lord, kindly cut this great doubt out of my heart with Your own words, which exhibit Your great skill in reasoning.

PURPORT

Śrī Uddhava requests Lord Kṛṣṇa to clearly demonstrate the difference between the material body and the spirit soul.

TEXT 28

त्वत्तो ज्ञानं हि जीवानां प्रमोषस्तेऽत्र शक्तितः ।
त्वमेव ह्यात्ममायाया गतिं वेत्थ न चापरः ॥२८॥

tvatto jñānaṁ hi jīvānāṁ
pramoṣas te 'tra śaktitaḥ
tvam eva hy ātma-māyāyā
gatiṁ vettha na cāparaḥ

tvattaḥ—from You; *jñānam*—knowledge; *hi*—indeed; *jīvānām*—of the living beings; *pramoṣaḥ*—stealing away; *te*—Your; *atra*—in this knowledge; *śaktitaḥ*—by the potency; *tvam*—You; *eva*—alone; *hi*—indeed; *ātma*—Your own; *māyāyāḥ*—of the illusory potency; *gatim*—the real nature; *vettha*—You know; *na*—not; *ca*—and; *aparaḥ*—any other person.

TRANSLATION

From You alone the knowledge of the living beings arises, and by Your potency that knowledge is stolen away. Indeed, no one but Yourself can understand the real nature of Your illusory potency.

PURPORT

As stated in *Bhagavad-gītā, mattaḥ smṛtir jñānam apohanaṁ ca:* "From Me come remembrance, knowledge and forgetfulness." By the Lord's causeless mercy one is enlightened with knowledge, and by the Lord's illusory potency that knowledge vanishes and one is merged into ignorance. Those bewildered by *māyā* cannot understand the difference between the material body and the spirit soul and thus should hear from the Lord Himself to remove this illusory covering.

TEXT 29

श्रीभगवानुवाच
प्रकृतिः पुरुषश्चेति विकल्पः पुरुषर्षभ ।
एष वैकारिकः सर्गो गुणव्यतिकरात्मकः ॥२९॥

śrī-bhagavān uvāca
prakṛtiḥ puruṣaś ceti
vikalpaḥ puruṣarṣabha
eṣa vaikārikaḥ sargo
guṇa-vyatikarātmakaḥ

śrī-bhagavān uvāca—the Supreme Personality of Godhead said; *prakṛtiḥ*—nature; *puruṣaḥ*—the enjoyer, living entity; *ca*—and; *iti*—thus; *vikalpaḥ*—complete distinction; *puruṣa-ṛṣabha*—O best among men; *eṣaḥ*—this; *vaikārikaḥ*—subject to transformation; *sargaḥ*—creation; *guṇa*—of the modes of nature; *vyatikara*—the agitation; *ātmakaḥ*—based upon.

TRANSLATION

The Supreme Personality of Godhead said: O best among men, material nature and its enjoyer are clearly distinct. This manifest creation undergoes constant transformation, being founded upon the agitation of the modes of nature.

PURPORT

The word *puruṣa* indicates the living entity and also the Supreme Lord, who is the supreme living entity. Material nature, subject to transformation, is full of duality, whereas the Lord is one and absolute. Material nature is dependent on its creator, maintainer and annihilator; the Lord, however, is completely self-reliant and independent. In the same way, material nature is unconscious and dull, lacking self-awareness, whereas the Supreme Lord is self-sufficient omniscience. The individual living entity shares the eternality, bliss and knowledge of the Personality of Godhead and is also completely distinct from material nature.

The word *sarga* here refers to the material amalgamation of the body, which covers the living entity. The material body undergoes constant transformation and is thus clearly different from the living entity, who is eternally the same. In the transcendental kingdom of God there is no conflict or agitation caused by creation, maintenance and destruction as exhibited in the material world. There all variety is resolved in the transcendental loving experience of Kṛṣṇa consciousness, the natural constitutional position of the soul.

TEXT 30

ममाङ्ग माया गुणमय्यनेकधा
विकल्पबुद्धीश्च गुणैर्विधत्ते ।
वैकारिकस्त्रिविधोऽध्यात्ममेक-
मथाधिदैवमधिभूतमन्यत् ॥३०॥

mamāṅga māyā guṇa-mayy anekadhā
vikalpa-buddhīś ca guṇair vidhatte
vaikārikas tri-vidho 'dhyātmam ekam
athādhidaivam adhibhūtam anyat

mama—My; *aṅga*—My dear Uddhava; *māyā*—material energy; *guṇa-mayī*—consisting of the three modes; *anekadhā*—manifold; *vikalpa*—different manifestations; *buddhīḥ*—and perceptions of these differences; *ca*—and; *guṇaiḥ*—by the modes; *vidhatte*—establishes; *vaikārikaḥ*—the full-blown manifestation of transformations; *tri-vidhaḥ*—having three aspects; *adhyātmam*—called *adhyātma; ekam*—one; *atha*—and; *adhidaivam*—*adhidaiva; adhibhūtam*—*adhibhūta; anyat*—another.

TRANSLATION

My dear Uddhava, My material energy, comprising three modes and acting through them, manifests the varieties of creation along with varieties of consciousness for perceiving them. The manifest result of material transformation is understood in three aspects: adhyātmic, adhidaivic and adhibhautic.

PURPORT

The word *vikalpa-buddhīḥ* indicates that consciousness within various material bodies reveals different aspects of the Lord's creation. Birds such as seagulls glide on the ocean breezes, experiencing the Lord's creation of wind and altitude. The fish experience life within the water, and other creatures intimately experience life within trees or within the earth. Human society affords its own varieties of awareness, and similarly in heaven and hell different experiences are available. All types of material consciousness are transformations of the three modes of material nature, the expansions of the Lord's illusory energy.

TEXT 31

दृग् रूपमार्कं वपुरत्र रन्ध्रे
परस्परं सिध्यति यः स्वतः खे ।
आत्मा यदेषामपरो य आद्यः
स्वयानुभूत्याखिलसिद्धसिद्धिः ॥३१॥

dṛg rūpam ārkaṁ vapur atra randhre
parasparaṁ sidhyati yaḥ svataḥ khe
ātmā yad eṣām aparo ya ādyaḥ
svayānubhūtyākhila-siddha-siddhiḥ

dṛk—the function of sight (as *adhyātma*); *rūpam*—visible form (as *adhibhūta*); *ārkam*—of the sun; *vapuḥ*—the partial image (as *adhidaiva*); *atra*—in this; *randhre*—aperture (of the eyeball); *parasparam*—mutually; *sidhyati*—cause the manifestation of each other; *yaḥ*—which; *svataḥ*—by its own power; *khe*—in the sky; *ātmā*—the Supersoul; *yat*—which; *eṣām*—of these (three features); *aparaḥ*—separate; *yaḥ*—who; *ādyaḥ*—the original cause; *svayā*—by His own; *anubhūtyā*—transcendental experience; *akhila*—of all; *siddha*—manifest phenomena; *siddhiḥ*—the source of manifestation.

TRANSLATION

Sight, visible form and the reflected image of the sun within the aperture of the eye all work together to reveal one another. But the original sun standing in the sky is self-manifest. Similarly, the Supreme Soul, the original cause of all entities, who is thus separate from all of them, acts by the illumination of His own transcendental experience as the ultimate source of manifestation of all mutually manifesting objects.

PURPORT

Form is recognized by the function of the eye, and the eye's function is understood by the presence of perceivable form. This interaction of sight and form further depends on the presence of light provided by the demigods, whose service of universal management depends on the presence of those who are to be managed, namely the living entities experiencing form with their eyes. Thus the three factors—*adhyātma,* represented by the senses such as the eye; *adhibhūta,* the sense objects such as form; and *adhidaiva,* the influence of the controlling deities—exist in an interdependent relationship.

The sun globe itself is said to be self-manifest, self-luminous and self-experiencing; it does not share the interdependence of the senses and sense objects although facilitating their function. Similarly, the

Supreme Personality of Godhead facilitates the interdependent experiences of all living entities. For example, newspapers, radio and television reveal world events to the mass of people. Parents reveal facts about life to their children, teachers to their students, friends to friends, and so on. The government manifests its will to the people and the people to their government. The sun and moon reveal the visual forms of all objects, and the perception of sound reveals audible form. The vibrations of particular types of music or rhetoric reveal the inner feelings of other living beings, and other types of knowledge are revealed by aroma, touch and taste. In this way, through the interaction of the senses and mind with innumerable sense objects, different types of knowledge are acquired. All such informative interactions, however, depend upon the supreme illuminating power of the Personality of Godhead. As stated in *Brahma-saṁhitā* (5.52), *yac-cakṣur eṣa savitā sakala-grahāṇām:* "Among all the planets the sun is considered the eye of the Supreme Lord." The Personality of Godhead is eternally omniscient by His own transcendental potency, and thus no one can reveal anything to the Lord about anything. Still, Lord Kṛṣṇa humbly accepts our prayers offered in Kṛṣṇa consciousness. In conclusion, Lord Kṛṣṇa clearly explains here that His sublime characteristics are completely different from those of the manifest universe. The Lord is therefore the supreme transcendental entity, free from all material influence.

TEXT 32

एवं त्वगादि श्रवणादि चक्षु-
जिह्वादि नासादि च चित्तयुक्तम् ॥३२॥

evaṁ tvag-ādi śravaṇādi cakṣur
jihvādi nāsādi ca citta-yuktam

evam—in the same way; *tvak-ādi*—the skin, the sensation of touch and the demigod of the wind, Vāyu; *śravaṇa-ādi*—the ears, the sensation of sound and the demigods of the directions; *cakṣuḥ*—the eyes (described in the previous verse); *jihvā-adi*—the tongue, the sensation of taste and the god of water, Varuṇa; *nāsa-ādi*—the nose, the sensation of smell and the Aśvinī-kumāras; *ca*—also; *citta-yuktam*—along with consciousness (implying not only conditioned consciousness together with the object of that consciousness and the presiding Deity Vāsudeva, but also the mind together with the object of thought and the moon-god Candra, intelligence with the object of intelligence and Lord Brahmā, and false ego together with the identification of false ego and Lord Rudra).

TRANSLATION

Similarly, the sense organs, namely the skin, ears, eyes, tongue and nose—as well as the functions of the subtle body, namely conditioned consciousness, mind, intelligence and false ego—can all be analyzed in terms of the threefold distinction of sense, object of perception and presiding deity.

PURPORT

The individual soul has no permanent relationship with the interdependent material functions of the senses, sense objects and controlling deities. The living entity is originally pure spirit soul and is meant to depend on the Personality of Godhead in the spiritual world. It is useless to try to analyze matter and spirit within the same categories, since they belong to different potencies of the Supreme Lord. Thus the act of spiritually perceiving the Supreme Lord, His abode and one's own self is an entirely antimaterial process realized within pure Kṛṣṇa consciousness.

TEXT 33

योऽसौ गुणक्षोभकृतो विकारः
प्रधानमूलान्महतः प्रसूतः ।
अहं त्रिवृन्मोहविकल्पहेतु-
वैकारिकस्तामस ऐन्द्रियश्च ॥३३॥

yo 'sau guṇa-kṣobha-kṛto vikāraḥ
pradhāna-mūlān mahataḥ prasūtaḥ
ahaṁ tri-vṛn moha-vikalpa-hetur
vaikārikas tāmasa aindriyaś ca

yaḥ asau—this; *guṇa*—of the modes of nature; *kṣobha*—by the agitation; *kṛtaḥ*—caused; *vikāraḥ*—transformation; *pradhāna-mūlāt*—which is generated from the *pradhāna,* the unmanifest form of the total material nature; *mahataḥ*—from the *mahat-tattva; prasūtaḥ*—generated; *aham*—false ego; *tri-vṛt*—in three phases; *moha*—of bewilderment; *vikalpa*—and material variety; *hetuḥ*—the cause; *vaikārikaḥ*—in the mode of goodness; *tāmasaḥ*—in the mode of ignorance; *aindriyaḥ*—in the mode of passion; *ca*—and.

TRANSLATION

When the three modes of nature are agitated, the resultant transformation appears as the element false ego in three phases—goodness, passion and ignorance. Generated from the *mahat-tattva,* which is itself produced from the unmanifest *pradhāna,* this false ego becomes the cause of all material illusion and duality.

PURPORT

By giving up one's false ego of identification with the three modes of nature, one can achieve Kṛṣṇa consciousness, the pure, original state of existence. The word *moha-vikalpa-hetuḥ* indicates that because of false ego one considers himself to be the enjoyer of nature and thus develops a false sense of material duality in terms of material happiness and distress. False ego is removed by identifying oneself as the Lord's eternal servitor in full Kṛṣṇa consciousness.

TEXT 34

आत्मापरिज्ञानमयो विवादो
ह्यस्तीति नास्तीति भिदार्थनिष्ठः ।
व्यर्थोऽपि नैवोपरमेत पुंसां
मत्तः परावृत्तधियां स्वलोकात् ॥३४॥

ātmāparijñāna-mayo vivādo
hy astīti nāstīti bhidārtha-niṣṭhaḥ
vyartho 'pi naivoparameta puṁsāṁ
mattaḥ parāvṛtta-dhiyāṁ sva-lokāt

ātma—of the Supreme Soul; *aparijñāna-mayaḥ*—based on lack of full knowledge; *vivādaḥ*—speculative argument; *hi*—indeed; *asti*—(this world) is real; *iti*—thus saying; *na asti*—it is not real; *iti*—thus saying; *bhidā*—material differences; *artha-niṣṭhaḥ*—having as its focus of discussion; *vyarthaḥ*—worthless; *api*—although; *na*—does not; *eva*—certainly; *uparameta*—cease; *puṁsām*—for persons; *mattaḥ*—from Me; *parāvṛtta*—who have turned; *dhiyām*—their attention; *sva-lokāt*—who am nondifferent from them.

TRANSLATION

The speculative argument of philosophers—"This world is real," "No, it is not real"—is based upon incomplete knowledge of the Supreme Soul and is simply aimed at understanding material dualities. Although such argument is useless, persons who have turned their attention away from Me, their own true Self, are unable to give it up.

PURPORT

If one doubts the existence of the Supreme Personality of Godhead, one will inevitably doubt the reality of the Lord's creation. Thus, without understanding Lord Kṛṣṇa, mere argument and debate over the reality and nonreality of the material world are useless. The material world is real specifically because it emanates from the supreme reality, Lord Kṛṣṇa. Without understanding the reality of Lord Kṛṣṇa one can never definitely ascertain the reality of His creation; one will always wonder if he is actually seeing something or merely thinking that he is seeing it. This kind of speculation can never be resolved without taking shelter of the Supreme Lord and is therefore useless. The devotees of the Lord are not inclined to such argument, because they are factually advancing in spiritual enlightenment and are fully satisfied with their progressively more beautiful experience of Kṛṣṇa consciousness.

TEXTS 35-36

श्री उद्धव उवाच

त्वत्तः परावृत्तधियः स्वकृतैः कर्मभिः प्रभो ।
उच्चावचान् यथा देहान् गृह्णन्ति विसृजन्ति च ॥३५॥

तन्ममाख्याहि गोविन्द दुर्विभाव्यमनात्मभिः ।
न ह्येतत् प्रायशो लोके विद्वांसः सन्ति वञ्चिताः ॥३६॥

śrī-uddhava uvāca
tvattaḥ parāvṛtta-dhiyaḥ
sva-kṛtaiḥ karmabhiḥ prabho
uccāvacān yathā dehān
gṛhṇanti visṛjanti ca

tan mamākhyāhi govinda
durvibhāvyam anātmabhiḥ
na hy etat prāyaśo loke
vidvāṁsaḥ santi vañcitāḥ

śrī-uddhavaḥ uvāca—Śrī Uddhava said; *tvattaḥ*—from You; *parāvṛtta*—diverted; *dhiyaḥ*—whose minds; *sva-kṛtaiḥ*—done by them; *karmabhiḥ*—by the fruitive activities; *prabho*—O supreme master; *ucca-avacān*—higher and lower; *yathā*—in which way; *dehān*—material bodies; *gṛhṇanti*—they accept; *visṛjanti*—give up; *ca*—and; *tat*—that; *mama*—to me; *ākhyāhi*—please explain; *govinda*—O Govinda; *durvibhāvyam*—impossible to understand; *anātmabhiḥ*—by those who are not intelligent; *na*—not; *hi*—indeed; *etat*—about this; *prāyaśaḥ*—for the most part; *loke*—in this world; *vidvāṁsaḥ*—knowledgeable; *santi*—they are; *vañcitāḥ*—who are cheated (by material illusion).

TRANSLATION

Śrī Uddhava said: O supreme master, the intelligence of those dedicated to fruitive activities is certainly deviated from You. Please explain to me how such persons accept superior and inferior bodies by their materialistic activities and then give up such bodies. O Govinda, this topic is very difficult for foolish persons to understand. Being cheated by illusion in this world, they generally do not become aware of these facts.

PURPORT

No one can be considered intelligent without understanding the science of God, which includes a description of the negative results of those who have forgotten their eternal relationship with Him. There are many so-called wise men in the world, but although considering themselves to be most intelligent, they generally do not surrender to the supreme intelligence of the Lord. Thus they concoct varieties of philosophies according to their positions within the modes of nature. However, one cannot escape the influence of material nature through philosophy generated from that same illusory nature. Liberation is achieved by perfect knowledge coming from the spiritual platform, the kingdom of God. By faithfully hearing from Lord Kṛṣṇa and His authorized representatives one can easily achieve liberation and go back home, back to Godhead.

TEXT 37

श्रीभगवानुवाच
मनः कर्ममयं नृणामिन्द्रियैः पञ्चभिर्युतम् ।
लोकाल्लोकं प्रयात्यन्य आत्मा तदनुवर्तते ॥३७॥

śrī-bhagavān uvāca
manaḥ karma-mayaṁ nṛṇām
indriyaiḥ pañcabhir yutam
lokāl lokaṁ prayāty anya
ātmā tad anuvartate

śrī-bhagavān uvāca—the Supreme Personality of Godhead said; *manaḥ*—the mind; *karma-mayam*—shaped by fruitive work; *nṛṇām*—of persons; *indriyaiḥ*—along with the senses; *pañcabhiḥ*—five; *yutam*—conjoined; *lokāt*—from one world; *lokam*—to another world; *prayāti*—travels; *anyaḥ*—separate; *ātmā*—the soul; *tat*—that mind; *anuvartate*—follows.

TRANSLATION

Lord Kṛṣṇa said: The material mind of men is shaped by the reactions of fruitive work. Along with the five senses, it travels from one material body to another. The spirit soul, although different from this mind, follows it.

TEXT 38

ध्यायन् मनोऽनु विषयान् दृष्टान् वानुश्रुतानथ।
उद्यत् सीदत् कर्मतन्त्रं स्मृतिस्तदनु शाम्यति ॥३८॥

dhyāyan mano 'nu viṣayān
dṛṣṭān vānuśrutān atha
udyat sīdat karma-tantraṁ
smṛtis tad anu śāmyati

dhyāyat—meditating; *manaḥ*—the mind; *anu*—regularly; *viṣayān*—on the sense objects; *dṛṣṭān*—seen; *vā*—or; *anuśrutān*—heard from Vedic authority; *atha*—subsequently; *udyat*—rising; *sīdat*—dissolving; *karma-tantram*—bound to the reactions of fruitive work; *smṛtiḥ*—remembrance; *tat anu*—after that; *śāmyati*—is destroyed.

TRANSLATION

The mind, bound to the reactions of fruitive work, always meditates on the objects of the senses, both those that are seen in this world and those that are heard about from Vedic authority. Consequently, the mind appears to come into being and to suffer annihilation along with its objects of perception, and thus its ability to distinguish past and future is lost.

PURPORT

One may ask how the subtle body, or mind, gives up its connection with one physical body and enters another. Such entering and leaving of physical bodies is called birth and death by conditioned souls. One utilizes his present senses to meditate on the visible objects of this world—beautiful women, palatial estates, and so on—and similarly one daydreams about the heavenly planets described in the *Vedas*. As death occurs, the mind is pulled away from the objects of its immediate experience and enters another body to experience a new set of sense objects. As the mind undergoes total reorientation there is the apparent loss of one's previous mentality and creation of a new mind, though actually the same mind is experiencing, but in a different way.

The conditioned soul is overwhelmed by the constant flow of material experience consisting of direct perception and abstract contemplation of the objects of this world. One thereby loses his transcendental memory of his relationship with God. As soon as one identifies with this world he forgets his eternal identity and surrenders to the false ego created by *māyā*.

TEXT 39

विषयाभिनिवेशेन नात्मानं यत् स्मरेत् पुनः ।
जन्तोर्वै कस्यचिद्धेतोर्मृत्युरत्यन्तविस्मृतिः ॥३९॥

viṣayābhiniveśena
nātmānaṁ yat smaret punaḥ
jantor vai kasyacid dhetor
mṛtyur atyanta-vismṛtiḥ

viṣaya—in (new) objects of perception; *abhiniveśena*—because of absorption; *na*—not; *ātmānam*—his previous self; *yat*—the situation in which; *smaret*—remembers; *punaḥ*—any more; *jantoḥ*—of the living entity; *vai*—indeed; *kasyacit hetoḥ*—for any reason or other; *mṛtyuḥ*—known as death; *atyanta*—total; *vismṛtiḥ*—forgetfulness.

TRANSLATION

When the living entity passes from the present body to the next body created by his own *karma*, he becomes absorbed in the pleasurable and painful sensations of the new body and completely forgets the experience of the previous body. This total forgetfulness for one reason or another of one's previous material identity is called death.

PURPORT

Depending on one's *karma*, or fruitive activities, one may achieve a beautiful, wealthy or powerful body or be degraded to an abominable condition of life. Taking birth in heaven or in hell, the living entity learns to completely identify his ego with the new body and thus becomes absorbed in the pleasure, fear, opulence or suffering of the new body, completely forgetting the experiences of the previous body. Death occurs when the specific *karma* allotted to a physical body is finished. Since that particular body's *karma* is used up, it can no longer act upon one's mind; in that way one forgets the previous body. The new body is created by nature so that one can experience the *karma* currently in effect. Consequently one's entire consciousness becomes absorbed in one's current body in order that one can fully experience the results of his previous activities. Because the living entity falsely identifies himself as the body, bodily death is experienced as death of the soul. Actually, however, the soul is eternal and is never subject to creation or annihilation. This analytic knowledge of self-realization is easily understood in Kṛṣṇa consciousness.

TEXT 40

जन्म त्वात्मतया पुंसः सर्वभावेन भूरिद ।
विषयस्वीकृतिं प्राहुर्यथा स्वप्नमनोरथः ॥४०॥

janma tv ātmatayā puṁsaḥ
sarva-bhāvena bhūri-da
viṣaya-svīkṛtiṁ prāhur
yathā svapna-manorathaḥ

janma—birth; *tu*—and; *ātmatayā*—by identification with oneself; *puṁsaḥ*—of a person; *sarva-bhāvena*—completely; *bhūri-da*—O most charitable Uddhava; *viṣaya*—of the body; *svī-kṛtim*—the acceptance; *prāhuḥ*—is called; *yathā*—just as; *svapna*—a dream; *manaḥ-rathaḥ*—or a mental fantasy.

TRANSLATION

O most charitable Uddhava, what is called birth is simply a person's total identification with a new body. One accepts the new body just as one completely accepts the experience of a dream or a fantasy as reality.

PURPORT

Identification with one's material body surpasses the mere affection and attachment one feels for the bodies of relatives or friends. The word *sarva-bhāvena* here shows that one totally accepts the material body to be oneself, just as one completely accepts the experience of a dream as real. Mere imagination without practical action is called a daydream; the mental concoction that occurs in a sleeping state is called a dream. Our identification with our own body and our blind acceptance of bodily relationships as permanent constitute a prolonged form of dreaming or fantasy in which one imagines oneself to be separate from the Supreme Personality of Godhead. The term birth, therefore, does not refer to the generation of a new entity but to the blind acceptance by the spirit soul of a new material body.

TEXT 41

स्वप्नं मनोरथं चेत्थं प्राक्तनं न स्मरत्यसौ ।
तत्र पूर्वमिवात्मानमपूर्वं चानुपश्यति ॥४१॥

svapnaṁ manorathaṁ cetthaṁ
prāktanaṁ na smaraty asau
tatra pūrvam ivātmānam
apūrvam cānupaśyati

svapnam—a dream; *manaḥ-ratham*—a daydream; *ca*—and; *ittham*—thus; *prāktanam*—previous; *na smarati*—does not remember; *asau*—he; *tatra*—in that (present body); *pūrvam*—the previous; *iva*—as if; *ātmānam*—himself; *apūrvam*—having no past; *ca*—and; *anupaśyati*—he views.

TRANSLATION

Just as a person experiencing a dream or daydream does not remember his previous dreams or daydreams, a person situated in his present body, although having existed previously to it, thinks that he has only recently come into being.

PURPORT

The objection may be raised that sometimes when experiencing a dream one actually remembers a previous dream. Śrīla Viśvanātha Cakravartī Ṭhākura replies that by the mystic power of *jāti-smara* one can remember one's previous body, and as is well known, "The exception establishes the rule." Normally, conditioned souls do not perceive their past existence; they think, "I am six years old" or "I am thirty years old," and "previous to this birth I did not exist." In such material ignorance one cannot understand the actual situation of the soul.

TEXT 42

इन्द्रियायनसृष्ट्येदं त्रैविध्यं भाति वस्तुनि ।
बहिरन्तर्भिदाहेतुर्जनोऽसज्जनकृद् यथा ॥४२॥

indriyāyana-sṛṣṭyedaṁ
trai-vidhyaṁ bhāti vastuni
bahir-antar-bhidā-hetur
jano 'saj-jana-kṛd yathā

indriya-ayana—by the resting place of the senses (the mind); *sṛṣṭyā*—because of the creation (of identification with a new body); *idam*—this; *trai-vidhyam*—threefold variety (of high, middle and low class); *bhāti*—appears; *vastuni*—in the reality (the soul); *bahiḥ*—external; *antaḥ*—and internal; *bhidā*—of the differences; *hetuḥ*—the cause; *janaḥ*—a person; *asat-jana*—of a bad person; *kṛt*—the progenitor; *yathā*—as.

TRANSLATION

Because the mind, which is the resting place of the senses, has created the identification with a new body, the threefold material variety of high, middle and low class appears as if present within the reality of the soul. The self thus becomes the creator of external and internal duality, just like a man who gives birth to a bad son.

PURPORT

The wealth, beauty, strength, intelligence, fame and detachment of different bodies are considered to be excellent, normal or inferior according to the material situation. The spirit soul acquires a particular body and thus judges himself and others to be high, middle or low class according to their material situation. Actually, the eternal soul exists beyond material duality but falsely mistakes the material situation to be his own. The words *asaj-jana-kṛd yathā* are significant. A father may by nature be peaceful, but because his bad son gets into trouble the father is forced to defend his son and consider his son's enemies to be enemies of the entire family. Thus the bad son implicates the father in troublesome conflicts. Similarly, the spirit soul has no intrinsic problems, but by creating a false identification with the material body the soul becomes involved in the happiness and distress of the body. With this verse the Lord summarizes His discussion of the difference between the body and the soul.

TEXT 43

नित्यदा ह्यङ्ग भूतानि भवन्ति न भवन्ति च ।
कालेनालक्ष्यवेगेन सूक्ष्मत्वात्तन्न दृश्यते ॥४३॥

nityadā hy aṅga bhūtāni
bhavanti na bhavanti ca
kālenālakṣya-vegena
sūkṣmatvāt tan na dṛśyate

nityadā—constantly; *hi*—indeed; *aṅga*—My dear Uddhava; *bhūtāni*—created bodies; *bhavanti*—come into being; *na bhavanti*—go out of being; *ca*—and; *kālena*—by time; *alakṣya*—imperceptible; *vegena*—whose speed; *sūkṣmatvāt*—because of being very subtle; *tat*—that; *na dṛśyate*—is not seen.

TRANSLATION

My dear Uddhava, material bodies are constantly undergoing creation and destruction by the force of time, whose swiftness is imperceptible. But because of the subtle nature of time, no one sees this.

TEXT 44

यथार्चिषां स्रोतसां च फलानां वा वनस्पतेः ।
तथैव सर्वभूतानां वयोऽवस्थादयः कृताः ॥४४॥

yathārciṣāṁ srotasāṁ ca
phalānāṁ vā vanaspateḥ
tathaiva sarva-bhūtānāṁ
vayo-'vasthādayaḥ kṛtāḥ

yathā—as; *arciṣām*—of the flames of a candle; *srotasām*—of the currents of a river; *ca*—and; *phalānām*—of fruits; *vā*—or; *vanaspateḥ*—of a tree; *tathā*—thus; *eva*—certainly; *sarva-bhūtānām*—of all material bodies; *vayaḥ*—of different ages; *avasthā*—situations; *ādayaḥ*—and so on; *kṛtāḥ*—are created.

TRANSLATION

The different stages of transformation of all material bodies occur just like those of the flame of a candle, the current of a river, or the fruits of a tree.

PURPORT

The wavering flame of a candle sometimes waxes brightly and again becomes weak. Finally it vanishes altogether. The waves of a flowing river rise and fall, creating innumerable shapes and patterns. The fruits of a tree gradually take birth, grow, ripen, sweeten and eventually rot and die. Similarly, one can easily understand that one's own body is undergoing constant transformation, and that the body is certainly subject to old age, disease and death. At different times of life the body exhibits degrees of sexual potency, physical strength, desire, wisdom and so on. As the body grows old, physical strength diminishes, but one's knowledge may increase even as the body undergoes such transformation.

Material birth and death occur within the realm of segmented time. The birth, creation or production of a material object immediately connects it with a segmented sequence of subtle time within the material world. Thus its destruction or death is inevitable. The irresistible force of time moves so subtly that only the most intelligent can perceive it. Just as the candle flame gradually diminishes, as the flowing currents move within the river or as fruits gradually ripen on a tree, the material body is steadily moving toward inevitable death. The temporary body should therefore never be confused with the eternal, unchanging spirit soul.

TEXT 45

सोऽयं दीपोऽर्चिषां यद्वत्स्रोतसां तदिदं जलम् ।
सोऽयं पुमानिति नृणां मृषा गीर्धीर्मृषायुषाम् ॥४५॥

so 'yaṁ dīpo 'rciṣāṁ yadvat
srotasāṁ tad idaṁ jalam
so 'yaṁ pumān iti nṛṇāṁ
mṛṣā gīr dhīr mṛṣāyuṣām

saḥ—this; *ayam*—the same; *dīpaḥ*—light; *arciṣām*—of the radiation of a lamp; *yadvat*—just as; *srotasām*—of the currents flowing in a river; *tat*—that; *idam*—the same; *jalam*—water; *saḥ*—this; *ayam*—the same; *pumān*—person; *iti*—thus; *nṛṇām*—of men; *mṛṣā*—false; *gīḥ*—statement; *dhīḥ*—thought; *mṛṣā-āyuṣām*—of those who are wasting their life.

TRANSLATION

Although the illumination of a lamp consists of innumerable rays of light undergoing constant creation, transformation and destruction, a person with illusory intelligence speaks falsely, saying, "This very light is still shining." As one observes a flowing river, ever-new water passes by and goes far away, but still, observing the same point in the river, a foolish person falsely states, "This is *the* water of the river." And although the material body of a human being is constantly undergoing transformation, those who are simply wasting their lives falsely think and say that each particular stage of the body is the real identity of the person.

PURPORT

Although one may say, "This is *the* light of the lamp," there are innumerable rays of light being created, transformed and destroyed at every moment; and although one may speak of *the* water of the river, there is an ever-new supply of different water molecules passing by. Similarly, when one meets a young child, one accepts that particular transitory phase of the body as the actual identity of the person, considering him to be a child. One also considers an old body to be an old person. In fact, however, the material body of a human being, just like the waves of a river or the radiation of a lamp, is merely a transformation of the three modes of material nature, the potency of the Supreme Lord. The real identity of a person is spirit soul, part and parcel of Lord Kṛṣṇa, but as Lord Kṛṣṇa proves in this verse, a conditioned soul is incapable of observing or understanding the subtle movements of time. With the gross vision of material consciousness one cannot ascertain the subtle segments of material manifestation, which are impelled by the Lord Himself as time. The word *mṛṣāyuṣām* in this verse indicates those who are uselessly wasting their time in ignorance without understanding the instructions of the Lord. Such persons gullibly accept any particular phase of the body to be the actual identity of the spirit soul within the body. Because the spirit soul is not subject to material transformation, when he engages himself in the eternal variegated pleasure of Kṛṣṇa consciousness, loving service to the Supreme Lord, he will experience no further ignorance and suffering.

TEXT 46

मा स्वस्य कर्मबीजेन जायते सोऽप्ययं पुमान् ।
म्रियते वामरो भ्रान्त्या यथाग्निर्दारुसंयुतः ॥४६॥

mā svasya karma-bījena
jāyate so 'py ayaṁ pumān
mriyate vāmaro bhrāntyā
yathāgnir dāru-saṁyutaḥ

mā—does not; *svasya*—of the self; *karma-bījena*—by the seed of his activities; *jāyate*—take birth; *saḥ*—he; *api*—indeed; *ayam*—this; *pumān*—personality; *mriyate*—dies; *vā*—or; *amaraḥ*—immortal; *bhrāntyā*—because of illusion; *yathā*—as; *agniḥ*—fire; *dāru*—with wood; *saṁyutaḥ*—joined.

TRANSLATION

A person does not actually take birth out of the seed of past activities, nor, being immortal, does he die. By illusion the living being appears to be born and to die, just as fire in connection with firewood appears to begin and then cease to exist.

PURPORT

The element fire exists perpetually within the material creation, but in connection with a particular piece of wood fire apparently comes into existence and ceases to exist. Similarly, the living entity is eternal, but in connection with a particular body apparently takes birth and dies. The reactions of *karma* thus impose an illusory suffering or enjoyment upon the living entity, but they do not cause the entity himself to change his eternal nature. In other words, *karma* represents a cycle of illusion in which each illusory activity produces another. Kṛṣṇa consciousness stops this cycle of *karma* by engaging the living being in spiritual activities in the loving service of the Lord. By such Kṛṣṇa consciousness one can escape the illusory chain of fruitive reactions.

TEXT 47

निषेकगर्भजन्मानि बाल्यकौमारयौवनम् ।
वयोमध्यं जरा मृत्युरित्यवस्थास्तनोर्नव ॥४७॥

niṣeka-garbha-janmāni
bālya-kaumāra-yauvanam
vayo-madhyaṁ jarā mṛtyur
ity avasthās tanor nava

niṣeka—impregnation; *garbha*—gestation; *janmāni*—and birth; *bālya*—infancy; *kaumāra*—childhood; *yauvanam*—and youth; *vayaḥ-madhyam*—middle age; *jarā*—old age; *mṛtyuḥ*—death; *iti*—thus; *avasthāḥ*—ages; *tanoḥ*—of the body; *nava*—nine.

TRANSLATION

Impregnation, gestation, birth, infancy, childhood, youth, middle age, old age and death are the nine ages of the body.

TEXT 48

एता मनोरथमयीर्हन्यस्योच्चावचास्तनूः ।
गुणसङ्गादुपादत्ते क्वचित् कश्चिज्जहाति च ॥४८॥

etā manoratha-mayīr
hānyasyoccāvacās tanūḥ
guṇa-saṅgād upādatte
kvacit kaścij jahāti ca

etāḥ—these; *manaḥ-rathaḥ-mayīḥ*—achieved by meditation of the mind; *ha*—certainly; *anyasya*—of the body (who is separate from the self); *ucca*—greater; *avacāḥ*—and lesser; *tanūḥ*—bodily conditions; *guṇa-saṅgāt*—because of associating with the modes of nature; *upādatte*—he accepts; *kvacit*—sometimes; *kaścit*—someone; *jahāti*—gives up; *ca*—and.

TRANSLATION

Although the material body is different from the self, because of the ignorance of material association one falsely identifies oneself with the superior and inferior bodily conditions. Sometimes a fortunate person is able to give up such mental concoction.

PURPORT

One who has received the special mercy of the Supreme Lord is able to give up the mental concoction of bodily identification. Thus there is always a chance of escaping the cycle of birth and death.

TEXT 49

आत्मनः पितृपुत्राभ्यामनुमेयौ भवाप्ययौ ।
न भवाप्ययवस्तूनामभिज्ञो द्वयलक्षणः ॥४९॥

ātmanaḥ pitṛ-putrābhyām
anumeyau bhavāpyayau
na bhavāpyaya-vastūnām
abhijño dvaya-lakṣaṇaḥ

ātmanaḥ—one's own; *pitṛ*—from the father or ancestors; *putrābhyām*—and the son; *anumeyau*—can be surmised; *bhava*—birth; *apyayau*—and death; *na*—is no longer; *bhava-apyaya-vastūnām*—of all that is subject to generation and destruction; *abhijñaḥ*—one who is in proper knowledge; *dvaya*—by these dualities; *lakṣaṇaḥ*—characterized.

TRANSLATION

By the death of one's father or grandfather one can surmise one's own death, and by the birth of one's son one can understand the condition of one's own birth. A person who thus realistically understands the creation and destruction of material bodies is no longer subject to these dualities.

PURPORT

The Lord has described the nine stages of the material body, beginning with impregnation, gestation and birth. One may argue that a living entity cannot remember his presence in the mother's womb nor his birth and early infancy. The Lord therefore states here that one can experience these phases of bodily existence by studying one's own child. Similarly, although one may hope to live forever, by experiencing the death of one's father, grandfather or great-grandfather, one has definite proof that the material body will die. A sober person, knowing the soul to be eternal, therefore gives up false identification with the temporary, unreliable body and takes shelter of the devotional service of the Lord. By this process one can escape the artificial imposition of birth and death.

TEXT 50

तरोर्बीजविपाकाभ्यां यो विद्वाञ्जन्मसंयमौ ।
तरोर्विलक्षणो द्रष्टा एवं द्रष्टा तनोः पृथक् ॥५०॥

taror bīja-vipākābhyāṁ
yo vidvāñ janma-saṁyamau
taror vilakṣaṇo draṣṭā
evaṁ draṣṭā tanoḥ pṛthak

taroḥ—of a tree; *bīja*—(birth from) its seed; *vipākābhyām*—(destruction subsequent to) maturity; *yaḥ*—one who; *vidvān*—in knowledge; *janma*—of birth; *saṁyamau*—and death; *taroḥ*—from the tree;

vilakṣaṇaḥ—distinct; *draṣṭā*—the witness; *evam*—in the same way; *draṣṭā*—the witness; *tanoḥ*—of the material body; *pṛthak*—is separate.

TRANSLATION

One who observes the birth of a tree from its seed and the ultimate death of the tree after maturity certainly remains a distinct observer separate from the tree. In the same way, the witness of the birth and death of the material body remains separate from it.

PURPORT

As a reference to trees, *vipāka* indicates the final transformation called death. In reference to other types of plants such as rice, *vipāka* indicates the stage of maturity, in which death also occurs. Thus by common observation one can understand the actual position of one's material body and one's own position as the transcendental observer.

TEXT 51

प्रकृतेरेवमात्मानमविविच्याबुधः पुमान् ।
तत्त्वेन स्पर्शसम्मूढः संसारं प्रतिपद्यते ॥५१॥

prakṛter evam ātmānam
avivicyābudhaḥ pumān
tattvena sparśa-sammūḍhaḥ
saṁsāraṁ pratipadyate

prakṛteḥ—from material nature; *evam*—in this way; *ātmānam*—the self; *avivicya*—failing to distinguish; *abudhaḥ*—the unintelligent; *pumān*—person; *tattvena*—because of thinking (material things) to be real; *sparśa*—by material contact; *sammūḍhaḥ*—completely bewildered; *saṁsāram*—the cycle of material existence; *pratipadyate*—attains.

TRANSLATION

An unintelligent man, failing to distinguish himself from material nature, thinks nature to be real. By contact with it he becomes completely bewildered and enters into the cycle of material existence.

PURPORT

A similar verse is found in *Śrīmad-Bhāgavatam* (1.7.5):

yayā sammohito jīva
ātmānaṁ tri-guṇātmakam
paro 'pi manute 'narthaṁ
tat-kṛtaṁ cābhipadyate

"Due to this external energy, the living entity, although transcendental to the three modes of material nature, thinks of himself as a material product and thus undergoes the reactions of material miseries."

TEXT 52

सत्त्वसङ्गादृषीन् देवान् रजसासुरमानुषान् ।
तमसा भूततिर्यक्त्वं भ्रामितो याति कर्मभिः ॥५२॥

sattva-saṅgād ṛṣīn devān
rajasāsura-mānuṣān
tamasā bhūta-tiryaktvaṁ
bhrāmito yāti karmabhiḥ

sattva-saṅgāt—by association with the mode of goodness; *ṛṣīn*—to the sages; *devān*—to the demigods; *rajasā*—by the mode of passion; *asura*—to the demons; *mānuṣān*—and to human beings; *tamasā*—by the mode of ignorance; *bhūta*—to the ghostly spirits; *tiryaktvam*—or the animal kingdom; *bhrāmitaḥ*—made to wander; *yāti*—he goes; *karmabhiḥ*—because of his fruitive activities.

TRANSLATION

Made to wander as the reaction of his fruitive work, the conditioned soul, by contact with the mode of goodness, takes birth among the sages or demigods. By contact with the mode of passion he becomes a demon or human being, and by association with the mode of ignorance he takes birth as a ghost or in the animal kingdom.

PURPORT

The word *tiryaktvam* means "the status of an animal," which includes all lower forms of life, such as beasts, birds, insects, fish and plants.

TEXT 53

नृत्यतो गायतः पश्यन् यथैवानुकरोति तान् ।
एवं बुद्धिगुणान् पश्यन्ननीहोऽप्यनुकार्यते ॥५३॥

nṛtyato gāyataḥ paśyan
yathaivānukaroti tān
evaṁ buddhi-guṇān paśyann
anīho 'py anukāryate

nṛtyataḥ—persons who are dancing; *gāyataḥ*—and singing; *paśyan*—observing; *yathā*—just as; *eva*—indeed; *anukaroti*—imitates; *tān*—them; *evam*—thus; *buddhi*—of the material intelligence; *guṇān*—the acquired qualities; *paśyan*—seeing; *anīhaḥ*—although not himself engaged in activity; *api*—nevertheless; *anukāryate*—is made to imitate.

TRANSLATION

Just as one may imitate persons whom one sees dancing and singing, similarly the soul, although never the doer of material activities, becomes captivated by material intelligence and is thus forced to imitate its qualities.

PURPORT

Sometimes people are captivated by professional singers and dancers and imitate within their minds the musical rhythms and melodies of the performers along with their romantic, humorous or heroic emotions. People sing songs heard on the radio and imitate dances and dramatic performances seen on television or in movies and theaters, entering into the emotions and art of the performer. The conditioned soul is similarly captivated by the concoctions of the material mind and intelligence, which convince him that he can become the enjoyer of the material world. Although different from the material body and never the actual performer of its activities, the conditioned soul is induced to engage his body in material activities, which entangle him in the cycle of birth and death. One should not accept the illicit propositions of material intelligence, but rather should engage himself fully in the service of the Lord in Kṛṣṇa consciousness.

TEXTS 54-55

यथाम्भसा प्रचलता तरवोऽपि चला इव ।
चक्षुषा भ्राम्यमाणेन दृश्यते भ्रमतीव भूः ॥५४॥
यथा मनोरथधियो विषयानुभवो मृषा ।
स्वप्नदृष्टाश्च दाशार्ह तथा संसार आत्मनः ॥५५॥

yathāmbhasā pracalatā
taravo 'pi calā iva
cakṣuṣā bhrāmyamāṇena
dṛśyate bhramatīva bhūḥ

yathā manoratha-dhiyo
viṣayānubhavo mṛṣā
svapna-dṛṣṭāś ca dāśārha
tathā saṁsāra ātmanaḥ

yathā—as; *ambhasā*—by water; *pracalatā*—moving, agitated; *taravaḥ*—trees; *api*—indeed; *calāḥ*—moving; *iva*—as if; *cakṣuṣā*—by the eyes; *bhrāmyamāṇena*—which are being turned about; *dṛśyate*—appears; *bhramatī*—moving; *iva*—as if; *bhūḥ*—the earth; *yathā*—as; *manaḥ-ratha*—of a mental fantasy; *dhiyaḥ*—the ideas; *viṣaya*—of sense gratification; *anubhavaḥ*—the experience; *mṛṣā*—false; *svapna-dṛṣṭāḥ*—things seen in a dream; *ca*—and; *dāśārha*—O descendant of Daśārha; *tathā*—thus; *saṁsāraḥ*—the material life; *ātmanaḥ*—of the soul.

TRANSLATION

Just as trees appear to be quivering by their reflection in agitated water, or as the earth appears to be spinning to one who has spun his eyes around, or as the world of a fantasy or dream appears to be real, O descendant of Daśārha, in the same way the soul's material life, his experience of sense gratification, is actually false.

PURPORT

Trees appear to be swaying when reflected in agitated water, and similarly, when one is sitting on a moving boat the trees on the shore appear to be moving. When the wind whips up the water, creating waves, the water appears to have movement of its own, although it is actually being moved by the wind. The conditioned soul in material life does not perform any activities, but rather the material body, with the consent of the illusioned living entity, is being moved by the modes of nature. One imposes this external movement upon oneself, considering oneself to be dancing, singing, running, dying, conquering and so on, although these are merely interactions of the external body with the modes of nature.

TEXT 56

अर्थे ह्यविद्यमानेऽपि संसृतिर्न निवर्तते ।
ध्यायतो विषयानस्य स्वप्नेऽनर्थागमो यथा ॥५६॥

arthe hy avidyamāne 'pi
saṁsṛtir na nivartate
dhyāyato viṣayān asya
svapne 'narthāgamo yathā

arthe—in truth; *hi*—certainly; *avidyamāne*—not existing; *api*—even though; *saṁsṛtiḥ*—material existence; *na nivartate*—does not stop; *dhyāyataḥ*—who is meditating; *viṣayān*—on the objects of sense gratification; *asya*—for him; *svapne*—in a dream; *anartha*—of unwanted things; *āgamaḥ*—the coming; *yathā*—just as.

TRANSLATION

For one who is meditating on sense gratification, material life, although lacking factual existence, does not go away, just as the unpleasant experiences of a dream do not.

PURPORT

One may object that if Lord Kṛṣṇa insists that material life is false, then why should one endeavor to stop it? The Lord therefore explains here that although not factual, material life stubbornly continues for one addicted to sense gratification, just as a frightening dream continues for one merged in sleep. The word *avidyamāna,* "not existing," means that material life is based on mental concoction, in which one thinks, "I am a man," "I am a woman," "I am a doctor," "I am a senator," "I am a street sweeper" and so on. A conditioned soul enthusiastically performs his activities based on the imaginary identification with the body. Thus although the spirit soul exists and the body exists, the false identification with the body does not exist. Material life, based on a false idea, has no factual existence.

After one awakens from a dream, the dim reflection of the dream may linger in one's memory. Similarly, one engaging in the devotional service of the Lord may be troubled sometimes by the dim reflection of sinful life. One should therefore become strong in Kṛṣṇa consciousness by hearing the Lord's instructions to Śrī Uddhava.

TEXT 57

तस्मादुद्धव मा भुङ्क्ष्व विषयानसदिन्द्रियैः ।
आत्माग्रहणनिर्भातं पश्य वैकल्पिकं भ्रमम् ॥५७॥

tasmād uddhava mā bhuṅkṣva
viṣayān asad-indriyaiḥ
ātmāgrahaṇa-nirbhātaṁ
paśya vaikalpikaṁ bhramam

tasmāt—therefore; *uddhava*—My dear Uddhava; *mā bhuṅkṣva*—do not enjoy; *viṣayān*—the objects of sense gratification; *asat*—impure; *indriyaiḥ*—with senses; *ātma*—of the self; *agrahaṇa*—inability to realize; *nirbhātam*—in which is manifest; *paśya*—see it; *vaikalpikam*—based on material duality; *bhramam*—the illusion.

TRANSLATION

Therefore, O Uddhava, do not try to enjoy sense gratification with the material senses. See how illusion based on material dualities prevents one from realizing the self.

PURPORT

Everything that exists is the potency and property of the Supreme Lord, meant to be used in His loving service. Seeing material objects as separate from the Lord and thus meant to be possessed and enjoyed by oneself is called *vaikalpikaṁ bhramam,* the illusion of material duality. When selecting one's personal object of enjoyment, such as food, clothing, residence or vehicle, one considers the relative quality of the object to be acquired. Consequently, in material life one is in constant anxiety, trying to acquire the most excellent sense gratification for one's personal pleasure. If one realizes everything as the property of the Lord, however, he will see everything as meant for the Lord's pleasure. He will feel no personal anxiety, because he is satisfied simply to be engaged in the Lord's loving service. It is not possible to exploit the property of the Lord and at the same time advance in self-realization.

TEXTS 58-59

क्षिप्तोऽवमानितोऽसद्भिः प्रलब्धोऽसूयितोऽथ वा ।
ताडितः सन्निबद्धो वा वृत्त्या वा परिहापितः ॥५८॥
निष्ठ्युतो मूत्रितो वाज्ञैर्बहुधैवं प्रकम्पितः ।
श्रेयस्कामः कृच्छ्रगत आत्मनात्मानमुद्धरेत् ॥५९॥

kṣipto 'vamānito 'sadbhiḥ
pralabdho 'sūyito 'tha vā
tāḍitaḥ sanniruddho vā
vṛttyā vā parihāpitaḥ

niṣṭhyuto mūtrito vājñair
bahudhaivaṁ prakampitaḥ
śreyas-kāmaḥ kṛcchra-gata
ātmanātmānam uddharet

kṣiptaḥ—insulted; *avamānitaḥ*—neglected; *asadbhiḥ*—by bad men; *pralabdhaḥ*—ridiculed; *asūyitaḥ*—envied; *atha vā*—or else; *tāḍitaḥ*—chastised; *sanniruddhaḥ*—tied up; *vā*—or; *vṛttyā*—of his means of livelihood; *vā*—or; *parihāpitaḥ*—deprived; *niṣṭhyutaḥ*—spat upon; *mūtritaḥ*—polluted with urine; *vā*—or; *ajñaiḥ*—by foolish men; *bahudhā*—

repeatedly; *evam*—thus; *prakampitaḥ*—agitated; *śreyaḥ-kāmaḥ*—one who desires the highest goal in life; *kṛcchra-gataḥ*—experiencing difficulty; *ātmanā*—by his intelligence; *ātmānam*—himself; *uddharet*—should save.

TRANSLATION

Even though neglected, insulted, ridiculed or envied by bad men, or even though repeatedly agitated by being beaten, tied up or deprived of one's occupation, spat upon or polluted with urine by ignorant people, one who desires the highest goal in life should in spite of all these difficulties use his intelligence to keep himself safe on the spiritual platform.

PURPORT

Throughout history many of the above-mentioned inconveniences have been experienced by devotees of the Lord. One who is advanced in God consciousness does not allow himself to become obsessed with the material body even in such conditions, but rather keeps the mind fixed on the spiritual platform through proper intelligence.

TEXT 60

श्री उद्धव उवाच
यथैवमनुबुध्येयं वद नो वदतां वर ॥६०॥

śrī-uddhava uvāca
yathaivam anubudhyeyaṁ
vada no vadatāṁ vara

śrī-uddhavaḥ uvāca—Śrī Uddhava said; *yathā*—how; *evam*—thus; *anubudhyeyam*—I may properly understand; *vada*—please speak; *naḥ*—to us; *vadatām*—of all speakers; *vara*—O You who are the best.

TRANSLATION

Śrī Uddhava said: O best of all speakers, please explain to me how I may properly understand this.

TEXT 61

सुदुःसहमिमं मन्य आत्मन्यसदतिक्रमम्
विदुषामपि विश्वात्मन् प्रकृतिर्हि बलीयसी ।
ऋते त्वद्धर्मनिरतान् शान्तांस्ते चरणालयान् ॥६१॥

su-duḥsaham imaṁ manya
ātmany asad-atikramam
viduṣām api viśvātman
prakṛtir hi balīyasī
ṛte tvad-dharma-niratān
śāntāṁs te caraṇālayān

su-duḥsaham—most difficult to tolerate; *imam*—this; *manye*—I consider; *ātmani*—upon oneself; *asat*—by ignorant people; *atikramam*—the attacks; *viduṣām*—for those who are learned; *api*—even; *viśva-ātman*—O soul of the universe; *prakṛtiḥ*—one's conditioned personality; *hi*—certainly; *balīyasī*—very strong; *ṛte*—except for; *tvat-dharma*—in Your devotional service; *niratān*—those who are fixed; *śāntān*—peaceful; *te*—Your; *caraṇa-ālayān*—who reside at the lotus feet.

TRANSLATION

O soul of the universe, the conditioning of one's personality in material life is very strong, and therefore it is very difficult even for learned men to tolerate the offenses committed against them by ignorant people. Only Your devotees, who are fixed in Your loving service and who have achieved peace by residing at Your lotus feet, are able to tolerate such offenses.

PURPORT

Unless one becomes advanced in the process of hearing and chanting the glories of the Supreme Lord, theoretical learning cannot make one actually saintly. One's conditioned personality, the result of long material association, is very difficult to overcome. Therefore we should humbly take shelter of the lotus feet of the Supreme Lord, who has so wonderfully explained to Śrī Uddhava the real meaning of knowledge.

Thus end the purports of the humble servant of His Divine Grace A. C. Bhaktivedanta Swami Prabhupāda to the Eleventh Canto, Twenty-second Chapter, of the Śrīmad-Bhāgavatam, *entitled "Enumeration of the Elements of Material Creation."*

CHAPTER TWENTY-THREE

The Song of the Avantī *Brāhmaṇa*

This chapter tells the story of a mendicant *sannyāsī* from the Avantī country as an example of how one should tolerate the disturbances and offenses created by evil persons.

The harsh words of uncouth persons pierce the heart even more severely than arrows. Yet a mendicant *brāhmaṇa* from the city of Avantī, even while being attacked by wicked men, considered this trouble to be simply the consequence of his own past deeds and tolerated it with utmost sobriety. Previously the *brāhmaṇa* had been an agriculturalist and merchant. He had been extremely greedy, miserly and prone to anger. As a result, his wife, sons, daughters, relatives and servants were all deprived of every kind of enjoyment and gradually came to behave unaffectionately toward him. In due course of time, thieves, family members and providence took away the sum total of his wealth. Finding himself without any property and abandoned by everyone, the *brāhmaṇa* developed a deep sense of renunciation.

He considered how the earning and preservation of wealth involve great effort, fear, anxiety and confusion. Because of wealth, there arise fifteen unwanted items—thievery, violence, lying, deception, lust, anger, pride, feverishness, disagreement, hatred, distrust, conflict, attachment to women, gambling and intoxication. When this meditation arose in his heart, the *brāhmaṇa* could understand that the Supreme Lord Śrī Hari had somehow become satisfied with him. He felt that only because the Lord was pleased with him had the apparently unfavorable turn of events in his life occurred. He was grateful that a sense of detachment had arisen in his heart and considered it the factual means for delivering his soul. In this condition he determined to engage the duration of his life in the worship of Lord Hari and thus accepted the mendicant order of *tridaṇḍi-sannyāsa*. Subsequently, he would enter different villages to beg charity, but the people would harass and disturb him. But he simply tolerated all this, remaining firm as a mountain. He remained fixed in his chosen spiritual practice and sang a song renowned as the *Bhikṣu-gīta*.

Neither mortal persons, the demigods, the soul, the ruling planets, the reactions of work nor time are the causes of one's happiness and distress. Rather, the mind alone is their cause, because it is the mind that makes the spirit soul wander in the cycle of material life. The real purpose of all charity, religiosity and so forth is to bring the mind under control. A person who has already composed his mind in meditation has no need for these other processes, and for a person who is incapable of fixing his mind they are of no practical use. The false conception of material ego binds the transcendental soul to material sense objects. The Avantī *brāhmaṇa* therefore became determined to bring himself over the insurmountable ocean of material existence by rendering service to the lotus feet of the Supreme Lord, Mukunda, with the same perfect faith in the Lord exhibited by the great devotees of the past.

Only when one can focus his intelligence on the lotus feet of the Supreme Personality of Godhead can the mind be completely subdued; this is the essence of all practical prescriptions for spiritual advancement.

TEXT 1

श्री बादरायणिरुवाच
स एवमाशंसित उद्धवेन
भागवतमुख्येन दाशार्हमुख्यः ।
सभाजयन् भृत्यवचो मुकुन्द-
स्तमाबभाषे श्रवणीयवीर्यः ॥ १ ॥

śrī-bādarāyaṇir uvāca
sa evam āśaṁsita uddhavena
bhāgavata-mukhyena dāśārha-mukhyaḥ
sabhājayan bhṛtya-vaco mukundas
tam ābabhāṣe śravaṇīya-vīryaḥ

śrī-bādarāyaṇiḥ uvāca—Śrī Śukadeva Gosvāmī said; *saḥ*—He; *evam*—thus; *āśaṁsitaḥ*—respectfully requested; *uddhavena*—by Uddhava; *bhāgavata*—of the devotees; *mukhyena*—by the greatest; *dāśārha*—of the dynasty of Dāśārha (the Yadus); *mukhyaḥ*—the chief; *sabhājayan*—

praising; *bhṛtya*—of His servant; *vacaḥ*—the words; *mukundaḥ*—Lord Mukunda, Kṛṣṇa; *tam*—to him; *ābabhāṣe*—began to speak; *śravaṇīya*—most worthy of hearing about; *vīryaḥ*—whose omnipotency.

TRANSLATION

Śukadeva Gosvāmī said: Lord Mukunda, the chief of the Dāśārhas, having thus been respectfully requested by the best of His devotees, Śrī Uddhava, first acknowledged the fitness of his servant's statements. Then the Lord, whose glorious exploits are most worthy of being heard, began to reply to him.

TEXT 2

श्रीभगवानुवाच

बार्हस्पत्य स नास्त्यत्र साधुर्वै दुर्जनेरितैः ।
दुरुक्तैर्भिन्नमात्मानं यः समाधातुमीश्वरः ॥ २ ॥

śrī-bhagavān uvāca
bārhaspatya sa nāsty atra
sādhur vai durjaneritaiḥ
duruktair bhinnam ātmānaṁ
yaḥ samādhātum īśvaraḥ

śrī-bhagavān uvāca—the Supreme Personality of Godhead said; *bārhaspatya*—O disciple of Bṛhaspati; *saḥ*—he; *na asti*—there is not; *atra*—in this world; *sādhuḥ*—a saintly person; *vai*—indeed; *durjana*—by uncivilized men; *īritaiḥ*—used; *duruktaiḥ*—by insulting words; *bhinnam*—disturbed; *ātmānam*—his mind; *yaḥ*—who; *samādhātum*—to compose; *īśvaraḥ*—is capable.

TRANSLATION

Lord Śrī Kṛṣṇa said: O disciple of Bṛhaspati, there is virtually no saintly man in this world capable of resettling his own mind after it has been disturbed by the insulting words of uncivilized men.

PURPORT

In the modern age there is widespread propaganda ridiculing the path of spiritual realization, and thus even saintly devotees are disturbed to see the progress of human society being obstructed. Still, a devotee of the Lord must tolerate any personal insult, though he cannot tolerate offense against the Lord Himself or the Lord's pure devotee.

TEXT 3

न तथा तप्यते विद्धः पुमान् बाणैः तु मर्मगैः ।
यथा तुदन्ति मर्मस्था ह्यसतां परुषेषवः ॥ ३ ॥

na tathā tapyate viddhaḥ
pumān bāṇais tu marma-gaiḥ
yathā tudanti marma-sthā
hy asatāṁ paruṣeṣavaḥ

na—not; *tathā*—in the same way; *tapyate*—is caused pain; *viddhaḥ*—pierced; *pumān*—a person; *bāṇaiḥ*—by arrows; *tu*—however; *marma-gaiḥ*—going to the heart; *yathā*—as; *tudanti*—prick; *marma-sthāḥ*—attaching within the heart; *hi*—indeed; *asatām*—of evil persons; *paruṣa*—harsh (words); *iṣavaḥ*—the arrows.

TRANSLATION

Sharp arrows which pierce one's chest and reach the heart do not cause as much suffering as the arrows of harsh, insulting words that become lodged within the heart when spoken by uncivilized men.

TEXT 4

कथयन्ति महत्पुण्यमितिहासमिहोद्धव ।
तमहं वर्णयिष्यामि निबोध सुसमाहितः ॥ ४ ॥

kathayanti mahat puṇyam
itihāsam ihoddhava
tam ahaṁ varṇayiṣyāmi
nibodha su-samāhitaḥ

kathayanti—they tell; *mahat*—greatly; *puṇyam*—pious; *itihāsam*—story; *iha*—in this regard; *uddhava*—My dear Uddhava; *tam*—that; *aham*—I; *varṇayiṣyāmi*—will describe; *nibodha*—please listen; *su-samāhitaḥ*—with careful attention.

TRANSLATION

My dear Uddhava, in this regard a most pious story is told, and I shall now describe it to you. Please listen with careful attention.

PURPORT

The Lord will now relate to Uddhava a historical account which teaches how to tolerate the insults of others.

TEXT 5

केनचिद् भिक्षुणा गीतं परिभूतेन दुर्जनैः ।
स्मरता धृतियुक्तेन विपाकं निजकर्मणाम् ॥ ५ ॥

kenacid bhikṣuṇā gītaṁ
paribhūtena durjanaiḥ
smaratā dhṛti-yuktena
vipākaṁ nija-karmaṇām

kenacit—by a certain; *bhikṣuṇā*—*sannyāsī;* *gītam*—sung; *paribhūtena*—who was insulted; *durjanaiḥ*—by impious persons; *smaratā*—remembering; *dhṛti-yuktena*—fixing his resolution; *vipākam*—the consequences; *nija-karmaṇām*—of his own past activities.

TRANSLATION

Once a certain *sannyāsī* was insulted in many ways by impious men. However, with determination he remembered that he was suffering the fruit of his own previous *karma*. I will narrate to you his story and that which he spoke.

PURPORT

Śrīla Bhaktisiddhānta Sarasvatī Ṭhākura comments as follows. "Often those who give up the materialistic path and devote themselves to renunciation are attacked by impious persons. This analysis, however, is superficial, since the punishment is actually the cumulative result of one's past *karma*. Some renunciants show lack of tolerance when presented with the remnants of their previous sins and thus are forced to enter again onto the path of impious life. Śrī Caitanya Mahāprabhu therefore instructs that one should become as tolerant as a tree. If a neophyte on the path of devotional service to the Lord's pure devotees is attacked by envious persons, he must accept it as a consequence of his previous fruitive activities. One should be intelligent and avoid future unhappiness by rejecting the ethic of An eye for an eye, a tooth for a tooth. If one refuses to enter into enmity with envious men, they will automatically leave him alone."

TEXT 6

अवन्तिषु द्विजः कश्चिदासीदाढ्यतमः श्रिया ।
वार्तावृत्तिः कदर्यस्तु कामी लुब्धोऽतिकोपनः ॥ ६ ॥

avantiṣu dvijaḥ kaścid
āsīd āḍhyatamaḥ śriyā
vārtā-vṛttiḥ kadaryas tu
kāmī lubdho 'ti-kopanaḥ

avantiṣu—in the Avantī country; *dvijaḥ*—*brāhmaṇa; kaścit*—a certain; *āsīt*—there was; *āḍhya-tamaḥ*—very rich; *śriyā*—with opulences; *vārtā*—by business; *vṛttiḥ*—earning his livelihood; *kadaryaḥ*—miserly; *tu*—but; *kāmī*—lusty; *lubdhaḥ*—greedy; *ati-kopanaḥ*—very prone to anger.

TRANSLATION

In the country of Avantī there once lived a certain *brāhmaṇa* who was very rich and gifted with all opulences, and who was engaged in the occupation of commerce. But he was a miserly person—lusty, greedy and very prone to anger.

PURPORT

According to Śrīla Śrīdhara Svāmī, the Avantī country is the district of Malwa. This *brāhmaṇa* was extremely wealthy, doing business in agriculture, banking and so on. Being a miser, he suffered agony when his hard-earned wealth was lost, as will be described by the Lord Himself.

TEXT 7

ज्ञातयोऽतिथयस्तस्य वाङ्मात्रेणापि नार्चिताः ।
शून्यावसथ आत्मापि काले कामैरनर्चितः ॥ ७ ॥

jñātayo 'tithayas tasya
vāṅ-mātreṇāpi nārcitāḥ
śūnyāvasatha ātmāpi
kāle kāmair anarcitaḥ

jñātayaḥ—the relatives; *atithayaḥ*—and guests; *tasya*—his; *vāk-mātreṇa api*—even by words; *na arcitāḥ*—were not shown respect; *śūnya-avasathe*—in his home deprived of religiosity and sense gratification; *ātmā*—himself; *api*—even; *kāle*—at the suitable times; *kāmaiḥ*—with sensory enjoyment; *anarcitaḥ*—not gratified.

TRANSLATION

In his home devoid of religiosity and lawful sense gratification, the family members and guests were never properly respected, even with words. He would not even allow sufficient gratification for his own body at the suitable times.

TEXT 8

दुःशीलस्य कदर्यस्य द्रुह्यन्ते पुत्रबान्धवाः ।
दारा दुहितरो भृत्या विषण्णा नाचरन् प्रियम् ॥ ८ ॥

duḥśīlasya kadaryasya
druhyante putra-bāndhavāḥ
dārā duhitaro bhṛtyā
viṣaṇṇā nācaran priyam

duḥśīlasya—having a bad character; *kadaryasya*—toward the miser; *druhyante*—they developed enmity; *putra*—his sons; *bāndhavāḥ*—and in-laws; *dārāḥ*—his wife; *duhitaraḥ*—his daughters; *bhṛtyāḥ*—the servants; *visaṇṇāḥ*—disgusted; *na ācaran*—they did not act; *priyam*—affectionately.

TRANSLATION

Since he was so hardhearted and miserly, his sons, in-laws, wife, daughters and servants began to feel inimical toward him. Becoming disgusted, they would never treat him with affection.

TEXT 9

तस्यैवं यक्षवित्तस्य च्युतस्योभयलोकतः ।
धर्मकामविहीनस्य चुक्रुधुः पञ्चभागिनः ॥ ९ ॥

tasyaivaṁ yakṣa-vittasya
cyutasyobhaya-lokataḥ
dharma-kāma-vihīnasya
cukrudhuḥ pañca-bhāginaḥ

tasya—at him; *evam*—in this way; *yakṣa-vittasya*—who simply kept his wealth without spending it, like the Yakṣas, who guard the treasury of Kuvera; *cyutasya*—who was deprived; *ubhaya*—of both; *lokataḥ*—worlds (this life and the next); *dharma*—religiosity; *kāma*—and sense gratification; *vihīnasya*—lacking; *cukrudhuḥ*—they became angry; *pañca-bhāginaḥ*—the deities of the five prescribed household sacrifices.

TRANSLATION

In this way the presiding deities of the five family sacrifices became angry at the *brāhmaṇa*, who was niggardly guarding his wealth like a Yakṣa, had no good destination either in this world or the next, and was totally deprived of religiosity and sense enjoyment.

TEXT 10

तदवध्यानविस्रस्तपुण्यस्कन्धस्य भूरिद ।
अर्थोऽप्यगच्छन्निधनं बह्वायासपरिश्रमः ॥ १० ॥

tad-avadhyāna-visrasta-
puṇya-skandhasya bhūri-da
artho 'py agacchan nidhanaṁ
bahv-āyāsa-pariśramaḥ

tat—of them; *avadhyāna*—because of his neglect; *visrasta*—depleted; *puṇya*—of piety; *skandhasya*—whose portion; *bhūri-da*—O magnanimous Uddhava; *arthaḥ*—the wealth; *api*—indeed; *agacchat nidhanam*—became lost; *bahu*—much; *āyāsa*—of endeavor; *pariśramaḥ*—which consisted only of the labor.

TRANSLATION

O magnanimous Uddhava, by his neglect of these demigods he depleted his stock of piety and all his wealth. The accumulation of his repeated exhaustive endeavors was totally lost.

PURPORT

The *brāhmaṇa's* stock of piety became like a withered branch that no longer gives fruits or flowers. Śrīla Jīva Gosvāmī comments that the *brāhmaṇa* had a trace of piety directed at the Supreme Lord with hopes of liberation. That pure portion of the branch of his piety remained unwithered, eventually giving the fruit of knowledge.

TEXT 11

ज्ञातयो जगृहुः किञ्चित् किञ्चिद् दस्यव उद्धव ।
दैवतः कालतः किञ्चिद् ब्रह्मबन्धोर्नृपार्थिवात् ॥ ११ ॥

jñātyo jagṛhuḥ kiñcit
kiñcid dasyava uddhava
daivataḥ kālataḥ kiñcid
brahma-bandhor nṛ-pārthivāt

jñātayaḥ—the relatives; *jagṛhuḥ*—took away; *kiñcit*—some; *kiñcit*—some; *dasyavaḥ*—thieves; *uddhava*—O Uddhava; *daivataḥ*—by providence; *kālataḥ*—by time; *kiñcit*—some; *brahma-bandhoḥ*—of the so-called *brāhmaṇa; nṛ*—by common men; *pārthivāt*—and by elevated government officials.

TRANSLATION

Some of the wealth of this so-called *brāhmaṇa* was taken away by his relatives, My dear Uddhava, some by thieves, some by the whims of providence, some by the effects of time, some by ordinary men and some by government authorities.

PURPORT

It appears that even though the so-called *brāhmaṇa* was determined not to spend his money, his wife and other relatives managed to squeeze out a portion. According to Śrīla Śrīdhara Svāmī, *providence* here refers to fires in the home and other types of occasional misfortune. *Effects of time* here refers to the destruction of agricultural crops through seasonal irregularities and other such occurrences. Śrīla Bhaktisiddhānta Sarasvatī Ṭhākura points out that one should not merely proclaim oneself to be a *brāhmaṇa* but should actually understand one's original identity as a servant of the Lord. One declaring himself to be a *brāhmaṇa* but maintaining a materialistic mentality is not a real *brāhmaṇa*, but rather a *brahma-bandhu*, or so-called *brāhmaṇa*. The humble devotees of Lord Viṣṇu, following the indications of the Vedic scriptures, refer to themselves as unfortunate and unable to understand the kingdom of God; they do not proudly proclaim themselves to be *brāhmaṇas*. Those who are wise, however, know that such humble devotees are actually *brāhmaṇas* whose hearts are cleansed by the pure mode of goodness.

TEXT 12

स एवं द्रविणे नष्टे धर्मकामविवर्जितः ।
उपेक्षितश्च स्वजनैश्चिन्तामाप दुरत्ययाम् ॥ १२ ॥

sa evaṁ draviṇe naṣṭe
dharma-kāma-vivarjitaḥ
upekṣitaś ca sva-janaiś
cintām āpa duratyayām

saḥ—he; *evam*—thus; *draviṇe*—when his property; *naṣṭe*—was lost; *dharma*—religiosity; *kāma*—and sense enjoyment; *vivarjitaḥ*—devoid of; *upekṣitaḥ*—neglected; *ca*—and; *sva-janaiḥ*—by his family members; *cintām*—anxiety; *āpa*—he obtained; *duratyayām*—insurmountable.

TRANSLATION

Finally, when his property was completely lost, he who never engaged in religiosity or sense enjoyment became ignored by his family members. Thus he began to feel unbearable anxiety.

TEXT 13

तस्यैवं ध्यायतो दीर्घं नष्टरायस्तपस्विनः ।
खिद्यतो बाष्पकण्ठस्य निर्वेदः सुमहानभूत् ॥ १३ ॥

tasyaivaṁ dhyāyato dīrghaṁ
naṣṭa-rāyas tapasvinaḥ
khidyato bāṣpa-kaṇṭhasya
nirvedaḥ su-mahān abhūt

tasya—of him; *evam*—thus; *dhyāyataḥ*—thinking; *dīrgham*—for a long time; *naṣṭa-rāyaḥ*—his wealth lost; *tapasvinaḥ*—experiencing agony; *khidyataḥ*—lamenting; *bāṣpa-kaṇṭhasya*—his throat choked with tears; *nirvedaḥ*—a sense of renunciation; *su-mahān*—very great; *abhūt*—arose.

TRANSLATION

Having lost all his wealth, he felt great pain and lamentation. His throat choked up with tears, and he meditated for a long time on his fortune. Then a powerful feeling of renunciation came over him.

PURPORT

The *brāhmaṇa* had previously been trained in pious life, but his past goodness was covered by his offensive behavior. Finally, his previous purity was reawakened within him.

TEXT 14

स चाहेदमहो कष्टं वृथात्मा मेऽनुतापितः ।
न धर्माय न कामाय यस्यार्थायास ईदृशः ॥१४॥

sa cāhedam aho kaṣṭaṁ
vṛthātmā me 'nutāpitaḥ
na dharmāya na kāmāya
yasyārthāyāsa īdṛśaḥ

saḥ—he; *ca*—and; *āha*—spoke; *idam*—this; *aho*—alas; *kaṣṭam*—the painful misfortune; *vṛthā*—vainly; *ātmā*—the self; *me*—my; *anutāpitaḥ*—distressed; *na*—not; *dharmāya*—for religiosity; *na*—nor; *kāmāya*—for sense gratification; *yasya*—whose; *artha*—for wealth; *āyāsaḥ*—labor; *īdṛśaḥ*—such as this.

TRANSLATION

The *brāhmaṇa* spoke as follows: O what great misfortune! I have simply tormented myself uselessly, struggling so hard for money that was not even intended for religiosity or material enjoyment.

TEXT 15

प्रायेणार्थाः कदर्याणां न सुखाय कदाचन ।
इह चात्मोपतापाय मृतस्य नरकाय च ॥ १५ ॥

prāyeṇārthāḥ kadaryāṇāṁ
na sukhāya kadācana
iha cātmopatāpāya
mṛtasya narakāya ca

prāyeṇa—generally; *arthāḥ*—items of wealth; *kadaryāṇām*—of those who are misers; *na*—do not; *sukhāya*—lead to happiness; *kadācana*—at any time; *iha*—in this life; *ca*—both; *ātma*—of himself; *upatāpāya*—result in the torment; *mṛtasya*—and of him when he has died; *narakāya*—in the attainment of hell; *ca*—and.

TRANSLATION

Generally, the wealth of misers never allows them any happiness. In this life it causes their self-torment, and when they die it sends them to hell.

PURPORT

A miser is afraid to spend his money even for obligatory religious and social duties. Offending God and people in general, he goes to hell.

TEXT 16

यशो यशस्विनां शुद्धं श्लाघ्या ये गुणिनां गुणाः ।
लोभः स्वल्पोऽपि तान् हन्ति श्वित्रो रूपमिवेप्सितम् ॥१६॥

yaśo yaśasvināṁ śuddhaṁ
ślāghyā ye guṇināṁ guṇāḥ
lobhaḥ sv-alpo 'pi tān hanti
śvitro rūpam ivepsitam

yaśaḥ—the fame; *yaśasvinām*— of those who are famous; *śuddham*—pure; *ślāghyāḥ*—praiseworthy; *ye*—which; *guṇinām*—of those endowed with good qualities; *guṇāḥ*—the qualities; *lobhaḥ*—greed; *su-alpaḥ*—a little; *api*—even; *tān*—these; *hanti*—destroys; *śvitraḥ*—white leprosy; *rūpam*—physical beauty; *iva*—just as; *īpsitam*—enchanting.

TRANSLATION

Whatever pure fame is possessed by the famous and whatever praiseworthy qualities are found in the virtuous are destroyed by even a small amount of greed, just as one's attractive physical beauty is ruined by a trace of white leprosy.

TEXT 17

अर्थस्य साधने सिद्धे उत्कर्षे रक्षणे व्यये ।
नाशोपभोग आयासस्त्रासश्चिन्ता भ्रमो नृणाम् ॥१७॥

arthasya sādhane siddhe
utkarṣe rakṣaṇe vyaye
nāśopabhoga āyāsas
trāsaś cintā bhramo nṛṇām

arthaysa—of wealth; *sādhane*—in the earning; *siddhe*—in the attainment; *utkarṣe*—in the increasing; *rakṣaṇe*—in the protecting; *vyaye*—in the expending; *nāśa*—in the loss; *upabhoge*—and in the enjoyment; *āyāsaḥ*—labor; *trāsaḥ*—fear; *cintā*—anxiety; *bhramaḥ*—confusion; *nṛṇām*—for men.

TRANSLATION

In the earning, attainment, increase, protection, expense, loss and enjoyment of wealth, all men experience great labor, fear, anxiety and delusion.

TEXTS 18-19

स्तेयं हिंसानृतं दम्भः कामः क्रोधः स्मयो मदः ।
भेदो वैरमविश्वासः संस्पर्धा व्यसनानि च ॥ १८ ॥
एते पञ्चदशानर्था ह्यर्थमूला मता नृणाम् ।
तस्मादनर्थमर्थाख्यं श्रेयोऽर्थी दूरतस्त्यजेत् ॥ १९ ॥

steyaṁ hiṁsānṛtaṁ dambhaḥ
kāmaḥ krodhaḥ smayo madaḥ
bhedo vairam aviśvāsaḥ
saṁspardhā vyasanāni ca

ete pañcadaśānarthā
hy artha-mūlā matā nṛṇām
tasmād anartham arthākhyaṁ
śreyo-'rthī dūratas tyajet

steyam—theft; *hiṁsā*—violence; *anṛtam*—lying; *dambhaḥ*—duplicity; *kāmaḥ*—lust; *krodhaḥ*—anger; *smayaḥ*—perplexity; *madaḥ*—pride; *bhedaḥ*—disagreement; *vairam*—emnity; *aviśvāsaḥ*—lack of faith; *saṁspardhā*—rivalry; *vyasanāni*—the dangers (coming from women, gambling and intoxication); *ca*—and; *ete*—these; *pañcadaśa*—fifteen; *anarthāḥ*—unwanted things; *hi*—indeed; *artha-mūlāḥ*—based on wealth; *matāḥ*—are known; *nṛṇām*—by men; *tasmāt*—therefore; *anartham*—that which is undesirable; *artha-ākhyam*—wealth, spoken of as if desirable; *śreyaḥ-arthī*—one who desires the ultimate benefit of life; *dūrataḥ*—at a great distance; *tyajet*—should leave.

TRANSLATION

Theft, violence, speaking lies, duplicity, lust, anger, perplexity, pride, quarreling, emnity, faithlessness, envy and the dangers caused by women, gambling and intoxication are the fifteen undesirable qualities that contaminate men because of greed for wealth. Although these qualities are undesirable, men falsely ascribe value to them. One desiring to achieve the real benefit of life should therefore remain aloof from undesirable material wealth.

PURPORT

The words *anartham arthākhyam,* or "undesirable wealth," indicate wealth that cannot be efficiently engaged in the loving service of the Lord. Such superfluous money or property will undoubtedly pollute a man with all of the above-mentioned qualities and therefore should be given up.

TEXT 20

भिद्यन्ते भ्रातरो दाराः पितरः सुहृदस्तथा ।
एकास्निग्धाः काकिणिना सद्यः सर्वेऽरयः कृताः ॥ २० ॥

bhidyante bhrātaro dārāḥ
pitaraḥ suhṛdas tathā
ekāsnigdhāḥ kākiṇinā
sadyaḥ sarve 'rayaḥ kṛtāḥ

bhidyante—they break off; *bhrātaraḥ*—the brothers; *dārāḥ*—wife; *pitaraḥ*—parents; *suhṛdaḥ*—friends; *tathā*—and; *eka*—as if one; *āsnigdhāḥ*—very dear; *kākiṇinā*—by a small coin; *sadyaḥ*—immediately; *sarve*—all of them; *arayaḥ*—enemies; *kṛtāḥ*—made.

TRANSLATION

Even a man's brothers, wife, parents and friends united with him in love will immediately break off their affectionate relationships and become enemies over a single coin.

TEXT 21

अर्थेनाल्पीयसा ह्येते संरब्धा दीप्तमन्यवः ।
त्यजन्त्याशु स्पृधो घ्नन्ति सहसोत्सृज्य सौहृदम् ॥ २१ ॥

arthenālpīyasā hy ete
saṁrabdhā dīpta-manyavaḥ
tyajanty āśu spṛdho ghnanti
sahasotsṛjya sauhṛdam

arthena—by wealth; *alpīyasā*—insignificant; *hi*—even; *ete*—they; *saṁrabdhāḥ*—agitated; *dīpta*—inflamed; *manyavaḥ*—their anger; *tyajanti*—they give up; *āśu*—very quickly; *spṛdhaḥ*—becoming quarrelsome; *ghnanti*—they destroy; *sahasā*—quickly; *utsṛjya*—rejecting; *sauhṛdam*—goodwill.

TRANSLATION

For even a small amount of money these relatives and friends become very agitated and their anger is inflamed. Acting as rivals, they quickly give up all sentiments of goodwill and will reject one at a moment's notice, even to the point of committing murder.

TEXT 22

लब्ध्वा जन्मामरप्रार्थ्यं मानुष्यं तद् द्विजाग्र्यताम् ।
तदनादृत्य ये स्वार्थं घ्नन्ति यान्त्यशुभां गतिम् ॥ २२ ॥

labdhvā janmāmara-prārthyaṁ
mānuṣyaṁ tad dvijāgryatām
tad anādṛtya ye svārthaṁ
ghnanti yānty aśubhāṁ gatim

labdhvā—having attained; *janma*—the birth; *amara*—by the demigods; *prārthyam*—prayed for; *mānuṣyam*—human; *tat*—and in that; *dvija-āgryatām*—the status of being the best of the twice-born; *tat*—that; *anādṛtya*—not appreciating; *ye*—those who; *sva-artham*—their own best interest; *ghnanti*—destroy; *yānti*—they go; *aśubhām*—to an inauspicious; *gatim*—destination.

TRANSLATION

Those who obtain human life, which is prayed for even by the demigods, and in that human birth become situated as first-class *brāhmaṇas,* are extremely fortunate. If they disregard this important opportunity, they are certainly killing their own self-interest and thus achieve a most unfortunate end.

PURPORT

Śrīla Bhaktisiddhānta Sarasvatī Ṭhākura comments as follows. "Human birth is better than that of the demigods, ghosts, spirits, animals, trees, lifeless stones, and so forth, because the demigods simply enjoy celestial pleasures, and in other forms of life there is excessive suffering. It is only in human life that one deeply considers one's ultimate benefit in life. Human birth is therefore more desirable than even that of the demigods." Within human life the position of a high-class *brāhmaṇa* is certainly most desirable. If a *brāhmaṇa,* however, gives up the devotional service of the Lord and works hard like a *śūdra* simply for the prestige of his community, he is certainly on the platform of material sense gratification. The special qualification of the *brāhmaṇas* is the spiritual knowledge by which they recognize every living entity to be an eternal servant of the Lord. A *brāhmaṇa,* free from false ego, thus feels himself lower than a blade of grass and tolerantly offers respect to all living entities. All human beings, and especially the *brāhmaṇas,* should avoid becoming killers of their own self-interest by neglecting Kṛṣṇa consciousness, the loving service of the Lord. Such neglect paves the way for future suffering.

TEXT 23

स्वर्गापवर्गयोर्द्वारं प्राप्य लोकमिमं पुमान् ।
द्रविणे कोऽनुषज्जेत मर्त्योऽनर्थस्य धामनि ॥ २३ ॥

svargāpavargayor dvāraṁ
prāpya lokam imaṁ pumān
draviṇe ko 'nuṣajjeta
martyo 'narthasya dhāmani

svarga—of heaven; *apavargayoḥ*—and liberation; *dvāram*—the gateway; *prāpya*—achieving; *lokam*—the human life; *imam*—this; *pumān*—a person; *draviṇe*—to property; *kaḥ*—who; *anuṣajjeta*—will become attached; *martyaḥ*—prone to death; *anarthasya*—of worthlessness; *dhāmani*—in the realm.

TRANSLATION

What mortal man, having achieved this human life, which is the very gateway to both heaven and liberation, would willingly become attached to that abode of worthlessness, material property?

PURPORT

That which one intends to use for one's personal sense gratification is called material property, whereas paraphernalia to be used in the Lord's loving service is understood to be spiritual. One should give up all one's material property by utilizing it completely in the devotional service of the Lord. A person who owns a luxurious mansion should install the Deity of the Lord and hold regular programs to propagate Kṛṣṇa consciousness. Similarly, wealth should be used to build temples of the Lord and publish literature scientifically explaining the Personality of Godhead. One who blindly renounces material property without utilizing it in the service of the Lord does not understand that everything belongs to the Personality of Godhead. Such blind renunciation is based on the material idea that "This property could belong to me, but I don't want it." Everything, in fact, belongs to God; knowing this one neither tries to enjoy nor to reject the things of this world, but peacefully engages them in the service of the Lord.

TEXT 24

देवर्षिपितृभूतानि ज्ञातीन् बन्धूंश्च भागिनः ।
असंविभज्य चात्मानं यक्षवित्तः पतत्यधः ॥ २४ ॥

devarṣi-pitṛ-bhūtāni
jñātīn bandhūṁś ca bhāginaḥ
asaṁvibhajya cātmānaṁ
yakṣa-vittaḥ pataty adhaḥ

deva—the demigods; *ṛṣi*—sages; *pitṛ*—departed forefathers; *bhūtāni*—and living entities in general; *jñātīn*—one's immediate relatives; *bandhūn*—extended family; *ca*—and; *bhāginaḥ*—to the shareholders; *asaṁvibhajya*—not distributing; *ca*—and; *ātmānam*—to oneself; *yakṣa-vittaḥ*—whose wealth is simply like that of a Yakṣa; *patati*—he falls; *adhaḥ*—down.

TRANSLATION

One who fails to distribute his wealth to the proper shareholders—the demigods, sages, forefathers and ordinary living entities, as well as his immediate relatives, in-laws and own self—is maintaining his wealth simply like a Yakṣa and will fall down.

PURPORT

One who does not share his wealth with the above-mentioned authorized persons and does not even enjoy the wealth himself will certainly suffer unlimited problems in life.

TEXT 25

व्यर्थयार्थेहया वित्तं प्रमत्तस्य वयो बलम् ।
कुशला येन सिध्यन्ति जरठः किं नु साधये ॥२५॥

vyarthayārthehayā vittaṁ
pramattasya vayo balam
kuśalā yena sidhyanti
jaraṭhaḥ kiṁ nu sādhaye

vyarthayā—useless; *artha*—for wealth; *īhayā*—by the endeavor; *vittam*—money; *pramattasya*—of the maddened; *vayaḥ*—youth; *balam*—strength; *kuśalāḥ*—those who are discriminating; *yena*—by means of which; *sidhyanti*—become perfect; *jaraṭhaḥ*—an old man; *kim*—what; *nu*—indeed; *sādhaye*—can I achieve.

TRANSLATION

Discriminating persons are able to utilize their money, youth and strength to achieve perfection. But I have feverishly squandered these in the useless endeavor for further wealth. Now that I am an old man, what can I achieve?

TEXT 26

कस्मात् संक्लिश्यते विद्वान् व्यर्थयार्थेहयासकृत् ।
कस्यचिन्मायया नूनं लोकोऽयं सुविमोहितः ॥२६॥

kasmāt saṅkliśyate vidvān
vyarthayārthehayāsakṛt
kasyacin māyayā nūnaṁ
loko 'yaṁ su-vimohitaḥ

kasmāt—why; *saṅkliśyate*—suffers; *vidvān*—one who is wise; *vyarthayā*—vain; *artha-īhayā*—in the pursuit of wealth; *asakṛt*—constantly; *kasyacit*—of someone; *māyayā*—by the illusory potency; *nūnam*—certainly; *lokaḥ*—the world; *ayam*—this; *su-vimohitaḥ*—very much bewildered.

TRANSLATION

Why must an intelligent man suffer by his constant vain efforts to get wealth? Indeed, this whole world is most bewildered by someone's illusory potency.

TEXT 27

किं धनैर्धनदैर्वा किं कामैर्वा कामदैरुत ।
मृत्युना ग्रस्यमानस्य कर्मभिर्वोत जन्मदैः ॥२७॥

kiṁ dhanair dhana-dair vā kiṁ
kāmair vā kāma-dair uta

mṛtyunā grasyamānasya
karmabhir vota janma-daiḥ

kim—of what use; *dhanaiḥ*—are different kinds of wealth; *dhana-daiḥ*—the givers of wealth; *vā*—or; *kim*—what is the use; *kāmaiḥ*—of the objects of sense gratification; *vā*—or; *kāma-daiḥ*—those who give such sense gratification; *uta*—or; *mṛtyunā*—by death; *grasyamānasya*—for one who is being seized; *karmabhiḥ*—by fruitive activities; *vā uta*—or else; *janma-daiḥ*—which give him his next birth.

TRANSLATION

For one who is in the grips of death, what is the use of wealth or those who offer it, sense gratification or those who offer it, or, for that matter, any type of fruitive activity, which simply causes one to again take birth in the material world?

TEXT 28

नूनं मे भगवांस्तुष्टः सर्वदेवमयो हरिः ।
येन नीतो दशामेतां निर्वेदश्चात्मनः प्लवः ॥२८॥

nūnaṁ me bhagavāṁs tuṣṭaḥ
sarva-deva-mayo hariḥ
yena nīto daśām etāṁ
nirvedaś cātmanaḥ plavaḥ

nūnam—certainly; *me*—with Me; *bhagavān*—the Supreme Personality of Godhead; *tuṣṭaḥ*—is satisfied; *sarva-deva-mayaḥ*—who comprises all the demigods; *hariḥ*—Lord Viṣṇu; *yena*—by whom; *nītaḥ*—I have been brought; *daśām*—to the condition; *etām*—this; *nirvedaḥ*—detachment; *ca*—and; *ātmanaḥ*—of the self; *plavaḥ*—the boat (to carry me over the ocean of material suffering).

TRANSLATION

The Supreme Personality of Godhead, Lord Hari, who contains within Himself all the demigods, must be satisfied with me.

Indeed, He has brought me to this suffering condition and forced me to experience detachment, which is the boat to carry me over this ocean of material life.

PURPORT

The *brāhmaṇa* could understand that the demigods, who award different types of sense gratification as the result of one's fruitive activities, cannot bestow the highest benefit in life. When the *brāhmaṇa* lost all his property he could understand that the Supreme Personality of Godhead, who comprises all the demigods, had given him the highest perfection, not by awarding sense gratification but by saving him from the ocean of material enjoyment. Being thus deprived of the opportunity to cultivate religiosity, wealth, sense gratification and liberation, the *brāhmaṇa* became detached, and transcendental knowledge awakened within his heart.

TEXT 29

सोऽहं कालावशेषेण शोषयिष्येऽङ्गमात्मनः ।
अप्रमत्तोऽखिलस्वार्थे यदि स्यात् सिद्ध आत्मनि॥२९॥

so 'haṁ kālāvaśeṣeṇa
śoṣayiṣye 'ṅgam ātmanaḥ
apramatto 'khila-svārthe
yadi syāt siddha ātmani

saḥ aham—I; *kāla-avaśeṣeṇa*—with whatever time remains; *śoṣayiṣye*—shall reduce to the minimum; *aṅgam*—this body; *ātmanaḥ*—my; *apramattaḥ*—unbewildered; *akhila*—entire; *sva-arthe*—in the real self-interest; *yadi*—if; *syāt*—there remains any (time); *siddhaḥ*—satisfied; *ātmani*—within myself.

TRANSLATION

If there is any time remaining in my life, I will perform austerities and force my body to subsist on the bare necessities. Without

further confusion I shall pursue that which constitutes my entire self-interest in life, and I shall remain satisfied within the self.

TEXT 30

तत्र मामनुमोदेरन् देवास्त्रिभुवनेश्वराः ।
मुहूर्तेन ब्रह्मलोकं खट्वाङ्गः समसाधयत् ॥३०॥

tatra mām anumoderan
devās tri-bhuvaneśvarāḥ
muhūrtena brahma-lokaṁ
khaṭvāṅgaḥ samasādhayat

tatra—in this regard; *mām*—with me; *anumoderan*—may they kindly be pleased; *devāḥ*—the demigods; *tri-bhuvana*—of the three worlds; *īśvarāḥ*—the controllers; *muhūrtena*—in a single moment; *brahma-lokam*—the spiritual world; *khaṭvāṅga*—King Khaṭvāṅga; *samasādhayat*—achieved.

TRANSLATION

Thus may the presiding demigods of these three worlds kindly show their mercy upon me. Indeed, Mahārāja Khaṭvāṅga was able to achieve the spiritual world in a single moment.

PURPORT

The *brāhmaṇa* of Avantī thought that although he was an old man who might die at any moment he could follow the example of Mahārāja Khaṭvāṅga, who achieved the Lord's mercy in a single moment. Mahārāja Khaṭvāṅga, as described in the Second Canto of *Śrīmad-Bhāgavatam*, fought valiantly on behalf of the demigods, and they offered the king any benediction he might desire. Khaṭvāṅga Mahārāja chose to find out the remaining duration of his life, which unfortunately was a single moment. The king therefore immediately surrendered to Lord Kṛṣṇa and achieved the spiritual world. The *brāhmaṇa* of Avantī desired to follow this example; with the blessings of the demigods, who are all devotees of the Lord, he hoped to become fully Kṛṣṇa conscious before giving up his body.

TEXT 31

श्रीभगवानुवाच
इत्यभिप्रेत्य मनसा ह्यावन्त्यो द्विजसत्तमः ।
उन्मुच्य हृदयग्रन्थीन् शान्तो भिक्षुरभून्मुनिः ॥३१॥

śrī-bhagavān uvāca
ity abhipretya manasā
hy āvantyo dvija-sattamaḥ
unmucya hṛdaya-granthīn
śānto bhikṣur abhūn muniḥ

śrī-bhagavān uvāca—the Supreme Lord said; *iti*—thus; *abhipretya*—concluding; *manasā*—within his mind; *hi*—indeed; *āvantyaḥ*—of the district of Avantī; *dvija-sat-tamaḥ*—now the most pious *brāhmaṇa; unmucya*—untying; *hṛdaya*—in his heart; *granthīn*—the knots (of desire); *śāntaḥ*—peaceful; *bhikṣuḥ*—a mendicant *sannyāsī; abhūt*—he became; *muniḥ*—silent.

TRANSLATION

Lord Śrī Kṛṣṇa continued: His mind thus determined, that most excellent Avantī *brāhmaṇa* was able to untie the knots of desire within his heart. He then assumed the role of a peaceful and silent *sannyāsī* mendicant.

TEXT 32

स चचार महीमेतां संयतात्मेन्द्रियानिलः ।
भिक्षार्थं नगरग्रामानसङ्गोऽलक्षितोऽविशत् ॥३२॥

sa cacāra mahīm etāṁ
saṁyatātmendriyānilaḥ
bhikṣārthaṁ nagara-grāmān
asaṅgo 'lakṣito 'viśat

saḥ—he; *cacāra*—wandered; *mahīm*—the earth; *etām*—this; *saṁyata*—controlled; *ātma*—his consciousness; *indriya*—senses; *anilaḥ*—and vital air; *bhikṣā-artham*—for the purpose of taking charity; *nagara*—the cities; *grāmān*—and villages; *asaṅgaḥ*—without any association; *alakṣitaḥ*—not making himself prominent, thus unrecognized; *aviśat*—he entered.

TRANSLATION

He wandered about the earth, keeping his intelligence, senses and life air under control. To beg charity he traveled alone to various cities and villages. He did not advertise his advanced spiritual position and thus was not recognized by others.

PURPORT

According to Śrīla Bhaktisiddhānta Sarasvatī Ṭhākura, the acceptance of the *tridaṇḍi-sannyāsa* order of life is the chief indication that one has actually taken shelter of the Supreme Personality of Godhead. The three rods of the *daṇḍa,* or staff, of the Vaiṣṇava *sannyāsī* indicate control of the body, mind and words by engaging them only in the loving service of the Lord. This procedure helps one to become more tolerant than a tree, as recommended by Śrī Caitanya Mahāprabhu. By strict control of one's body, mind and speech, the quality of tolerance becomes strengthened, and thus one manifests the further qualities of forgiving others, never wasting one's time, detachment from sense gratification, lack of false pride in one's work and not hankering for liberation. One in this way gives up the mentality of materialistic persons, who establish so-called affectionate relationships of mutual flattery and exploit each other for sense gratification. One who adopts the strict path of Kṛṣṇa consciousness, following in the footsteps of great souls, can achieve the shelter of the Lord.

TEXT 33

तं वै प्रवयसं भिक्षुमवधूतमसज्जनाः ।
दृष्ट्वा पर्यभवन् भद्र बह्वीभिः परिभूतिभिः ॥३३॥

taṁ vai pravayasaṁ bhikṣum
avadhūtam asaj-janāḥ

dṛṣṭvā paryabhavan bhadra
bahvībhiḥ paribhūtibhiḥ

tam—him; *vai*—indeed; *pravayasam*—old; *bhikṣum*—the beggar; *avadhūtam*—unclean; *asat*—low-class; *janāḥ*—persons; *dṛṣṭvā*—seeing; *paryabhavan*—dishonored; *bhadra*—O kind Uddhava; *bahvībhiḥ*—with many; *paribhūtibhiḥ*—insults.

TRANSLATION

O kind Uddhava, seeing him as an old, dirty beggar, rowdy persons would dishonor him with many insults.

TEXT 34

केचित्त्रिवेणुं जगृहुरेके पात्रं कमण्डलुम् ।
पीठं चैकेऽक्षसूत्रं च कन्थां चीराणि केचन ।
प्रदाय च पुनस्तानि दर्शितान्याददुर्मुनेः ॥३४॥

kecit tri-veṇuṁ jagṛhur
eke pātraṁ kamaṇḍalum
pīṭhaṁ caike 'kṣa-sūtraṁ ca
kanthāṁ cīrāṇi kecana
pradāya ca punas tāni
darśitāny ādadur muneḥ

kecit—some of them; *tri-veṇum*—his *sannyāsī* triple staff; *jagṛhuḥ*—they took away; *eke*—some; *pātram*—his begging bowl; *kamaṇḍalum*—waterpot; *pīṭham*—seat; *ca*—and; *eke*—some; *akṣa-sūtram*—chanting beads; *ca*—and; *kanthām*—rags; *cīrāṇi*—torn; *kecana*—some of them; *pradāya*—offering back; *ca*—and; *punaḥ*—again; *tāni*—they; *darśitāni*—which were being shown; *ādaduḥ*—they took away; *muneḥ*—of the sage.

TRANSLATION

Some of these persons would take away his *sannyāsī* rod, and some the waterpot which he was using as a begging bowl. Some took his deerskin seat, some his chanting beads, and some would

steal his torn, ragged clothing. Displaying these things before him, they would pretend to offer them back but would then hide them again.

TEXT 35

अन्नं च भैक्ष्यसम्पन्नं भुञ्जानस्य सरित्तटे ।
मूत्रयन्ति च पापिष्ठाः ष्ठीवन्त्यस्य च मूर्धनि ॥३५॥

annaṁ ca bhaikṣya-sampannaṁ
bhuñjānasya sarit-taṭe
mūtrayanti ca pāpiṣṭhāḥ
ṣṭhīvanty asya ca mūrdhani

annam—food; *ca*—and; *bhaikṣya*—by his begging; *sampannam*—acquired; *bhuñjānasya*—of him who was about to partake; *sarit*—of a river; *taṭe*—on the shore; *mūtrayanti*—they urinate upon; *ca*—and; *pāpiṣṭhāḥ*—most sinful persons; *ṣṭhīvanti*—they spit; *asya*—his; *ca*—and; *mūrdhani*—on his head.

TRANSLATION

When he was sitting on the bank of a river about to partake of the food that he had collected by his begging, such sinful rascals would come and pass urine on it, and they would dare to spit on his head.

TEXT 36

यतवाचं वाचयन्ति ताडयन्ति न वक्ति चेत् ।
तर्जयन्त्यपरे वाग्भिः स्तेनोऽयमिति वादिनः ।
बध्नन्ति रज्ज्वा तं केचिद् बध्यतां बध्यतामिति ॥३६॥

yata-vācaṁ vācayanti
tāḍayanti na vakti cet
tarjayanty apare vāgbhiḥ
steno 'yam iti vādinaḥ
badhnanti rajjvā taṁ kecid
badhyatāṁ badhyatām iti

yata-vācam—who had taken a vow of silence; *vācayanti*—they try to make speak; *tāḍayanti*—they beat; *na vakti*—he does not speak; *cet*—if; *tarjayanti*—they cajole; *apare*—others; *vāgbhiḥ*—with their words; *stenaḥ*—thief; *ayam*—this person; *iti*—thus; *vādinaḥ*—saying; *badhnanti*—they bind up; *rajjvā*—with rope; *tam*—him; *kecit*—some; *badhyatām badhyatām*—"Bind him up! Bind him up!"; *iti*—thus saying.

TRANSLATION

Although he had taken a vow of silence, they would try to make him speak, and if he did not speak they would beat him with sticks. Others would chastise him, saying, "This man is just a thief." And others would bind him up with rope, shouting, "Tie him up! Tie him up!"

TEXT 37

क्षिपन्त्येकेऽवजानन्त एष धर्मध्वजः शठः ।
क्षीणवित्त इमां वृत्तिमग्रहीत् स्वजनोज्झितः ॥३७॥

kṣipanty eke 'vajānanta
eṣa dharma-dhvajaḥ śaṭhaḥ
kṣīṇa-vitta imāṁ vṛttim
agrahīt sva-janojjhitaḥ

kṣipanti—they criticize; *eke*—some; *avajānantaḥ*—committing insults; *eṣaḥ*—this person; *dharma-dhvajaḥ*—a religious hypocrite; *śaṭhaḥ*—a cheater; *kṣīṇa-vittaḥ*—having lost his wealth; *imām*—this; *vṛttim*—occupation; *agrahīt*—has taken; *sva-jana*—by his family; *ujjhitaḥ*—turned out.

TRANSLATION

They would criticize and insult him, saying, "This man is just a hypocrite and a cheat. He makes a business of religion simply because he lost all his wealth and his family threw him out."

TEXTS 38-39

अहो एष महासारो धृतिमान् गिरिराडिव ।
मौनेन साधयत्यर्थं बकवद् दृढनिश्चयः ॥३८॥

इत्येके विहसन्त्येनमेके दुर्वातयन्ति च ।
तं बबन्धुर्निरुरुधुर्यथा क्रीडनकं द्विजम् ॥३९॥

aho eṣa mahā-sāro
dhṛtimān giri-rāḍ iva
maunena sādhayaty arthaṁ
baka-vad dṛḍha-niścayaḥ

ity eke vihasanty enam
eke durvātayanti ca
taṁ babandhur nirurudhur
yathā krīḍanakaṁ dvijam

aho—just see; *eṣaḥ*—this person; *mahā-sāraḥ*—very powerful; *dhṛtimān*—steadfast; *giri-rāṭ*—the Himalaya Mountains; *iva*—just like; *maunena*—with his vow of silence; *sādhayati*—he is striving; *artham*—for his goal; *baka-vat*—just like a duck; *dṛḍha*—firm; *niścayaḥ*—his determination; *iti*—thus speaking; *eke*—some; *vihasanti*—ridicule; *enam*—him; *eke*—some; *durvātayanti*—pass foul air; *ca*—and; *tam*—him; *babandhuḥ*—they bound in chains; *nirurudhuḥ*—kept captive; *yathā*—as; *krīḍanakam*—a pet animal; *dvijam*—that *brāhmaṇa.*

TRANSLATION

Some would ridicule him by saying, "Just see this greatly powerful sage! He is as steadfast as the Himalaya Mountains. By practice of silence he strives for his goal with great determination, just like a duck." Other persons would pass foul air upon him, and sometimes others would bind this twice-born *brāhmaṇa* in chains and keep him captive like a pet animal.

TEXT 40

एवं स भौतिकं दुःखं दैविकं दैहिकं च यत् ।
भोक्तव्यमात्मनो दिष्टं प्राप्तं प्राप्तमबुध्यत ॥४०॥

evaṁ sa bhautikaṁ duḥkhaṁ
daivikaṁ daihikaṁ ca yat

bhoktavyam ātmano diṣṭaṁ
prāptaṁ prāptam abudhyata

evam—thus; *saḥ*—he; *bhautikam*—due to other living entities; *duḥkham*—suffering; *daivikam*—due to higher powers; *daihikam*—due to his own body; *ca*—and; *yat*—whatever; *bhoktavyam*—destined to be suffered; *ātmanaḥ*—his own; *diṣṭam*—allotted by destiny; *prāptam prāptam*—whatever was received; *abudhyata*—he understood.

TRANSLATION

The *brāhmaṇa* understood that all his suffering—from other living beings, from the higher forces of nature and from his own body—was unavoidable, being allotted to him by providence.

PURPORT

Many cruel persons harassed the *brāhmaṇa*, and his own body caused him suffering in the form of fever, hunger, thirst, fatigue, etc. The higher forces of nature are those that cause excessive heat, cold, wind and rain. The *brāhmaṇa* realized that his suffering was due to his false identification with his material body, and not to the interaction of his body with external phenomena. Rather than try to adjust his external situation, he tried to adjust his Kṛṣṇa consciousness and thus realize his actual identity as eternal spirit soul.

TEXT 41

परिभूत इमां गाथामगायत नराधमैः ।
पातयद्भिः स्वधर्मस्थो धृतिमास्थाय सात्त्विकीम् ॥४१॥

paribhūta imāṁ gāthām
agāyata narādhamaiḥ
pātayadbhiḥ sva-dharma-stho
dhṛtim āsthāya sāttvikīm

paribhūtaḥ—insulted; *imām*—this; *gāthām*—song; *agāyata*—he sang; *nara-adhamaiḥ*—by low-class men; *pātayadbhiḥ*—who were trying to make him fall down; *sva-dharma*—in his own duty; *sthaḥ*—remaining firm; *dhṛtim*—his resolution; *āsthāya*—fixing; *sāttvikīm*—in the mode of goodness.

TRANSLATION

Even while being insulted by these low-class men who were trying to effect his downfall, he remained steady in his spiritual duties. Fixing his resolution in the mode of goodness, he began to chant the following song.

PURPORT

Resolution in the mode of goodness is described in *Bhagavad-gītā* (18:33):

dhṛtyā yayā dhārayate
manaḥ-prāṇendriya-kriyāḥ
yogenāvyabhicāriṇyā
dhṛtiḥ sā pārtha sāttvikī

"O son of Pṛthā, that determination which is unbreakable, which is sustained with steadfastness by *yoga* practice, and thus controls the mind, life and the acts of the senses, is in the mode of goodness."

Atheists who are envious of the devotees of the Supreme Lord are called *narādhamas,* or the lowest of men, and undoubtedly are enroute to hell. By all means at their disposal they disturb the devotional service of the Lord, sometimes by direct attack and sometimes by mockery. The devotees, however, remain tolerant, fixing their determination in the mode of goodness. As described by Śrīla Rūpa Gosvāmī in *Śrī Upadeśāmṛta* (1),

vāco vegaṁ manasaḥ krodha-vegaṁ
jihvā-vegam udaropastha-vegam
etān vegān yo viṣaheta dhīraḥ
sarvām apīmāṁ pṛthivīṁ sa śiṣyāt

"A sober person who can tolerate the urge to speak, the mind's demands, the actions of anger and the urges of the tongue, belly and genitals is qualified to make disciples all over the world."

TEXT 42

द्विज उवाच
नायं जनो मे सुखदुःखहेतु-
र्न देवतात्मा ग्रहकर्मकालाः ।
मनः परं कारणमामनन्ति
संसारचक्रं परिवर्तयेद् यत् ॥ ४२ ॥

dvija uvāca
nāyaṁ jano me sukha-duḥkha-hetur
na devatātmā graha-karma-kālāḥ
manaḥ paraṁ kāraṇam āmananti
saṁsāra-cakraṁ parivartayed yat

dvijaḥ uvāca—the *brāhmaṇa* said; *na*—not; *ayam*—these; *janaḥ*—people; *me*—my; *sukha*—of happiness; *duḥkha*—and distress; *hetuḥ*—the cause; *na*—nor; *devatā*—the demigods; *ātmā*—my own body; *graha*—the controlling planets; *karma*—my past work; *kālāḥ*—or time; *manaḥ*—the mind; *param*—rather only; *kāraṇam*—the cause; *āmananti*—is called by standard authorities; *saṁsāra*—of material life; *cakram*—the cycle; *parivartayet*—causes to rotate; *yat*—which.

TRANSLATION

The *brāhmaṇa* said: These people are not the cause of my happiness and distress. Neither are the demigods, my own body, the planets, my past work, or time. Rather, it is the mind alone that causes happiness and distress and perpetuates the rotation of material life.

TEXT 43

मनो गुणान् वै सृजते बलीय-
स्ततश्च कर्माणि विलक्षणानि ।
शुक्लानि कृष्णान्यथ लोहितानि
तेभ्यः सवर्णाः सृतयो भवन्ति ॥ ४३ ॥

mano guṇān vai sṛjate balīyas
tataś ca karmāṇi vilakṣaṇāni
śuklāni kṛṣṇāny atha lohitāni
tebhyaḥ sa-varṇāḥ sṛtayo bhavanti

manaḥ—the mind; *guṇān*—the activities of the modes of nature; *vai*—indeed; *sṛjate*—manifests; *balīyaḥ*—very strong; *tataḥ*—by those qualities; *ca*—and; *karmāṇi*—material activities; *vilakṣaṇāni*—of different varieties; *śuklāni*—white (in the mode of goodness); *kṛṣṇāni*—black (in the mode of ignorance); *atha*—and; *lohitāni*—red (in the mode of passion); *tebhyaḥ*—from those activities; *sa-varṇāḥ*—having the same corresponding colors; *sṛtayaḥ*—created conditions; *bhavanti*—arise.

TRANSLATION

The powerful mind actuates the functions of the material modes, from which evolve the different kinds of material activities in the modes of goodness, ignorance and passion. From the activities in each of these modes develop the corresponding statuses of life.

PURPORT

In the mode of goodness one considers oneself to be a saintly or wise person, in the mode of passion one struggles for material success, and in the mode of ignorance one becomes cruel, lazy and sinful. By the combination of the material modes one identifies oneself as a demigod, a king, a rich capitalist, a wise scholar, etc. These conceptions are material designations generated from the modes of nature, and they arrange themselves according to the tendency of the powerful mind to enjoy temporary sense gratification. The word *balīyas* in this verse, meaning "very strong," indicates that the material mind becomes insensitive to intelligent advice. Even if we are informed that we are committing many sins and offenses in order to earn money, we may still think that money should be acquired at all costs, since without it one can neither perform religious ceremonies nor gratify the senses with beautiful women, mansions and vehicles. Once the money is achieved, one suffers further problems, but the stubborn mind will never heed good advice in this regard. One must therefore give up mental concoction and control the mind in Kṛṣṇa consciousness, as exemplified here by the *brāhmaṇa* from Avantī.

TEXT 44

अनीह आत्मा मनसा समीहता
हिरण्मयो मत्सख उद्विचष्टे ।
मनः स्वलिङ्गं परिगृह्य कामान्
जुषन् निबद्धो गुणसङ्गतोऽसौ ॥ ४४ ॥

anīha ātmā manasā samīhatā
hiraṇ-mayo mat-sakha udvicaṣṭe
manaḥ sva-liṅgaṁ parigṛhya kāmān
juṣan nibaddho guṇa-saṅgato 'sau

anīhaḥ—not endeavoring; *ātmā*—the Supreme Soul; *manasā*—along with the mind; *samīhatā*—which is struggling; *hiraṇ-mayaḥ*—exhibiting transcendental enlightenment; *mat-sakhaḥ*—my friend; *udvicaṣṭe*—looks down from above; *manaḥ*—the mind; *sva-liṅgam*—which projects the image of the material world upon him (the soul); *parigṛhya*—embracing; *kāmān*—objects of desire; *juṣan*—engaging with; *nibaddhaḥ*—becomes bound; *guṇa-saṅgataḥ*—because of association with the modes of nature; *asau*—that infinitesimal spirit soul.

TRANSLATION

Although present along with the struggling mind within the material body, the Supersoul is not endeavoring, because He is already endowed with transcendental enlightenment. Acting as my friend, He simply witnesses from His transcendental position. I, the infinitesimal spirit soul, on the other hand, have embraced this mind, which is the mirror reflecting the image of the material world. Thus I have become engaged in enjoying objects of desire and am entangled due to contact with the modes of nature.

TEXT 45

दानं स्वधर्मो नियमो यमश्च
श्रुतं च कर्माणि च सद्व्रतानि ।
सर्वे मनोनिग्रहलक्षणान्ताः
परो हि योगो मनसः समाधिः ॥४५॥

dānaṁ sva-dharmo niyamo yamaś ca
śrutaṁ ca karmāṇi ca sad-vratāni
sarve mano-nigraha-lakṣaṇāntāḥ
paro hi yogo manasaḥ samādhiḥ

dānam—giving of charity; *sva-dharmaḥ*—carrying out one's prescribed duties; *niyamaḥ*—the regulations of day-to-day life; *yamaḥ*—the major regulations of spiritual practice; *ca*—and; *śrutam*—listening to scripture; *ca*—and; *karmāṇi*—pious work; *ca*—and; *sat*—pure; *vratāni*—vows; *sarve*—all; *manaḥ-nigrahaḥ*—the subduing of the mind; *lakṣaṇa*—consisting of; *antāḥ*—their aim; *paraḥ*—supreme; *hi*—indeed; *yogaḥ*—transcendental knowledge; *manasaḥ*—of the mind; *samādhiḥ*—meditation on the Supreme in trance.

TRANSLATION

Charity, prescribed duties, observance of major and minor regulative principles, hearing from scripture, pious works and purifying vows all have as their final aim the subduing of the mind. Indeed, concentration of the mind on the Supreme is the highest *yoga*.

TEXT 46

समाहितं यस्य मनः प्रशान्तं
दानादिभिः किं वद तस्य कृत्यम् ।
असंयतं यस्य मनो विनश्यद्
दानादिभिश्चेदपरं किमेभिः ॥ ४६ ॥

samāhitaṁ yasya manaḥ praśāntaṁ
dānādibhiḥ kiṁ vada tasya kṛtyam
asaṁyataṁ yasya mano vinaśyad
dānādibhiś ced aparaṁ kim ebhiḥ

samāhitam—perfectly fixed; *yasya*—whose; *manaḥ*—mind; *praśāntam*—pacified; *dāna-ādibhiḥ*—by charity and the other processes; *kim*—what; *vada*—please tell; *tasya*—of those processes; *kṛtyam*—use; *asaṁyatam*—uncontrolled; *yasya*—whose; *manaḥ*—mind; *vinaśyat*—dissolving; *dāna-ādibhiḥ*—by these processes of charity and so on; *cet*—if; *aparam*—further; *kim*—what use; *ebhiḥ*—of these.

TRANSLATION

If one's mind is perfectly fixed and pacified, then tell me what need does one have to perform ritualistic charity and other pious rituals? And if one's mind remains uncontrolled, lost in ignorance, then of what use are these engagements for him?

TEXT 47

मनोवशेऽन्ये ह्यभवन् स्म देवा
मनश्च नान्यस्य वशं समेति ।
भीष्मो हि देवः सहसः सहीयान्
युञ्ज्याद् वशे तं स हि देवदेवः ॥ ४७ ॥

mano-vaśe 'nye hy abhavan sma devā
manaś ca nānyasya vaśaṁ sameti
bhīṣmo hi devaḥ sahasaḥ sahīyān
yuñjyād vaśe taṁ sa hi deva-devaḥ

manaḥ—of the mind; *vaśe*—under the control; *anye*—others; *hi*—indeed; *abhavan*—have become; *sma*—in the past; *devāḥ*—the senses (represented by their presiding deities); *manaḥ*—the mind; *ca*—and; *na*—never; *anyasya*—of another; *vaśam*—under the control; *sameti*—comes; *bhīṣmaḥ*—fearsome; *hi*—indeed; *devaḥ*—the godlike power; *sahasaḥ*—than the strongest; *sahīyān*—stronger; *yuñjyāt*—can fix;

vaśe—under control; *tam*—that mind; *saḥ*—such a person; *hi*—indeed; *deva-devaḥ*—the master of all the senses.

TRANSLATION

All the senses have been under the control of the mind since time immemorial, and the mind himself never comes under the sway of any other. He is stronger than the strongest, and his godlike power is fearsome. Therefore, anyone who can bring the mind under control becomes the master of all the senses.

TEXT 48

तं दुर्जयं शत्रुमसह्यवेग-
मरुन्तुदं तन्न विजित्य केचित् ।
कुर्वन्त्यसद्विग्रहमत्र मर्त्यै-
र्मित्राण्युदासीनरिपून् विमूढाः ॥४८॥

taṁ durjayaṁ śatrum asahya-vegam
arun-tudaṁ tan na vijitya kecit
kurvanty asad-vigraham atra martyair
mitrāṇy udāsīna-ripūn vimūḍhāḥ

tam—that; *durjayam*—difficult to conquer; *śatrum*—enemy; *asahya*—intolerable; *vegam*—whose urges; *arum-tudam*—capable of tormenting the heart; *tat*—therefore; *na vijitya*—failing to conquer over; *kecit*—some people; *kurvanti*—they create; *asat*—useless; *vigraham*—quarrel; *atra*—in this world; *martyaiḥ*—with mortal living beings; *mitrāṇi*—friends; *udāsīna*—indifferent persons; *ripūn*—and rivals; *vimūḍhāḥ*—completely bewildered.

TRANSLATION

Failing to conquer this irrepressible enemy, the mind, whose urges are intolerable and who torments the heart, many people are completely bewildered and create useless quarrel with others. Thus they conclude that other people are either their friends, their enemies or parties indifferent to them.

PURPORT

Falsely identifying oneself as the material body, and accepting bodily expansions such as children and grandchildren to be one's eternal property, one completely forgets that every living being is qualitatively one with God. There is no essential difference between one individual being and another, since all are eternal expansions of the Supreme Lord. The mind absorbed in false ego creates the material body, and by identification with the body, the conditioned soul is overwhelmed by false pride and ignorance, as described here.

TEXT 49

देहं मनोमात्रमिमं गृहीत्वा
ममाहमित्यन्धधियो मनुष्याः ।
एषोऽहमन्योऽयमिति भ्रमेण
दुरन्तपारे तमसि भ्रमन्ति ॥४९॥

dehaṁ mano-mātram imaṁ gṛhītvā
mamāham ity andha-dhiyo manuṣyāḥ
eṣo 'ham anyo 'yam iti bhrameṇa
duranta-pāre tamasi bhramanti

deham—the material body; *manaḥ-mātram*—coming simply from the mind; *imam*—this; *gṛhītvā*—having accepted; *mama*—mine; *aham*—I; *iti*—thus; *andha*—blinded; *dhiyaḥ*—their intelligence; *manuṣyāḥ*—human beings; *eṣaḥ*—this; *aham*—I am; *anyaḥ*—someone else; *ayam*—this is; *iti*—thus; *bhrameṇa*—by the illusion; *duranta-pāre*—unsurpassable; *tamasi*—within the darkness; *bhramanti*—they wander.

TRANSLATION

Persons who identify with this body, which is simply the product of the material mind, are blinded in their intelligence, thinking in terms of "I" and "mine." Because of their illusion of "this is I, but that is someone else," they wander in endless darkness.

TEXT 50

जनस्तु हेतुः सुखदुःखयोश्चेत्
किमात्मनश्चात्र ह भौमयोस्तत् ।
जिह्वां क्वचित् संदशति स्वदद्भि-
स्तद्वेदनायां कतमाय कुप्येत् ॥५०॥

janas tu hetuḥ sukha-duḥkhayoś cet
kim ātmanaś cātra hi bhaumayos tat
jihvāṁ kvacit sandaśati sva-dadbhis
tad-vedanāyāṁ katamāya kupyet

janaḥ—these people; *tu*—but; *hetuḥ*—the cause; *sukha-duḥkhayoḥ*—of my happiness and distress; *cet*—if; *kim*—what; *ātmanaḥ*—for the self; *ca*—and; *atra*—in this conception; *hi*—indeed; *bhaumayoḥ*—they pertain to the material bodies; *tat*—that (status of being the performer and the sufferer); *jihvām*—the tongue; *kvacit*—sometimes; *sandaśati*—is bitten; *sva*—by one's own; *dadbhiḥ*—teeth; *tat*—of that; *vedanāyām*—in the distress; *katamāya*—with whom; *kupyet*—can one get angry.

TRANSLATION

If you say that these people are the cause of my happiness and distress, then where is the place of the soul in such a conception? This happiness and distress pertain not to the soul but to the interactions of material bodies. If someone bites his tongue with his own teeth, at whom can he become angry in his suffering?

PURPORT

Although bodily pleasure and pain are felt by the soul, one must tolerate such duality, understanding it to be a creation of one's own material mind. If one accidentally bites his own tongue or lip, he cannot become angry and pull out his own teeth. Similarly, all living beings are individual parts and parcels of God, and thus nondifferent from each other. All of them are meant to serve the Supreme Lord in spiritual equality. If the living beings give up their master's service and instead quarrel among themselves, they will be forced to suffer by the laws of nature. If the conditioned souls establish artificial relationships of affection based on the material body and having nothing to do with God, then time itself will destroy such relationships, and they will be subjected to further suffering. But if the individual living entities understand each other to be of the same family, all having connection with the Supreme Lord, their mutual friendship will develop. Thus one should not exhibit anger that will be harmful to oneself and others. Although the *brāhmaṇa* was receiving kind offerings of charity from some people and being harassed and beaten by others, he denied that these people were the ultimate cause of his happiness and distress, for he was fixed on the platform of self-realization beyond the material body and mind.

TEXT 51

दुःखस्य हेतुर्यदि देवतास्तु
किमात्मनस्तत्र विकारयोस्तत् ।
यदङ्गमङ्गेन निहन्यते क्वचित्
क्रुध्येत कस्मै पुरुषः स्वदेहे ॥ ५१ ॥

duḥkhasya hetur yadi devatās tu
kim ātmanas tatra vikārayos tat
yad aṅgam aṅgena nihanyate kvacit
krudhyeta kasmai puruṣaḥ sva-dehe

duḥkhasya—of suffering; *hetuḥ*—the cause; *yadi*—if; *devatāḥ*—the demigods (who rule over the different senses within the body); *tu*—but; *kim*—what; *ātmanaḥ*—for the soul; *tatra*—in that connection; *vikārayoḥ*—which pertain to the transformable (senses and their deities); *tat*—that (acting and being acted upon); *yat*—when; *aṅgam*—a limb; *aṅgena*—by another limb; *nihanyate*—is hurt; *kvacit*—ever; *krudhyeta*—should become angry; *kasmai*—at whom; *puruṣaḥ*—the living entity; *sva-dehe*—within his own body.

TRANSLATION

If you say that the demigods who rule the bodily senses cause suffering, still, how can such suffering apply to the spirit soul?

This acting and being acted upon are merely interactions of the changeable senses and their presiding deities. When one limb of the body attacks another, with whom can the person in that body be angry?

PURPORT

The *brāhmaṇa* is elaborately explaining the condition of self-realization, in which one understands oneself to be totally distinct from the material body and mind and the demigods who control them. By cultivating bodily happiness we are forced to accept bodily pain. Foolish conditioned souls endeavor to eliminate distress and enjoy happiness, but material happiness and distress are two sides of the same coin. One cannot relish bodily happiness without identifying oneself as the body. But as soon as such identification occurs, one is harassed by the innumerable pains and sufferings also inevitably present within the same body. Bodily happiness and distress are administered by the demigods, who can never be brought under our control; thus one remains subject to the whims of providence on the material platform. If, however, one surrenders to the Personality of Godhead, Lord Kṛṣṇa, the reservoir of all pleasure, one can reach the spiritual platform, where transcendental bliss enlivens the liberated souls without any interrupting anxiety or unhappiness.

TEXT 52

आत्मा यदि स्यात् सुखदुःखहेतुः
किमन्यतस्तत्र निजस्वभावः ।
न ह्यात्मनोऽन्यद् यदि तन्मृषा स्यात्
क्रुध्येत कस्मान्न सुखं न दुःखम् ॥ ५२ ॥

ātmā yadi syāt sukha-duḥkha-hetuḥ
kim anyatas tatra nija-svabhāvaḥ
na hy ātmano 'nyad yadi tan mṛṣā syāt
krudhyeta kasmān na sukhaṁ na duḥkham

ātmā—the soul himself; *yadi*—if; *syāt*—should be; *sukha-duḥkha*—of happiness and distress; *hetuḥ*—the cause; *kim*—what; *anyataḥ*—other; *tatra*—in that theory; *nija*—his own; *svabhāvaḥ*—nature;

na—not; *hi*—indeed; *ātmanaḥ*—than the soul; *anyat*—anything separate; *yadi*—if; *tat*—that; *mṛṣā*—false; *syāt*—would be; *krudhyeta*—one can become angry; *kasmāt*—at whom; *na*—there is no; *sukham*—happiness; *na*—nor; *duḥkham*—misery.

TRANSLATION

If the soul himself were the cause of happiness and distress, then we could not blame others, since happiness and distress would be simply the nature of the soul. According to this theory, nothing except the soul actually exists, and if we were to perceive something besides the soul, that would be illusion. Therefore, since happiness and distress do not actually exist in this concept, why become angry at oneself or others?

PURPORT

Because a dead body does not feel pleasure or pain, our happiness and distress are due to our own consciousness, which is the nature of the soul. It is not, however, the original function of the soul to enjoy material happiness and suffer material distress. These are produced by ignorant material affection and enmity based on false ego. Our involvement in sense gratification drags our consciousness into the material body, where it is shocked by the inevitable bodily pains and problems.

On the spiritual platform there is neither material happiness nor distress because there the living consciousness is fully engaged, without personal desire, in the devotional service of the Supreme Lord. This is the actual position of happiness, aloof from false bodily identification. Rather than uselessly becoming enraged with others for one's own foolishness, one should take to self-realization and solve the problems of life.

TEXT 53

ग्रहा निमित्तं सुखदुःखयोश्चेत्
किमात्मनोऽजस्य जनस्य ते वै ।
ग्रहैर्ग्रहस्यैव वदन्ति पीडां
क्रुध्येत कस्मै पुरुषस्ततोऽन्यः ॥५३॥

grahā nimittaṁ sukha-duḥkhayoś cet
kim ātmano 'jasya janasya te vai
grahair grahasyaiva vadanti pīḍāṁ
krudhyeta kasmai puruṣas tato 'nyaḥ

grahāḥ—the controlling planets; *nimittam*—the immediate cause; *sukha-duḥkhayoḥ*—of happiness and distress; *cet*—if; *kim*—what; *ātmanaḥ*—for the soul; *ajasya*—who is unborn; *janasya*—of that which is born; *te*—those planets; *vai*—indeed; *grahaiḥ*—by other planets; *grahasya*—of a planet; *eva*—only; *vadanti*—(expert astrologers) say; *pīḍām*—suffering; *krudhyeta*—should become angry; *kasmai*—at whom; *puruṣaḥ*—the living entity; *tataḥ*—from that material body; *anyaḥ*—distinct.

TRANSLATION

And if we examine the hypothesis that the planets are the immediate cause of suffering and happiness, then also where is the relationship with the soul, who is eternal? After all, the effect of the planets applies only to things that have taken birth. Expert astrologers have moreover explained how the planets are only causing pain to each other. Therefore, since the living entity is distinct from these planets and from the material body, against whom should he vent his anger?

TEXT 54

कर्मास्तु हेतुः सुखदुःखयोश्चेत्
किमात्मनस्तद्धि जडाजडत्वे ।
देहस्त्वचित् पुरुषोऽयं सुपर्णः
क्रुध्येत कस्मै न हि कर्ममूलम् ॥५४॥

karmāstu hetuḥ sukha-duḥkhayoś cet
kim ātmanas tad dhi jaḍājaḍatve
dehas tv acit puruṣo 'yaṁ suparṇaḥ
krudhyeta kasmai na hi karma mūlam

karma—one's fruitive activities; *astu*—hypothetically granted; *hetuḥ*—the cause; *sukha-duḥkhayoḥ*—of happiness and distress; *cet*—if; *kim*—what; *ātmanaḥ*—for the soul; *tat*—that *karma; hi*—certainly; *jaḍa-ajaḍatve*—in being both material and not material; *dehaḥ*—the body; *tu*—on the one hand; *acit*—not living; *puruṣaḥ*—the person; *ayam*—this; *su-parṇaḥ*—endowed with living consciousness; *krudhyeta*—one should become angry; *kasmai*—at whom; *na*—are not; *hi*—certainly; *karma*—fruitive activities; *mūlam*—the root cause.

TRANSLATION

If we assume that fruitive work is the cause of happiness and distress, we still are not dealing with the soul. The idea of material work arises when there is a spiritual actor who is conscious and a material body that undergoes the transformation of happiness and distress as a reaction to such work. Since the body has no life, it cannot be the actual recipient of happiness and distress, nor can the soul, who is ultimately completely spiritual and aloof from the material body. Since *karma* thus has no ultimate basis in either the body or the soul, at whom can one become angry?

PURPORT

The material body is composed of earth, water, fire and air, just like bricks, stones and other objects. Our consciousness, falsely absorbed in the body, experiences happiness and distress, and fruitive work (*karma*) is performed when we falsely consider ourselves to be the enjoyers of the material world. False ego is thus the illusory combination within our minds of the self and the body, which are actually two separate objects. Since *karma,* or material work, is based on illusory consciousness, these activities are also illusory and have no factual basis in either the body or the soul. When a conditioned soul falsely considers himself to be the body, and consequently the enjoyer of the material world, he tries to find pleasure in illicit connection with women. Such sinful activity is based on his false concept of being the body and thus the enjoyer of women and of the world. Since he is not the body, his activity of enjoying a woman does not actually exist. There is merely the interaction of two machines, namely the two bodies, and the interaction of the illusory consciousness of the man and woman. The sensation of illicit sex occurs within the material body and is falsely assimilated by the false ego as its own experience. Thus the miserable or pleasurable reactions of *karma* ultimately act upon the false ego and not upon the body, which is composed of dull matter, nor upon the soul, which has nothing to do with matter. False ego is the illusory concoction of the mind; it is specifically this false ego that is suffering happiness and distress. The soul cannot become angry at others, since he is not personally enjoying or suffering. Rather, the false ego is doing this.

TEXT 55

कालस्तु हेतुः सुखदुःखयोश्चेत्
किमात्मनस्तत्र तदात्मकोऽसौ ।
नाग्नेर्हि तापो न हिमस्य तत् स्यात्
क्रुध्येत कस्मै न परस्य द्वन्द्वम् ॥५५॥

kālas tu hetuḥ sukha-duḥkhayoś cet
kim ātmanas tatra tad-ātmako 'sau
nāgner hi tāpo na himasya tat syāt
krudhyeta kasmai na parasya dvandvam

kālaḥ—time; *tu*—but; *hetuḥ*—the cause; *sukha-duḥkhayoḥ*—of happiness and distress; *cet*—if; *kim*—what; *ātmanaḥ*—for the soul; *tatra*—in that idea; *tat-ātmakaḥ*—based on time; *asau*—the soul; *na*—not; *agneḥ*—from fire; *hi*—indeed; *tāpaḥ*—burning; *na*—not; *himasya*—of snow; *tat*—that; *syāt*—becomes; *krudhyeta*—should become angry; *kasmai*—at whom; *na*—there is not; *parasya*—for the transcendental soul; *dvandvam*—duality.

TRANSLATION

If we accept time as the cause of happiness and distress, that experience still cannot apply to the spirit soul, since time is a manifestation of the Lord's spiritual potency and the living entities are also expansions of the Lord's spiritual potency manifesting through time. Certainly a fire does not burn its own flames or sparks, nor does the cold harm its own snowflakes or hail. In fact,

the spirit soul is transcendental and beyond the experience of material happiness and distress. At whom, therefore, should one become angry?

PURPORT

The material body is dull matter and does not experience happiness, distress or anything else. Because the spirit soul is completely transcendental, he should fix his consciousness on the transcendental Lord, who is beyond material happiness and distress. It is only when transcendental consciousness falsely identifies with dull matter that the living entity imagines he is enjoying and suffering in the material world. This illusory identification of consciousness with matter is called false ego and is the cause of material existence.

TEXT 56

न केनचित् क्वापि कथञ्चनास्य
द्वन्द्वोपरागः परतः परस्य ।
यथाहमः संसृतिरूपिणः स्या-
देवं प्रबुद्धो न बिभेति भूतैः ॥५६॥

na kenacit kvāpi kathañcanāsya
dvandvoparāgaḥ parataḥ parasya
yathāhamaḥ saṁsṛti-rūpiṇaḥ syād
evaṁ prabuddho na bibheti bhūtaiḥ

na—there is not; *kenacit*—by the agency of anyone; *kva api*—anywhere; *kathañcana*—by any means; *asya*—for him, the soul; *dvandva*—of the duality (of happiness and distress); *uparāgaḥ*—the influence; *parataḥ parasya*—who is transcendental to material nature; *yathā*—in the same way as; *ahamaḥ*—for the false ego; *saṁsṛti*—to material existence; *rūpiṇaḥ*—which give shape; *syāt*—arises; *evam*—thus; *prabuddhaḥ*—one whose intelligence is awakened; *na bibheti*—does not fear; *bhūtaiḥ*—on the basis of material creation.

TRANSLATION

The false ego gives shape to illusory material existence and thus experiences material happiness and distress. The spirit

soul, however, is transcendental to material nature; he can never actually be affected by material happiness and distress in any place, under any circumstance or by the agency of any person. A person who understands this has nothing whatsoever to fear from the material creation.

PURPORT

The *brāhmaṇa* has refuted six specific explanations of the happiness and distress of the living entity, and now he refutes any other explanation that might be given. On the basis of false ego, the bodily covering factually overwhelms the spirit soul, and thus one falsely enjoys and suffers that which has no real relationship with oneself. One who can understand this sublime teaching of the *brāhmaṇa*, spoken by the Lord to Uddhava, will never again suffer the terrible anxiety of fear within the material world.

TEXT 57

एतां स आस्थाय परात्मनिष्ठा-
मध्यासितां पूर्वतमैर्महर्षिभिः ।
अहं तरिष्यामि दुरन्तपारं
तमो मुकुन्दाङ्घ्रिनिषेवयैव ॥५७॥

etāṁ sa āsthāya parātma-niṣṭhām
adhyāsitāṁ pūrvatamair maharṣibhiḥ
ahaṁ tariṣyāmi duranta-pāraṁ
tamo mukundāṅghri-niṣevayaiva

etām—this; *saḥ*—such; *āsthāya*—becoming completely fixed in; *para-ātma-niṣṭhām*—devotion to the Supreme Person, Kṛṣṇa; *adhyāsitām*—worshiped; *pūrva-tamaiḥ*—by previous; *mahā-ṛṣibhiḥ*—*ācāryas; aham*—I; *tariṣyāmi*—shall cross over; *duranta-pāram*—the insurmountable; *tamaḥ*—the ocean of nescience; *mukunda-aṅghri*—of the lotus feet of Mukunda; *niṣevayā*—by worship; *eva*—certainly.

TRANSLATION

I shall cross over the insurmountable ocean of nescience by being firmly fixed in the service of the lotus feet of Kṛṣṇa. This

was approved by the previous *ācāryas*, who were fixed in firm devotion to the Lord, Paramātmā, the Supreme Personality of Godhead.

PURPORT

This verse is quoted by Kṛṣṇadāsa Kavirāja in his *Caitanya-caritāmṛta* (*Madhya-līlā* 3.6). Śrīla Prabhupāda comments as follows. "In connection with this verse, which is a quotation from *Śrīmad-Bhāgavatam* (11.23.57), Śrīla Bhaktisiddhānta Sarasvatī Ṭhākura says that of the sixty-four items required for rendering devotional service, acceptance of the symbolic marks of *sannyāsa* is a regulative principle. If one accepts the *sannyāsa* order, his main business is to devote his life completely to the service of Mukunda, Kṛṣṇa. If one does not completely devote his mind and body to the service of the Lord, he does not actually become a *sannyāsī*. It is not simply a matter of changing dress. In *Bhagavad-gītā* (6.1) it is also stated, *anāśritaḥ karma-phalaṁ kāryaṁ karma karoti yaḥ/ sa sannyāsī ca yogī ca:* one who works devotedly for the satisfaction of Kṛṣṇa is a *sannyāsī*. The dress is not *sannyāsa,* but the attitude of service to Kṛṣṇa is.

"The word *parātma-niṣṭhā* means being a devotee of Lord Kṛṣṇa. *Parātmā,* the Supreme Person, is Kṛṣṇa. *Īśvaraḥ paramaḥ kṛṣṇaḥ sac-cid-ānanda-vigrahaḥ.* Those who are completely dedicated to the lotus feet of Kṛṣṇa in service are actually *sannyāsīs.* As a matter of formality, the devotee accepts the *sannyāsa* dress as previous *ācāryas* did. He also accepts the three *daṇḍas.* Later Viṣṇusvāmī considered that accepting the dress of a *tri-daṇḍī* was *parātma-niṣṭhā.* Therefore sincere devotees add another *daṇḍa,* the *jīva-daṇḍa,* to the three existing *daṇḍas.* The Vaiṣṇava *sannyāsī* is known as a *tridaṇḍi-sannyāsī.* The Māyāvādī *sannyāsī* accepts only one *daṇḍa,* not understanding the purpose of *tri-daṇḍa.* Later, many persons in the community of Śiva Svāmī gave up the *ātma-niṣṭhā* (devotional service) of the Lord and followed the path of Śaṅkarācārya. Instead of accepting 108 names, those in the Śiva Svāmī *sampradāya* follow the path of Śaṅkarācārya and accept the ten names of *sannyāsa.* Although Śrī Caitanya Mahāprabhu accepted the then-existing order of *sannyāsa* (namely *eka-daṇḍa),* He still recited a verse from *Śrīmad-Bhāgavatam* about the *tridaṇḍa-sannyāsa* accepted by the *brāhmaṇa* of Avantīpura. Indirectly He declared that within that *ekadaṇḍa* (one *daṇḍa*), four *daṇḍas* existed as one. Accepting *ekadaṇḍa-sannyāsa* without *parātma-niṣṭhā* (devotional service to Lord Kṛṣṇa) is not acceptable to Śrī Caitanya Mahāprabhu. In addition, according to the exact regulative principles, one should add the *jīva-daṇḍa* to the *tri-daṇḍa*. These four *daṇḍas*, bound together as one, are symbolic of unalloyed devotional service to the Lord. Because the *ekadaṇḍi-sannyāsīs* of the Māyāvāda school are not devoted to the service of Kṛṣṇa, they try to merge into the Brahman effulgence, which is a marginal position between material and spiritual existence. They accept this impersonal position as liberation. Māyāvādī *sannyāsīs*, not knowing that Śrī Caitanya Mahāprabhu was a *tri-daṇḍī*, think of Caitanya Mahāprabhu as an *ekadaṇḍi-sannyāsī*. This is due to their *vivarta*, bewilderment. In *Śrīmad-Bhāgavatam* there is no such thing as an *ekadaṇḍi-sannyāsī;* indeed, the *tridaṇḍi-sannyāsī* is accepted as the symbolic representation of the *sannyāsa* order. By citing this verse from *Śrīmad-Bhāgavatam*, Śrī Caitanya Mahāprabhu accepted the *sannyāsa* order recommended in *Śrīmad-Bhāgavatam*. The Māyāvādī *sannyāsīs*, who are enamored of the external energy of the Lord, cannot understand the mind of Śrī Caitanya Mahāprabhu.

"To date, all the devotees of Śrī Caitanya Mahāprabhu, following in His footsteps, accept the *sannyāsa* order and keep the sacred thread and tuft of unshaved hair. The *ekadaṇḍi-sannyāsīs* of the Māyāvādī school give up the sacred thread and do not keep any tuft of hair. Therefore they are unable to understand the purport of *tridaṇḍa-sannyāsa*, and as such they are not inclined to dedicate their lives to the service of Mukunda. They simply think of merging into the existence of Brahman because of their disgust with the material existence. The *ācāryas* who advocate the *daiva-varṇāśrama* (the social order of *cātur-varṇyam* mentioned in *Bhagavad-gītā*) do not accept the proposition of *āsura-varṇāśrama*, which maintains that the social order of *varṇa* is indicated by birth.

"The most intimate devotee of Śrī Caitanya Mahāprabhu, namely Gadādhara Paṇḍita, accepted the *tridaṇḍa-sannyāsa* and also accepted Mādhava Upādhyāya as his *tridaṇḍi-sannyāsī* disciple. It is said that from this Mādhavācārya the *sampradāya* known in western India as the

Vallabhācārya-sampradāya has begun. Śrīla Gopāla Bhaṭṭa Vasu, who is known as a *smṛty-ācārya* in the Gauḍīya Vaiṣṇava-sampradāya, later accepted the *tridaṇḍa-sannyāsa* order from Tridaṇḍipāda Prabodhānanda Sarasvatī. Although acceptance of *tridaṇḍa-sannyāsa* is not distinctly mentioned in the Gauḍīya Vaiṣṇava literature, the first verse of Śrīla Rūpa Gosvāmī's *Upadeśāmṛta* advocates that one should accept the *tridaṇḍa-sannyāsa* order by controlling the six forces:

vāco vegaṁ manasaḥ krodha-vegaṁ
jihvā-vegam udaropastha-vegam
etān vegān yo viṣaheta dhīraḥ
sarvām apīmāṁ pṛthivīṁ sa śiṣyāt

'One who can control the forces of speech, mind, anger, belly, tongue and genitals is known as a *gosvāmī* and is competent to accept disciples all over the world.' The followers of Śrī Caitanya Mahāprabhu never accepted the Māyāvāda order of *sannyāsa*, and for this they cannot be blamed. Śrī Caitanya Mahāprabhu accepted Śrīdhara Svāmī, who was a *tridaṇḍi-sannyāsī*, but the Māyāvādī *sannyāsīs*, not understanding Śrīdhara Svāmī, sometimes think that Śrīdhara Svāmī belonged to the Māyāvāda *ekadaṇḍa-sannyāsa* community. Actually this was not the case."

TEXT 58

श्रीभगवानुवाच
निर्विद्य नष्टद्रविणे गतक्लमः
प्रव्रज्य गां पर्यटमान इत्थम् ।
निराकृतोऽसद्भिरपि स्वधर्मा-
दकम्पितोऽमुं मुनिराह गाथाम् ॥५८॥

śrī-bhagavān uvāca
nirvidya naṣṭa-draviṇe gata-klamaḥ
pravrajya gāṁ paryaṭamāna ittham
nirākṛto 'sadbhir api sva-dharmād
akampito 'mūṁ munir āha gāthām

śrī-bhagavān uvāca—the Supreme Personality of Godhead said; *nirvidya*—becoming detached; *naṣṭa-draviṇe*—his wealth having been destroyed; *gata-klamaḥ*—free from moroseness; *pravrajya*—leaving home; *gām*—the earth; *paryaṭamānaḥ*—traveling; *ittham*—in this way; *nirākṛtaḥ*—insulted; *asadbhiḥ*—by rascals; *api*—even though; *sva-dharmāt*—from his prescribed duties; *akampitaḥ*—unswerved; *amūm*—this; *muniḥ*—the sage; *āha*—spoke; *gāthām*—song.

TRANSLATION

Lord Śrī Kṛṣṇa said: Thus becoming detached upon the loss of his property, this sage gave up his moroseness. He left home, taking *sannyāsa*, and began to travel about the earth. Even when insulted by foolish rascals he remained unswerved from his duty and chanted this song.

PURPORT

Those becoming free from the materialistic way of life, which involves grueling austerities performed to acquire money, may chant the preceding song of the Vaiṣṇava *sannyāsī*. Śrīla Bhaktisiddhānta Sarasvatī Ṭhākura states that if one is not capable of listening to the song of this *sannyāsī*, then one will certainly remain an obedient servant of material illusion.

TEXT 59

सुखदुःखप्रदो नान्यः पुरुषस्यात्मविभ्रमः ।
मित्रोदासीनरिपवः संसारस्तमसः कृतः ॥५९॥

sukha-duḥkha-prado nānyaḥ
puruṣasyātma-vibhramaḥ
mitrodāsīna-ripavaḥ
saṁsāras tamasaḥ kṛtaḥ

sukha-duḥkha-pradaḥ—giver of happiness and distress; *na*—there is no; *anyaḥ*—other; *puruṣasya*—of the soul; *ātma*—of the mind; *vibhramaḥ*—bewilderment; *mitra*—friends; *udāsīna*—indifferent parties; *ripavaḥ*—and enemies; *saṁsāraḥ*—material life; *tamasaḥ*—out of ignorance; *kṛtaḥ*—created.

TRANSLATION

No other force besides his own mental confusion makes the soul experience happiness and distress. His perception of friends, neutral parties and enemies and the whole material life he builds around this perception are simply created out of ignorance.

PURPORT

Everyone is working hard to please their friends, defeat their enemies and maintain the status quo with neutral parties. These relations are certainly based on the material body and do not exist beyond the body's inevitable demise. They are called ignorance, or material illusion.

TEXT 60

तस्मात् सर्वात्मना तात निगृहाण मनो धिया ।
मय्यावेशितया युक्त एतावान् योगसंग्रहः ॥६०॥

tasmāt sarvātmanā tāta
nigṛhāṇa mano dhiyā
mayy āveśitayā yukta
etāvān yoga-saṅgrahaḥ

tasmāt—therefore; *sarva-ātmanā*—in all respects; *tāta*—My dear Uddhava; *nigṛhāṇa*—bring under control; *manaḥ*—the mind; *dhiyā*—with intelligence; *mayi*—in Me; *āveśitayā*—which is absorbed; *yuktaḥ*—linked up; *etāvān*—thus; *yoga-saṅgrahaḥ*—the essence of spiritual practice.

TRANSLATION

My dear Uddhava, fixing your intelligence in Me, you should thus completely control the mind. This is the essence of the science of *yoga*.

TEXT 61

य एतां भिक्षुणा गीतां ब्रह्मनिष्ठां समाहितः ।
धारयञ्छ्रावयञ्छृण्वन् द्वन्द्वैर्नैवाभिभूयते ॥६१॥

ya etāṁ bhikṣuṇā gītāṁ
brahma-niṣṭhāṁ samāhitaḥ
dhārayañ chrāvayañ chṛṇvan
dvandvair naivābhibhūyate

yaḥ—whoever; *etām*—this; *bhikṣuṇā*—by the *sannyāsī; gītām*—sung; *brahma*—knowledge of the Absolute; *niṣṭhām*—based upon; *samāhitaḥ*—with full attention; *dhārayan*—meditating; *śrāvayan*—causing others to hear; *śṛṇvan*—himself hearing; *dvandvaiḥ*—by dualities; *na*—never; *eva*—indeed; *abhibhūyate*—will become overwhelmed.

TRANSLATION

Anyone who listens to or recites to others this song of the *sannyāsī*, which presents scientific knowledge of the Absolute, and who thus meditates upon it with full attention, will never again be overwhelmed by the dualities of material happiness and distress.

PURPORT

The Vaiṣṇava *sannyāsī* took shelter of the devotional service of the Lord and thus could overcome the illusory potency of his worshipable object, the Supreme Personality of Godhead. He himself meditated upon and heard this song, and also taught it to others. Having received the Lord's mercy, he enlightened other conditioned souls with transcendental intelligence so that they could also follow in the footsteps of the devotees of the Lord. Religion actually means to become a pure devotee of the Supreme Lord in loving service. Those who are trying to enjoy the material world or merely renounce it to avoid personal inconvenience cannot actually understand love of Godhead, in which the only objective is the satisfaction of the Lord.

Thus end the purports of the humble servant of His Divine Grace A. C. Bhaktivedanta Swami Prabhupāda to the Eleventh Canto, Twenty-third Chapter, of the Śrīmad-Bhāgavatam, *entitled "The Song of the Avantī* Brāhmaṇa."

CHAPTER TWENTY-FOUR

The Philosophy of Sāṅkhya

In this chapter Lord Kṛṣṇa gives instruction how bewilderment of the mind can be dispelled by the science of Sāṅkhya. Herein the Supreme Lord again imparts to Uddhava instruction about the analysis of material nature. By assimilating this knowledge the spirit soul can drive away his confusion based on false dualities.

In the beginning of creation, the seer and seen are one and indistinguishable. This Supreme Absolute Truth, one without a second and inaccessible to words and mind, then separates into two—the seer, which means consciousness or personality, and the seen, which means substance or nature. The material nature, which comprises the three modes of matter, is agitated by the controlling male factor. The *mahat-tattva* then becomes manifest together with the energies of consciousness and activity. From these come the principle of false ego in its three aspects of goodness, passion and ignorance. From false ego in the mode of ignorance arise fifteen subtle forms of sense perception, followed by the fifteen physical elements. From false ego in the mode of passion come the ten senses, and from false ego in the mode of goodness come the mind and the eleven demigods who preside over the senses. By the conglomeration of all of these elements grows the universal egg, in the midst of which the Supreme Personality of Godhead as the creating Lord of the universe takes up residence in the role of indwelling Supersoul. From the navel of this ultimate creator comes a lotus, upon which Brahmā takes birth. Lord Brahmā, invested with the mode of passion, executes austerities by the grace of the Supreme Personality of Godhead, and on the strength of these penances he is able to create all the planets of the universe. The region of heaven is meant for the demigods, that of inner space for ghostly spirits and that of the earth for human beings and others. In the region above these three planetary systems are the places of advanced sages, and in the lower worlds are those of the demons, Nāga serpents and so forth. The goals achieved by activities based on the three modes of material nature are all within the three mortal worlds. The destinations of *yoga,* severe austerity and the renounced order of life are the worlds known as Mahar, Janas, Tapas and Satya. The goal of devotional service to the Supreme Lord, on the other hand, is the lotus feet of the Personality of Godhead in His abode, Vaikuṇṭha. This universe of material action and reaction is constituted under the control of time and the three modes of material nature. Moreover, whatever exists in this universe is simply the product of the combination of material nature and her Lord. In the same way that creation proceeds gradually from the one and supremely subtle to the multitudinous and very gross, the process of annihilation proceeds from the grossest to the subtlest manifestation of nature, leaving only the eternal spiritual substance. This ultimate Soul remains situated within Himself, alone and without end. The mind of a person who meditates on these ideas does not become bewildered by material dualities. This science of Sāṅkhya, narrated in alternating sequences of creation and annihilation, serves to cut off all doubts and bondage.

TEXT 1

श्रीभगवानुवाच
अथ ते संप्रवक्ष्यामि सांख्यं पूर्वैर्विनिश्चितम् ।
यद् विज्ञाय पुमान् सद्यो जह्याद् वैकल्पिकं भ्रमम् ॥ १ ॥

śrī-bhagavān uvāca
atha te sampravakṣyāmi
sāṅkhyaṁ pūrvair viniścitam
yad vijñāya pumān sadyo
jahyād vaikalpikaṁ bhramam

śrī-bhagavān uvāca—the Supreme Personality of Godhead said; *atha*—now; *te*—unto you; *sampravakṣyāmi*—I shall speak; *sāṅkhyam*—the knowledge of the evolution of the elements of creation; *pūrvaiḥ*—by previous authorities; *viniścitam*—ascertained; *yat*—which; *vijñāya*—knowing; *pumān*—a person; *sadyaḥ*—immediately; *jahyāt*—can give up; *vaikalpikam*—based on false duality; *bhramam*—the illusion.

TRANSLATION

Lord Śrī Kṛṣṇa said: Now I shall describe to you the science of Sāṅkhya, which has been perfectly established by ancient authorities. By understanding this science a person can immediately give up the illusion of material duality.

PURPORT

In the previous chapter the Lord explained that one can give up material duality by controlling the mind and fixing it in Kṛṣṇa consciousness. This chapter describes the Sāṅkhya system, in which the difference between matter and spirit is elaborately explained. By hearing this knowledge one can easily separate the mind from material contamination and fix it on the spiritual platform in Kṛṣṇa consciousness. The Sāṅkhya philosophy system mentioned here is that presented by Lord Kapila in the Third Canto of *Śrīmad-Bhāgavatam* and not the atheistic Sāṅkhya presented later by materialists and Māyāvādīs. The material elements, which emanate from the potency of the Lord, evolve in a progressive sequence. One should not foolishly think that such evolution begins from an original material element without the assistance of the Lord. This speculative theory is generated from the false ego of conditioned life and constitutes gross ignorance, unacceptable to the Personality of Godhead and His followers.

TEXT 2

आसीज्ज्ञानमथो अर्थ एकमेवाविकल्पितम् ।
यदा विवेकनिपुणा आदौ कृतयुगेऽयुगे ॥ २ ॥

āsīj jñānam atho artha
ekam evāvikalpitam
yadā viveka-nipuṇā
ādau kṛta-yuge 'yuge

āsīt—there existed; *jñānam*—the seer; *atha u*—thus; *arthaḥ*—the seen; *ekam*—one; *eva*—simply; *avikalpitam*—undifferentiated; *yadā*—

when; *viveka*—in discrimination; *nipuṇāḥ*—persons who were expert; *ādau*—in the beginning; *kṛta-yuge*—in the age of purity; *ayuge*—and before that, during the time of annihilation.

TRANSLATION

Originally, during the Kṛta-yuga, when all men were very expert in spiritual discrimination, and also previous to that, during the period of annihilation, the seer existed alone, non-different from the seen object.

PURPORT

Kṛta-yuga is the first age, also known as Satya-yuga, in which knowledge, being perfect, is not different from its object. In modern society, knowledge is highly speculative and constantly changing. There is often a vast difference between people's theoretical ideas and actual reality. In Satya-yuga, however, people are *viveka-nipuṇāḥ,* or expert in intelligent discrimination, and thus there is no difference between their vision and reality. In Satya-yuga, the population in general is self-realized. Seeing everything as the potency of the Supreme Lord, they do not artificially create duality between themselves and other living entities. This is a further aspect of the oneness of Satya-yuga. At the time of annihilation, everything merges to rest within the Lord, and at that time also there is no difference between the Lord, who becomes the only seer, and the objects of knowledge, which are contained within the Lord. The liberated living entities in the eternal spiritual world are never subject to such merging but remain forever undisturbed in their spiritual forms. Because they are voluntarily one with the Lord in love, their abode is never annihilated.

TEXT 3

तन्मायाफलरूपेण केवलं निर्विकल्पितम् ।
वाङ्मनोऽगोचरं सत्यं द्विधा समभवद् बृहत् ।। ३ ।।

tan māyā-phala-rūpeṇa
kevalaṁ nirvikalpitam
vāṅ-mano-'gocaraṁ satyaṁ
dvidhā samabhavad bṛhat

tat—that (Supreme); *māyā*—of the material nature; *phala*—and the enjoyer of its manifestations; *rūpeṇa*—in the two forms; *kevalam*—one; *nirvikalpitam*—nondifferentiated; *vāk*—to speech; *manaḥ*—and the mind; *agocaram*—inaccessible; *satyam*—true; *dvidhā*—twofold; *samabhavat*—He became; *bṛhat*—the Absolute Truth.

TRANSLATION

That one Absolute Truth, remaining free from material dualities and inaccessible to ordinary speech and mind, divided Himself into two categories—the material nature and the living entities who are trying to enjoy the manifestations of that nature.

PURPORT

Both material nature and the living entity are potencies of the Supreme Personality of Godhead.

TEXT 4

तयोरेकतरो ह्यर्थः प्रकृतिः सोभयात्मिका ।
ज्ञानं त्वन्यतमो भावः पुरुषः सोऽभिधीयते ॥ ४ ॥

tayor ekataro hy arthaḥ
prakṛtiḥ sobhayātmikā
jñānaṁ tv anyatamo bhāvaḥ
puruṣaḥ so 'bhidhīyate

tayoḥ—of the two; *ekataraḥ*—one; *hi*—indeed; *arthaḥ*—entity; *prakṛtiḥ*—nature; *sā*—she; *ubhaya-ātmikā*—consisting of both the subtle causes and their manifest products; *jñānam*—(who possesses) consciousness; *tu*—and; *anyatamaḥ*—the other; *bhāvaḥ*—entity; *puruṣaḥ*—the living soul; *saḥ*—he; *abhidhīyate*—is called.

TRANSLATION

Of these two categories of manifestation, one is material nature, which embodies both the subtle causes and manifests products of matter. The other is the conscious living entity, designated as the enjoyer.

PURPORT

According to Śrīla Jīva Gosvāmī, *prakṛti* here refers to the subtle *pradhāna*, which later becomes manifest as *mahat-tattva*.

TEXT 5

तमो रजः सत्त्वमिति प्रकृतेरभवन् गुणाः ।
मया प्रक्षोभ्यमाणायाः पुरुषानुमतेन च ॥ ५ ॥

tamo rajaḥ sattvam iti
prakṛter abhavan guṇāḥ
mayā prakṣobhyamāṇāyāḥ
puruṣānumatena ca

tamaḥ—ignorance; *rajaḥ*—passion; *sattvam*—goodness; *iti*—thus; *prakṛteḥ*—from nature; *abhavan*—became manifest; *guṇāḥ*—the modes; *mayā*—by Me; *prakṣobhyamāṇāyāḥ*—who was being agitated; *puruṣa*—of the living entity; *anumatena*—in order to fulfill the desires; *ca*—and.

TRANSLATION

When material nature was agitated by My glance, the three material modes of goodness, passion and ignorance became manifest to fulfill the pending desires of the conditioned souls.

PURPORT

The Lord casts His glance over material nature to remind her that the conditioned souls have not worked out their chain of fruitive activity and mental speculation and that creation is therefore again necessary. The Lord desires that the conditioned souls get the opportunity to become Kṛṣṇa conscious in love of Godhead by understanding the futility of life without the Lord. The modes of nature arise after the glance of the Lord and become inimical to one another, each mode attempting to conquer the other two. There is constant competition between birth, maintenance and annihilation. Although a child desires to take birth, the cruel mother may desire to kill the child through abortion. Although we may desire to kill the weeds in a field, they stubbornly take birth again and again. Similarly, we often desire to maintain our physical status quo, but still deterioration sets in. Thus there is constant competition among the modes of nature, and by their combinations and permutations the living entities try to enjoy innumerable material situations without Kṛṣṇa consciousness. The word *puruṣānumatena* indicates that the Lord sets the stage for such material futility so that the conditioned souls will eventually come back home, back to Godhead.

TEXT 6

तेभ्यः समभवत् सूत्रं महान् सूत्रेण संयुतः ।
ततो विकुर्वतो जातो यो ऽहङ्कारो विमोहनः ॥ ६ ॥

tebhyaḥ samabhavat sūtraṁ
mahān sūtreṇa saṁyutaḥ
tato vikurvato jāto
yo 'haṅkāro vimohanaḥ

tebhyaḥ—from those modes; *samabhavat*—arose; *sūtram*—the first transformation of nature, endowed with the potency of activity; *mahān*—primeval nature endowed with the potency of knowledge; *sūtreṇa*—with this *sūtra-tattva; saṁyutaḥ*—conjoined; *tataḥ*—from the *mahat; vikurvataḥ*—transforming; *jātaḥ*—was generated; *yaḥ*—which; *ahaṅkāraḥ*—false ego; *vimohanaḥ*—the cause of bewilderment.

TRANSLATION

From these modes arose the primeval *sūtra*, along with the *mahat-tattva*. By the transformation of the *mahat-tattva* was generated the false ego, the cause of the living entities' bewilderment.

PURPORT

According to Śrīla Śrīdhara Svāmī, *sūtra* is the first transformation of material nature that manifests the potency of activity, and it is accompanied by the *mahat-tattva*, which is endowed with the potency of knowledge. In the material world, one's real knowledge is covered by fruitive activity and mental speculation. As one's devotional service to the Lord slackens, these two tendencies grow automatically, just as the diminishing of light automatically brings an increase in darkness.

TEXT 7

वैकारिकस्तैजसश्च तामसश्चेत्यहं त्रिवृत् ।
तन्मात्रेन्द्रियमनसां कारणं चिदचिन्मयः ॥ ७ ॥

vaikārikas taijasaś ca
tāmasaś cety ahaṁ tri-vṛt
tan-mātrendriya-manasāṁ
kāraṇaṁ cid-acin-mayaḥ

vaikārikaḥ—in the mode of goodness; *taijasaḥ*—in the mode of passion; *ca*—and; *tāmasaḥ*—in the mode of ignorance; *ca*—also; *iti*—thus; *aham*—false ego; *tri-vṛt*—in three categories; *tat-mātra*—of the subtle forms of sense objects; *indriya*—of the senses; *manasām*—and of the mind; *kāraṇam*—the cause; *cit-acit*—both spirit and matter; *mayaḥ*—encompassing.

TRANSLATION

False ego, which is the cause of physical sensation, the senses and the mind, encompasses both spirit and matter and manifests in three varieties: in the modes of goodness, passion and ignorance.

PURPORT

The word *cid-acin-maya,* "encompassing both spirit and matter," is significant in this regard. The false ego is the illusory combination of the eternal conscious soul and the temporary unconscious body. Because the spirit soul desires to exploit illicitly the creation of God, he is bewildered by the three modes of nature and assumes an illusory identity within the material world. Struggling to enjoy, he becomes more and more entangled in the complexities of illusion and only increases his anxiety. This hopeless situation can be overcome by taking to pure Kṛṣṇa consciousness, in which the pleasure of the Supreme Lord becomes the only goal of one's life.

TEXT 8

अर्थस्तन्मात्रिकाज्जज्ञे तामसादिन्द्रियाणि च ।
तैजसाद् देवता आसन्नेकादश च वैकृतात् ॥ ८ ॥

arthas tan-mātrikāj jajñe
tāmasād indriyāṇi ca
taijasād devatā āsann
ekādaśa ca vaikṛtāt

arthaḥ—the gross elements; *tat-mātrikāt*—from the subtle sensations (which themselves are derived from false ego in the mode of goodness); *jajñe*—became generated; *tāmasāt*—from false ego in the mode of ignorance; *indriyāṇi*—the senses; *ca*—and; *taijasāt*—from false ego in the mode of passion; *devatāḥ*—the demigods; *āsan*—arose; *ekādaśa*—eleven; *ca*—and; *vaikṛtāt*—from false ego in the mode of goodness.

TRANSLATION

From false ego in the mode of ignorance, the subtle physical perceptions and thus the gross elements were generated. From false ego in the mode of passion came the senses, and from false ego in the mode of goodness arose the eleven demigods.

PURPORT

From false ego in the mode of ignorance, sound is generated along with the sense of hearing to receive it and the sky as its medium. Next, the sensation of touch, air and the sense of touch are generated, and thus from subtle to gross all of the elements and their perceptions are generated. The senses, because they are busily engaged in activity, are created from false ego in the mode of passion. From false ego in goodness come eleven demigods: the deities of the directions, the wind and the sun, Varuṇa, the Aśvinī deities, Agni, Indra, Upendra, Mitra, Brahmā and Candra.

TEXT 9

मया सञ्चोदिता भावाः सर्वे संहत्यकारिणः ।
अण्डमुत्पादयामासुर्ममायतनमुत्तमम् ॥ ९ ॥

mayā sañcoditā bhāvāḥ
sarve saṁhatya-kāriṇaḥ
aṇḍam utpādayām āsur
mamāyatanam uttamam

mayā—by Me; *sañcoditāḥ*—impelled; *bhāvāḥ*—elements; *sarve*—all; *saṁhatya*—by amalgamation; *kāriṇaḥ*—functioning; *aṇḍam*—the egg of the universe; *utpādayām āsuḥ*—they brought into being; *mama*—My; *āyatanam*—residence; *uttamam*—superior.

TRANSLATION

Impelled by Me, all these elements combined to function in an orderly fashion and together gave birth to the universal egg, which is My excellent place of residence.

TEXT 10

तस्मिन्नहं समभवमण्डे सलिलसंस्थितौ ।
मम नाभ्यामभूत् पद्मं विश्वाख्यं तत्र चात्मभूः ॥१०॥

tasminn ahaṁ samabhavam
aṇḍe salila-saṁsthitau
mama nābhyām abhūt padmaṁ
viśvākhyaṁ tatra cātma-bhūḥ

tasmin—within that; *aham*—I; *samabhavam*—appeared; *aṇḍe*—in the egg of the universe; *salila*—in the water of the Causal Ocean; *saṁsthitau*—which was situated; *mama*—My; *nābhyām*—from the navel; *abhūt*—arose; *padmam*—a lotus; *viśva-ākhyam*—known as universal; *tatra*—in that; *ca*—and; *ātma-bhūḥ*—self-born Brahmā.

TRANSLATION

I Myself appeared within that egg, which was floating on the causal water, and from My navel arose the universal lotus, the birthplace of self-born Brahmā.

PURPORT

The Supreme Lord here describes His appearance in His transcendental pastime form of Śrī Nārāyaṇa. Lord Nārāyaṇa enters within the universe but does not give up His purely transcendental body of knowledge and bliss. Lord Brahmā, however, born from the Lord's navel lotus, has a material body. Although Lord Brahmā is the most powerful mystic, his body, which pervades all material existence, is material, whereas the body of the Supreme Lord Hari, Nārāyaṇa, is always transcendental.

TEXT 11

सोऽसृजत्तपसा युक्तो रजसा मदनुग्रहात् ।
लोकान् सपालान् विश्वात्मा भूर्भुवः स्वरिति त्रिधा ॥११॥

so 'sṛjat tapasā yukto
rajasā mad-anugrahāt
lokān sa-pālān viśvātmā
bhūr bhuvaḥ svar iti tridhā

saḥ—he, Brahmā; *asṛjat*—created; *tapasā*—by his austerity; *yuktaḥ*—endowed; *rajasā*—with the potency of the mode of passion; *mat*—My; *anugrahāt*—because of the mercy; *lokān*—the different planets; *sa-pālān*—along with their presiding demigods; *viśva*—of the universe; *ātmā*—the soul; *bhūḥ bhuvaḥ svaḥ iti*—called Bhūr, Bhuvar and Svar; *tridhā*—three divisions.

TRANSLATION

Lord Brahmā, the soul of the universe, being endowed with the mode of passion, performed great austerities by My mercy and thus created the three planetary divisions called Bhūr, Bhuvar and Svar, along with their presiding deities.

TEXT 12

देवानामोक आसीत् स्वर्भूतानां च भुवः पदम् ।
मर्त्यादीनां च भूर्लोकः सिद्धानां त्रितयात् परम् ॥१२॥

devānām oka āsīt svar
bhūtānāṁ ca bhuvaḥ padam
martyādīnāṁ ca bhūr lokaḥ
siddhānāṁ tritayāt param

devānām—of the demigods; *okaḥ*—the home; *āsīt*—became; *svaḥ*—heaven; *bhūtānām*—of ghostly spirits; *ca*—and; *bhuvaḥ*—Bhuvar; *padam*—the place; *martya-ādīnām*—of ordinary mortal humans and other beings; *ca*—and; *bhūḥ lokaḥ*—the planet called Bhūr; *siddhānām*—(the place) of those striving for liberation; *tritayāt*—these three divisions; *param*—beyond.

TRANSLATION

Heaven was established as the residence of the demigods, Bhuvarloka as that of the ghostly spirits, and the earth system as the place of human beings and other mortal creatures. Those mystics who strive for liberation are promoted beyond these three divisions.

PURPORT

Planets such as Indraloka and Candraloka are meant for the heavenly enjoyment of the most pious fruitive workers. The highest four planets, however, Satyaloka, Maharloka, Janoloka and Tapoloka, are meant for those who are most perfectly endeavoring for liberation. Caitanya Mahāprabhu is so inconceivably merciful that He is promoting the most fallen victims of Kali-yuga beyond these four planets and even beyond Vaikuṇṭha, to the supreme planet of Lord Kṛṣṇa in the spiritual sky, called Goloka Vṛndāvana. Śrīla Bhaktisiddhānta Sarasvatī Ṭhākura explains that heaven is the residence of the demigods, the earth is the residence of the human beings, and in between is a temporary residence for both classes of beings.

TEXT 13

अधोऽसुराणां नागानां भूमेरोकोऽसृजत् प्रभुः ।
त्रिलोक्यां गतयः सर्वाः कर्मणां त्रिगुणात्मनाम् ॥१३॥

adho 'surāṇāṁ nāgānāṁ
bhūmer oko 'sṛjat prabhuḥ

tri-lokyāṁ gatayaḥ sarvāḥ
karmaṇāṁ tri-guṇātmanām

adhaḥ—below; *asurāṇām*—of the demons; *nāgānām*—of the celestial snakes; *bhūmeḥ*—from the earth; *okaḥ*—the residence; *asṛjat*—created; *prabhuḥ*—Lord Brahmā; *tri-lokyām*—of the three worlds; *gatayaḥ*—the destinations; *sarvāḥ*—all; *karmaṇām*—of fruitive activities; *tri-guṇa-ātmanām*—partaking of the three modes.

TRANSLATION

Lord Brahmā created the region below the earth for the demons and the Nāga snakes. In this way the destinations of the three worlds were arranged as the corresponding reactions for different kinds of work performed within the three modes of nature.

TEXT 14

योगस्य तपसश्चैव न्यासस्य गतयोऽमलाः ।
महर्जनस्तपः सत्यं भक्तियोगस्य मद्गतिः ॥१४॥

yogasya tapasaś caiva
nyāsasya gatayo 'malāḥ
mahar janas tapaḥ satyaṁ
bhakti-yogasya mad-gatiḥ

yogasya—of mystic *yoga; tapasaḥ*—of great austerity; *ca*—and; *eva*—certainly; *nyāsasya*—of the renounced order of life; *gatayaḥ*—the destinations; *amalāḥ*—spotless; *mahaḥ*—Mahar; *janaḥ*—Janas; *tapaḥ*—Tapas; *satyam*—Satya; *bhakti-yogasya*—of devotional service; *mat*—My; *gatiḥ*—destination.

TRANSLATION

By mystic *yoga*, great austerities and the renounced order of life, the pure destinations of Maharloka, Janoloka, Tapoloka and Satyaloka are attained. But by devotional *yoga*, one achieves My transcendental abode.

PURPORT

Śrīla Jīva Gosvāmī explains that the word *tapasaḥ* in this verse refers to austerities performed by *brahmacārīs* and *vānaprasthas.* A *brahmacārī* who practices celibacy perfectly in some particular stage of his life achieves Maharloka, and one who perfectly practices lifelong celibacy achieves Janoloka. By perfect execution of *vānaprastha* one may achieve Tapoloka, and one in the renounced order of life goes to Satyaloka. These different destinations certainly depend on one's seriousness in the *yoga* system. In the Third Canto of the *Bhāgavatam,* Lord Brahmā explains to the demigods, "The inhabitants of Vaikuṇṭha travel in their airplanes made of lapis lazuli, emeralds and gold. Although crowded by their consorts, who have large hips and beautiful smiling faces, they cannot be stimulated to passion by their mirth and beautiful charms." (*Bhāg.* 3.15.20) Thus in the spiritual world, the kingdom of God, the inhabitants have absolutely no desire for personal satisfaction, since they are completely satisfied in love of Godhead. Because they only think of the Lord's pleasure, there is no possibility of cheating, anxiety, lust, disappointment, and so on. As described in *Bhagavad-gītā* (18.62),

tam eva śaraṇaṁ gaccha
sarva-bhāvena bhārata
tat-prasādāt parāṁ śāntiṁ
sthānaṁ prāpsyasi śāśvatam

"O scion of Bharata, surrender unto Him utterly. By His grace you will attain transcendental peace and the supreme and eternal abode."

TEXT 15

मया कालात्मना धात्रा कर्मयुक्तमिदं जगत् ।
गुणप्रवाह एतस्मिन्नुन्मज्जति निमज्जति ॥१५॥

mayā kālātmanā dhātrā
karma-yuktam idaṁ jagat
guṇa-pravāha etasminn
unmajjati nimajjati

mayā—by Me; *kāla-ātmanā*—who contains the energy of time; *dhātrā*—the creator; *karma-yuktam*—full of fruitive activities; *idam*—this; *jagat*—world; *guṇa-pravāhe*—in the mighty current of the modes; *etasmin*—in this; *unmajjati*—one rises up; *nimajjati*—one drowns.

TRANSLATION

All results of fruitive work have been arranged within this world by Me, the supreme creator acting as the force of time. Thus one sometimes rises up toward the surface of this mighty river of the modes of nature and sometimes again submerges.

PURPORT

Unmajjati refers to one's promotion to the higher planetary systems, as mentioned in previous verses, and *nimajjati* refers to being submerged in a miserable condition of life by impious activities. In both cases one is drowning within the mighty river of material existence, which carries one far away from one's real home in the kingdom of God.

TEXT 16

अणुर्बृहत् कृशः स्थूलो यो यो भावः प्रसिध्यति ।
सर्वोऽप्युभयसंयुक्तः प्रकृत्या पुरुषेण च ॥१६॥

aṇur bṛhat kṛśaḥ sthūlo
yo yo bhāvaḥ prasidhyati
sarvo 'py ubhaya-saṁyuktaḥ
prakṛtyā puruṣeṇa ca

aṇuḥ—small; *bṛhat*—great; *kṛśaḥ*—thin; *sthūlaḥ*—stout; *yaḥ yaḥ*—whatever; *bhāvaḥ*—manifestation; *prasidhyati*—is established; *sarvaḥ*—all; *api*—indeed; *ubhaya*—by both; *saṁyuktaḥ*—conjoined; *prakṛtyā*—by nature; *puruṣeṇa*—by the enjoying spirit soul; *ca*—and.

TRANSLATION

Whatever features visibly exist within this world—small or great, thin or stout—certainly contain both the material nature and its enjoyer, the spirit soul.

TEXT 17

यस्तु यस्यादिरन्तश्च स वै मध्यं च तस्य सन् ।
विकारो व्यवहारार्थो यथा तैजसपार्थिवाः ॥१७॥

yas tu yasyādir antaś ca
sa vai madhyaṁ ca tasya san
vikāro vyavahārārtho
yathā taijasa-pārthivāḥ

yaḥ—which (cause); *tu*—and; *yasya*—of which (product); *ādiḥ*—the beginning; *antaḥ*—the end; *ca*—and; *saḥ*—that; *vai*—indeed; *madhyam*—the middle; *ca*—and; *tasya*—of that product; *san*—being (real); *vikāraḥ*—the transformation; *vyavahāra-arthaḥ*—for ordinary purposes; *yathā*—as; *taijasa*—things produced from gold (which is itself derived from fire); *pārthivāḥ*—and things produced from earth.

TRANSLATION

Gold and earth are originally existing as ingredients. From gold one may fashion golden ornaments such as bracelets and earrings, and from earth one may fashion clay pots and saucers. The original ingredients gold and earth exist before the products made from them, and when the products are eventually destroyed, the original ingredients, gold and earth, will remain. Thus, since the ingredients are present in the beginning and at the end, they must also be present in the middle phase, taking the form of a particular product to which we assign for convenience a particular name, such as bracelet, earring, pot or saucer. We can therefore understand that since the ingredient cause exists before the creation of a product and after the product's destruction, the same ingredient cause must be present during the manifest phase, supporting the product as the basis of its reality.

PURPORT

The Lord here explains that the original cause is certainly present in its effect, citing the example of gold and clay functioning as the causal ingredients of many different products in which gold and clay continue to be present. For our convenience, we assign different names to temporary products, although their essential nature continues to be that of the ingredient, and not of the temporary product.

TEXT 18

यदुपादाय पूर्वस्तु भावो विकुरुतेऽपरम् ।
आदिरन्तो यदा यस्य तत् सत्यमभिधीयते ॥१८॥

yad upādāya pūrvas tu
bhāvo vikurute 'param
ādir anto yadā yasya
tat satyam abhidhīyate

yat—which (form); *upādāya*—accepting as the ingredient cause; *pūrvaḥ*—the previous cause (such as the *mahat-tattva*); *tu*—and; *bhāvaḥ*—thing; *vikurute*—produces as transformation; *aparam*—the second thing (such as the element *ahaṅkāra*); *ādiḥ*—the beginning; *antaḥ*—the end; *yadā*—when; *yasya*—of which (product); *tat*—that (cause); *satyam*—real; *abhidhīyate*—is called.

TRANSLATION

A material object, itself composed of an essential ingredient, creates another material object through transformation. Thus one created object becomes the cause and basis of another created object. A particular thing may thus be called real in that it possesses the basic nature of another object that constitutes its origin and final state.

PURPORT

One may understand the purport of this verse through the simple analogy of a clay pot. A clay pot is formed from a lump of clay, which is itself prepared from the earth. In this case earth is the original ingredient forming the clay lump, and the clay lump is in a sense the original cause of the pot. When the pot is destroyed, it will again assume the designation clay and ultimately merge back into the earth, its original cause. In relation to the clay pot, clay is the beginning and final state;

thus the pot is called real, for it possesses the essential characteristics of clay, which exists before and after the existence of the functioning instrument known as the pot. Similarly, earth exists before and after the clay, and thus clay may be considered real because it possesses the essential characteristics of earth, which exists before and after the existence of the clay. Similarly, earth and other elements are created from the *mahat-tattva*, which exists before and after the existence of the elements, which may be considered real because they possess the essential characteristics of the *mahat-tattva*. The *mahat-tattva* is ultimately the creation of the Supreme Personality of Godhead, the cause of all causes, who exists after all is annihilated. The Absolute Truth is the Supreme Lord Himself, who step by step gives meaning and character to all that exists.

TEXT 19

प्रकृतिर्यस्योपादानमाधारः पुरुषः परः ।
सतोऽभिव्यञ्जकः कालो ब्रह्म तत्त्रितयं त्वहम् ॥१९॥

prakṛtir yasyopādānam
ādhāraḥ puruṣaḥ paraḥ
sato 'bhivyañjakaḥ kālo
brahma tat tritayaṁ tv aham

prakṛtiḥ—material nature; *yasya*—of which (produced manifestation of the universe); *upādānam*—the ingredient cause; *ādhāraḥ*—the foundation; *puruṣaḥ*—the Personality of Godhead; *paraḥ*—Supreme; *sataḥ*—of the real (nature); *abhivyañjakaḥ*—the agitating agent; *kālaḥ*—time; *brahma*—the Absolute Truth; *tat*—this; *tritayam*—group of three; *tu*—but; *aham*—I.

TRANSLATION

The material universe may be considered real, having nature as its original ingredient and final state. Lord Mahā-Viṣṇu is the resting place of nature, which becomes manifest by the power of time. Thus nature, the almighty Viṣṇu and time are not different from Me, the Supreme Absolute Truth.

PURPORT

Material nature is the energy of the Lord, Mahā-Viṣṇu is His plenary portion, and time represents the Lord's activity. In this way, time and nature are always subservient to the Supreme Personality of Godhead, who creates, maintains and annihilates all that exists through the agency of His potencies and plenary portions. In other words, Lord Kṛṣṇa is the Absolute Truth because He contains all existence within Himself.

TEXT 20

सर्गः प्रवर्तते तावत् पौर्वापर्येण नित्यशः ।
महान् गुणविसर्गार्थः स्थित्यन्तो यावदीक्षणम् ॥२०॥

sargaḥ pravartate tāvat
paurvāparyeṇa nityaśaḥ
mahān guṇa-visargārthaḥ
sthity-anto yāvad īkṣaṇam

sargaḥ—the creation; *pravartate*—continues to exist; *tāvat*—to that extent; *paurva-aparyeṇa*—in the form of parents and children; *nityaśaḥ*—perpetually; *mahān*—bountiful; *guṇa-visarga*—of the variegated manifestation of the material modes; *arthaḥ*—for the purpose; *sthiti-antaḥ*—until the end of its maintenance; *yāvat*—as long as; *īkṣaṇam*—the glance of the Supreme Personality of Godhead.

TRANSLATION

As long as the Supreme Personality of Godhead continues to glance upon nature, the material world continues to exist, perpetually manifesting through procreation the great and variegated flow of universal creation.

PURPORT

Although the *mahat-tattva,* impelled by the force of time, is the ingredient cause of this world, it is clearly explained here that the Supreme Lord is personally the only ultimate cause of all that exists. Time and nature are powerless to act without the glance of the

Personality of Godhead. He creates unlimited material variety for the sense gratification of the conditioned souls, who try to enjoy life as the children of particular parents and as the parents of particular children, throughout the 8,400,000 species of life.

TEXT 21

विराण्मयासाद्यमानो लोककल्पविकल्पकः ।
पञ्चत्वाय विशेषाय कल्पते भुवनैः सह ॥२१॥

virāṇ mayāsādyamāno
loka-kalpa-vikalpakaḥ
pañcatvāya viśeṣāya
kalpate bhuvanaiḥ saha

virāṭ—the universal form; *mayā*—by Me; *āsādyamānaḥ*—being pervaded; *loka*—of the planets; *kalpa*—of repeated creation, maintenance and destruction; *vikalpakaḥ*—manifesting the variety; *pañcatvāya*—the elemental manifestation of creation of the five elements; *viśeṣāya*—in varieties; *kalpate*—is capable of displaying; *bhuvanaiḥ*—with the different planets; *saha*—being endowed.

TRANSLATION

I am the basis of the universal form, which displays endless variety through the repeated creation, maintenance and destruction of the planetary systems. Originally containing within itself all planets in their dormant state, My universal form manifests the varieties of created existence by arranging the coordinated combination of the five elements.

PURPORT

According to Śrīla Śrīdhara Svāmī, the word *mayā* refers to the Lord in His form as eternal time.

TEXTS 22-27

अन्ने प्रलीयते मर्त्यमन्नं धानासु लीयते ।
धाना भूमौ प्रलीयन्ते भूमिर्गन्धे प्रलीयते ॥२२॥

अप्सु प्रलीयते गन्ध आपश्च स्वगुणे रसे ।
लीयते ज्योतिषि रसो ज्योती रूपे प्रलीयते ॥२३॥
रूपं वायौ स च स्पर्शे लीयते सोऽपि चाम्बरे ।
अम्बरं शब्दतन्मात्र इन्द्रियाणि स्वयोनिषु ॥२४॥
योनिर्वैकारिके सौम्य लीयते मनसीश्वरे ।
शब्दो भूतादिमप्येति भूतादिर्महति प्रभुः ॥२५॥
स लीयते महान् स्वेषु गुणेषु गुणवत्तमः ।
तेऽव्यक्ते संप्रलीयन्ते तत् काले लीयतेऽव्यये ॥२६॥
कालो मायामये जीवे जीव आत्मनि मय्यजे ।
आत्मा केवल आत्मस्थो विकल्पापायलक्षणः ॥२७॥

anne pralīyate martyam
annaṁ dhānāsu līyate
dhānā bhūmau pralīyante
bhūmir gandhe pralīyate

apsu pralīyate gandha
āpaś ca sva-guṇe rase
līyate jyotiṣi raso
jyotī rūpe pralīyate

rūpaṁ vāyau sa ca sparśe
līyate so 'pi cāmbare
ambaraṁ śabda-tan-mātra
indriyāṇi sva-yoniṣu

yonir vaikārike saumya
līyate manasīśvare
śabdo bhūtādim apyeti
bhūtādir mahati prabhuḥ

sa līyate mahān sveṣu
guṇesu guṇa-vattamaḥ
te 'vyakte sampralīyante
tat kāle līyate 'vyaye

kālo māyā-maye jīve
jīva ātmani mayy aje
ātmā kevala ātma-stho
vikalpāpāya-lakṣaṇaḥ

anne—in food; *pralīyate*—becomes merged; *martyam*—the mortal body; *annam*—food; *dhānāsu*—within the grains; *līyate*—becomes merged; *dhānāḥ*—the grains; *bhūmau*—in the earth; *pralīyante*—become merged; *bhūmiḥ*—the earth; *gandhe*—within fragrance; *pralīyate*—becomes merged; *apsu*—in water; *pralīyate*—becomes merged; *gandhaḥ*—fragrance; *āpaḥ*—water; *ca*—and; *sva-guṇe*—within its own quality; *rase*—taste; *līyate*—becomes merged; *jyotiṣi*—within fire; *rasaḥ*—taste; *jyotiḥ*—fire; *rūpe*—within form; *pralīyate*—becomes merged; *rūpam*—form; *vāyau*—in air; *saḥ*—it; *ca*—and; *sparśe*—in touch; *līyate*—becomes merged; *saḥ*—it; *api*—also; *ca*—and; *ambare*—in ether; *ambaram*—ether; *śabda*—in sound; *tat-mātre*—its corresponding subtle sensation; *indriyāṇi*—the senses; *sva-yoniṣu*—in their sources, the demigods; *yoniḥ*—the demigods; *vaikārike*—in false ego in the mode of goodness; *saumya*—My dear Uddhava; *līyate*—become merged; *manasi*—in the mind; *īśvare*—which is the controller; *śabdaḥ*—sound; *bhūta-ādim*—in the original false ego; *apyeti*—becomes merged; *bhūta-ādiḥ*—false ego; *mahati*—in the total material nature; *prabhuḥ*—powerful; *saḥ*—that; *līyate*—becomes merged; *mahān*—the total material nature; *sveṣu*—in its own; *guṇeṣu*—three modes; *guṇa-vat-tamaḥ*—being the ultimate abode of these modes; *te*—they; *avyakte*—in the unmanifest form of nature; *sampralīyante*—become completely merged; *tat*—that; *kāle*—in time; *līyate*—become merged; *avyaye*—in the infallible; *kālaḥ*—time; *māyā-maye*—who is full of transcendental knowledge; *jīve*—in the Supreme Lord, who activates all living beings; *jīvaḥ*—that Lord; *ātmani*—in the Supreme Self; *mayi*—in Me; *aje*—the unborn; *ātmā*—the original Self; *kevalaḥ*—alone; *ātma-sthaḥ*—self-situated; *vikalpa*—by creation; *apāya*—and annihilation; *lakṣaṇaḥ*—characterized.

TRANSLATION

At the time of annihilation, the mortal body of the living being becomes merged into food. Food merges into the grains, and the

grains merge back into the earth. The earth merges into its subtle sensation, fragrance. Fragrance merges into water, and water further merges into its own quality, taste. That taste merges into fire, which merges into form. Form merges into touch, and touch merges into ether. Ether finally merges into the sensation of sound. The senses all merge into their own origins, the presiding demigods, and they, O gentle Uddhava, merge into the controlling mind, which itself merges into false ego in the mode of goodness. Sound becomes one with false ego in the mode of ignorance, and all-powerful false ego, the first of all the physical elements, merges into the total nature. The total material nature, the primary repository of the three basic modes, dissolves into the modes. These modes of nature then merge into the unmanifest form of nature, and that unmanifest form merges into time. Time merges into the Supreme Lord, present in the form of the omniscient Mahā-puruṣa, the original activator of all living beings. That origin of all life merges into Me, the unborn Supreme Soul, who remains alone, established within Himself. It is from Him that all creation and annihilation are manifested.

PURPORT

The annihilation of the material world is the reversal of the process of creation, and ultimately everything is merged to rest within the Supreme Lord, who remains full in His absolute position.

TEXT 28

एवमन्वीक्षमाणस्य कथं वैकल्पिको भ्रमः ।
मनसो हृदि तिष्ठेत व्योम्नीवार्कोदये तमः ॥२८॥

evam anvīkṣamāṇasya
kathaṁ vaikalpiko bhramaḥ
manaso hṛdi tiṣṭheta
vyomnīvārkodaye tamaḥ

evam—in this way; *anvīkṣamāṇasya*—of one who is carefully examining; *katham*—how; *vaikalpikaḥ*—based on duality; *bhramaḥ*—illusion;

manasaḥ—of his mind; *hṛdi*—in the heart; *tiṣṭheta*—can remain; *vyomni*—in the sky; *iva*—just as; *arka*—of the sun; *udaye*—upon the rising; *tamaḥ*—darkness.

TRANSLATION

Just as the rising sun removes the darkness of the sky, similarly, this scientific knowledge of cosmic annihilation removes all illusory duality from the mind of a serious student. Even if illusion somehow enters his heart, it cannot remain there.

PURPORT

Just as the brilliant sun removes all darkness from the sky, a clear understanding of the knowledge spoken by Lord Kṛṣṇa to Uddhava removes all ignorance concocted by the material mind. One will then no longer accept the material body as the self. Even if such illusion temporarily manifests within one's consciousness, it will be driven away by the resurgence of one's spiritual knowledge.

TEXT 29

एष सांख्यविधिः प्रोक्तः संशयग्रन्थिभेदनः ।
प्रतिलोमानुलोमाभ्यां परावरदृशा मया ॥२९॥

eṣa sāṅkhya-vidhiḥ proktaḥ
saṁśaya-granthi-bhedanaḥ
pratilomānulomābhyāṁ
parāvara-dṛśā mayā

eṣaḥ—this; *sāṅkhya-vidhiḥ*—method of Sāṅkhya (analytic philosophy); *proktaḥ*—spoken; *saṁśaya*—of doubts; *granthi*—the bondage; *bhedanaḥ*—which breaks; *pratiloma-anulomābhyām*—in both direct and reverse order; *para*—the situation of the spiritual world; *avara*—and the inferior situation of the material world; *dṛśā*—by Him who sees perfectly; *mayā*—by Me.

TRANSLATION

Thus I, the perfect seer of everything material and spiritual, have spoken this knowledge of Sāṅkhya, which destroys the illusion of doubt by scientific analysis of creation and annihilation.

PURPORT

Lord Śrī Kṛṣṇa has explained that the material mind accepts and rejects many different concepts of life, generating innumerable false arguments about the actual process of perfection. But a person who takes shelter of the lotus feet of the Supreme Personality of Godhead can see everything with clear intelligence. One who understands how the Supreme Lord creates and annihilates can be liberated from material bondage and devote himself to the eternal service of the Supreme Lord.

Thus end the purports of the humble servant of His Divine Grace A. C. Bhaktivedanta Swami Prabhupāda to the Eleventh Canto, Twenty-fourth Chapter, of the Śrīmad-Bhāgavatam, *entitled "The Philosophy of Sāṅkhya."*

Appendixes

The Author

His Divine Grace Śrīla Hridayananda dāsa Goswami Ācāryadeva is one of the foremost spiritual leaders of the International Society for Krishna Consciousness. He enjoys the unique status of being among the first Western-born members of the authorized chain of disciplic succession descending from the Supreme Lord, Kṛṣṇa. In modern times, the most essential task of Kṛṣṇa conscious spiritual masters has been to translate the Vedic scriptures of ancient India into modern languages and distribute them widely throughout the world. Śrīla Ācāryadeva has made this mission his life and soul.

Śrīla Ācāryadeva appeared in this world on November 5, 1948, in Los Angeles, California. As an academically gifted student at the University of California, Berkeley, he attended a talk given by His Divine Grace A. C. Bhaktivedanta Swami Prabhupāda, the founder and spiritual master of the Kṛṣṇa consciousness movement. Impresssed by Śrīla Prabhupāda's scholarship and saintliness, Śrīla Ācāryadeva became a member of the Kṛṣṇa consciousness community in Berkeley and, shortly thereafter, on February 8, 1970, was initiated as Śrīla Prabhupāda's disciple.

From the beginning, Śrīla Ācāryadeva distinguished himself by his oratorical skills, his spiritual dedication and his devotion to studying the writings of his spiritual master, through which he acquired a deep knowledge of Sanskrit. He quickly gained recognition from Śrīla Prabhupāda himself, who marked him as "a literary man" and in 1970 sent him to Boston to accept responsibilities with ISKCON's publishing activities there. Later, Śrīla Ācāryadeva served as president in ISKCON's center in Gainesville, Florida, and Houston, Texas, and made a significant contribution to the rapid expansion of the Kṛṣṇa consciousness movement there in the early 1970s. In 1972, he adopted the renounced order (*sannyāsa*) in order to fully dedicate himself to serving the mission of his spiritual master: the propagation of the Kṛṣṇa consciousness movement throughout the world. For the next two years he traveled widely, speaking at colleges and universities throughout the United States.

In 1974, Śrīla Ācāryadeva was appointed to the Governing Body Commission of ISKCON and entrusted with the development of the Kṛṣṇa consciousness movement in Latin America. Over the following three years, he established twenty-five centers of the Society and attracted thousands of Latin Americans to the movement, as predicted by Śrīla Prabhupāda himself. In the course of his travels he met with numerous heads of state, government ministers and high religious leaders, conversing with them in fluent Spanish and Portuguese. He also founded the Spanish- and Portuguese-language divisions of the Bhaktivedanta Book trust for the translation and publication of Śrīla Prabhupāda's books. At present, more than 20 million books in these two languages have been distributed throughout Latin America and abroad.

Shortly before his departure from this world in November, 1977, His Divine Grace Śrīla Prabhupāda chose Śrīla Ācāryadeva, along with ten other senior disciples, to accept the role of spiritual master and to initiate disciples. Currently, Śrīla Ācāryadeva serves as the Governing Body Commissioner for Brazil and the state of Florida and as one of the initiating spiritual masters for Latin America and the southern United States. His most challenging assignment came, however, in 1979 when the leaders of ISKCON, in recognition of his devotional scholarship, commissioned him to complete Śrīla Prabhupāda's monumental translation of and commentary on the *Śrīmad-Bhāgavatam*. For thousands of years in India, great spiritual masters have presented commentaries on the *Bhāgavatam* to make its urgent message clear to the people of their times. Śrīla Ācāryadeva is the first Westerner to be entrusted with this demanding task, and his success in communicating the essence of India's spiritual heritage to modern readers has already been noted by scholars and religionists around the world.

His Divine Grace A. C. Bhaktivedanta Swami Prabhupāda

His Divine Grace A. C. Bhaktivedanta Swami Prabhupāda appeared in this world in 1896 in Calcutta, India. He first met his spiritual master, Śrīla Bhaktisiddhānta Sarasvatī Gosvāmī, in Calcutta in 1922. Bhaktisiddhānta Sarasvatī, a prominent religious scholar and the founder of sixty-four Gauḍīya Maṭhas (Vedic institutes), liked this educated young man and convinced him to dedicate his life to teaching Vedic knowledge. Śrīla Prabhupāda became his student, and eleven years later (1933) at Allahabad he became his formally initiated disciple.

At their first meeting, in 1922, Śrīla Bhaktisiddhānta Sarasvatī Ṭhākura requested Śrīla Prabhupāda to broadcast Vedic knowledge through the English language. In the years that followed, Śrīla Prabhupāda wrote a commentary on the *Bhagavad-gītā,* assisted the Gauḍīya Maṭha in its work and, in 1944, without assistance, started *Back to Godhead,* an English fortnightly magazine, edited it, typed the manuscripts and checked the galley proofs. He even distributed the individual copies and struggled to maintain the publication. Once begun, the magazine never stopped; it is now being continued by his disciples in the West and is published in over thirty languages.

Recognizing Śrīla Prabhupāda's philosophical learning and devotion, the Gauḍīya Vaiṣṇava Society honored him in 1947 with the title "Bhaktivedanta." In 1950, at the age of fifty-four, Śrīla Prabhupāda retired from married life, adopting the *vānaprastha* (retired) order to devote more time to his studies and writing. Śrīla Prabhupāda traveled to the holy city of Vṛndāvana, where he lived in very humble circumstances in the historic medieval temple of Rādhā-Dāmodara. There he engaged for several years in deep study and writing. He accepted the renounced order of life (*sannyāsa*) in 1959. At Rādhā-Dāmodara, Śrīla Prabhupāda began work on his life's masterpiece: a multivolume translation of and commentary on the eighteen-thousand-verse *Śrīmad-Bhāgavatam* (*Bhāgavata Purāṇa*). He also wrote *Easy Journey to Other Planets.*

After publishing three volumes of the *Bhāgavatam*, Śrīla Prabhupāda came to the United States, in 1965, to fulfill the mission of his spiritual master. Subsequently, His Divine Grace wrote more than sixty volumes of authoritative translations, commentaries and summary studies of the philosophical and religious classics of India.

In 1965, when he first arrived by freighter in New York City, Śrīla Prabhupāda was practically penniless. It was after almost a year of great difficulty that he established the International Society for Krishna Consciousness in July of 1966. Before his passing away on November 14, 1977, he guided the Society and saw it grow to a worldwide confederation of more than one hundred *āśramas*, schools, temples, institutes and farm communities.

In 1968, Śrīla Prabhupāda created New Vrindaban, an experimental Vedic community in the hills of West Virginia. Inspired by the success of New Vrindaban, now a thriving farm community of more than two thousand acres, his students have since founded several similar communities in the United States and abroad.

In 1972, His Divine Grace introduced the Vedic system of primary and secondary education in the West by founding the Gurukula school in Dallas, Texas. Since then, under his supervision, his disciples have established children's schools throughout the United States and the rest of the world, with the principal educational center now located in Vṛndāvana, India.

Śrīla Prabhupāda also inspired the construction of several large international cultural centers in India. The center at Śrīdhāma Māyāpur in West Bengal is the site for a planned spiritual city, an ambitious project for which construction will extend over the next decade. In Vṛndāvana, India, is the magnificent Kṛṣṇa-Balarāma Temple and International Guesthouse. There is also a major cultural and educational center in Bombay. Other centers are planned in a dozen other important locations on the Indian subcontinent.

Śrīla Prabhupāda's most significant contribution, however, is his books. Highly respected by the academic community for their authoritativeness, depth and clarity, they are used as standard textbooks in numerous college courses. His writings have been translated into over thirty languages. The Bhaktivedanta Book Trust, established in 1972 exclusively to publish the works of His Divine Grace, has thus become the world's largest publisher of books in the field of Indian religion and philosophy.

In just twelve years, in spite of his advanced age, Śrīla Prabhupāda circled the globe fourteen times on lecture tours that took him to six continents. In spite of such a vigorous schedule, Śrīla Prabhupāda continued to write prolifically. His writings constitute a veritable library of Vedic philosophy, religion, literature and culture.

References

The purports of *Śrīmad-Bhāgavatam* are all confirmed by standard Vedic authorities. The following authentic scriptures are specifically cited in this volume. For specific page references, consult the general index.

Bhagavad-gītā

Bhakti-rasāmṛta-sindhu

Brahma-saṁhitā

Caitanya-caritāmṛta

Garuḍa Purāṇa

Manu-saṁhitā

Pañcarātra

Ṛg Veda

Skanda Purāṇa

Śrīmad-Bhāgavatam

Upadeśāmṛta

Vedānta-sūtra

Vedas

Glossary

A

Ācamana—process of purification performed before worship or sacrifice.
Ācārya—a spiritual master who teaches by example.
Adhibhautic—of the material sense objects.
Adhidaivic—of the controlling demigods.
Adhyātmic—of the material senses.
Agni—demigod of fire.
Anilāyāma—the discipline of controlling the breathing process.
Aṇimā-siddhi—the mystic power of becoming very small.
Arjuna—Lord Kṛṣṇa's friend and devotee, to whom He spoke *Bhagavad-gītā.*
Āśrama—a spiritual order of life.
Aśvinī deities—demigods in charge of the nostrils and sense of smell.

B

Battle of Kurukṣetra—a battle between the Kurus and the Pāṇḍavas, which took place five thousand years ago and before which Lord Kṛṣṇa spoke *Bhagavad-gītā* to Arjuna.
Bengal—province in northwestern India.
Bhagavad-gītā—the basic directions for spiritual life spoken by the Lord Himself.
Bhagavān—the Supreme Lord, who is full of all opulences.
Bhakti-rasāmṛta-sindhu—a book by Rūpa Gosvāmī outlining the practice of devotional service to Lord Kṛṣṇa.
Bhaktisiddhānta Sarasvatī Ṭhākura—the spiritual master of His Divine Grace A. C. Bhaktivedanta Swami Prabhupāda.
Bhakti-yoga—the *yoga* of devotional service to the Supreme Lord, Kṛṣṇa.
Bharata—a king of ancient India.

Bhīṣmadeva—a great devotee and senior family member of the Kuru dynasty.

Bhūr—the lower material planets.

Bhuvar—the middle material planets.

Bihar—a state in northwestern India.

Brahmā, Lord—the first created being; chief of the demigods and creator of the universe.

Brahmacārī—a celibate student under the care of a bona fide spiritual master.

Brahmaloka—the abode of Lord Brahmā, in the highest planetary system of the material universe.

Brahman—the all-pervading impersonal aspect of Kṛṣṇa.

Brāhmaṇa—the intelligent class of men, according to the system of social and spiritual orders.

Bṛhaspati—the spiritual master of the demigods.

C

Caitanya-caritāmṛta—the biography of Lord Caitanya by Kṛṣṇadāsa Kavirāja.

Caitanya Mahāprabhu—the incarnation of Kṛṣṇa who appeared in India five hundred years ago to propagate the congregational chanting of the Hare Kṛṣṇa *mantra.*

Candra—the demigod of the moon.

Candraloka—the moon planet.

Cāturmāsya—a four-month period of fasting and austerities.

Cātur-varṇyam—the four occupational divisions of society (*brāhmaṇas, kṣatriyas, vaiśyas,* and *śūdras*).

Citraketu—a great king and devotee of Lord Kṛṣṇa.

D

Daiva-varṇāśrama—the system of dividing society into four occupational and four spiritual divisions, according to actual qualification rather than birth.

Daṇḍa—the staff of a member of the renounced order (*sannyāsa*).

Deity—the incarnation of the Lord in an apparently material form to facilitate personal service by the devotee.

Demigods—residents of the heavenly planets.

Devotional service—the process of worshiping Lord Kṛṣṇa by dedicating one's thoughts, words and actions to Him with love.

E

Ekadaṇḍa—the staff, made of a single rod, carried by a *sannyāsī* of the Māyāvāda (impersonalist) school.

Ekādaśī—A special fast day for increased remembrance of Kṛṣṇa, which comes on the eleventh day of both the waxing and waning moon.

F

False ego—identification with the material body rather than the soul.

G

Gauḍīya Vaiṣṇava-sampradāya—the line of spiritual masters descending from Lord Caitanya.

Gaura-pūrṇimā—the appearance day of Lord Caitanya.

Gāyatrī mantra—a transcendental vibration chanted by *brāhmaṇas*.

Govinda—Kṛṣṇa, who gives pleasure to the senses and the cows.

Gṛhastha-āśrama—the householder order of spiritual life.

Guru—a spiritual master.

H

Hanumān—the great monkey devotee of Lord Rāmacandra.

Hare Kṛṣṇa mantra—the great chanting for deliverance: Hare Kṛṣṇa, Hare Kṛṣṇa, Kṛṣṇa Kṛṣṇa, Hare Hare/ Hare Rāma, Hare Rāma, Rāma Rāma, Hare Hare.

Hari, Lord—Kṛṣṇa, who takes away the distress of His devotees.

I

Indra—the king of the heavenly planets and chief of the administrative demigods.

Indraloka—the planet of Indra.

J

Janaloka—a heavenly planet.

Janas—*See:* Janaloka.

Janmāṣṭamī—the appearance day of Lord Kṛṣṇa.

Japa—the soft recitation of the Lord's holy names as a private meditation.

Jayadeva—a great Kṛṣṇa conscious poet.

Jīva—the soul or atomic living entity.

Jīva Gosvāmī—one of the six Gosvāmīs; author of many authoritative books on the philosophy of Kṛṣṇa consciousness.

Jīva-tattva—of the nature of *jīva.*

Jñāna—theoretical knowledge.

Jñāna-kāṇḍa—the sections of the *Vedas* dealing with philosophical analysis of matter and spirit.

Jñāna-yoga—the practice of self-realization by intellectual analysis of matter and spirit.

K

Kali, age of—*See:* Kali-yuga

Kali-yuga—the present age of quarrel and hypocrisy.

Kapila, Lord—an incarnation of Kṛṣṇa who appeared as the son of Devahūti and Kardama to propound the Sāṅkhya philosophy.

Karma—one's situation in life resulting from past material actions; the universal principle of action and reaction; work performed for material results.

Karma-kāṇḍa—the part of the *Vedas* that prescribes modes of action for obtaining material benedictions.

Karma-yoga—material action performed according to scriptural regulations.

Kaupīna—the thick belt and underwear worn by saintly persons.

Keśava—Kṛṣṇa, who has beautiful dark hair.

Kikaṭa—the present state of Gaya, in north-central India.

Kṛṣṇa, Lord—the Supreme Personality of Godhead, appearing in His original, two-armed form, which is the origin of all the Lord's other forms and incarnations.

Kṛṣṇadāsa Kavirāja—the author of *Caitanya-caritāmṛta,* a biography of Lord Caitanya.

Kṛṣṇa-kīrtana—the chanting of Kṛṣṇa's name and pastimes.

Kṣatriya—the administrative and protective occupation according to the system of social and spiritual orders.

Kumāras—four young sons of Brahmā who became great authorities on devotional service.

Kuntī—*See:* Pṛthā.

Kurukṣetra—a pilgrimage place in northern India, site of the Battle of Kurukṣetra, where Lord Kṛṣṇa spoke *Bhagavad-gītā.*

L

Locana dāsa Ṭhākura—a great Kṛṣṇa conscious spiritual master.

M

Mādhava, Lord—Kṛṣṇa, the husband of the goddess of fortune.

Madhvācārya—a thirteenth-century Vaiṣṇava spiritual master who preached the theistic philosophy of "pure dualism," which maintains that the Lord and the living entities are always distinct from one another.

Mahābhārata—the epic history of India, of which *Bhagavad-gītā* is part.

Mahā-prasādam—the remnants of food directly offered to the Deity of Lord Kṛṣṇa.

Maharloka—a heavenly planet.

Mahat-tattva—the total material energy.

Mahā-Viṣṇu—the Viṣṇu expansion from whom all material universes emanate.

Mantra—a combination of transcendental sounds that has the effect of purifying consciousness of material contamination.

Manu-saṁhitā—the legal code for human society compiled by Manu.

Māyā—illusion; forgetfulness of one's relationship with Kṛṣṇa.

Māyāvādī—an impersonalist or voidist.

Mitra—demigod who controls death.

Mukunda—Kṛṣṇa, the giver of liberation.

Mystic yoga—*yoga* performed for the purpose of developing subtle material powers.

N

Nārada—a great devotee who travels through space to preach the Lord's glories.

Nārāyaṇa, Lord—the four-handed expansion of the Lord who resides in the spiritual world, Vaikuṇṭha.

Niyama—strict principles of spiritual regulation.

O

Oṁ—*See:* oṁkāra.

Oṁkāra—the impersonal sound representation of the Lord.

P

Pañcarātra—a class of scriptures that gives instructions for executing devotional service.

Paramahaṁsa—the topmost class of devotees.

Paramātmā—the Supersoul, or localized aspect of the Supreme Lord.

Phala-śrutis—Sanskrit verses granting various benedictions.

Pradhāna—the material elements in their unmanifest state.

Prakṛti—the material elements in their manifest state.

Prāṇa—the life air.

Prāṇāyāma—the process of regulating the life air.

Prasādam—food offered to Kṛṣṇa, the remnants of which are spiritual and can purify any living entity.

Prema-bhakti—the highest perfectional stage of love of God.

Pṛthā—the wife of Pāṇḍu, mother of the Pāṇḍavas and aunt of Lord Kṛṣṇa.

Pṛthu Mahārāja—a partial incarnation of Kṛṣṇa, who appeared as a great king.

Puruṣa—an enjoying personality (either the individual living entity or the supreme living entity, Kṛṣṇa.)

R

Ratha-yātrā—an annual festival in which Deities of the Supreme Lord are drawn in procession upon huge, gaily decorated canopied chariots.

Rudra, Lord—a name of Lord Śiva.

Rūpa Gosvāmī—the chief of the six Vaiṣṇava spiritual masters who directly followed Lord Caitanya Mahāprabhu and systematically presented His teachings.

S

Sacred thread—a thread worn by persons initiated into the chanting of the Gāyatrī *mantra.*

Śālagrāma-śilā—a Deity of the Supreme Lord manifest in the form of a round, black stone.

Sampradāya—a disciplic succession of spiritual masters.

Śaṅkarācārya—an incarnation of Lord Siva, who expounded the doctrine of impersonalism.

Sāṅkhya—analytical study of the elements of the universe.

Sāṅkhya-yoga—practice of self-realization by analytical study of the body and soul.

Sannyāsa—the renounced order of life.

Śāstras—scriptures.

Satya—*See:* Satyaloka.

Satyaloka—a heavenly planet.

Satya-yuga—the first of the four ages, lasting 1,728,000 years.

Śiva, Lord—the personality in charge of the mode of ignorance and the destruction of the material universe.

Smṛty-ācārya—a spiritual master expert in the supplementary Vedic literatures.

Sparṣas—the consonants in the Sanskrit alphabet.

Śravaṇaṁ kīrtanaṁ viṣṇoḥ—the process of hearing and chanting the names and glories of the Supreme Lord, Viṣṇu.

Śrī—*See:* Śrīla.

Śrīdhara Svāmī—a great Kṛṣṇa conscious scholar who wrote the original commentary on *Śrīmad-Bhāgavatam.*

Śrī Gurudeva—the spiritual master.

Śrīla—a title indicating possession of exceptional spiritual qualities.

Śrīla Prabhupāda—His Divine Grace A. C. Bhaktivedanta Swami Prabhupāda.

Śūdras—the laborer class of men according to the system of social and spiritual orders.

Śukadeva Gosvāmī—the sage who spoke *Śrīmad-Bhāgavatam* to Parīkṣit Mahārāja.
Supersoul—*See:* Paramātmā.
Svar—the upper material planets.

T

Tapas—*See:* Tapoloka
Tapoloka—a heavenly planet.
Tri-daṇḍa—a staff, made of three rods, carried by *sannyāsīs* who are devotees of Lord Kṛṣṇa, signifying service with mind, body and words.
Tridaṇḍi-sannyāsī—a member of the renounced order of life who carries a *tridaṇḍa.*

U

Uddhava—a great friend and devotee of Lord Kṛṣṇa.
Upadeśāmṛta—a short Sanskrit work by Rūpa Gosvāmī containing important instructions about devotional service to Lord Kṛṣṇa.
Upāsanā-kāṇḍa—the section of the *Vedas* describing worship of demigods.

V

Vaikuṇṭha—the spiritual kingdom of Lord Nārāyaṇa.
Vaiṣṇava—a devotee of the Supreme Lord, Viṣṇu, or Kṛṣṇa.
Vaiśyas—the class of men engaged in business and farming according to the system of social and spiritual orders.
Vānaprastha—retired life.
Varṇa—one of the social orders in the *varṇāśrama* system.
Varṇāśrama—the Vedic institution dividing the human population into four social orders (*varṇas*) and four spiritual orders (*āśramas*).
Varuṇa—the demigod of bodies of water.
Vāsudeva—Kṛṣṇa, the son of Vasudeva.
Vāyu—the demigod of the air.

Veda-cakṣuḥ—literally, seeing through the eyes of the *Vedas.*

Vedānta—a philosophical work summarizing the conclusions of the *Vedas.*

Vedas—the original revealed scriptures first spoken by the Lord Himself.

Veda-vāda-rata—persons attached to the portions of the *Vedas* prescribing actions to attain favorable material results.

Viṣṇu, Lord—the four-armed expansion of the Supreme Lord who maintains the material creation.

Viṣṇu-tattva—the original Personality of Godhead's primary expansions, each of whom is equally God.

Viśvanātha Cakravartī Ṭhākura—a great Kṛṣṇa conscious spiritual master who wrote a famous commentary on *Śrīmad-Bhāgavatam.*

Vyāsa—*See:* Vyāsadeva.

Vyāsadeva—an incarnation of Viṣṇu who compiled the *Vedas, Purāṇas, Mahābhārata, Vedānta-sūtra,* etc.

Y

Yakṣas—supernatural beings who guard the wealth of Kuvera, treasurer of the demigods.

Yama—the process of controlling the senses.

Yoga—various processes of spiritual realization, all ultimately meant for attaining the Supreme.

Yudhiṣṭhira—the eldest of the Pāṇḍava brothers; Lord Kṛṣṇa established him as king after the Battle of Kurukṣetra.

Sanskrit Pronunciation Guide

Throughout the centuries, the Sanskrit language has been written in a variety of alphabets. The mode of writing most widely used throughout India, however, is called *devanāgarī*, which means, literally, the writing used in "the cities of the demigods." The *devanāgarī* alphabet consists of forty-eight characters: thirteen vowels and thirty-five consonants. Ancient Sanskrit grammarians arranged this alphabet according to practical linguistic principles, and this order has been accepted by all Western scholars. The system of transliteration used in this book conforms to a system that scholars in the last fifty years have accepted to indicate the pronunciation of each Sanskrit sound.

Vowels

अ a आ ā इ i ई ī उ u ऊ ū ऋ ṛ
ॠ ṝ ऌ ḷ ए e ऐ ai ओ o औ au

Consonants

Gutturals:	क ka	ख kha	ग ga	घ gha	ङ ṅa
Palatals:	च ca	छ cha	ज ja	झ jha	ञ ña
Cerebrals:	ट ṭa	ठ ṭha	ड ḍa	ढ ḍha	ण ṇa
Dentals:	त ta	थ tha	द da	ध dha	न na
Labials:	प pa	फ pha	ब ba	भ bha	म ma
Semivowels:	य ya	र ra	ल la	व va	
Sibilants:	श śa	ष ṣa	स sa		
Aspirate:	ह ha	Anusvāra: ं ṁ	Visarga: ः ḥ		

Numerals

० -0 १ -1 २ -2 ३ -3 ४ -4 ५ -5 ६ -6 ७ -7 ८ -8 ९ -9

The vowels are written as follows after a consonant:

ा ā ि i ी ī ु u ू ū ृ ṛ ॄ ṝ े e ै ai ो o ौ au

For example: क ka का kā कि ki की kī कु ku कू kū

कृ kṛ कॄ kṝ के ke कै kai को ko कौ kau

Generally two or more consonants in conjunction are written together in a special form, as for example: क्ष kṣa त्र tra

The vowel "**a**" is implied after a consonant with no vowel symbol.

The symbol virāma (्) indicates that there is no final vowel: क्

The vowels are pronounced as follows:

a — as in **but**
ā — as in **far** but held twice as long as **a**
ai — as in **aisle**
au — as in **how**
e — as in **they**
i — as in **pin**
ī — as in **pique** but held twice as long as **i**
ḷ — as in **lree**
o — as in **go**
ṛ — as in **rim**
ṝ — as in **reed** but held twice as long as **ṛ**
u — as in **push**
ū — as in **rule** but held twice as long as **u**

The consonants are pronounced as follows:

Gutturals
(pronounced from the throat)
k — as in **kite**
kh — as in **Eckhart**
g — as in **give**
gh — as in **dig-hard**
ṅ — as in **sing**

Labials
(pronounced with the lips)
p — as in **pine**
ph — as in **up-hill** (not **f**)
b — as in **bird**
bh — as in **rub-hard**
m — as in **mother**

Cerebrals
(pronounced with tip of tongue against roof of mouth)

ṭ — as in **t**ub
ṭh — as in ligh**t-h**eart
ḍ — as in **d**ove
ḍh — as in re**d-h**ot
ṇ — as in si**n**g

Dentals
(pronounced as cerebrals but with tongue against teeth)

t — as in **t**ub
th — as in ligh**t-h**eart
d — as in **d**ove
dh — as in re**d-h**ot
n — as in **n**ut

Aspirate

h — as in **h**ome

Anusvāra

ṁ — a resonant nasal sound like in the French word *bon*

Palatals
(pronounced with middle of tongue against palate)

c — as in **ch**air
ch — as in staun**ch-h**eart
j — as in **j**oy
jh — as in he**dgeh**og
ñ — as in ca**ny**on

Semivowels

y — as in **y**es
r — as in **r**un
l — as in **l**ight
v — as in **v**ine, except when preceded in the same syllable by a consonant, then like in s**w**an

Sibilants

ś — as in the German word *s**p**rechen*
ṣ — as in **sh**ine
s — as in **s**un

Visarga

ḥ — a final **h**-sound: **aḥ** is pronounced like **aha**; **iḥ** like **ihi**

There is no strong accentuation of syllables in Sanskrit, or pausing between words in a line, only a flowing of short and long (twice as long as the short) syllables. A long syllable is one whose vowel is long (**ā, ai, au, e, ī, o, ṝ, ū**) or whose short vowel is followed by more than one consonant (including **ḥ** and **ṁ**). Aspirated consonants (consonants followed by an **h**) count as single consonants.

Index of Sanskrit Verses

This index constitutes a complete listing of the first and third lines of each of the Sanskrit poetry verses of this volume of *Śrīmad-Bhāgavatam*, arranged in English alphabetical order. The first column gives the Sanskrit transliteration, and the second and third columns, respectively, list the chapter-verse reference and page number for each verse.

A

abhyāsenātmano yogī	20.18	117
ābrahma-sthāvarādīnaāṁ	21.5	152
ādaraḥ paricaryāyāṁ	19.21	76
ādāv ante ca madhye ca	19.16	72
ā-dehāntāt kvacit khyātis	18.37	40
adho 'surāṇāṁ nāgānāṁ	24.13	322
ādir anto yadā yasya	24.18	327
aghaṁ kurvanti hi yathā	21.11	161
agnihotraṁ carśaś ca	18.8	10
agni-mugdhā dhūma-tāntāḥ	21.27	179
agnīn sva-prāṇa āveśya	18.13	14
agni-pakvaṁ samaśnīyāt	18.5	7
ahaṁ tariṣyāmi duranta-pāraṁ	23.57	303
agaṁ tri-vṛn moha-vikalpa-hetur	22.33	229
āhārārthaṁ samīheta	18.34	37
ahiṁsā satyam asteyam	19.33	84
aho eṣa mahaā-sāro	23.38	285
aho-rātraiś chidyamānaṁ	20.16	114
ajāta-śatruḥ papraccha	19.11	67
ajijñāsita-mad dharmo	18.38	42
ākaṇṭha-majjaḥ śiśira	18.4	6
ākāśād ghoṣavān prāṇo	21.38	190
ākhyāhi viśveśvara viśva-mūrte	19.8	63
akṛṣṇa-sāro deśānām	21.8	156
alabdhvā na viṣīdeta	18.33	36
ambaraṁ śabda-tan-mātra	24.24	331
amedhya-liptaṁ yad yena	21.13	163
anādy-avidyā-yuktasya	22.10	207
ananta-pārāṁ bṛhatīṁ	21.40	191
ananta-pāraṁ gambhīraṁ	21.36	188
aṇḍam utpādayām āsur	24.9	320
anīha ātmā manasā samīhatā	23.44	290
annaṁ ca bhaikṣya-sampannaṁ	23.35	283
anne pralīyate martyam	24.22	331
aṇur bṛhat kṛśaḥ sthūlo	24.16	325
anvīkṣetātmano bandhaṁ	18.22	25
anyac ca sunṛtā vāṇī	19.38	86
anyāṁś ca niyamān jñānī	18.36	39
anyonyāpāśrayāt kṛṣṇa	22.26	222
apramatta idaṁ jñātvā	20.14	113
apramatto 'khila-svārthe	23.29	278
apsu pralīyate gandha	24.23	331
arthas tan-maātrikāj jajñe	24.8	319
arthasya sādhane siddhe	23.17	269
arthe hy avidyamāno 'pi	22.56	250
arthenālpīyasā hy ete	23.21	272
artho 'py agacchan nidhanaṁ	23.10	265
asakta-citto viramed	18.26	29
āsakta-manaso martyā	21.24	175
asaṁvibhajya cātmānaṁ	23.24	275
asaṁyataṁ yasya mano vinaśyad	23.46	292
āsīj jñānam atho artha	24.2	313
āśiṣo hṛdi saṅkalpya	21.31	183
asmin loke vartamānaḥ	20.11	110
aṣṭau prakṛtayaś caiva	22.24	220
āstikyaṁ brahmacaryaṁ ca	19.33	84
atandrito 'nurodhena	20.19	117
atha te sampravakṣyāmi	24.1	312
ati-vādāṁs titikṣeta	18.31	34
ātmāgrahaṇa-nirbhātaṁ	22.57	251

ātmā kevala ātma-stho 24.27 332
ātma-krīḍa ātma-rata 18.20 21
ātmanaḥ pitṛ-putrābhyām 22.49 244
ātmānaṁ cintayed ekam 18.21 24
ātmany agnīn samāropya 18.11 12

ātmāparijñāna-mayo vivādo 22.34 230
ātmā yad eṣām aparo ya ādyaḥ 22.31 227
ātmā yadi syāt sukha-duḥkha-hetuḥ 23.52 297
autpattilo guṇaḥ saṅgo 21.17 168
avantiṣu dvijaḥ kaścid 23.6 262
avekṣate 'ravindākṣa 20.1 98
avipakva-kaṣāyo 'smād 18.41 44

B

badhnanti rajjvā taṁ kecid 23.36 283
bahir-antar-bhidā-hetur 22.42 238
bahir jalāśayaṁ gatvā 18.19 20
bandha indriya-vikṣepo 18.22 25
bārhaspatya sa nāsty atra 23.2 259

bhago ma aiśvaro bhāvo 19.40 90
bhajate prakṛtiṁ tasya 21.13 163
bhakti-yogaḥ puraivoktaḥ 19.19 75
bhaktyoddhavānapāyinyā 18.45 49
bhavāpyayāv anudhyāyen 20.22 121

bhedo vairam aviśvāsaḥ 23.18 270
bhidyante bhrātaro dārāḥ 23.20 271
bhidyate hṛdaya-granthiś 20.30 131
bhikṣāṁ caturṣu varṇeṣu 18.18 19
bhikṣārthaṁ nagara-grāmān 23.32 280

bhikṣor dharmaḥ śamo 'hiṁsā 18.42 45
bhīṣmo hi devaḥ sahasaḥ sahīyān 23.47 292
bhoktavyam ātmano diṣṭaṁ 23.40 286
bhūmy-ambv-agny-anilākāśā 21.5 152
bhūtendriyāṇi pañcaiva 22.23 219

bhūteṣu ghoṣa-rūpeṇa 21.37 189
bibhṛyāc cen munir vāsaḥ 18.15 16
brahmacaryaṁ tapaḥ śaucaṁ 18.43 46
budho bālaka-vat krīḍet 18.29 32

C

cakṣuṣā bhrāmyamāṇena 22.54 249
cāturmāsyāni ca muner 18.8 10
catvāry eveti tatrāpi 22.21 218
chando-mayo 'mṛta-mayaḥ 21.39 190
chettum arhasi sarva-jña 22.27 223

chidyamānaṁ yamair etaiḥ 20.15 114

D

daivataḥ kālataḥ kiñcid 23.11 265
dakṣiṇā jñāna-sandeśaḥ 19.39 86
dānaṁ sva-dharmo niyamo yamaś ca 23.45 291
daṇḍa-nyāsaḥ paraṁ dānaṁ 19.37 86
dārā duhitaro bhṛtyā 23.8 263

daridro yas tv asantuṣṭaḥ 19.44 90
darśito 'yaṁ mayācāro 21.4 150
daṣṭaṁ janaṁ sampatitaṁ bile 'smin 19.10 65
dehaṁ mano-mātram imaṁ gṛhītvā 23.49 294
deham uddiśya paśu-vad 18.31 34

dehas tv acit puruṣo 'yaṁ suparṇaḥ 23.54 299
deśa-kāla-balābhijño 18.6 8
deśa-kālādi-bhāvānāṁ 21.7 155
devānām oka āsī svar 24.12 322
devarṣi-pitṛ-bhūtāni 23.24 275

dhānā bhūmau pralīyante 24.22 331
dhānya-dārv-asthi-tantūnāṁ 21.12 162
dhārayan śrāvayan śṛṇvan 23.61 309
dharmaḥ sampadyate ṣaḍbhir 21.15 165
dharma iṣṭaṁ dhanaṁ nṛṇāṁ 19.39 86

dharma-kāma-vihīnasya 23.9 264
dharmaṁ jñānaṁ sa vairāgyam 19.25 79
dharmārthaṁ vyavahārārthaṁ 21.3 148
dharmo mad-bhakti-kṛt prokto 19.27 81
dhāryamāṇaṁ mano yarhi 20.19 117

dhātuṣūddhava kalpyanta 21.6 153
dhyāyan mano 'nu viṣayān 22.38 234
dhyāyato viṣayān asya 22.56 250
draviṇe ko 'nuṣajjeta 23.23 274
dravya-deśa-vayaḥ-kālān 20.2 98

dravyasya śuddhy-aśuddhī ca 21.10 159
dravyasya vicikitsārthaṁ 21.3 148
dṛg rūpam ārkam vapur atra randhre 22.31 227
dṛṣṭi-pūtaṁ nyaset pādaṁ 18.16 16
dṛṣṭvā paryabhavan bhadra 23.33 282

duḥkhaṁ kāma-sukhāpekṣā 19.41 90
duḥkhasya hetur yadi devatās tu 23.51 296
duḥkhodarkeṣu kāmeṣu 18.38 42
duḥśīlasya kadaryasya 23.8 263
duruktair bhinnam ātmānaṁ 23.2 259

E

ekādaśatva ātmāsau 22.24 220
eka eva paro hy ātmā 18.32 36
ekaś caren mahīm etāṁ 18.20 21
ekasminn api dṛśyante 22.8 205
ekāsnigdhāḥ kākiṇinā 23.20 271

eṣa dharmo nṛṇāṁ kṣemaḥ 21.18 169
eṣa sāṅkhya-vidhiḥ proktaḥ 24.29 334
eṣa vaikārikaḥ sargo 22.29 224
eṣa vai paramo yogo 20.21 119
eṣo 'ham anyo 'yam iti bhrameṇa 23.49 294

etad eva hi vijñānaṁ 19.15 70
etad vidvān purā mṛtyor 20.14 113
etā manoratha-mayīr 22.48 244
etāṁ sa āsthāya parātma-niṣṭhām 23.57 303
etān praśnān mama brūhi 19.32 83

etat te 'bhihitaṁ sādho 18.48 51
eta uddhava te praśnāḥ 19.45 90
etāvān sarva-vedārthaḥ 21.43 194
etāvattvaṁ hi saṅkhyānāṁ 22.3 199
ete pañcadaśānarthā 23.19 270

ete yamāḥ sa-niyamā 19.35 85
evam anvīkṣamāṇasya 24.28 333
evaṁ buddhi-guṇān paśyann 22.53 248
evaṁ cīrṇena tapasā 18.9 11
evaṁ dharmair manuṣyāṇāṁ 19.24 77

evam etān mayā diṣṭān 20.37 141
evaṁ me puṇḍarīkākṣa 22.27 223
evaṁ puṣpitayā vācā 21.34 185
evaṁ sa bhautikaṁ duḥkhaṁ 23.40 285
evaṁ tvag-ādi śravaṇādi cakṣur 22.32 228

evaṁ vivadatāṁ hetuṁ 22.5 202
evaṁ vyavasitaṁ decid 21.26 178

G

gāyanti pṛthag āyuṣmann 22.3 199
gāyatry uṣṇig anuṣṭup ca 21.41 192
gaty-ukty-utsarga-śilpāni 22.16 214
grahair grahasyaiva vadanti pīḍāṁ 23.53 299
grahā nimittaṁ sukha-duḥkhayoś cet 23.53 299

gāhaṁ śarīraṁ mānuṣyaṁ 19.43 90
gṛhasthasyāpy ṛtau gantuḥ 18.43 46
gṛhiṇo bhūta-rakṣejyā 18.42 45
grīṣme tapyeta pañcāgnīn 18.4 6
guṇa-doṣa-dṛśir doṣo 19.45 90

guṇa-doṣa-bhidā-dṛṣṭim 20.3 99
guṇa-doṣa-bhidā-dṛṣṭir 20.5 101
guṇa-doṣārtha-niyamas 21.16 166
guṇa-doṣau vidhīyete 21.7 155
guṇa-doṣa-vidhānena 20.26 126

guṇa-pravāha etasminn 24.15 324
guṇa-saṅgād upādatte 22.48 244
guṇa-vyatikaraḥ kālaḥ 22.13 212
guṇeṣv asakta-dhīr īśo 19.44 90
guṇesv asaṅgo vairāgyam 19.27 81

H

hiṁsā-vihārā hy ālabdhaiḥ 21.30 181
hiṁsāyāṁ yadi rāgaḥ syād 21.29 181
hṛdaya-jñatvam anvicchan 20.21 119

I

iha cātmopatāpāya 23.15 268
īkṣetāthaikam apy eṣu 19.14 69
indriyāyana-sṛṣṭyedaṁ 22.42 238
iṣṭaṁ dattaṁ hutaṁ japtaṁ 19.23 77
iṣṭvā yathopadeśaṁ māṁ 18.13 14

iṣṭveha devatā yajñair 21.33 185
iti māṁ yaḥ sva-dharmeṇa 18.44 47
iti nānā-prasaṅkhyānaṁ 22.25 221
iti sva-dharma-nirṇikta- 18.46 50
ittham etat purā rājā 19.11 67

ity abhipretya manasā 23.31 280
ity asyā hṛdayaṁ loke 21.42 193
ity eke vihasanty enam 23.39 285

J

janas tu hetuḥ sukha-duḥkhayoś cet 23.50 295
janmādayo 'sya yad amī tava tasya kiṁ syur 19.7 61
janma tva ātmatayā puṁsaḥ 22.40 236
jantor vai kasyacid dhetor 22.39 235
jātāni tair idaṁ jātaṁ 22.21 218

jāta-śraddho mat-kathāsau 20.27 127
jihvāṁ kvacit sandaśati sva-dadbhis 23.50 295
jñānam ātmobhayādhāras 22.19 216
jñānaṁ karma ca bhaktiś ca 20.6 103
jñānaṁ tv anyatamo bhāvaḥ 24.4 315

jñānaṁ viśuddham āpnoti 20.11 110
jñānaṁ viśuddhaṁ vipulaṁ yathaitad 19.8 63
jñāna-niṣṭho virakto vā 18.28 30
jñāna-vairāgya-rahitas 18.40 44
jñāna-vairāgya-vijñāna- 19.13 68

jñāna-vijñāna-sampanno 18.46 50
jñāna-vijñāna-sampanno 19.5 60
jñāna-vijñāna-saṁsiddhāḥ 19.3 57
jñāna-vijñāna-yajñena 19.6 61
jñāninas tva aham eve ṣṭaḥ 19.2 55

jñānī priyatamo 'to me 19.3 57
jñātayo 'tithayas tasya 23.7 263
jñātyo jagṛhuḥ kiñcit 23.11 265
juṣamāṇaś ca tān kāmān 20.28 127
jyotir āpaḥ kṣitir iti 22.14 213

K

ka āḍhyaḥ ko daridro vā 19.32 83
kaḥ paṇḍitaḥ kaś ca mūrkhaḥ 19.31 82
kaḥ śamaḥ ko damaḥ kṛṣṇa 19.28 82
kaḥ svargo narakaḥ kaḥ svit 19.31 82
kālas tu hetuḥ sukha-duḥkhayoś cet 23.55 301

kāla-vāyv-agni-mṛt-toyaiḥ 21.12 162
kālenālakṣya-vegena 22.43 239
kaler durviṣahaḥ krodhas 21.20 172
kālo māyā-maye jīve 24.27 332
kāmā hṛdayyā naśyanti 20.29 130

kāmāyālpīyase yuñjyād 18.10 12
kāminaḥ kṛpaṇā lubdhāḥ 21.27 179
kanda-mūla-phalair vanyair 18.2 4
karmaṇāṁ jāty-aśuddhānām 20.26 126
karmaṇāṁ pariṇāmitvād 19.18 74

karmaṇyo guṇavān kālo 21.9 158
karmāstu hetuḥ sukha-duḥkhayoś cet 23.54 299
karmasv asaṅgamaḥ śaucaṁ 19.38 86
kasmāt saṅkliśyate vidvān 23.26 276
kas tyāgaḥ kiṁ dhanaṁ ceṣṭaṁ 19.29 82

kasyacin māyayā nūnaṁ 23.26 276
kathaṁ yuñjyāt punas teṣu 21.25 176
kathayanti mahat puṇyam 23.4 260
kati tattvāni viśveśa 22.1 199
kā vidyā hrīḥ parā kā śrīḥ 19.30 82

kecit ṣaḍ-viṁśatiṁ prāhur 22.2 199
kecit saptadaśa prāhuḥ 22.2 199
kecit tri-veṇuṁ jagṛhur 23.34 282
kenacid bhikṣuṇā gītaṁ 23.5 261
keśa-roma-nakha-śmaśru- 18.3 5

khagaḥ sva-ketam utsṛjya 20.15 114
khidyato bāṣpa-kaṇṭhasya 23.13 267
kiṁ dānaṁ kiṁ tapaḥ śauryaṁ 19.29 82
kiṁ dhanair dhana-dair vā kiṁ 23.27 276
kiṁ varṇitena bahunā 19.45 90

kiṁ vidhatte kim ācaṣṭe 21.42 19
kṛṣṇa-sāro 'py asauvīra- 21.8 15
kṣemaṁ vindanti mat-sthānaṁ 20.37 14
kṣīṇa-vitta imāṁ vṛttim 23.37 28
kṣipanty eke 'vajānanta 23.37 28

kṣipto 'vamānito 'sadbhiḥ 22.58 25
kṣīyante cāsya karmāṇi 20.30 13
kṣudrān kāmāṁś calaiḥ prāṇair 21.1 14
kurvanty asad-vigraham atra martyair 23.48 29
kuśalā yena sidhyanti 23.25 27
kvacid guṇo 'pi doṣaḥ syād 21.16 16

L

labdha-vīryāḥ sṛjanty aṇḍaṁ 22.18 21
labdhvā janmāmara-prārthyaṁ 23.22 27

labdhvā na hṛṣyed dhṛti-mān 18.33 37
līyate jyotiṣi raso 24.23 331
lobhaḥ sv-alpo 'pi tān hanti 23.16 269
lokāl lokaṁ prayāyy anya 22.37 237
lokān sa-pālān viśvātmā 24.11 321

M

mad-arthe 'rtha-parityāgo 19.23 77
mad-artheṣv aṅga-ceṣṭā ca 19.22 77
mad-bhakta-pūjābhyadhikā 19.21 76
mahān guṇa-visargārthaḥ 24.20 329
mahar janas tapaḥ satyaṁ 24.14 323

mama nābhyām abhūt padmaṁ 24.10 320
mamāṅga māyā guṇa-mayy anekadhā 22.30 226
mamārcopāsanābhir vā 20.24 123
māṁ tapo-mayam ārādhya 18.9 11
māṁ vidhatte 'bhidhatte māṁ 21.43 194

manaḥ karma-mayaṁ nṝṇām 22.37 237
manaḥ paraṁ kāraṇam āmananti 23.42 288
manaḥ sva-liṅgaṁ parigṛhya kāmān 23.44 290
manaso hṛdi tiṣṭheta 24.28 333
manas tyajati daurātmyaṁ 20.23 122

māninām cāti-lubdhānāṁ 21.34 185
mano-gatiṁ na visṛjej 20.20 118
mano guṇām vai sṛjate balīyas 23.43 289
mano-vaśe 'nye hy abhavan sma devā 23.47 292
mantrasya ca parijñānaṁ 21.15 165

mā svasya karma-bījena 22.46 242
martyādīnāṁ ca bhūr lokaḥ 24.12 322
mat-kathā-śravaṇādau vā 20.9 107
mat-smṛtyā cātmanaḥ śaucaṁ 21.14 164
maunānīhānilāyāmā 18.17 17

maunena sādhayaty arthaṁ 23.38 285
mayā kālātmanā dhātrā 24.15 324
māyā-mātram anūdyānte 21.43 194
māyā-mātram idaṁ jñātvā 19.1 54
māyāṁ madīyām udgṛhya 22.4 201

mayānukūlena nabhasvateritaṁ 20.17 115
mayā prakṣobhyamāṇāyāḥ 24.5 316
mayā sañcoditā bhāvāḥ 24.9 320

mayi sañjāyate bhaktiḥ 19.24 77
mayopabṛṁhitaṁ bhūmnā 21.37 189
mayy arpanaṁ ca manasaḥ 19.22 77
mayy āveśitayā yukta 23.60 308
mitrodāsīna-ripavaḥ 23.59 307
mriyate vāmaro bhrāntyā 22.46 242
mṛtyunā grasyamānasya 23.27 277

muhūrtena brahma-lokaṁ 23.30 279
mukta-saṅgaḥ paraṁ buddhvā 20.16 114
mūrkho dehādy-ahaṁ-buddhiḥ 19.42 90
mūtrayanti ca pāpiṣṭhāḥ 23.35 283

na bhavāpyaya-vastūnām 22.49 244
na dharmāya na kāmāya 23.14 268
na dhāved apsu majjeta 18.3 5
nāgner hi tāpo na himasya tat syāt 23.55 301
na hi tasya vikalpākhyā 18.37 40

na hy ātmano 'nyad yadi tan mṛṣā syāt 23.52 297
na hy etat prāyaśo loke 22.36 232
na hy ete yasya santy aṅga 18.17 17
nairapekṣyaṁ paraṁ prāhur 20.35 138
naitad evaṁ yathāttha tvaṁ 22.5 202

naitad vastutayā paśyed 18.26 29
na jñānaṁ na ca vairāgyaṁ 20.31 133
na kenacit kvāpi kathañcanāsya 23.56 302
na kiñcit sādhavo dhīrā 20.34 137
nālaṁ kurvanti tāṁ siddhiṁ 19.4 59

na mayy ekānta-bhaktānaāṁ 20.36 139
na naraḥ svar-gatiṁ kāṅkṣen 20.13 112
na nirviṇṇo nāti-sakto 20.8 106
narakas tama-unnāho 19.43 90
nāśopabhoga āyāsas 23.17 269

natān aviduṣaḥ svārthaṁ 21.25 176
na tathā tapyate viddhaḥ 23.3 260
na te māṁ aṅga jānanti 21.28 180
na tu śrautena paśunā 18.7 9
navaikādaśa pañca trīn 19.14 69

navaikādaśa pañca trīṇy	22.1	199
nāyaṁ jano me sukha-duḥkha-hetur	23.42	288
na yāti svarga-narakau	20.10	109
nemaṁ lokaṁ ca kāṅkṣeta	20.13	112
nirākṛto 'sadbhir api sva-dharmād	23.58	306
nigamenāpavādaś ca	20.5	101
niḥśreyasaṁ kathaṁ nṛṇāṁ	20.3	99
nirvidya naṣṭa-draviṇe gata-klamaḥ	23.58	306
nirviṇṇānāṁ jñāna-yogo	20.7	105
nirviṇṇasya viraktasya	20.23	122
niṣeka-garbha-janmāni	22.47	243
niṣṭhyuto mūtrito vājñair	22.59	252
nityadā hy aṅga bhūtāni	22.43	239
nivṛtte bhārate yuddhe	19.12	68
nodvijeta janād dhīro	18.31	34
nṛ-deham ādyaṁ su-labhaṁ su-durlabhaṁ	20.17	115
nṛtyato gāyataḥ paśyan	22.53	248
nūnaṁ me bhagavāṁs tuṣṭaḥ	23.28	279

O

oṁkārād vyañjita-sparśa-	21.39	191

P

pañca pañcaika-manasā	22.22	219
pañcatvāya viśeṣāya	24.21	330
parasparānupraveśāt	22.7	205
paribhūta imāṁ gāthām	23.41	286
pariniṣṭā ca pūjāyāṁ	19.20	76
parokṣa-vādā ṛṣayaḥ	21.35	186
paśyāmi nānyac charaṇaṁ tavāṅghri-	19.9	64
pātayadbhiḥ sva-dharma-stho	23.41	286
paurvāparyam ato 'mīṣāṁ	22.9	207
paurvāparya-prasaṅkhyānaṁ	22.7	205
phala-śrutiṁ kusumitāṁ	21.26	178
phala-śrutir iyaṁ nṛṇāṁ	21.23	174
pīṭhaṁ caike 'kṣa-sūtraṁ ca	23.34	282
pitṛ-deva-manuṣyāṇāṁ	20.4	100
pradāya ca punas tāni	23.34	282
prakṛtau lakṣyate hy ātmā	22.26	222
prakṛter evam ātmānam	22.51	246
prakṛtiḥ puruṣaś ceti	22.29	224
prakṛtiḥ puruṣaś cobhau	22.26	221
prakṛtir guṇa-sāmyaṁ vai	22.12	210
prakṛtir yasyopādānam	24.19	328
pramāṇeṣv anavasthānād	19.17	73
prāpte śama-dame 'pyeti	22.6	203
pratilomānulomābhyāṁ	24.29	334
prāyeṇārthāḥ kadaryāṇāṁ	23.15	268
proktena bhakti-yogena	20.29	130
puṁsaḥ kiṁ svid balaṁ śrīman	19.30	82
puṁsām upāsitās tāta	19.35	85
punaś ca kathayiṣyāmi	19.19	75
punas tat-pratisaṅkrāme	19.16	72
puṇya-deśa-saric-chaila-	18.24	27
pura-grāma-vrajān sārthān	18.24	26
puruṣaḥ prakṛtir vyaktam	22.14	213
puruṣeśvarayor atra	22.11	209
pūrvasmin vā parasmin vā	22.8	206

R

rajaḥ-sattva-tamo-niṣṭhā	21.32	184
rajas-valaṁ cāsan-niṣṭhaṁ	19.26	80
ṛte tvad-dharma-niratān	22.61	254
rūpaṁ vāyau sa ca sparśe	24.24	331
śabda-brahma su-durbodhaṁ	21.36	18[illegible]
śabdaḥ sparśo raso gandho	22.16	214
śabdo bhūtādim apyeti	24.25	331
sabhājayan bhṛtya-vaco mukundas	23.1	25[illegible]
sa cacāra mahīm etāṁ	23.32	28[illegible]
sa cāhedam aho kaṣṭaṁ	23.14	26[illegible]
sādhakaṁ jñāna-bhaktibhyām	20.12	111
sādhūnāṁ sama-cittānāṁ	20.36	13[illegible]
ṣaḍ ity atrāpi bhūtāni	22.20	21[illegible]
sa eva mad-bhakti-yuto	18.47	5[illegible]
sa evam āśaṁsita uddhavena	23.1	25[illegible]
sa evaṁ draviṇe nāṣṭe	23.12	26[illegible]

śaktyāśaktyātha vā buddhyā 21.11 161
sa-liṅgān āśramāṁs tyaktvā 18.28 31
sa līyate mahān sveṣu 24.26 331
samāhitaṁ yasya manaḥ praśātaṁ 23.46 292
samāna-karmācaraṇaṁ 21.17 168
śamo man-niṣṭhatā buddher 19.36 86
saṁsidhyaty āśv asammohaḥ 18.25 28
saṁskāreṇātha kālena 21.10 159

samuddharainaṁ kṛpayāpavargyair 19.10 65
saṅgāt tatra bhavet kāmaḥ 21.19 170
saṅkhyāne saptadaśake 22.22 219
sāṅkhyena sarva-bhāvānaṁ 20.22 121
saptāgārān asaṅklptāṁs 18.18 19

saptaike mava ṣaṭ kecic 22.2 199
saptaiva dhātava iti 22.19 216
sargādau prakṛtir hy asya 22.17 215
sargaḥ pravartate tāvat 24.20 329
sarva-bhūteṣu mad-bhāvo 18.44 47

sarvaṁ mad-bhakti-yogena 20.33 135
sarvaṁ māyeti tarkeṇa 18.27 29
sarvaṁ nyāyyaṁ yuktimattvād 22.25 221
sarva-yajña-patim māṁ vai 19.6 61
sarve mano-nigraha-lakṣaṇāntāḥ 23.45 291

sarvo 'py ubhaya-saṁyuktaḥ 24.16 325
sarvotpatty-apyayaṁ brahma 18.45 49
sato 'bhivyañjakaḥ kālo 24.19 328
sattvādibhir guṇair dhatte 22.17 215
sattvaṁ jñānaṁ rajaḥ karma 22.13 212

sattvaṁ rajas tama iti 22.12 210
sattva-sampannayā buddhyā 20.20 119
sattva-saṅgād ṛṣīn devān 22.52 247
satya-pūtāṁ vaded vācaṁ 18.16 16
śaucam ācamanaṁ snānaṁ 18.36 39

śaucaṁ japas tapo homaḥ 19.34 85
smaratā dhṛti-yuktena 23.5 261
snāna-dāna-tapo-'vasthā- 21.14 164
so 'haṁ kālāvaśeṣeṇa 23.29 278
so 'sṛjat tapasā yukto 24.11 321

so 'yaṁ dīpo 'rciṣāṁ yadvat 22.45 241
so 'yam pumān iti nṛṇāṁ 22.45 241
śraddhāmṛta-kathāyāṁ me 19.20 76

śreyas-kāmaḥ kṛcchra-gata 22.59 252
śreyas tv anupalabdhe 'rthe 20.4 100
śreyo-vivakṣayā proktaṁ 21.23 174
śrīr guṇā nairapekṣyādyāḥ 19.41 90
śrotraṁ tvag darśanaṁ ghrāṇo 22.15 214
śrutiḥ pratyakṣam atihyam 19.17 73
śrutvā dharmān bahūn paścān 19.12 68

steyaṁ hiṁsānṛtaṁ dambhaḥ 23.18 270
sthity-utpatty-apyayān paśyed 19.15 70
śuddhy-aśuddhī vidhīyete 21.3 148
su-duḥsaham imaṁ manya 22.61 254
sukha-duḥkha-prado nānyaḥ 23.59 307

śuklāni kṛṣṇāny atha lohitāni 23.43 289
śūnyāvasatha ātmāpi 23.7 263
surān ātmānam ātma-sthaṁ 18.41 44
śuṣka-vāda-vivāde na 18.30 33
svabhāva-vijayaḥ śauryaṁ 19.37 86

sva-dharma-stho yajan yajñair 20.10 109
svapna-dṛṣṭāś ca dāśārha 22.55 249
svapnaṁ manorathaṁ cetthaṁ 22.41 237
svapnopamam amuṁ lokam 21.31 183
svargāpavargaṁ mad-dhāma 20.33 135

svargāpavargayor dvāraṁ 23.23 274
svargaś caivāpavargaś ca 19.2 55
svargiṇo 'py etam icchanti 20.12 111
svato na sambhavād anyas 22.10 208
svayaṁ sañcinuyāt sarvam 18.6 8

sve sve 'dhikāre yā niṣṭhā 20.26 126
sve sve 'dhikāre yā niṣṭhā 21.2 146

T

tad anādṛtya ye svārthaṁ 23.22 272
tad-anya-kalpanāpārthā 22.11 209
tad-avadhyāna-visrasta- 23.10 265
tāḍitaḥ sanniruddho vā 22.58 252
tadvat ṣoḍaśa-saṅkhyāne 22.23 219

taijasād devatā āsann 24.8 319
tair yukta ātma-sambhūtaiḥ 22.20 217
tamasā bhūta-tiryaktvaṁ 22.52 247
tamasā grasyate puṁsaś 21.20 172
taṁ babandhur nirurudhur 23.39 285

taṁ durjayaṁ śatrum asahya-vegam 23.48 293
tamo rajaḥ sattvam iti 24.5 316
taṁ vai pravayasaṁ bhikṣum 23.33 281
tān ahaṁ te 'bhidhāsyāmi 19.13 68
tan ahaṁ varṇayiṣyāmi 23.4 260

tan mamākhyāhi govinda 22.36 232
tan-mātrendriya-manasāṁ 24.7 318
tan māyā-phala-ṛupeṇa 24.3 314
tapas tīrthaṁ japo dānaṁ 19.4 59
tāpa-trayeṇābhihatasya ghore 19.9 64

tarjayanty apare vāgbhiḥ 23.36 283
taror bīja-vipākābhyāṁ 22.50 245
taror vilakṣaṇo dṛṣṭā 22.50 245
tasmād anartham arthākhyaṁ 23.19 270
tasmād uddhava mā bhuṅkṣva 22.57 251

tasmāj jñānena sahitaṁ 19.5 60
tasmān mad-bhakti-yuktasya 20.31 133
tasmān nirāśiṣo bhaktir 20.35 138
tasmān niyamya ṣaḍ-vargaṁ 18.23 26
tasmāt sarvātmanā tāta 23.60 308

tasminn ahaṁ samabhavam 24.10 320
tasyaivaṁ dhyāyato dīrghaṁ 23.13 267
tasyaivaṁ yakṣa-vittasya 23.9 264
tasyānta iha bhūyāsma 21.33 185
tathaiva sarva-bhūtānāṁ 22.44 240

tathā vāsas tathā śayyāṁ 18.35 38
tato bhajeta māṁ prītaḥ 20.28 127
tato 'sya svārtha-vibhraṁśo 21.21 172
tato vikurvato jāto 24.6 317
tatra māma anumoderan 23.30 279

tatra pūrvam ivātmānam 22.41 237
tattvaṁ vimṛśyate tena 18.34 37
tattvena sparśa-sammūḍhaḥ 22.51 246
tāvat karmāṇi kurvīta 20.9 107
tāvat paricared bhaktaḥ 18.39 43

tayā virahitaḥ sādho 21.21 172
tayor ekataro hy arthaḥ 24.4 315
tebhyaḥ samabhavat sūtraṁ 24.6 317
te me matam avijñāya 21.29 181
teṣv anirviṇṇa-cittānāṁ 20.7 105

te 'vyakte sampralīyante 24.26 331
tīrthāṭanaṁ parārthehā 19.34 85
titikṣā duḥkha-sammarṣo 19.36 86
tri-lokyāṁ gatayaḥ sarvāḥ 24.13 323
triṣṭub jagaty aticchando 21.41 192

tvam eva hy ātma-māyāyā 22.28 223
tvattaḥ parāvṛtta-dhiyaḥ 22.35 232
tvatto jñānaṁ hi jīvānāṁ 22.28 223
tvayy uddhavāśrayati yas tri-vidho vikāro 19.7 61
tyajanty āśu spṛdho ghnanti 23.21 272

tyaktaṁ na daṇḍa-pātrābhyām 18.15 16

U

uccāvacān yathā dehān 22.35 232
udyat sīdat karma-tantraṁ 22.38 234
uktha-śastrā hy asu-tṛpo 21.28 180
ulūkhalāśma-kuṭṭo vā 18.5 7
unmucya hṛdaya-granthīn 23.31 280

upāsata indra-mukhyān 21.32 184
upekṣitaś ca sva-janaiś 23.12 266
utpathaś citta-vikṣepaḥ 19.42 90
utpattyaiva hi kāmeṣu 21.24 175

V

vaded unmatta-vad vidvān 18.29 32
vaikārikas taijasaś ca 24.7 318
vaikārikas tri-vidho 'dhyātmam ekam 22.30 226
vāk-pāṇy-upastha-pāyv-aṅghriḥ 22.15 214
vana eva vasec chāntas 18.1 4

vanaṁ vivikṣuḥ putreṣu 18.1 4
vānaprasthāśrama-padeṣv 18.25 27
vāñchanty api mayā dattaṁ 20.34 137
vāṅ-mano-'gocaraṁ satyaṁ 24.3 314
vanyaiś caru-puroḍāśair 18.7 9

varṇāśramavatāṁ dharma 18.47 50
varṇāśrama-vikalpaṁ ca 20.2 98
vārtā-vṛttiḥ kadaryas tu 23.6 262
vasīta valkalaṁ vāsas 18.2 4
vayo-madhyaṁ jarā mṛtyur 22.47 243

vedā brahmātma-viṣayās	21.35	186
veda duḥkhātmakān kāmān	20.27	127
veda-vāda-rato na syān	18.30	33
vedena nāma-rūpāṇi	21.6	153
vibhajya pāvitaṁ śeṣaṁ	18.19	21
vicitra-bhāṣā-vitatāṁ	21.40	191
vidhiś ca pratiṣedhaś ca	20.1	99
viduṣām api viśvātman	22.61	254
vidyātmani bhidā-bādho	19.40	90
vighnaṁ kurvanty ayaṁ hy asmān	18.14	15
vikāro vyavahārātho	24.17	326
viparyayas tu doṣaḥ syād	21.2	146
vipaścin naśvaraṁ paśyed	19.18	74
viprasya vai sannyasato	18.14	15
virāgo jāyate samyaṅ	18.12	13
viraktaḥ kṣudra-kāmebhyo	18.23	26
virāṇ mayāsādyamāno	24.21	33
viṣayābhiniveśena	21.22	173
viṣayābhiniveśena	22.39	235
viṣaya-svīkṛtiṁ prāhur	22.40	236
viṣayeṣu guṇādhyāsāt	21.19	170
vivikta-kṣema-śaraṇo	18.21	24
vṛkṣa-jīcikayā jīvan	21.22	173
vyaktādayo vikurvāṇā	22.18	216
vyarthayārthehayā vittaṁ	23.25	275
vyartho 'pi naivoparameta puṁsāṁ	22.34	230

Y

yadā karma-vipākeṣu	18.12	13
yad aṅgam aṅgena nihanyate kvacit	23.51	296
yadārambheṣu nirviṇṇo	20.18	117
yad arpitaṁ tad vikalpe	19.26	80
yadāsau niyame 'kalpo	18.11	12
yadātmany arpitaṁ cittaṁ	19.25	79
yadāviveka-nipuṇā	24.2	313
yad etad ātmani jagan	18.27	29
yadi kuryāt pramādena	20.25	124
yadṛcchayā mat-kathādau	20.8	106
yadṛcchayopapannānnam	18.35	38
yad upādāya pūrvas tu	24.18	327
yad vijñāya pumān sadyo	24.1	312
ya etāṁ bhikṣuṇā gītāṁ	23.61	309
ya etān mat-patho hitvā	21.1	145
yajante devatā yajñaiḥ	21.30	182
yamādibhir yoga-pathair	20.24	123
yamaḥ kati-vidhaḥ prokto	19.28	82
yāsāṁ vyatikarād āsīd	22.6	203
yaśo yaśavināṁ śuddhaṁ	23.16	269
yas tu yasyādir antaś ca	24.17	326
yas tv asaṁyata-ṣaḍ-vargaḥ	18.40	44
yas tv etat kṛcchrataś cīrṇaṁ	18.10	12
yata-vācaṁ vācayanti	23.36	283
yathāhamaḥ saṁsṛti-rūpiṇaḥ syād	23.56	302
yathaivam anubudhyeyaṁ	22.60	253
yathā manoratha-dhiyo	22.55	249
yathāmbhasā pracalatā	22.54	249
yathāriciṣāṁ srotasāṁ ca	22.44	240
yathā sva-dharma-saṁyukto	18.48	51
yathā tudanti marma-sthā	23.3	260
yathā viviktaṁ yad-vaktraṁ	22.9	207
yathendur uda-pātreṣu	18.32	36
yathorṇanābhir hṛdayād	21.38	190
yat karmabhir yat tapasā	20.32	135
yato nivartate karma	21.9	158
yato yato nivarteta	21.18	169
yāvad brahma vijānīyān	18.39	43
yena nīto daśām etāṁ	23.28	277
yogās trayo mayā proktā	20.6	103
yogasya tapasaś caiva	24.14	323
yogena dāna-dharmeṇa	20.32	135
yogenaiva dahed aṁho	20.25	124
yonir vaikārike saumya	24.25	331
yo 'sau guṇa-kṣobha-kṛto vikāraḥ	22.33	229
yo vidyā-śruta-sampanna	19.1	53
yuktaṁ ca santi sarvatra	22.4	201

General Index

Numerals in boldface type indicate references to translations of the verses of *Śrīmad-Bhāgavatam.*

A

Abortion, 316
Absolute Truth. *See:* Supreme Lord; Spiritual world
Ācārya(s). See: Spiritual master
Acintya-bhedābheda-tattva
quoted, 210
Ādhāra-cakra, 188
Adhibhūta defined, 227
Adhidaiva defined, 227
Adhyātma defined, 227
Administrators, universal. *See:* Demigods
Advancement, spiritual, stages of, 146–47, 196
Affection for body as self-defeating, 176
Age
of body, nine stages of, **243**
of responsibility, 14 years, 167
Ages of time. *See:* Satya-yuga; Tretā-yuga; Dvāpara-yuga; Kali-yuga
Agnihotra, **10**
Ahaṅkāra-vimūḍhātmā
verse quoted, 211
Ājñā-cchedi mama dveṣi
verse quoted, 108
Akāmaḥ sarva-kāmo vā
quoted, 136, 138
Alcohol, drinking of, relative sinfulness of, 168
Allegory. *See:* Analogies
Alms. *See:* Begging
Amāninā māna-dena
verse quoted, 35
Ambaṣṭhas defined, 98
America, false worshipers in, 183
Anāhata-cakra, 189

Analogies
bellows & dull person, **174**
bird in tree & soul in body, **114**
boat & human body, **116**
businessmen & demigods, 101
candles, waves and fruits & body transformations, **240, 241**-42
digestive fire & *bhakti-yoga,* 132
father's pride & Kṛṣṇa's happiness, 59
fiber of lotus & *oṁkāra,* **190**
fire & fruitive action, 132
firewood & body, **242,** 243
foolish businessmen & false worshipers, **183,** 184
greed & white leprosy, 269
horse & mind, **120,** 121
itching sensation & illusory desires, 56, 57
Lord in heart & moon's reflection, **36**
medicine & Viṣṇu worship, 175, 177
mud in pot & elements' interaction, 206
parents' forgiveness & Lord's mercy, 140–41
reflection on water & sense gratification, **249**
river & nature's modes, **325**
rope as snake & body as self, 62
safe driver & devotee, 31
sannyāsī's heart & flower garden, 14–15
snake's hole & material world, 66
spider's web & Vedic sound, **191-92**
sun & knowledge, **334**
sun & Kṛṣṇa, 131
sun & Lord, 131, 154, **227**
sun's rays & *bhakti,* 139
taming horse & mind control, **120,** 121

Ananta-pāra defined, 188
Anāvṛtti-śabdāt
quoted, 187
Anger
cause of, 171
heroes conquer, 88
misdirected, **295-302**
as unjustifiable, 36
Animal killing. *See:* Animal sacrifices; Killing of animals
Animals
irresponsible, 167
types of, 248
Animal sacrifices condemned for *vānaprastha,* **9**
Annihilation of universe, **332-33**
Antar bahir yadi
verse quoted, 7
Antelope in holy places, **157**
Ānukūlyena kṛṣṇānu
verse quoted, 162
Anuṣṭup, **192**
Anyābhilāṣitā-śūnyaṁ
verse quoted, 162
Apavitraḥ paviyto vā
verse quoted, 165
Api cet su-durācāro
quoted, 125, 140
Ārādhito yadi haris
verse quoted, 7
Argument amongst philosophers, **200-7**
Asaṅkḷptān defined, 20
Association with devotees, 22-23, 107
Asthitaḥ sa hi yuktātmā
quoted, 58
Atheistic literature, devotee avoids, 34
Atheists
attack devotees, 287
See also: Demons; Impersonalists
Aticchanda, **192**
Atijagatī, **192**
Ativirāṭ, **192**
Atonement for sinful activities, 125
Attachment, material
to body, 176, 236-37
as disease of soul, 56
Attachment, material (*continued*)
two extremes of, 107
See also: Desires, material; False ego; Identification with body; Illusion; Lust; Sense gratification
Atyaṣṭi, 192
Austerity
artificial, 151
defined, 87, 88
extremes of, rejected, 118, 120
promotion to heaven via, 323
of *vānaprastha,* **6,** 11
See also: Penance; Renunciation
Authority, supreme, 84
Author quoted on self, 28
Avantī *Brāhmaṇa,* story of, **261-309**
Avidhi-pūrvakam
defined, 184

B

Bamboo rods of *sannyāsī,* 18
Beauty, leprosy destroys, **269**
Begging
humbling process, 28
types of, **19**-20
Bhagavad-gītā, quotations from
on attaining Lord's abode, 324
on *bhakti* as easy, 150
on birth and death, 121-22
on determination, 287
on devotee's falldown, 140
on falldown, 125
on *karma,* 108
on Lord's influence, 224
on Lord's obscurity, 187
on Lord's splendor, 194
on Lord within, 120
on peity, 170
on pure devotion, 58
on religion, 150
on surrender, 103-4
on three modes, 211
on *Vedas,* 102, 180
Bhakti-rasāmṛta-sindhu, quoted on devotional service, 162

Caitanya Mahāprabhu (*continued*)
  quoted
    on chanting, 35
    on oneness and difference, 210
  special mercy of, **322**
Caste system. *See: Varṇāśrama-dharma*
Causal water, 320
Cause and effect explained, **72**
Cause of all causes, **70,** 71
Celibacy
  of householder, 47
  promotion to heaven via, 324
  See also: Brahmacārī; Sannyāsa; Sannyāsī
Chanting the holy names of the Lord
  humility in, 35
  purpose of, 166
  to remember Lord, 165
  sublime process, 150–51
  See also: Hare Kṛṣṇa *mantra*
Charity
  defined, **87,** 88
  purpose of, **291**
  See also: Dependence on others
Childbirth, impure period after, 161
Children
  innocent to age 14, 167
  purpose of begetting, **46**
Cheaters, 45
Citraketu, 136
Cleanliness defined, **87**
Clothing for renunciates, 5
Collecting (too much), 8
Conditioned soul. *See:* Living entities; Soul, conditioned
Conditioning as very strong, **254**
Consciousness
  pure, spiritual. *See:* Kṛṣṇa consciousness
  varieties of, 226
Creation of material world
  as chain reaction, 205, 206
  explained, **215-16, 315-30**
  theories of, described, **217-21**
  See also: Elements; Material world
Criticism of neophyte devotees, 148

D

Dadāmi buddhi-yogaṁ taṁ
  quoted, 120
Dadāti prahgṛhṇāti
  quoted, 22
Daily duties, **85-86**
Daṇḍa
  defined, 281
  purpose of, 18
Dārśa, **10**
Daydream defined, 237
Death
  correct perception of, **114, 115**
  misusing life as, **173, 174**
  process of, described, 234–47
  of soul, **116**
  subtle approach of, 240, **241**
  vārnaprastha accepts, 13
  See also: Annihilation; Transmigration
Deer (antelopes) in holy places, **157**
Deity worship by householders, 46
Demigods
  administer pleasure and pain, 297
  compared to businessman, 101
  as devotees, 179
  humans superior to, **273**
  origins and identities of, **319**
  sannyāsīs hindered by, **15**
  Vedas essential to, **100,** 101
  worship to, 48, **186**
Demons, insults by, **253, 254**
Dependence
  on Lord, 8
  on others, condemned, 8–9
Depression to be avoided in Kṛṣṇa consciousness, 129
Descent of soul. *See:* Falldown
Designations, material, as illusory, **62**
Desire
  as cause of creation, **316**
  of devotees, Lord fulfills, **135-36**
  spiritual vs. material, 137–38
  unfulfilled, **105,** 106

Desires, material
compared to itching sensation, 56, 57
Kṛṣṇa in heart destroys, 131
sannyāsī in danger of, 14–15
See also: Attachment, material
Desire, spiritual, Lord fulfills, **135,** 136, 138
Destiny (providence), types of, **266**
Detachment
in extreme situations, **253, 254**
via frustration, **117, 123**
via *karma-yoga,* 106
vs. positive loving service, 129-30
realization causes, 71
See also: Liberation; Renunciation
Determination to bear insults, **282-87**
Devarṣi-bhūtāpta-nṛṇāṁ pitṝṇāṁ
verse quoted, 109
Devotees of the Supreme Lord (Vaiṣṇavas)
accidental falldown of, 140–41
association with, 22–23, 107
avoid atheistic literature, 34
beyond radical penances, 6
beyond useless debating, 231
compared to safe driver, 31
criticism of, 148
depend on Kṛṣṇa, 151
desire only one thing, **137**
desires of, Lord fulfills, **135**-36
determination of, 128–30
eating too little hinders, 38
exchanges between, 22–23
free from debt, 8–9
free from obligation, 109
humility of, 35
Kṛṣṇa in heart of, 131
levels of advancement of, 196
mercy of, 27
outwit stubborn mind, **120,** 121
personal existence for, 107
preaching of, 27
real vs. imposters, 140
repent past sinful life, 128–29
see Kṛṣṇa everywhere, **41**
tolerate extremes, **253, 254**
Devotees (*continued*)
tolerate insults, 262
value of, 22–23
See also: Paramahaṁsa; Pure devotees; Transcendentalists
Devotional service to the Supreme Lord (*bhakti-yoga*)
anyone can perform, 139
beyond Vedic injunctions, **107-8,** 109
candidate for, described, 107
compared to digestive fire, 132
compared to sun rays, 139
defined, 162
depression in, 128–30
vs. detachment, 129–30
determination for, 128–29
as final stage, 196
goal of *Varṇāśrama* system, 48
highest form of, 43
methods of, described, **78**
mixed, **75,** 76, 111
motivated, vs. pure devotional service, 137, 139, 148
one of three paths, **103,** 104
power of, **133,** 136, 138–39
pure
vs. motivated, 137, 139, 148
vs. regulative, **31,** 32, 40
See also: Paramahaṁsa; Pure devotees
relaxation within, 118, 120
spontaneous vs. regulative, **31,** 32, 40
sublime process, 150–51
tri-daṇḍa indicates, 305
as ultimate goal, **63,** 64
untruths detrimental to, 17
as worthwhile activity, 17
Dhṛtyā yayā dhārayate
verse quoted, 287
Diet. *See:* Food
Dīkṣā defined, 168
Disciple(s)
neophyte and advanced, 43
qualifications for accepting, 306

Discipline
defined, 87, 88
principles of, **85**
of *sannyāsī,* 18
See also: Austerity; Regulative principles; Renunciation
Discrimination in life, 149
Disease of the soul, 56
Distress
via bodily identification, 239
from material hankering, **66**-67
mind as sole cause of, **288**
real cause of, **295-303,** 308
See also: Frustration; Misery; Pain; Suffering
Dovetailing property in Lord's service, 274
Dreaming, bodily identification as, 176, **236-37,** 251
Drugs, 5
Duality
destroys self-realization, **251**
in everyday dealings, 149
formula for conquering, **309**
mind creates, 295
of mundane knowledge, 74
removed by spiritual knowledge, **334**
seeing good & bad as, **92, 97**
See also: False ego; Illusion
Duty
of four *āśramas,* **45-46**
occupational, 154
types of, 85
Duty, prescribed
as offering to Kṛṣṇa, 170
purpose of, **109, 110**
Duties, religious, as troublesome, 150

E

Earth element. *See:* Elements, material
Earth planet
one of the three systems, **322**
special opportunity on, **111, 112**
Ekadaṇḍi-sannyāsī, 304–5
Elements, material
described, **69**-70, **152, 200-22**
evolution of, **319**
interaction of, compared to mud in pot, 206
Enemies, mind creates, **293,** 296
Energies of the Supreme Lord, 222
Enjoyment
difficult to renounce, 128–29
as impediment, **111,** 112
real platform of, 213
See also: Happiness; Pleasure; Sense gratification
Envy
falldown caused by, 23
as unjustifiable, 36
Equality described, 88, 294
Etān vegān yo viṣaheta dhīraḥ
verse quoted, 287, 306
Eternality of the soul, **242,** 243
Evolution
of material world, 316–28
See also: Body, human
Eyesight, cause of, **227**

F

Faith, power of, 130
Falldown
accidental, 140–41
atonement for, 126–27
deviation causes, 134
of living entity, **66**
Lord forgives, 140–41
relativity of, 168
transcendence of, 125
False ego
defined, **318**
as knot in heart, 132
origin of, **230**
as ultimate sufferer and enjoyer, 300–1, 302
False identification, 241, 244, **246, 249,** 294
Fame, greed destroys, **269**

Family
  affection for, 176
  devotee's obligation to, 109
  money can destroy, **272**
  perfection in, 106
  real and false, 296
  See also: Gṛhastha
Family planning, **98-99**
Fate. *See: Karma;* Providence
Faultfinding, 88, 89, 148
Fear
  formula to conquer, **302-3**
  as passing of time, **115**
Fire sacrifices, 180
Food
  detachment from, 37
  endeavoring for, 38, 39
  obtained by *sannyāsī,* 19
  prasādam, spiritual food, 118
  purity of, 160
  in renounced order, 5, 7, 8
  in retirement, **7**
  rules for eating, 21
  sage accepts, 39
  Vedas prescribe, 156
Food distribution in Vedic system, **19**-20
Forefathers
  Vedas essential to, **100**
  worship of, 51
Forgetfulness of previous lifetimes, 235–38
Free will, **39,** 40
Friends, mind creates, **293,** 296
Frustration
  cause of, 177
  leads to detachment, **117, 123**
  leads to *jñāna-yoga,* **105,** 106, 107
  men and demigods experience, 100–1
  See also: Distress; Misery; Pain; Suffering

G

Gadādhara Paṇḍita, 305
Gambling, 56
Garuḍa Purāṇa, quoted on purification, 165
Gauḍīya Vaiṣṇava-sampradāya, 306
Gāyatrī, **192**
Ghosts, **322**
Goal of life, **114-16,** 175
Godhead. *See:* Supreme Lord; Kṛṣṇa; Spiritual world
Godhead, returning to
  eligibility for, 156
  via Lord's mercy, 66–67
  See also: Liberation
Good and bad, discriminating between, 149–50
Good deeds. *See:* Pious activities
Goodness, mode of
  oneness perceived in, **209,** 210
  two kinds of, 79, 80
Goodness, spiritual mode of, vision in, 210
Gopāla Baṭṭa Vasu, 306
Gosvāmī
  defined, 306
  See also: Sannyāsī
Grains, **7**
Greed
  heros conquer, 88
  poisonous effect of, 269
  See also: Lust; Wealth
Gṛhasthas. See: Householders
Guru
  qualifications for, 287
  See also: Spiritual master
Gurus (bogus)
  artificially justify immoral acts, 140
  foolish followers of, 45

H

Habits, bad, 128–29
Hallucinogens, 5
Happiness
  via bodily identification, 239
  material
    hopeless pursuit of, **117**
    as insignificant, **66**
    See also: Enjoyment; Sense gratification

Happiness (*continued*)
misers cannot have, **268**
real cause of, 56, **92, 295-303,** 308
See also: Bliss; Pleasure
Hare Kṛṣṇa *mantra* (*Mahā-mantra*)
purpose of, 166, 173
surpasses Vedic sacrifices, 10
See also: Chanting the holy names of the Lord
Health to be maintained, **38**
Hearing and chanting stressed, 11
Heart
cleansing of, **131**
oṁkāra within, **190**
Heaven & hell, devotees bypass, **109-10**
Heavenly planets
dreamlike, **183**
elevation to, 12
as impediment, **111, 112**
indirect purpose of, 175
Maharloka (Ṛṣiloka), 11, 12, **323,** 324
one of three planetary systems, **322**
temporary, **74,** 75
Vedas direct one to, 177-79
See also: Brahmaloka
Hell
envious persons enroute to, 287
as impediment, **11, 112**
lower modes lead to, 185
Herbs, intoxicating, 5
Hero, qualification for, 87, **293**
Hippies contrasted to saintly beggars, 28
Hlādinī, defined, 211
Holy names of the Lord
as ultimate Vedic sound, 189
See also: Chanting; Hare Kṛṣṇa *mantra*
Holy places, deer at, 157
Homestead
proper and improper, 157-58
See also: Family; Householders
Hoarding condemned, 8
Honesty, 17
Horseradish, 5
Householder life, renunciation of. *See: Vānaprastha, Sannyāsa*
Householders (*Gṛhasthas*)
alms given by, 19
duty of, **45-46**
See also: Family
Human form of life
compared to boat, **116**
liberation facilitated by, 112, **116**
misuse of, 167
purpose of, **173, 174**
special opportunity in, **111, 112-116**
superior status of, **273**
See also: Body, material; Living entities; Society, human; Soul
Human society. *See:* Society, human
Humility
via begging, 28
of *sannyāsī,* 35
Hygiene in *Vānaprastha-āśrama,* **6**

I

Identification with body
as dreaming, 236-37, **249, 250,** 251
See also: False ego; Illusion
Illicit sex, 56
See also: Sex life
Illusion
birth and death as, **242,** 243
devotee may appear under, 41
function of, **41**
material body as, 30, 62
material hankering as, 66-67
material world not, 231
sannyāsī careful of, 15
of sex attraction, 132
six forms of, **44**
See also: False ego
Illusory energy defined, 23
Impersonalism
contaminates heart, 17
degrades society, 153
denies personal existence, 107
increases illusion, 58-59
vs. Kṛṣṇa consciousness, 65

Impersonalism (*continued*)
  moroseness causes, 129–30
  See also: Merging; Oneness
Impersonalists
  plight of, 209
  See also: Atheists
Insane person, *Paramahaṁsa* imitates, 32
Insects, killing of, **17**
Insults
  effect of, 259
  spiritualists must endure, **253, 254**
Intelligence
  self-control requires, **119,** 120
  soul captivated by, **248,** 249
  Vedic phase of, 189
Intoxicants, sages avoid, 5
Intoxication
  compared to hopeless scratching, 56
  relative sinfulness of, 168
Īśvaraḥ paramaḥ kṛṣṇaḥ
  quoted, 304
Itching disease of the soul, 56

J

Jagad-guru defined, 93
Jagatī, **192**
Janaloka, **323,** 324
Janayaty āśu vairāgyaṁ
  verse quoted, 108
Jarayaty āśu yā
  quoted, 132
Jātasya hi dhruvo mṛtyur
  quoted, 121
Jayadeva, 157
Jīva-daṇḍa, 304, 305
Jñāna
  defined, 58
  as preliminary knowledge, 71
  secondary to devotion, 133–34
Jñāna-kāṇḍa, 193, 195
Jñāna-yoga (philosophical speculation)
  described, 147
  ends in confusion, 151
Jñāna-yoga (*continued*)
  frustrated persons adopt, 105, 106, 107
  one of three paths, 104
Jñānī acts with free will, 40

K

Kali-yuga
  fallen people of, 139
  sannyāsa accepted early in, 4
Kapila, Lord, quoted on *bhakti's* effect, 132
Karaṇa defined, 98
Karma
  compared to fire, 132
  defined, 243
  harsh insults as, **261,** 262
  new body caused by, **235**
  See also: Sinful reactions; Transmigration
Karma-kāṇḍa, 193, 195
Karma-mīmāṁsā philosophy, 178
Karma-yoga
  described, 146–47
  detachment via, 106
  fruitive persons adopt, **105,** 106, 107
  uncertainty of, 104–5
  See also: Work
Khaṭvāṅga Mahārāja, story of, **279**
Kikaṭa (Bihar), 157
Killing of animals
  saints avoid, 5, **17**
  in *Vedas,* 182
Killing of unborn, 316
Knowledge
  actual, **81**
  compared to sun, **334**
  as deviation, 130
  four methods of acquiring, **73**
  Lord gives and takes away, 224
  material
    controversial systems of, **200-7**
    necessity of, 122

Knowledge (*continued*)
philosophical
ultimate perfection of, **54**-57
See also: Jñāna
of self
via spiritual master, 42
See also: Self-realization
Kṛṣṇa, Lord (Supreme Personality of Godhead)
compared to proud father, 59
compared to sun, 131
encourages *sannyāsīs,* 15
enthroned in one's heart, 131
faith in, 129-30
source of pleasure, 297
three features of, 49
true object of worship, 23
Kṛṣṇa consciousness
actions which hinder, **33-34**
avoiding weeds in, 15
beyond mundane good & bad, 149-50, 167-68
defined, 151-52
essence of human life, 51
foremost enemy of, 171
scientific understanding via, 206
seriousness of, 127
Kṛṣṇa consciousness movement
preachers of, 27
preaching mission of, 43
Kṛta-yuga, **314**
Kurvanti caiṣāṁ muhur
verse quoted, 203
Kuṭī defined, 20

L

Land, suitability of, 158
Laziness
as abominable, 20
See also: Dependence
Leaders, spiritual. *See: Guru;* Spiritual master
Leprosy destroys beauty, **269**
Liberation (*mukti*)
bhakti awards, 132-33
complete vs. incomplete, 11
Liberation (*continued*)
devotees reject, **137**
devotional service includes, 111
guaranteed for devotees, 41
human body facilitates, 112, **116**
in one moment, **279**
three paths of, **103,** 104
types of, 49
via Vedic knowledge, **99, 100,** 101
See also: Godhead, returning to; Merging; Oneness; Self-realization
Life. *See:* Consciousness; Living entity; Soul
Life air (*prāṇa*) as Vedic sound, 188
Life, goal of. *See:* Goal of life
Light from demigods, **227**
Literature, atheistic, 34
Living entities
compared to bird in tree, **114**
equality of, 36, 294
as potency of Lord, **315**
as servants, 213
See also: Body, material; Human form of life, Soul
Locana dāsa Ṭhākura quoted on Lord Caitanya, 151
Logic
to acquire knowledge, **73**
within controversy, 207
of skeptic, irrelevant, 34
Loss of wealth, story about, **261-309**
Love, material, money destroys, **272**
Lust
heroes conquer, 88
result of, **171**

M

Mādhava Upādhyāya, 305
Mādhukara defined, 20
Madhvācārya, 157, 305
Madhyamā defined, 189
Mahā-mantra. See: Hare Kṛṣṇa *mantra*
Mahā-māyā defined, 202
Mahāprabhura bhakta-gaṇera
verse quoted, 169

Mahā-prasādam, 118
Maharloka, 11, 12, **323,** 324
Mahat defined, 64
Mahat-tattva, **212-13, 317, 329**
Mahā-Viṣṇu, **328,** 329
Mama vartmānuvartante
quoted, 104
Maṇipūraka-cakra, 189
Mantra
described, 166
See also: Chanting; Hare Kṛṣṇa *mantra*
Manu-saṁhitā quoted on sage's diet, 5
Marriage
mixed castes in, 98
not to be renounced, 148
Vedic, **98,** 99
See also: Family; Householders
Material body. *See:* Body, material
Material desires. *See:* Desires, material; Lust; sense gratification
Materialists
dreamlike condition of, 176
dullness of, **173, 174**
imitate devotees sometimes, 140
motivated religionists as, 151
philosophy of, 210
tricked into submission, 177
varṇāśrama system for, 154
See also: Atheists; Material life
Material life
compared to snake's hole, **66**
insulation from, 23
See also: Sense gratification
Material world
analytical study of, **121,** 122, 147, 148
annihilation of, **332-33**
categories within, 212
as causes and effects, 72
compared to mighty river, **325**
compared to snake's hole, 66
composition of, **69**-70
constantly shifting, 24
dead nature of, 225
discriminating right and wrong in, 149
elements of. *See:* Elements
engaged in Lord's service, 274
fear of, 303
Material world (*continued*)
as Lord's property, 252
mind reflects image of, 290
purpose of, 102
as real, 231, **328**
substance and forms of, **326**
temporary nature of, **73, 74,** 75, **115, 326, 327**
two potencies in, **315**
See also: Creation; Universe, material
Mattaḥ smṛtir jñānam
quoted, 224
Maturity, age of, 167
Maya defined, 330
Māyā. *See:* Illusion
Māyāvādīs
accept *eka-daṇḍa*, 304–5
See also: Atheists; Impersonalists
Meat eating
compared to hopeless scratching, 56
See also: Killing of animals
Medhyaiḥ defined, 5
Medicine, intoxicating, prohibited, 5
Memory loss, cause of, **234**
Mental equilibrium defined, **87,** 88
Mercy
of devotees, 27
See also: Supreme Lord, mercy of
Merging
during annihilation, **332-33**
bliss of, 65
See also: Impersonalism
Mind
body created by, **294**
compared to horse, **120,** 121
controlling, method of, **118**-21, 123
as mirror, **290**
pleasure and pain caused by, 295
power of, **293**
sannyāsī controls, 18
shape of, cause of, **233-34,** 235
as sole cause of misery, **288**
stubborness of, 289
subduing of, **291**
Vedic phase of, 189
Mirror, mind as, **290**
Miser, story of, **261-309**

Misery
cruel nature causes, 174
false identification causes, **286**
on heavenly planets, **74**, 75
passion mode causes, **80**, 81
sense gratification causes, 128–29
See also: Depression; Frustration; Suffering
Modes of nature
body types created by, **247**
compared to river, **325**
described, 211–12
destiny affected by, 185
generate false ego, **230**
mind actuates, **289**
origin of, **316**
in process of creation, 319
rotation within, 165
Money
desire for, 289
See also: Wealth
Moon's reflection compared to Lord in heart, **36**
Morality, two types of, 102–3
Mūrdhāvasikta defined, 98
Mushrooms, 5
Mystic *yoga*
destinations of, **323**
as highest opulence, **81**
See also: Yoga

N

Na bhajanty avajānanti
quoted, 47
Nāga snakes, **323**
Nāhaṁ prakāśaḥ sarvasya
quoted, 187
Nature, material. *See:* Material world; Modes of nature; Universe, material
Nondevotees
association of, rejected, 23
See also: Atheists; Demons; Impersonalists; Materialists
Nonexistence, self-neglect as, 173
Nonviolence
in devotees, 35
as discipline, **85**
in saintly persons, 5, **17**

O

Occupational duties. *See:* Duty; *Varṇāśrama-dharma*
Offenses
tolerance of, **253, 254**
See also: Faultfinding
Old age
in *vānaprastha-āśrama,* 13
See also: Sannyāsa; Vānaprastha
Oṁ (Oṁkāra)
compared to fiber of lotus, **190**
Vedas expand from, **191**
within all beings, **190**
Oneness
of Lord and *jīva* soul, 210
spiritual paths in, **103**, 104
See also: Impersonalism; Merging

P

Pain
cause of, 117, **295**
See also: Frustration; Misery; Suffering
Pañcarātra, quoted on penances, 6–7
Paramahaṁsa
conceals exalted position, **32, 33,** 34
described, 31, 32
rules for, 34
status of, 40
See also: Saints; *Sannyāsī*
Parama-karuṇa, pahuṅ dui jana
verse quoted, 151
Para-tattva defined, 204
Paro 'pi manute 'narthaṁ
verse quoted, 247
Paṅkti, Vedic meter, **192**
Pāṣaṇḍī defined, 10
Passion mode
result of, **80,** 81
See also: Modes of nature

Paśyantī defined, 189
Paths to liberation, **103,** 104
  See also: Liberation; *Yoga*
Patience in awaiting Lord's mercy, 129
Paurṇamāsa, **10**
Peacefulness. *See:* Mental equilibrium
Peace on spiritual platform only, 177–78
Penance(s)
  two types of, 126
  of *vānaprastha,* **6**
  See also: Austerity
Perfection
  via Lord's mercy, 67
  See also: Devotional service to the Supreme Lord, pure
Personal existence, devotee aspires for, 107
Personalism. *See:* Devotional service to the Supreme Lord
Pervasiveness of the Lord, **69**-70
Philanthropy, modern, false basis of, 153
Philosophers
  controversy amongst, **200-7**
  creation theories of, **217-21**
  debate real and unreal, **231**
  mixed up, 209
  ultimate goal of, 58
  under laws of nature, 233
  See also: Self-realization
Philosophical speculation. *See:* *Jñāna-yoga*
Piety
  can expire, **265**
  purpose of, **291**
  relativity of, **167**
Pious activities
  defined, **126,** 127
  life's goal is beyond, 113
  transcending of, 140
Planets, material
  influence body, **299**
  See also: Heavenly planets; Universe, material
Pleasure
  from bodily interaction, **295**
  desire for, leads to *karma-yoga,* **105,** 106, 107
Pleasure (*continued*)
  seeking of, causes misery, 252
  from scratching itch, 56
  See also: Bliss; Happiness; Sense gratification
Pollution of body and mind, 89
Prabhupāda, A. C. Bhaktivedanta Swami, quoted on power of *bhakti,* 139
Prabodhānanda Sarasvatī Tridaṇḍipāda, 306
Pradhāna defined, 212
Prakṛteḥ kriyamāṇāni
  verse quoted, 211
Prakṛti defined, 213
Prāṇa (life air) as Vedic sound, 188
Prāṇāyāma
  defined, 18
  as strength, **87,** 89
Prasādam, mahā-, pacifies mind, 118
Preachers of Kṛṣṇa consciousness, 27
Preaching Kṛṣṇa consciousness
  as highest service, 43
  without personal motive, 33
Priyo hi jñānino 'ty-artham
  verse quoted, 58
Property used in Lord's service, 274
Providence
  brings misery, **286**
  types of, **266**
  See also: Karma
Pure devotees of the Supreme Lord
  association with, 107
  no material hindrance for, 24
  worship of, recommended, **78**
  See also: Devotees of the Supreme Lord; *Paramahaṁsa;* Saints
Pure devotional service. *See:* Devotional service to the Supreme Lord, *appropriate topics;* Pure devotees
Purification
  of heart, 14–15, 131
  via humility and begging, 28
  via remembrance of Supreme Lord, 165
  two types of, 134
Purity, of objects, described, **159,** 160
Puruṣa defined, 213, 225

Q

Quarrel
amongst philosophers, **200-7**
mind creates, **293**

R

Rainwater, purity of, 160
Rāja-guhyam defined, 187
Reality
defined, **87,** 88
of material world, 29, 231
Reawakening of religious life, **267**
Regulative principles
four, described, 151
paramahaṁsa beyond, 40
purpose of, **107-8,** 109, 291
See also: Discipline, principles of; Duty
Reincarnation. *See:* Transmigration of the soul
Relaxation in spiritual life, 118, 120
Religion
actual process of, **78**
basis of, **169**
defined, 309
as devotional service, **81**
mundane, as troublesome, 150–51
as real wealth, **87,** 89
See also: Devotional service to the Supreme Lord; Morality
Religious principles. *See:* Discipline; Regulative principles
Remembrance of previous lifetime, 237–38
Renunciant. *See: Sannyāsī; Vānaprastha*
Renunciation
Caitanya pleased by, 169
defined, **87,** 88
via material loss, **267-80**
of philosophical knowledge, 54–55
of property, 274
purpose of, **29**
via recognizing illusion, 30
regulative and spontaneous, 31, 32
by *sannyāsī,* **14-27**
Renunciation (*continued*)
secondary to devotion, 133–34
See also: Austerity; Detachment; *Sannyāsa; Vānaprastha*
Repentance
of devotees, **128**
See also: Atonement; Austerity
Residences, pure and impure, 157–58
Responsibility
for sins, age of, 167
toward others, 109
See also: Duty; Regulative principles; *Varṇāśrama-dharma*
Retaliation (eye for an eye) rejected, 262
Retirement. *See:* Renunciation; *Sannyāsa; Vānaprastha*
Ṛg Veda quoted on demigods, 179
Rituals condemned, 125
Ṛṣiloka, 11
See also: Maharloka
Rules. *See:* Regulative principles
Rūpa Gosvāmī, quotations from. *See: Upadeśāmṛta*

S

Saba avatāra, sāra-śiromaṇi quoted, 151
Sacrifices (Vedic)
described, **9, 10**
materialists perform, 177–82
require deerskin, 157
Sādhur eva sa mantavyaḥ quoted, 125, 140
Saints
greed destroys, 269
qualities of, **17**
seek solitude, 27
See also: Devotee(s) of the Supreme Lord; *Paramahaṁsa; Sannyāsī*
Śālagrāma-śilā, 157
Salvation. *See:* Liberation
Samādhi defined, 137
Saṁvit defined, 211
Sandhinī defined, 211
Sāṅkhya philosophy delineated, **313-35**

Saṅkīrtana. See: Preaching Kṛṣṇa consciousness
Sannyāsa
defined, 304
falsely adopted, **44-45**
in Kali-yuga, accepted early, 4
purpose of, 281
time and circumstance for, 167
Sannyāsī (renounced saintly person)
avoids sense gratification, 27
clothing and food for, 5, 19–20, 39
criterion for, **14**-15, 18
demigods hinder, **15**
duty of, **45-46**
eating method of, 21
external features of, 32
heart of, compared to flower garden, 14–15
imitates bee, 20
possessions of, **16**
qualities of, **35**
regulations for, 20
See also: Paramahaṁsa; Renunciation; *Vānaprastha*
Sarva dharmān parityajya
quoted, 150
Sarva-kāma defined, 139
Sarvātmanā yaḥ śaraṇaṁ
verse quoted, 109
Satyaloka, **323,** 324
Satya-yuga (Kṛta-yuga), enlightened age, **314**
Sauvīram defined, 157
Scholars. *See:* Philosophers
Scientists, modern, society degraded by, 153
Scripture
defined, 150
purpose of, **291**
See also: Vedas; names of individual scriptures
Seer and seen become one, **314**
Self-control
defined, 87, 88
method of, **118, 119,** 120, **169**
Self-purification, means of, 164–65
Self-realization
vs. deathlike condition, 173, **174**
explained, 62, 222, 225, **295, 303**
in Satya-yuga, 314
via spiritual master, 42
ultimate perfection of, **54**-55
vision experienced in, **41, 241-45**
See also: Liberation; Self control; *Vijñāna*
Sense gratification
attachment to. *See:* Attachment, material
compared to reflection, **249**
detachment from. *See:* Detachment; Renunciation
devotees sometimes indulge in, **128,** 129
drags one down, 298
frustration with, **117,** 123
as impediment, 78
meditating on, result of, **250, 251,** 252
regulating, 118, 120
as scratching process, 56
social disharmony from, **171**
unsatiated desire for, 177
See also: Desire
Senses, material
categories of, **214, 215**
controlled or bound by, **25**
drag one, 26
evolution of, 319
interaction of, 226–29
training of, **120,** 121
travel from body to body, **233**
Service to God. *See:* Devotional service
Sex life
absent in Vaikuṇṭha, 324
for begetting children, **46**
both good and bad, 168
desire for, insatiable, 171
futility of, 128–29
illicit, 300–1
Sincerity for repentance, 128–30

Sinful activities
conteraction of, 6, 125
defined, **126**
difficult to overcome, 128–29
refraining from, **169**
responsibility for, age of, 167
relativity of, 168
responsibility for, age of, 167
transcending, 140
See also: Sense gratification
Śiva Svāmī, 304
Skanda Purāṇa, quoted on residences, 157
Smṛty-ācārya, 306
Snake, time compared to, 66
Social interaction compared to scratching itch, 56
Society, human
in America, demonic, 183
beggars in, 19–20
bogus religious leaders disturb, 140
celibacy practiced in, 47
conflict in, cause of, **171,** 172
degradation of, cause of, 153
divisions in, of social and spiritual orders. *See: Varṇāśrama-dharma*
divisions in, purpose of, 154
marriage in. *See:* Family; Householders; Marriage
mixed marriages in, **98,** 99
in West, as dull, 28
Vedas essential to, 101, 155–56
See also: Human form of life
Son, bad, implicates father, **238-**39
Soul
beyond birth & death, **242,** 243, **244, 245, 249**
beyond matter, 213
beyond material motion, **249,** 250
beyond mundane designations, 62, 154
body types accepted by, **247**
bondage vs. liberation of, **25**
captivated by material intelligence, **248,** 249
compared to bird in tree, **114**
"death" of, **116**
eternality of, **242,** 243

Soul (*continued*)
identifies with mind, **290**
independent of material interaction, 229
material disease of, 56
pleasure and pain of, **295-303**
as problem-free, **239**
reincarnation of. *See:* Transmigration
separate from body, 222, 225
"suicide" of, **116**
& Supersoul, oneness of, 208, 209, 210
transcendental nature of, **295-303**
under influence of modes, 211
See also: Living entities
Sound, transcendental. *See:* Hare Kṛṣṇa *mantra*
Sound vibration of *Vedas,* 188, **191-92**
Species of life, numbered, 330
Speculation. *See: Jñāna-yoga*
Speech
insulting, **259**
two types of, 88, 89
Spirit
false ego encompasses, **318**
separate from matter, 229
See also: Soul
Spirit, Supreme. *See:* Supreme Personality of Godhead
Spiritual life
best time for, 158
compared to riding horse, **120,** 121
extreme situations in, **253, 254**
falldown in, 125
seriousness of, 119
stages of, 146–47, 196
undereating hinders, 38
See also: Devotional service; Kṛṣṇa consciousness
Spiritual master (*guru*)
as captain of ship, **116**
necessity of, **42,** 208
rescues fallen souls, 173
service to, **43**
See also: Gurus, bogus
Spiritual realization. *See:* Kṛṣṇa consciousness; Self-realization

Spiritual world (Vaikuṇṭha)
achieved in a moment, **279**
conflict absent in, 225
description of, 324
devotees enter, 23
variety in, 210
See also: Godhead, returning to
Śrīdhara Svāmī, 306
Śrīmad-Bhāgavatam, cited on three features of absolute, 49
Śrīmad-Bhāgavatam, quotations from
on devotee's independence, 109
on exclusive worship of Kṛṣṇa, 136, 138
on false identification, 247
on knowledge & detachment, 108
on liberation, 132
on philosophers, 203
on Vaikuṇṭha inhabitants, 324
on worship of the Lord, 47
See also: Vedas
Śruti-smṛtī mamaivājñe
verse quoted, 108
Staff of renunciant. *See: Daṇḍa*
Stage, world as, 317
Steadiness
from mind control, 119, **120,** 121
in one's duty, **146**
Strength, *prāṇāyāma* as, **87,** 89
Subtle body in transmigration process, **233-41**
Śūdra, intoxication accepted for, 168
Suffering
via attachment, 176
benefit from, **277-78**
cause of, 37, 56
from harsh speech, 260
as impediment, **111,** 112
past sins cause, 129
See also: Frustration; Misery
Suicide, spiritual, **116**
Śukadeva Gosvāmī, 136
Sun globe, status of, **227,** 228
Supersoul
pervades 28 elements, **69-**70
position of, **290**
Supreme Lord
abode of. *See:* Spiritual world
authority of, 84
awards devotees' desires, **135-**36
beyond cause and effect, **72**
beyond material conception, **139-40**
cause of all causes, **70-**71
compared to parent, 140–41
compared to sun, 131, 154, **227**
controversy dissolves within, 204
creation by. *See:* Creation
dependence on, 8, 19–20, 134
devotees of. *See:* Devotees of the Supreme Lord
devotonal service to. *See:* Devotional service to the Supreme Lord
energies of, 222
free will of, 39, 40
glance of, **215-16, 316, 329**
hearing about, 76, 130
in heart
devotee enthrones, 131
as *oṁkāra,* **190**
instructions of, as favorable winds, **116**
instructions of. *See also: Vedas*
Kṛṣṇa as. *See:* Kṛṣṇa
love for
as final stage, 147
via hearing and chanting, 11
humans can develop, **111,** 112
as only panacea, 76
three paths lead to, 104
See also: Devotional service to the Supreme Lord
lotus feet of, **58,** 65
mercy of, **66-**67, 129, 134, 159
mercy of, compared to parents' forgiveness, 140–41
as one and different from soul, 210
opulences of, **92**
pervades matter, 70
penance to achieve, 7
property of, everything as, 252
realization of, in stages, **70-**71
relationships to, described, 111

Supreme Lord (*continued*)
remembrance of, as most purifying, 164-65
as sacrifice personified **87,** 88
submission to, 177
sun as eye of, 228
surrender to, **54,** 55, 140
transcendentalists dear to, **58**
as twenty-sixth element, 208
as ultimate goal, **56,** 57
Vedas emanate from, 102
worship of, 48, **78,** 79
compared to medicine, 175, 177
See also: Devotional service to the Supreme Lord
See also: Kṛṣṇa, Lord
Supreme Personality of Godhead. *See:* Kṛṣṇa, Lord; Supreme Lord
Surrender of philosophical knowledge, **54**-55
Su-sukhaṁ kartum
quoted, 150
Sūtas defined, 98
Sūtra defined, 212, **317**
Suvīra defined, 157
Svar, **321**

T

Tad-arthaṁ karma kaunteya
quoted, 104
Tad tad evāvagaccha tvaṁ
verse quoted, 194
Tad viṣṇoḥ paramaṁ
quoted, 179
Tam eva śaraṇaṁ gaccha
verse quoted, 324
Tapaloka, **323,** 324
Tapasya. See: Austerity
Tasmād aparihārye 'rthe
quoted, 122
Tat-prasādāt parāṁ śāntiṁ
verse quoted, 324
Teachers, spiritual. *See: Guru;* Spiritual master
Te dvandva-moha-nirmuktā
verse quoted, 170
Teṣāṁ jñānī nitya-yukta
verse quoted, 58
Teṣāṁ satata-yuktānāṁ
quoted, 120
Theories of creation, **217-21**
Time-and-circumstance considerations, 161-62, 167
Time(s)
auspicious and inauspicious, **158**
compared to serpent, 66
in creation process, **328-30**
as cutting life short, **115**
defined, **301**
destruction caused by, 149, **239,** 241
force of, **325**
modes interact via, 212
Tīvena bhakti-yogena
quoted, 136, 138
Tolerance
defined, **87,** 88
of extreme offenses, **253, 254**
of harsh insults, **259-60, 282-88**
Transcendence
of mundane morality, 102-3
beyond sin and piety, 97
See also: Liberation; Self-realization; Spiritual world
Transcendentalist(s)
as dear to Lord, 58
outwit stubborn mind, **120**
qualifications of, 140
See also: Devotees; *Paramahaṁsas;* Saints; *Sannyāsī*
Transmigration of the soul (reincarnation)
into animal form, 167
forgetfulness of, 235-38
as mental process, 237-41
to repay debts, 8-9
Tri-daṇḍi-sannyāsī
compared to *eka-daṇḍi-sannyāsī,* 304, 305
defined, 281
Triṣṭup as Vedic meter, **192**

Tṛṇād api su-nīcena
verse quoted, 35
Truth, as virtue of saint, **17**
Truthfullness, defined, **87**

U

Udārāḥ sarva evāite
quoted, 58
Unhappiness
tolerance of, 87
See also: Misery; Suffering
Universe, material
administrators of. *See:* Demigods
heavenly planets of. *See:* Heavenly planets
three modes of, 211
See also: Creation; Elements; Material world
Upadeśāmṛta (Rūpa Gosvāmī) quoted
on devotee exchanges, 22
on devotional service, 162
on *sannyāsa,* 306
on tolerance, 287
Upāsanā-kāṇḍa, 193, 195
Uṣṇik Vedic meter, **192**

V

Vāco vegaṁ manasaḥ
verse quoted, 287, 306
Vaidehaka defined, 98
Vaikharī defined, 188
Vaikuṇṭha. *See:* Spiritual world
Vaiṣṇavas. See: Devotees of the Supreme Lord
Vallabhācārya-sampradāya, 306
Vānaprastha (retired householders)
austerities of, **6,** 11
avoids sense gratification, 27
death accepted by, 13
diet of, **7**
duty of, **45-46**
enters sacrificial fire, 13
heavenly destination of, 3, 24
hygiene of, **6**
sacrifices for, **10**
Vānaprastha (continued)
ultimate goal of, **12**
See also: Sannyāsī
Vānaprastha-āśrama
purpose of, 4
sustenance of, **5, 8**
Varṇāśrama-dharma (caste system)
begging restrictions within, **19**-20
divisions of, **45-46**, 154
duties within, **45-46**
goal of, 48
mixed marriages in, 98
See also: specific divisions of system
Vāsudeve bhagavati
verse quoted, 108
Vedaiś ca sarvair
quoted, 102, 180
Vedānta-sūtra quoted on *Vedas,* 187
Vedas
animal sacrifice in, **182**
compared to spider's web, **191-92**
confidential, 187, **193,** 194
devotees beyond, 140
divisions and complexity of, **188,** 189
exploitation of, 181
full knowledge within, 155–56
marriage system in, **98,** 99
men and demigods consult, **100,** 101
meters of, **192,** 193
must be transcended, 97
origin of, **191-92**
portions of, rejected, 74
purpose of, 154, **175,** 177, 178, 180, 187
quoted on obeying scripture, 108
regulations within. *See:* Regulative principles
rituals in, 126–27, 151
source of, 102
stages of advancement given in, 196
Veda-vāda-rata philosophy described, 177
Veda-vit defined, 193
Vedic knowledge, ultimate purpose of, 54–55
Vedic sacrifices, 10

Vedic society
opposers of, 20
See also: Varṇāśrama-dharma
Vijñāna
defined, 58
symptoms of, **70**-71
See also: Self-realization
Vīrarāghava Ācārya quoted on *sannyāsa*, 20
Virtue, greed destroys, **269**
Viṣṇu Svāmī cited on *tridaṇḍa-sannyāsa*, 304
Viśuddha-sattva defined, 210
Viśvanātha Cakravartī Ṭhākura quoted on *gurus'* mercy, 43
Voidism. *See:* Impersonalism; Nonexistence
Vows, purpose of, **291**

W

Wars as inferior heroism, 88
Water to be filtered, **17**
Wealth
contamination caused by, **271**
defined, **87,** 88
destroys family affection, **272**
as impediment, 66
loss of, story of, **261**
proper use of, 78, 274, **275**
real and false, 93
Welfare (dependence on others) condemned, 8-9
Western countries cannot distinguish saint, 28
Wife
demigods can appear as, **15**
deserts penniless husband, **272**
Women
impure period for, 159
stumbling block for *sannyāsī*, 15
vānaprastha stage for, **4**
Words, pure and impure, 160
Work
fruitive, soul distinct from, **300**
See also: Duty; *Karma-yoga*
Worship
according to modes, **184,** 185
to demigods, 48, **186**
to Supreme Lord. *See:* Devotional service to the Supreme Lord

Y

Yac-cakṣur eṣa
quoted, 228
Yac chaktayo vadatām
verse quoted, 203
Yad yad vibhūtimat sattvaṁ
verse quoted, 194
Yahā dekhi' prīta hana
verse quoted, 169
Yaḥ smaret puṇḍarīkākṣaṁ
verse quoted, 165
Yajñārthāt karmaṇo 'nyatra
quoted, 104
Yasya prasādād bhagavat-prasādaḥ
quoted, 43
Yayā sammohito jīva
verse quoted, 247
Yeṣāṁ tv anta-gataṁ pāpaṁ
verse quoted, 170
Ye yathā māṁ prapadyante
quoted, 103
Yoga
bhakti. See: Devotional service to the Supreme Lord
difficulties in, 151
essence of, 308
highest form of, **291**
three paths of, **103,** 104
ultimate goal of, **54-55**
See also: Devotional service to the Supreme Lord; *Jñāna-yoga; Karma-yoga*
Yogenāvyabhicāriṇyā
verse quoted, 287
Youth, purity of, 164
Yudhiṣṭhira, King, **68**
Yugas. *See: individual names*